For Sociology

Legacies and prospects

Edited by
John Eldridge, John MacInnes, Sue Scott,
Chris Warhurst and Anne Witz

sociologypress

Published by:
sociologypress
[c/o British Sociological Association,
Units 3F/G, Mountjoy Research Centre, Stockton Road, Durham, DH1 3UR
Or http://www.britsoc.org.uk/sociologypress]

sociologypress is supported by the British Sociological Association. It furthers the Association's aim of promoting the discipline of sociology and disseminating sociological knowledge.

© British Sociological Association 2000

All rights reserved. Except for the quotation of short passages for the purposes of criticism and review, no part of this publication may be reproduced, stored in a retrieval system, or transmitted in any form, or by any means, without the prior permission of the publisher.

This book may not be circulated in any other binding or cover and the same condition must be imposed on any acquiror.

British Library Cataloguing in Publication Data
A CIP catalogue record for this book is available from the British Library

ISBN 1 903457 01 7

Printed and bound by York Publishing Services Ltd, 64 Hallfield Road, Layerthorpe, York YO31 7ZQ

This book is dedicated to the memory of Alvin Gouldner without whom it would not have been possible

Acknowledgements

The papers in this book were originally presented at the British Sociological Association (BSA) Annual Conference, 'For Sociology', held in April 1999 at the University of Glasgow. The conference was organised by the editors, who would like to thank all those who contributed to its success. Special thanks are due to Nicola Boyne, Judith Mudd, Nicky Gibson and Debbie Brown of the BSA, to Teresa Witz for her design work, and to all the support staff at the University of Glasgow. In relation to the production of the book thanks are due to all the contributors, for being so helpful and conscientious, but especially to Anneliese Emmans Dean our copy-editor and Eva Fairnell at YPS, and to Elaine Blaxter of the University of Strathclyde library. We would also like to thank all the friends and colleagues, too numerous to list, who helped us through the stresses and strains of organising the conference and editing this volume – you know who you are.

John Eldridge, John MacInnes, Sue Scott, Chris Warhurst and Anne Witz
September 2000

Contents

Acknowledgements		vi
Overview		1
Anne Witz, John Eldridge, John MacInnes, Sue Scott and Chris Warhurst		
1	The new positivity Gregor McLennan	17
2	Sociology and its audience(s): changing perceptions of sociological argument John Holmwood	33
3	For sociology, Gouldner's and ours Liz Stanley	56
4	For postdisciplinary studies: sociology and the curse of disciplinary parochialism and imperialism Andrew Sayer	83
5	For a sociological feminism Stevi Jackson	92
6	Bourdieu and methodological polytheism: taking sociology forward in the twenty-first century David Inglis, Norman Stockman and Paula Surridge	107
7	Work and its narratives Richard Sennett	119
8	Sociology and the Third Way John Eldridge	131
9	Memory, violence and identity Larry Ray	145
10	Science, technology and the relevance of sociology Stephen Crook	160
11	The coming biological challenge to social theory and practice Steve Fuller	174
12	Putting sociology on the bioethics map Pat Spallone, Tom Wilkie, Elizabeth Ettorre, Erica Haimes, Tom Shakespeare and Meg Stacey	191
Notes on contributors		207

Overview
For Sociology: Legacies and Prospects
Anne Witz
John Eldridge, John MacInnes, Sue Scott and
Chris Warhurst

Fin-de-siècle anxieties

In April 1999 members of the British Sociological Association met for their 48th annual conference. The theme was *For Sociology*, evoking Alvin Gouldner's (1973) book of the same name, and addressing *fin-de-siècle* anxieties about the state of the discipline. Participants were encouraged to reflect, both critically and constructively, on sociology's past, present and future, and on its changing relationship with other disciplines and with wider social and political agendas. This volume brings together some of these reflections.

Anxieties about the state of a discipline often come from within, and it is perhaps the case that sociologists too readily speak of crisis, rather than seeing ups and downs as simply being 'the way of things'. Writing in 1975, Robert Merton suggested:

> *Sociology has typically been in an unstable state, alternating between planes of extravagant optimism and extravagant pessimism amongst its cultivators about its capacity then and there, or at least very soon, to find abiding solutions to the problems of human society and the problems of human sociology, that is, solutions to the major social ones and the major cognitive ones.*
> (1975: 22)

The essays in this book do not exhibit such extreme mood swings, but they do display the tensions and hopes of those who are aware of the complexities of the world in which we live and the difficulties encountered in trying to make sense of it.

Historically the relationship between sociology and its practitioners has been by no means straightforward. While nineteenth-century pioneers Comte and Durkheim had a mission to promote the subject, Marx did not define himself as a sociologist, and for the most part found himself in opposition to those who did. Weber only hesitatingly called himself a sociologist in the last decade or so of his life. He was an academic economist and lawyer and sceptical of much of what, at that time, was labelled as sociology. 'If I have become a sociologist', he wrote in a letter to Robert Liefmann in 1920, 'it is mainly to exorcise the spectre of collective conceptions which still lingers among us' (Mommsen, 1965: 25). Some thirty years earlier, the British economist Alfred Marshall reflected on the relationship of sociology to economics in his *Principles of Economics*. He acknowledged the contributions of Comte, Spencer and J.S. Mill to the study of society, and wished to remind disciplines such as economics not to become inward-looking specialisms, unaware of what was going on in neighbouring social sciences. Yet, as he reflected on the practice of the subject in Britain and the USA, he thought the use of the term sociology was premature:

> For it seems to claim that a unification of social sciences is already in sight and though some excellent intensive studies have been published under the name of Sociology, it is doubtful whether those efforts at unification have achieved any great success beyond that of preparing the way and erecting danger posts at its pitfalls for the guidance of later generations, whose resources will be less inadequate for the giant task than our own.
> (Marshall, 1961: 637)

As far as sociology in Britain at the beginning of the twentieth century is concerned, we need look no further than Philip Abrams' historical analysis (Abrams, 1968). He called attention to the first issue of the *Sociological Review*, published in 1908, in which L.T. Hobhouse published a paper entitled, *Sociology, General, Special and Scientific*. This, in Abrams' view, was 'as near to an agreed manifesto as British sociology had ever produced' (Abrams, 1968: 253). Hobhouse certainly offered a generous conspectus of the subject, urging that it should be embraced not only as a science, but also as a philosophy and an art. It should exist in conscious awareness of other social sciences, and on value questions always make a clear distinction between the 'is' and the 'ought'. The diversity of activity which sociology represented was seen by Hobhouse as a sign of health, not fragmentation.

Abrams was not so sure. For him the sheer range of activities occurring under the umbrella of sociology represented a splintering of the subject. Not only was there the heritage of Spencerian sociology and social Darwinism, but also the development of the eugenics movement, the claims of the social statisticians, the social reform surveys of Booth and Rowntree, and the interest of Geddes in urbanism. However, in their various ways, all of these impinged on the great social questions of their day. These included issues of socialism, class and poverty, as well as the emerging debates about the place of women in civil society. Cross-cutting these were questions about the significance of heredity and environment, of nature and nurture. The essays in this volume reflect some of the continuities and discontinuities that relate to these issues.

As John Holmwood (Chapter 2) points out, Gouldner's overriding concern when he wrote *For Sociology* in 1973 was that the discipline might degenerate into a technocratic science dominated by considerations of methodology, lacking ethical or political purpose, and becoming at best anodyne or at worst an unwitting servant of power and the status quo. This crisis of sociology was rooted in the very power of its promise to be a 'science of society', a system of thought that proffered 'rational' solutions to social and political questions which had previously been dominated by religious dogma, superstition, prejudice or simply the weight of tradition. It is not clear that this role was ever a real possibility for sociology in Britain. And, as Holmwood shows, in the event sociology's fate seemed to be threatened as much by those who were more concerned with the radicalism of their approach than with the sociological character of their endeavour.

Sociology has had various and variable relationships with a number of other disciplines: political economy, women's studies, cultural studies and politics, to name but a few, and its practitioners' views have ranged from seeing the discipline as central to the social sciences, to seeing it as parasitic on them (Urry, 1982). Stevi Jackson (Chapter 5) suggests that sociologists have developed an increasing tendency 'to genuflect towards theory from other disciplines while forgetting the insights which have been yielded by sociology'. Towards the other end of the spectrum, Andrew Sayer (Chapter 4) goes so far as to argue that disciplinary boundaries have done little for social science – but often the essence of the relationship has been a radical assault on the academy, on method or, as Holmwood argues, on any social structure characterised by the operation of power. Thus the problems faced by sociology have rarely been those of creeping technocracy or antiseptic value freedom, but have more often resulted from the search to reconcile social science with radical social commitment and intervention. Sometimes this search has led to a kind of theoretical sectarianism based on competing readings of key social theorists that have not always been careful to relate their concerns back to the objectives of sociological practice. Sometimes it has led to forms of radicalism which unwittingly reproduce the 'Parsonian' divorce of social science from social reform or engagement that Gouldner and other radical sociologists set out to challenge.

However, as John Eldridge (Chapter 8) shows, attempts to hitch the cause of social science to a 'third way' beyond those of interest or identity groups competing to control state policy are as old as the discipline itself, and have met with similar objections. Conversely, Holmwood draws attention to theoretical approaches that appear to set out from wildly different starting points, and quite opposed objectives, but achieve effects which, curiously, resemble each other. Rather than drawing on a better relationship between theory and practice, such approaches have too often resorted implicitly or explicitly to political calculations of 'balance' and pragmatism. It is useful to recall, in this context, Weber's (1949: 57) warning that the questions of value relevance and value freedom, objectivity and a scientific method had nothing to do with balance:

> It can, to be sure, be just as obligatory, subjectively, for the practical politician, in the individual case, to mediate between antagonistic points of view as to take sides with one of them. But this has nothing whatsoever to do with scientific 'objectivity'. Scientifically the middle course is not truer even by a hair's breadth, than the most extreme party ideals of left or right.

Inspired by Gouldner's call for reflexivity, sociology developed a new sensitivity to the social and institutional conditions of its production. Questions about the situated and interested positions of sociologists as knowledge producers have reverberated throughout the sociological community since the 1970s. A number of contributors to this volume address, or allude to, the issue of sociology's own internal critique and its legacy for the twenty-first century. This internal critique has been deeply troubling for some practitioners, but refreshingly transformative for others. These developments, which amount to a 'sociology of sociology', are surely in the spirit of Gouldner's rallying call, even if they move in directions – feminism, for example – that he could not have anticipated at the time. Gouldner's reflexive sociologist was, after all, manly to his very core:

> The quality of a social scientist's work remains dependent on the quality of his manhood
> (1971: 494)

Indeed, in his call for a reflexive sociology which applied its understandings to itself and its role in bolstering the status quo, Gouldner did not include an explicitly gendered reflexivity that addressed the role of male sociological persons in bolstering the patriarchal status quo. Yet one of the most discomforting and powerful critiques of modern sociology has been the feminist critique of sociology as an overwhelmingly masculinist project (Smith, 1987).

The internal feminist critique of sociology has moved the discipline in the direction Gouldner (1971: 494) advocated of 'a new praxis that transforms the person of the sociologist'. In the spirit of reflexivity, feminists exposed 'the relationship ... between being a sociologist and being a person' (Gouldner, 1971: 495), and how the institutional and historical dominance of male persons in academic sociology had led to a sociology written from a partial and interested standpoint. Feminist persons working both inside and outside sociology have taken up the gauntlet thrown down by Gouldner (1971, 1973). Pursuing explicitly partisan agendas, they have exposed the implicit partisanship of established, allegedly value-free and objective sociological practices which, behind the veil of objectivity and value neutrality, maintained the status quo – or, as Dorothy Smith (1987) puts it, participated in the relations of ruling. However this critique does not necessarily lead to a wholesale rejection of prefeminist sociological ideas. Indeed, as Stevi Jackson suggests (drawing on the example of social constructionism), it can lead to a rehabilitation of sociological ideas in response to some wheel-reinventing practices which are occurring elsewhere in the academy.

Feminism is not the only movement to have challenged the discipline's partial standpoint. Paul Gilroy (1994) describes how he struggled to relate canonised sociological theory texts to the experiences of black students studying sociology in the 1980s. Bob Connell (1997) charts how the concerns that marked early 'sociological' writings in the nineteenth-century were intimately connected to the position of Western sociologists at the centre of empire: 'whiteness' and 'maleness' were the unspoken, taken-for-granted subject positions of early sociologists. However, the institutionalisation of sociology in the twentieth-century entailed the retrospective reconstruction of a sociological canon, which selectively rehabilitated some topics as sociology's core concerns, whilst de-emphasising others, such as 'race' and 'sexuality', in its collective memory. As sociology became the chosen discipline for members of disenfranchised groups entering the academy, its own partisanship was unmasked. The experiences of socially and academically marginalised groups encountering sociology is captured eloquently in Franz Fanon's words of 1952:

> The black man among his own in the twentieth century does not know at what moment his inferiority comes into being through the other ... And then the occasion arose when I had to meet the white man's eyes. An unfamiliar weight burdened me.
> (1986: 110)

Similarly, it was not until the early 1970s that working class voices began to be heard within sociology. For instance, within the subdiscipline of what was at the time termed 'industrial sociology', a number of radical British sociologists (see for example, Beynon and Blackburn, 1972) began to articulate a sociology that was not for managers, but was sensitive to 'worker's [sic] wants and expectations' (1972: 4). The 'managerialism' which was beginning to threaten the legitimacy of the sociology of work had first been exposed by Lupton (1963), but was not theorised in terms of its relation to institutionalised power until a decade later – occurring, interestingly, in the case of Beynon and Blackburn, with reference to Gouldner's 1959 writings on organisations, which were themselves part of another, earlier, reflection on the state of sociology generally. This sociological retooling had its limitations: female working-class voices remained silent in this subdiscipline for a further decade, until the work of, for example, Cavendish (1982) and Pollert (1981).

A number of contributors to this volume consider the impact of feminism on sociology or, in Stevi Jackson's case, the impact of sociology on feminism and the place of a distinctly 'sociological feminism'. Has the feminist challenge to sociology been a fatal one, in the sense of necessarily undermining the integrity of sociological methodologies, theories and substantive concerns? Or has this challenge been as much *for* as against sociology, in the spirit of sociology after Gouldner? Liz Stanley (Chapter 3), Stevi Jackson, John Holmwood and Gregor McLennan (Chapter 1) all reflect on the feminist sociological project. Stanley and Holmwood deal specifically with the question (to paraphrase Gouldner, 1973) of whether feminist sociology begins *and* ends with disenchanting *sociology*, or whether it is *for* a sociology in the spirit of Gouldner.

If Gouldner's coming crisis has indeed arrived, then *for whom is it a crisis*? This is the issue addressed by Liz Stanley, for whom the spirit of Gouldner lives on. Both Stanley and Holmwood see sociology as an epistemic community, thus stressing its fundamentally social and pragmatic character. Clearly, the centre will cohere – both intellectually and institutionally – more than the periphery, which will be occupied by the voices not only of aspiring others, but also of marginalised others engaged in constant critique of the centre. For Stanley, part of the current perceived crisis of sociology is that the centre is being taken away from those who *used* to have and hold it. This generates insecurity, in the form of a lack of intellectual *and* institutional certainty. For those who cannot tolerate such insecurity, this represents a challenge to their authority as well as to the institutional composition of sociology, as 'they' increasingly challenge 'our' ideas. Liz Stanley alerts us, then, to the institutional as well as the intellectual practices of sociology, yet reminds us that no-one owns sociology, for if we work in the spirit of Gouldner, there are no centres which are inviolate, sealed off from comment, critique and change. She tells us that 'The discipline is ours, those of us who are all for it, all of us', and goes on to show that an internally differentiated discipline need not necessarily be perceived as a fatally fragmented one. Rather, it can be seen as a discipline engaged in the constant politics of renewal, both intellectually and institutionally, as well as in the sense of responding to the crises and challenges of the time, a role advocated by Gouldner and emphasised by Stanley in her call for a 'rapid-response sociology', where sociologists engage as public intellectuals with issues of the day.

Stanley clearly writes in the spirit of a reflexive sociology that is *for* sociology in the sense that, as she argues, many sociologists want to craft a position which is both sociologically creditable and can underpin some kind of transformative project. There are necessarily *partial connections* (Strathern, 1991) between being a sociologist and adopting a partisan stance. Thus, being a feminist will affect one's sociology, just as being a sociologist will affect one's feminism. Indeed, neither would be quite the way it is unless it were partially connected, but neither is wholly determined by the other. So how does what might be seen as feminist partisanship shape up under the influence of the sociological imagination? In her spirited advocacy of 'sociological feminism' – and the ordering of terms is crucial here – Stevi Jackson urges us to recognise, and indeed not to forget, how sociologists engaged in feminist praxis have made a *distinctive* contribution to feminist knowledge and politics. This has entailed a concern with the lived, material realities of women's lives and with the substantive shape of gender inequalities and hierarchies. Yet Jackson also expresses her concern about the way in which distinctly sociological perspectives have become eclipsed in recent years within the interdisciplinary mix that has come to characterise feminist theory. Both Jackson and Stanley are concerned about the 'have feminist theory, will travel' direction of contemporary academic feminism which seems, increasingly, to parallel the practices of male-dominated social theory.

The bonfire of the disciplines

For many sociologists, *fin-de-siècle* anxieties centre around the question of whether sociology has a future. Indeed, given that the contemporary intellectual landscape seems to be aglow with a bonfire of the disciplines, we might ask if the time has come to cast sociology onto that fire. Indeed Gregor McLennan asks whether we should see sociology 'as a sinking ship that we ought to be deserting and fast', whilst Stephen Crook (Chapter 10) explores the idea that 'sociology should simply recognise that its time is up and fade peacefully away'. There is a consensus that Parsons' (1954) optimistic and possibly naive dream of an 'age of sociology' has been shattered. Disarray and fragmentation do seem to be the order, or rather the disorder, of the sociological day – as John Holmwood makes abundantly clear.

However, in the midst of the 'crisis' that sociology has experienced from the 1970s onwards, it has nevertheless achieved a great deal, as this volume testifies. In part this has been because much of the time methodological polytheism, as David Inglis, Norman Stockman and Paula Surridge (Chapter 6) term it, has been practised, even by many of those who do not preach it. And their research has not reduced sociology to the role of intellectual assistant to the practical concerns of state policy. Nevertheless, the relationship between social science and the state has always been a difficult one, as John Eldridge shows.

For Andrew Sayer, sociology has no future if it becomes too introspectively obsessed with the nature of disciplinary boundaries. Sayer urges social scientists to embrace not merely interdisciplinary but *post*disciplinary studies in order to achieve a more coherent understanding of the social world. Because of their parochialism, he argues, disciplines such as sociology inhibit open and fruitful analysis by limiting the very questions that are asked, what counts as proof, and the methods used to generate knowledge. Furthermore, their imperialism leads them to try to establish the primacy of their own approach to defining and understanding the social. Sayer sees social science as something that is inevitably greater than individual disciplines. Its methods of analysis ought to be driven by the nature of the problem being confronted, and the evidence available. The nub of Sayer's objection to 'disciplines' is their methodological closure, the fact that, even if they push beyond the bounds of their given object, they can only bring themselves to look at new objects in a discipline-bound way, and so produce partial understandings. However, arguing that social problems, rather than institutional disciplinary boundaries, ought to drive our methods and analysis is all very well – and it is no accident that Holmwood's review of sociology urges us towards just such an approach – but as Sayer would probably be the first to admit, this does not tell us *how* this is to be achieved.

Paradoxically, Sayer presents Pierre Bourdieu's 1997 *The State Nobility* as an arch example of sociological imperialism, whilst David Inglis, Norman Stockman and Paula Surridge use the same study as a prime illustration of the methodological polytheism that they advocate. Inglis *et al.* applaud Bourdieu for employing a range of methods appropriate to the evidence available, and for pushing sociology into the exploration of new questions (particularly in relation to patterns of cognition); Sayer, by contrast, chides him for continually trying to get sociology to account for the greatest number of things possible. For Sayer, the methodological polytheism advocated by Inglis *et al.* would have to be part of a greater disciplinary polytheism.

Both Sayer and Fuller (Chapter 11) discuss 'predisciplinary studies'. Sayer, clearly seduced by the lure of the 'predisciplinary', invokes the encyclopaedic, free-ranging minds of thinkers such as Adam Smith and Karl Marx as both antidotes to the closed minds of twentieth-century disciplinarians, and exemplars of the spirit of postdisciplinarity. Steve Fuller, on the other hand, is not seduced by predisciplinarity. Considering the mutual antagonism between sociology and biology in the twentieth-century, he makes the point that the nineteenth-century predisciplinary mind *could* work with an inchoate notion of 'human nature' precisely because there was no generally accepted account of genetics to underwrite a more strictly biological conception of human nature. 'Nature' referred to a whole range of psychosocial aspects of the human condition, and did not evoke some notion of a specific physical substratum. Moreover, Fuller urges caution with regard to 'hybrid discourses'. His notion of interdisciplinary interchange preserves a clear sense of a discipline of sociology, at the same time as charting some ways in which this discipline must change in the light of new knowledges generated by other disciplines. There *is* a biological challenge to sociology, and Fuller urges us to confront this, not by rekindling 'an age-old turf war', but by *re*-engaging with matters 'biological'. Fuller is critical of the way in which sociologists have either ignored or rejected wholesale biological ones, particularly sociobiological and evolutionary theories. In advocating indisciplinary interchange, Fuller also retains a notion of sociology as being in part about the critique of how other disciplines 'do knowledge'. At the same time, he insists that insights from other disciplines may have implications for cherished sociological conventions, implications which sociologists must seriously consider.

Perhaps more than any other contributor to the debate in this volume, Gregor McLennan strikes the most positive note. Indeed, McLennan discerns a new mood of 'positivity' emerging, even within postmodernism, as some of its proponents finally face up to its 'principled, theorised, philosophical hopelessness' (Rorty, 1998: 37). In a similar vein, Stevi Jackson urges us not to give up on the hope of a better future, as some postmodern intellectuals would have us do, but to salvage a distinctly *sociological* feminist imagination, precisely because this gives us 'the ability to at least imagine that the social world could be radically other than it is. If we cannot do so we lose the cutting edge of sociology, its ability to make us think critically about the society in which we live'.

McLennan is also clear that he wants to 'retain and promote the broader idea of generic sociology' as centrally concerned with a logic of the social, which it confronts substantively and empirically. The crux of McLennan's conception of a generic sociology is that it must be concerned with substantive analysis, and so must necessarily embrace an 'everyday realism'. He goes on to insist that 'you don't have to be a philosophical realist to be an everyday realist, most of the time'.[1] McLennan's point – and it is one that chimes with other contributions such as Stanley's and Jackson's – is that sociology cannot retreat into the realm of purely theoretical reflection. The new challenges for the discipline are to be found in the new *situations* it turns its analytic gaze on, but it must embrace these new 'empiricities' as 'positivities' in the expectation that some understanding can, and indeed must, be achieved. We perceive in McLennan's notion of a 'new positivity' a reinvigorated sense of the 'positive' as being forward-looking and constructive. Sociological insights are 'hard-won', to the extent that they consist of a creative interplay between substantive developments or situations and analytical concepts. Sociological theory is born out of this creative interchange between situations and concepts. Thus sociological theory is not coterminus with social theory, nor should it be eclipsed by social theory. So from McLennan we gain a strong impression that social theory is not the seedbed out of which we grow or develop our analysis of the social; rather it is the mirror we hold up in order to reflect the social back for analysis.

There are many points of overlap between the contributions of McLennan and Holmwood. For example, there is a mutual concern that sociology post-Gouldner can become *too* reflexive and succumb to intellectual paralysis if it lets its focus stray too far from empirical, practical problems. For Holmwood, the crux of the dilemma currently facing sociology is that we have reached an impasse of our own making 'where, in an apparent openness to multiple voices and a reflexive application of sociology to its own undertaking, sociology has seemed to lose its own distinctive voice'. At the same time, he eschews any vision of a monologic sociology and any cure for a dangerously terminal reflexivity that might silence the plurality of new voices struggling to make themselves heard within the sociological community. Holmwood is certain that sociology must never seek closure in the service of some sort of illusory theoretical or paradigmatic security. Gouldner came to a similar conclusion in *The Coming Crisis of Western Sociology*: 'This crisis cannot be resolved by retreating to traditional conceptions of a "pure" sociology' (1971: 512). For Holmwood, as for Stanley, sociology must always be open to, and learn from, new voices. Holmwood embraces a postpositivist definition of sociological practice as a set of communal problem-solving practices which are nonetheless open to contestation and debate. For this reason, he insists that we must not be tempted to seek solutions to disarray which are recidivist, such as the 'back to basics' programmes of, amongst others, Alexander (1995) and Mouzelis (1991), with their talk of 'core' disciplinary concerns and distracting peripheries. Nor must we succumb to celebratory *'Vive la crise!'* positions, such as that of Bourdieu; nor to Lemert's (1995) sanguine and resigned view of the inevitability of crisis. Neither debilitating relativism nor terminal reflexivity will be avoided by attempts to 'hold the centre' in order to unite sociologists into a secure community under the umbrella of an overarching standpoint. Such unifying strategies tend to be pitched at such a level of abstraction that they immediately render invisible the standpoints of groups who championed the case for reflexivity in the first place. Stanley argues that sociologists need to develop analytical reflexivity, in the spirit of Gouldner. She thinks that 'piecemeal attempts to work out the articulation of an analytical reflexivity in specific pieces of work by particular sociologists are preferable as well as being what is possible at this point in sociological time'.

What do sociologists do when they do sociology?

What, then, do current 'sociologies' have in common *by virtue of being sociology*? Or, to put it another way: how do we recognise sociology when we see it? Such questions expose the underlying question of whether sociology has a distinctive voice and, indeed, a future.

There is a strong sense in which both McLennan and Holmwood share a vision of sociology as marked by its distinctive *practices*. McLennan's *new positivity*, which embraces new 'empiricities', implies that sociologists 'do' knowledge in a way that demands attention above all to everyday reality and that *some* sense, however provisional or partial, must be made out of this everyday reality. Holmwood similarly embraces a *postpositivity*, which begins to identify the core of any meaning of 'sociology' as the problem-solving *practices* of an epistemological community.

Sociology proceeds through *problem-solving*, but what the problems are and how they are to be solved derives from no single strategy, and certainly cannot be prescribed by theorists working at one level removed from the problem-solvers. Any 'core' of sociology consists of a minimal, working consensus among practitioners, where contestation and change are perpetual possibilities. Thus Holmwood argues, as does McLennan, that sociology is essentially about substantively grounded analysis of empirical, social problems that are relevant to 'the communities of which sociologists are members'. Holmwood, like Inglis *et al.* and Sayer, is reluctant to legislate for the scope and nature of the problems that are to be addressed. This, however, is to be expected, given Holmwood's insistence on the nature of the sociological enterprise as a set of knowledge constitutive practices, as well as his defence of the notion of a minimal consensus and a loose, polyvalent community.

Of course, a 'problem-solving' sociology brings us back to its relationship to state funding and public policy. Gouldner's fear was that, despite being underpinned by a more theoretically comprehensive Parsonian grand theory, the discipline might become a mere technocratic servant to the immediate public policy agenda. In contrast, Anthony Giddens, in his opening plenary address to the conference on which this collection is based, urged sociologists to become what he termed 'public intellectuals', engaged with public policy debate. Holmwood's concept of 'problem solving' starts out from an awareness of the inevitably political nature of any public policy agenda, of 'problems' to be solved and solutions proffered, an awareness which tended to be eclipsed in the search for 'the end of ideology' and the assertion of the 'scientific' status of sociology. While it is the role of politicians and the state to claim that the politics can be taken out of 'problem solving', it is sociology's role to show that it is always there - whether it tries to disguise itself as a 'third way' or as a 'common sense revolution'.

A sociology that sets out to solve problems, not in a technocratic spirit, but from the standpoint of critically analysing what qualifies as a problem in the first place, and transparently thinking through the costs to diverse social groups of alternative 'solutions', need not become a servant of the state. Sociology cannot offer omniscience. It cannot offer any final proof of how people must live in order to achieve enlightenment. This is itself proof of the discipline's disenchanted and democratic character. Sociology can offer insight, especially in terms of clarifying the choices and constraints which social actors face. Like theologians, sociologists might argue endlessly over the details of the true path, but the difference between a sect and a broader and more effective church has always been a practical concern with the profane life of its communicants and an ability to tolerate dissent and innovation. In an era of disenchantment and the rise of the risk society, sociology offers an approach to problem solving which recognises that conscious, planned social change is always possible.

The contribution of Inglis *et al.* is an unbridled celebration of 'methodological polytheism', and has echoes of both McLennan's and Holmwood's arguments. Inglis *et al.* engage with the issue of whether a wide range of methods of doing sociology necessarily signals disciplinary disarray, or even the end of sociology as a 'discipline'. Like McLennan and Holmwood, they define sociology as an *empirical* discipline. It must necessarily engage with 'the real'. The sense in which Inglis *et al.* understand sociology to be 'scientific' is insofar as it is 'a discipline which relies on empirical evidence as the basis for the development of its corpus of theory'. This view of sociology chimes with McLennan's notion of a substantive underpinning to its theoretical elaborations; and Inglis *et al.*'s advocacy of a methodological polytheism chimes with Holmwood's view of social scientific communities as communing around problem-solving activities rather than applying any particular method.

Inglis *et al.* want us to uncouple methodology from epistemology and embrace a more pragmatic approach, whereby the choice of method is dictated more by the problem at hand than by any pre-existing epistemological commitment. They insist that this leads to a productive 'methodological polytheism' rather than to a debilitating 'methodological anarchism', as in Feyerabend's (1978) advocacy of an 'anything goes' approach. Inglis *et al.* do not, however, pursue this point, and leave hanging in the air the question of how we know that we are 'doing sociology' rather than 'doing something else'.

Blurring boundaries

For nineteenth-century pioneers such as Durkheim and Simmel, the integrity of sociology as a discipline hinged on the designation of an epistemological object – *the social* – which was to be understood as distinct from the 'psychological' or 'biological'. Recent declarations about 'the end of the social' can therefore quickly be transmuted into manifestos for the death of sociology – though it may be that such declarations are simply for the end of the social *as we knew it.* Boundaries are blurring, both as they are lived and as they are thought. Perhaps no concept has been used more unreflectively than that of 'society' (Wallerstein, 1987). Indeed, John Urry (2000) calls for a twenty-first-century sociology that is 'beyond societies' and embraces the kinds of 'diverse mobilities' which, he argues, characterise contemporary social life. If societal boundaries are blurring, then so too are the boundaries between 'the natural' and 'the social'. The cyborg metaphor (Haraway, 1991) has become powerful, as has the actor-network metaphor (Law and Hassard, 1999), in attuning the contemporary intellectual mindset to the increasing complexity of technico–socio relations, and particularly the ways in which this is forcing sociologists to radically alter their sense of the social and – a point Fuller emphasises –the *moral* and *political.*

In their contributions, both Stephen Crook and Steve Fuller urge us to radically rework our concept of the social, whilst Pat Spallone and her co-authors (Chapter 12) urge sociologists to engage with the public debates and new practices that are emerging around biomedical technologies, insisting that sociologists can and do bring a distinctive perspective to bear on these matters. For Fuller and Crook it goes without saying that any residual Durkheimian ontological privileging of 'the social' must be abandoned in the face of new developments in scientific and technological practices, particularly the new human biotechnologies. Crook calls for a reworking of the idea of the social into the sociotechnical,[2] whilst Fuller, in a similar vein, calls for a reworking of the idea of the social into the biological. At the same time, both Fuller and Crook preserve a clear sense of the salience of sociology in the face of shifts which might seem to threaten its displacement.

Crook reflects on what remains of 'the social' after we have given away the idea of 'society'. For him, sociology as a discipline does not dissolve, but has to negotiate its way through the problems of 'nihilism' and 'quietism'. A reworked understanding of the social demands a reformed sociology that retains its capacity to engage over the long term and combine, or at least juxtapose, micro-analyses of the social with macro-analyses of change. At one level, this is the intractable problem that has always bedevilled sociology: nothing changes – but look again and everything changes. We are indeed witnessing a displacement of the social by developments in scientific and technical knowledges and practices, the most obvious example being the new human biotechnologies. The relation between 'humans', 'technologies' and 'nature' is increasingly one of interpenetration, and an understanding of human–natural–technical complexes demands an interdisciplinary division of labour. So, is there still a role for sociology in this new context, or does the demise of the purely social necessarily signal the death of sociology as a mode of knowing? Crook suggests that in order to preserve the salience of sociology, a rethinking of what the 'social' and the 'sociotechnical' are to mean is vital. At the same time, sociology continues to be relevant precisely because it provides us with models for the analysis of science and technology as practices – a point that is also made by Steve Fuller.

Sociologists should not only engage in a rethinking of boundaries, but must also engage practically and with a critical sense of sympathy in a social world where new biomedical technologies are making their presence felt and transforming taken-for-granted notions of personhood. Steve Fuller argues passionately that sociologists must engage intellectually and politically with the, sometimes, sinister ways in which the new biotechnical practices are becoming imbricated in the social. Biotechnical practices have the ability to transform our very conception of personhood, and even of who has a right to personhood. Fuller considers the radical and disturbing implications of such a prospect for those labelled as 'disabled' in society – a point echoed by Pat Spallone *et al.* who call for a partisan sociological engagement in bioethics. Fuller also charts the way in which we can develop a critical, sociological analysis of bioprospecting and 'offspring design', insisting that 'our sense of humanity is underwritten by the *sympathy* we can establish with the life circumstances of others', and that this constitutes a *moral* bond. He argues that it is imperative that a critical sense of sympathy become the basis for a new social bond; we cannot simply watch passively and intellectualise the end of the social as we knew it. Yet many sociological responses to biology have polarised unhelpfully either as wholesale dismissal or slavish adherence. While neither response is seen as helpful, Fuller produces a particularly hard-hitting critique of the neo-Darwinian Left. The stakes are high, and the questions raised by Fuller are urgent ones. They are questions that should intimately concern sociologists, as they are about the future of the social bond itself. Fuller insists that what is 'at stake here is no less than what it takes to constitute a normative social order and who counts as a member of such an order'.

Fuller's vision of a reworked sociology calls for an *interdisciplinary engagement*, as distinct from the *postdisciplinarity* advocated by Sayer. In much the same way as Crook calls for an engagement of sociology with scientific and technical practices, Fuller calls for an engagement between sociology and biology. But Fuller is not arguing that sociologists should turn into biologists. He is alerting us to developments in biological knowledge, particularly in the fields of genetics and ecology, which severely undermine ontologies of the social. Just as Crook argues that new scientific and technical practices diminish the possibility of anything remaining 'purely social', so Fuller warns that new forms of biological knowledge severely undermine the possibility of a 'purely sociological' explanation, for example by challenging the taken-for-granted, spatiotemporal perspective conventionally employed in sociology – such as who counts as the collective 'we' of which 'I' am a member?

Pat Spallone and her co-authors, Tom Wilkie, Elizabeth Ettorre, Erica

Haimes, Tom Shakespeare and Meg Stacey, address many of the issues discussed by Crook and Fuller, and argue that the time is ripe for a reinvigoration of bioethics. Their central concern is to establish how sociologists can engage in distinctive, and above all morally committed, ways with bioethics. The question of the relation between ethics and science is an urgent one; the media is filled with reports and discussions of a variety of biomedical practices and potentialities, such as fertility treatment, genetic screening and cloning. The position adopted by Spallone *et al.* has much in common with that of Steve Fuller, most especially in its advocacy of a *moral* engagement with these issues on the part of sociologists. After all, a social bioethics must necessarily be rooted in social relations and intersubjectivity, with each responsible for the other's condition.

Taken together, the three chapters by Crook, Fuller, and Spallone *et al.* show all too clearly how sociologists must urgently confront blurring boundaries, not as a purely intellectual exercise, but in a spirit of critical and moral engagement with the kinds of social and ethical questions that people are asking and grappling with in the twenty-first century. Alvin Gouldner would surely have approved.

Sociology in context

At this point it is instructive to draw attention to the symposium in the January 2000 issue of *Contemporary Sociology*. The symposium is entitled 'Utopian visions: engaged sociologies for the twenty-first century' (note the plural). The essays deal with issues of global significance which are highly resistant to resolution – genocide, hunger, violence. This is an example of sociology attempting to get to grips with 'the big picture'; it is humanistic in spirit and sharply aware of the vast amount of suffering experienced by the wretched of the earth. The underlying assumption in these essays is that an engaged sociology can and must address these large-scale human problems. Big problems rarely have simple solutions, and the contributors exhibit a wary utopianism, not a glib one. Something of this spirit is to be found in Larry Ray's contribution to this volume (Chapter 9). Just as Oberschall (2000), in his essay on genocide, stresses the importance of developing schemes of shared sovereignty, so Ray points to the importance of understanding the processes whereby collective memories and rituals are produced, and stresses their significace as a site for creating and sustaining violent predispositions. Although there are stated differences with Elias (1994), Ray emphasises the need to understand the long-term historical processes in order to understand and deal with contemporary problems. It is through such understandings and the ways in which they are linked to collective violence that, Ray argues, we can move towards a more nuanced understanding of the constitution of the social. The strong implication is, however, that this is not understanding for its own sake, but as a means of showing how processes of pacification may take place. These are matters that can engage sociologists on the local level (we have only to think of the arrival of refugees and asylum seekers in Britain), as well as on a more global terrain. Exploring the relationship between the two levels is an ongoing task for sociologists and will surely form a crucial part of the public agenda for the twenty-first century.

Even if 'social' theory is currently more in vogue than sociological theory (Mouzelis, 1993), sociological theorising is not purely historical. There are attempts to generate novel and insightful sociological frameworks of understanding. Richard Sennet (Chapter 7) offers to articulate the disjunctures currently occurring in people's lives as a result of the restructuring of economic activity. He draws on material from his 1998 book, *The Corrosion of Character*, which is in itself a fine example of accessible, relevant, theoretically informed sociology. Sennett argues that one of the most dramatic changes in people's work-history has been the displacement of a life-long 'career' by a succession of short-term jobs. A sociological theory of narrative, Sennett proposes, provides a technique by which this transformation can be articulated, and sociological analysis developed, enabling 'sociologists ... to redirect their habits of thinking about social reality'. In his contribution he returns to one of sociology's classic concerns – class – but with a novel analytical approach, that of 'a sociological theory of narrative' (inspired by the works of, for example, Calvino and Joyce). He examines the impact of changing labour markets on the problem of social order, and concludes with the warning that 'loss of work is modern capitalism's ticking bomb'. This, of course, is not the first time that sociologists have issued such proclamations. And there have not, so far, been any explosions. However this has not been, as Gouldner feared, because sociology has evolved into a hired army of intellectual bomb disposal teams. Nor is it because, as has sometimes been suggested on the further shores of postmodernism, there has been nothing to blow up. Rather, social order, at least in Western capitalism, has proved remarkably resilient and capable of substantial and rapid change. Sociology's analysis and criticism of social order have been central, not only to the charting of such change, but also in actively influencing the direction it has taken. For this, sociology deserves attention – both now and in the future.

However, as Holmwood's wide-ranging discussion highlights, sociology has lost both its voice and its memory. This problem of amnesia is echoed by Jackson, who argues, with reference to the attribution of the development of social constructionist analysis to recent poststructuralist and postmodern writers, that its 'effect is to obliterate sociology's past contributions from the collective scholarly memory'. Without a memory of other aspects of the sociological tradition, it is also possible to overestimate the novelty of the Third Way and the claims of New Labour to rejuvenate and transform social democracy (Thompson, 2000). Eldridge shows that attempts by sociologists to develop a third way – as distinct from interest or identity groups competing to control state policy – are as old as the discipline itself – starting with Durkheim, through to Mannheim and, more recently, Giddens. In making this case, Eldridge demonstrates the need for sociologists to remember the history of sociological theory. He also reminds us that British and Continental European sociologists have a long tradition of social concern and political engagement – of working for a better future.

All of the contributors to this volume look to the future, and most, if not all, see a future for sociology. But this will, of necessity, be a reworked sociology. As Crook portends, if sociology does not rework itself, then 'there is shelf space in the museum of nineteenth-century curiosities ready and waiting, just after phrenology and the rational dress movement'.

Notes

1 Even if this entails, as it does for McLennan, only a minimal sense of 'everyday', rather than a 'philosophical' sense of 'realism' as something always already there, however complexly constructed its 'thereness' and our understanding of it turns out to be.

2 This 'sociotechnical' is distinct from the previous sociotechnical approach or perspective as a conceptual framework and action research programme, which was promoted by Trist and then others within the sociology of organisations. That approach arose from the study of working patterns and problems in British coalmines in the 1950s (see, for example, Trist, 1981; Cherns, 1976).

References

Abrams, P. (1968) *The Origins of British Sociology 1834–1944*. London: University of Chicago Press

Alexander, J.C. (1995) *Fin-de-Siècle Social Theory*. London: Verso

Beynon, H. and Blackburn, R.M. (1972) *Perceptions of Work*. Cambridge: Cambridge University Press

Bourdieu, P. (1997) *The State Nobility: Elite Schools in the Field of Power*. Cambridge: Polity Press

Cavendish, R. (1982) *Women on the Line*. London: Routledge and Kegan Paul

Cherns, A. (1976) 'The principles of sociotechnical design, *Human Relations* 29, pp. 783–92

Connell, R.W. (1987) *Gender and Power*. Cambridge: Polity

Connell, R.W. (1997) 'Why is classical theory classical?', *American Journal of Sociology*, Vol. 102, No. 6, pp. 1511–57

Elias, W. (1994) *The Civilizing Process*, Oxford: Blackwell

Fanon, F. (1986) *Black Skin, White Masks*. London: Pluto Press

Feyerabend P. K. (1988) *Against Method*. London: Verso

Giddens, A. (1999) *Runaway World*. London: Profile

Gilroy, P. (1994) *The Black Atlantic*. London: Routledge

Gouldner, A.W. (1959) 'Organisational analysis', in R.K. Merton, L. Broom and L.S. Cottrell Jr. (eds) *Sociology Today: Problems and Prospects*. New York: Harper and Row

Gouldner, A.W. (1971) *The Coming Crisis of Western Sociology*. London: Heinemann

Gouldner, A.W. (1973) *For Sociology: Renewal and Critique in Sociology Today*. London: Allen Lane

Haraway, D. (1991) 'A cyborg manifesto: science, technology and socialist feminism in the late twentieth century', in *Simians, Cyborgs and Women: The Reinvention of Nature*. London: Free Association Books

Law, J. and Hassard, J. (eds) (1999) *Actor Network Theory and After*. Oxford: Blackwell

Lemert, C. (1995) *Sociology after the Crisis*. Boulder, Colorado: Westview

Lupton, T. (1963) *On the Shop Floor*. Oxford: Pergamon

Marshall, A. (1961) *Principles of Economics*. London: Macmillan

Merton, R.K. (1975) * title to be supplied in P. Blau, (ed.) *Approaches to the Study of Social Structure*. Glencoe: Free Press

Mommsen, W.J. (1965) 'Max Weber's political sociology and his philosophy of world history', *Int. Soc. Science Jnl*, Vol. 17

Mouzelis, N. (1991) *Back to Sociological Theory*. Basingstoke: Macmillan

Mouzelis, N. (1993) 'The poverty of sociological theory', *Sociology*, 27, pp. 675–95.

Oberschall, A. (2000) 'Theory and progress in social science', *Social Forces*, Vol. 78, No. 3, pp. 1188–90

Parsons, T. (1954) *Some Problems Confronting Sociology as a Profession in Essays in Sociological Theory*. New York: Free Press

Pollert, A. (1981) *Girls, Wives, Factory Lives*. London: Macmillan

Rorty, R. (1998) *Achieving Our Country*. Cambridge, Massachusetts: Harvard University Press

Sennett, R. (1998) *The Corrosion of Character*. London: W.W. Norton

Smith, D. (1987) *The Everyday World as Problematic*. Milton Keynes: Open University Press

Strathern, M. (1991) *Partial Connections*. Savage, Maryland: Rowman and Littlefield

Thompson, P. (2000) 'Living in the present, haunted by the past: New Labour and Year Zero', *Renewal*, 8, pp. 1–6

Trist, E.L. (1981) 'The sociotechnical perspective', in A.H. van de Ven and W.F. Joyce (eds) *Perspectives on Organisational Design and Behaviour*. New York: John Wiley

Urry, J. (1982) 'Sociology as a parasite', in P. Abrams, R. Deem, J. Finch and P. Rock (eds) *Practice and Progress: British Sociology 1950–1980*, London: Allen and Unwin

Urry, J. (2000) *Sociology Beyond Societies*. London: Routledge

Wallerstein, T. (1999) 'The heritage of sociology: the promise of social science', *Current Sociology*, Vol. 47, No. 1, pp. 1–41

Weber, M. (1949) *The Methodology of the Social Sciences*, New York: Free Press

Chapter 1
The new positivity
Gregor McLennan[1]

Cultures of Sociology

In the early 1770s, John Millar of Glasgow wrote:

> *When we contemplate the amazing diversity to be found in the laws of different countries, and even of the same country at different periods, our curiosity is naturally excited to enquire in what manner mankind have been led to embrace such different rules of conduct ... In searching for the causes of those peculiar systems of law and government which have appeared in the world, we must undoubtedly resort, first of all, to the differences of situation which have suggested different views and motives of action to the inhabitants of particular countries ... The variety that frequently occurs in these and such other particulars, must have a prodigious influence upon the great body of a people; as, by giving a peculiar direction to their inclinations and pursuits, it must be productive of correspondent habits, dispositions, and ways of thinking.*
> (cited in Lehman, 1960: 175)

Millar's statement is an energetic expression of what we might call 'generic sociology'. He is saying that we need to establish both the uniformities and the differences that characterise different situations, systems of rules, and popular views and motives. Wide-rangingly, he goes on to itemise the various elements of social situation: natural environments, types of labour and subsistence, demography, 'proficiency in arts', advantages of 'mutual transaction' and forms of 'intimate correspondence'. Let us note too that the relation between situation and views and motives is couched as only the first main move in an explanatory strategy, and that there is a felicitous avoidance of determinism in Millar's sense of exactly how situations 'influence' and 'give direction to' people's 'inclinations'. It is almost as if he foresaw, and forestalled, the protracted debates around these matters within the 'disciplinary Sociology' that came after.

Today, we are at the other end of that disciplinary tradition, and we are being urged by some to see Sociology as a sinking ship that we ought to be deserting – and fast. Immanuel Wallerstein, for example, in his capacity as president of the International Sociological Association, has urged us to 'unthink' the culture of Sociology (Wallerstein, 1999). Sociology, he suggests, might well be incapable of fully embracing the intellectual problems of our time: the concern to investigate new sorts of unconscious processes, to embrace radical complexity, and to articulate multilinear and compressed temporality. Sociology is culturally inadequate in a political sense too, Wallerstein asserts, failing to adjust properly to feminist, anti-Eurocentric and non-modern thinking. I agree with this sense of the challenges facing us, and feel no overwhelming need to protect and defend disciplinary Sociology as such – though it surely can be defended against facile versions of these objections.[2] I do however want to retain and promote the broader idea of generic sociology, from which none of the aspiring successor discourses to Sociology has managed to cut loose. For example, there seems to be a battle going on for the soul of postcolonial studies, between a recognisably sociologistic understanding of postimperial life and thought, and a more 'performative' mode of disrupting the 'Westernist' representational mentality. Within postfeminism too, there is a fundamental issue about the extent to which propositions about the primacy of knowable gendered social relations are being reaffirmed, and the extent to which this whole way of thinking is being circumvented, as feminism becomes philosophically and politically pluralised. Cultural studies, for its part, has undergone a heart-wrenching move out of 'Birmingham model' assumptions into those of 'postmodern conjuncturalism'. But does this mean that 'culture' and 'society' are being refigured here, or entirely thrown over, plunging us into a deep sea of discursive imaginaries? On my reading,[3] even the most urgent and antisociological advocates for the development of a postdisciplinary culture can be found making significant claims or assumptions about the way in which society is generally structured, and about how to understand subjectivities and discourses in relation to the wider social situations that they somehow express. A culture of inquiry around 'the logic of the social' – my baseline definition of generic sociology – is thus much harder to 'unthink' than many post-Sociologists imagine.

Indeed, it could be that sociology, if not necessarily Sociology, is actually making something of a come-back within the critical human sciences, in the form of a *new positivity* that made itself felt in a number of ways during the 1990s. The 1980s, we might say, was the decade in which deconstruction and 'negative' critique – of the various 'sins' of modernist thinking: objectivism, essentialism, reductionism, universalism, realism and so on (cf. McLennan, 1996) – held full sway, making any impulse to conventional sociological thinking look rather positivistic and naive. Whilst the 1990s of course remained formally postpositivist and even antirealist, nevertheless we can see retrospectively that a creeping positivism was at work, or at least a new positivity, in which the 'interminable self-critique' that Derrida himself (1994: 89) regards as the fatal weakness in deconstructionism was being moved along in favour of something more substantive and affirmative. That mood continues to swell at the millennium, and amongst other things this will ensure the vitality of generic sociology for some time to come.

Positivism reconsidered

Having mentioned positivism and positivity in one breath, let me immediately clarify that I am not advocating a return to positivism 'as we know it'. Many of the tenets of postpositivism as an account of social knowing seem to me entirely valid. At the same time, given the caricatures of positivism that prevail in the textbooks, it is salutary to look again at some of the forgotten and surprising aspects of positivist metatheory. These can be phrased in a summary way in terms of what positivism is *not* (necessarily), and they lead on to perhaps the main point that I want to emphasise in this context: that, strangely enough, there is considerable *continuity* between positivism and postpositivism.

- The first point about positivism is that it cannot be equated with *empiricism per se*, and certainly not inductivism. This is because the role of theory and science has always been crucial for positivists. Consequently, although positivism has always had a healthy respect for 'the facts', the notion that it is 'fact driven' is basically wrong. Moreover, many positivists have viewed theory as a creative, imaginative human faculty rather than some kind of abstract calculus or mirror to reality.

- Positivists are not necessarily scientifically *reductionist*. Comte, for one, did not view the unity of science as a matter of different scientific domains having the same basic laws of operation (cf. Pickering, 1997). Rather his argument was for the necessary interconnectedness of the various sciences, and the positivist assertion of the methodological unity of science has varied considerably from thinker to thinker in terms of tightness of specification.

- Positivists are not necessarily *rationalist* about motivation and culture, as is sometimes made out in critiques which strive to 'save' the psychodynamic richness of social phenomena from one-dimensional positivist images of the self-interested agent or (in a leftist version) the clear-sighted altruist. Pareto, for instance, was a systematic positivist in his formal presentation of the structure of society, and in his belief that its underlying forces could be empirically observed in their manifestations. Yet the content of Pareto's social theory had 'irrational' or non-rational, and even non-representable, social forces – the Paretian 'residues' and 'derivations' – at its very heart.

- Positivists have not been overly rationalist, either, in terms of the *purpose* of social science. Far from being disinterestedly 'scientistic' in this regard, positivists have generally followed a reformist impulse, accepting that the practice of social science is strongly governed by value-orientations. In the case of Comte and his British followers like Harriet Martineau, the predominantly humanist values of positivism took a liberal reformist hue, with honourable Victorians such as Edward Beesly being considerably more radical (cf. Wright, 1986). Otto Neurath of the Vienna Circle of logical positivists was a revolutionary socialist. Generally speaking, positivists have been Left-leaning, and their hope has been that science can be used – must be used – to create a more enlightened and egalitarian society. This picture of workaday positivism goes against the hackneyed picture of positivism as either ideologically conservative or doctrinally value-free. Indeed, many positivists, at least in the last century, declared their 'project' to be one of determined *synthesis* of the persistent dualisms within modern intellectual culture (theory/fact; science/faith; sociology/other disciplines) (cf. Vogeler, 1984).

We can go a little further than this in problematising the current status of positivism, for positivists have long been concerned to put forward claims that look remarkably *post*-positivist.[4] Perhaps the most characteristic feature of positivism has been its antipathy to metaphysical foundationalism. Hume, of course, immediately comes to mind here; and Comte too, for whom the cultural shift away from justification in terms of abstract absolutes was definitive of positivism. The Vienna Circle were also vehemently opposed to surplus reference to all manner of shadowy essences and deep forces operating behind observable connections.

Such articles of positivist faith need underlining when we hear so often that realism and objectivism are expressions of 'positivist' mythology. The logical positivists were emphatic on this matter. Moritz Schlick, the convenor of the

Circle, initially regarded all claims to know reality 'in itself' as irremediably metaphysical, and therefore false, though he subsequently softened up on this, suggesting that they were merely undecidable and irrelevant (Hanfling, 1981: 55). In his wavering over whether this was a principled position, or a 'strategic' one, Schlick's attitudes closely parallel those of antiessentialists today. The Vienna school held strongly to the idea that theory was underdetermined by evidence, and that the facts were overdetermined by theory, since claims about the nature of reality only made sense in and through particular discourses, especially scientific ones. This premise of linguistic relativity was summarised by Rudolph Carnap (1956: 206–7), the most systematic of the logical positivists, as the view that to be real meant to be 'an element in the system', a coherent part of the linguistic framework or system of scientific categories. Was there some *privileged* system of categories, a primary language of science? Certainly, *physicalism* came to be favoured because of its hard-science resonance, but this essentialist-sounding move has an interesting origin. It seems that Neurath persuaded Carnap to plump for a physicalist metatheoretical frame, because it was ideologically and politically progressive at the time, and Carnap, whose primary concern was for maximum intersubjective agreement, found this a plausible basis for consensus despite his own phenomenalist inclinations (see Neurath, 1973: 44–5). With this latter angle – an intersubjective and conventional approach to matters of ultimate truth and validity – we get a sense of how for these positivists 'objectivity' as such, which was certainly desirable, was mainly a matter of professional and instrumental effectivity, rather than something spontaneously prompted by the nature of reality itself. Much has been made, rightly, of the Vienna theorists' attempt to construct a basic 'observation language', a terminology that could be shared by all scientific endeavours, and strenuous-looking 'correspondence rules' were formalised for connecting the terms of the scientific theoretical language with 'primitive' observational sentences. But all the time, questions of basic observations and theoretical laws were couched by the positivists as in the first instance *terminologies*, that is, discursive conventions and constructs.

Logical positivism, then, was thoroughly antimetaphysical, irrealist and conventionalist, these also being core features of postpositivist or postpragmatist thinking at the present time. Obviously, there is no need to claim that the two perspectives are one and the same. The strong positivist assertion that general covering laws are required within and, ideally, across each domain of investigation, is no longer accepted in the social sciences. The related deductivism of positivism is also largely gone. And the insistence in some strands of positivism that there must be a clear line of demarcation between science and non-science has been abandoned too, though I am less sure about the associated separation of facts and values. As already suggested, this distinction may not have been so clear-cut in positivist practice anyway, and whilst there is much rhetorical opposition to it in antipositivist thought, critical theorists are as unlikely as positivists to concede that their own considered views and research results emanate directly from their ideological predilections.

Social theory and sociological theory

Lately, there has been a campaign to replace boring old sociological theory by new, stimulating social theory, on the grounds that Sociology remains mired in a commitment to positivistically conceived objectivity within an intellectually 'modernist' framework, whereas social theory is more free-spiritedly embracing of discursive constructionism, interdisciplinarity and postmodern/postcolonial disruptions. In Charles Lemert's formula (1997: 24, III), sociologists always want to be assured of objectivity and scientificity, whereas social theorists are 'constantly reflecting on the necessity and nature of interpretation itself', and in so doing, habitually transgressing its subject matter. The point of my previous section was to disallow any easy assumptions about what positivistic scientificity entails, even if Sociology was to be accepted as aspiring to it. But historically, the notion that sociological theory has been consistently scientistic is also open to question. After all, the 'big pictures' of classical social thought and their residues today are regarded with suspicion by postmodern social theorists as undemonstrable metanarratives, and ironically this seems like a decidedly positivist complaint.

I would also take issue with the assumption in arguments like␊ Lemert's that the move out of sociology and into social theory is automatically to be considered coherent and politically progressive. The prime candidates as replacements for scientism as a governing mentality for social thought appear to be 'reflexivity' and 'moral advocacy'. The latter is urged, for example, by Steven Seidman (1994), who desires sociological reflection to be less concerned with absolutes, abstractions and truth, and more concerned with local visions, practical effectivity and perspectival validity. Yet it is difficult to see how one can be rigorously relativist and perspectival with respect to a wide variety of worldviews or social values, *and* be the kind of passionate moral advocate for particular causes and movements that Seidman admires, since the latter normally involve a substantial degree of essentialism, both about how the world works and about the values that most need to be institutionalised.

Seidman's moralistic overtures are welcome for all that, because although the various bouts of reflexivity from the time of Gouldner onwards have been generally good for sociology, rightly holding in check any excessively scientistic inclinations, in the wrong hands reflexivity can result in intellectual paralysis. In my view, critical social theory is not to be sharply distinguished from, and preferred to, a narrower sort of sociological theory, precisely because a vital and necessary element of positivity tends to get lost along with all that positivism. Take Craig Calhoun's (1995: 35) account of critical theory, summarised as four main characteristics:

1. a critical engagement with the theorist's contemporary social world;
2. a critical awareness of the historico-cultural conditions in which theory is produced;
3. self-critical re-examination of one's own theoretical understanding;
4. a critical confrontation with other works of social explanation.

This declaration of critical reflexivity, alright as far as it goes perhaps, nevertheless seems blandly question-begging in its formulation. Moreover, there is almost nothing in it to indicate why the 'critical' in critical theory is connected to radical or reformist social politics rather than to the sensitive liberal intelligence. Seidman's call for urgency in clarifying what the point of sociological theory is today, is thus just as relevant for the social theory that he and others regard as obviously superior. Here we have to remember the paradox that positivism and antipositivism alike, each claiming to relieve us of metaphysical hang-ups, are *philosophical* programmes, that is, they form general conceptual accounts of proper intellectual practice which, however interesting and even occasionally transformative of cultural debate, are parasitical upon substantive and 'positive' practices of social knowledge. This is one reason why sociology cannot allow itself to be pensioned off under postpositivist pressure, any more than it needed to wilt embarrassingly when designated 'immature' by earlier positivists.

I want to touch on the trajectory of some important strands within social theory, as illustrations of a pattern whereby the hegemony of philosophy was firstly challenged by holistic sociological or social-theoretical alternatives to what was imagined to be positivism, with subsequent movement towards reflexivity, and then positivity.

The sociology of scientific knowledge

In the stimulating development of the sociology of scientific knowledge (SSK), for example, we see a first phase of radical critique whereby the leading role of philosophy in general, and philosophical positivism in particular, is challenged for delivering from on high a prescriptive formula for 'valid' knowledge production, quite outside any consideration of the processes through which science is practised and progressed by living scientists in specific social contexts. Famously asserting that true science and bad science must be treated equally in respect of their social production, the 'strong programmes' that emerged overturned sociology's dependence on philosophical models of knowledge, and indeed asserted a claim to primacy themselves, in that henceforth philosophy and science were to be seen as socially constructed and socially explicable.

In a second phase, SSK asked itself some questions. Was not the new primacy of the social in accounts of science and knowledge itself a kind of positivistic and legislative manoeuvre? Moreover, when we talk about the 'social' determinants of scientific knowledge, what exactly have we got in mind? Origins, causes, conditions, influences, expressions? And to what, concretely, do these projected origins, causes, conditions etc. refer? To class positions, pressure group interests, general ideological assumptions, gender bias? Finally, when we settle on a particular social storyline for the emergence or success of particular scientific episodes, what gives us the right to argue that this sense of the social, and that degree of conditioning or influence, are demonstrably valid, as against other contestable construals of the work of the social? All this, quite apart from the (not dissimilar) traditional philosophical response to SSK, attested that no amount of social explanation can account for the validity or invalidity of scientific claims.

An intense period of 'reflexivity' followed, with ever greater attention being paid to the way in which any assertions to knowledge or primacy were rhetorically advanced, and with some interesting experimentation with 'new literary forms' (NLF) going on as a means of reflexive debate. Here as in other spheres, the initial sociological impulse of SSK was giving way to literary deconstructionism. But again, as with formal deconstructionism and overgeneralised social constructionism elsewhere, in SSK it was quickly realised that such antipositivist and antiphilosophical strategies were largely framed as merely the 'other' of the mindsets they sought to challenge. Realism had been replaced by an equally totalising and quasi-metaphysical antirealism, determinism by principled indeterminacy, referentiality by constructionism, substantivity by all-pervasive rhetoric or textuality, and so on. Accordingly, SSK having earlier been transformed into NLF and generalised reflexivity, took on a new lease of life as STS – science and technology studies. The aim of this version was to leave philosophical considerations aside, their being an obstacle to understanding, and instead describe the way in which scientists go about constructing their worlds and conducting their material practices. This is typical of the new positivity: the concern is to describe and observe, to gain some knowledge of how scientific things in the social world are realised, in discourse and technology, without being filtered through 'deeper' background contrasts, however construed, between Science and Ideology, Society and Nature.

Feminism

The second 'case' of a tradition where we can see a new positivity developing is feminist metatheory. The fundamental, and culturally revolutionary, insights of feminist critique in the philosophical realm were firstly that images of Science and practices of science alike were profoundly masculinist, and secondly that modern epistemology – as the place where those images are systematised and legitimated – has been constitutively men-oriented in its prevailing model of the disinterested and disembodied inquirer into truth and justice. Understandably, this led to a search for a wholly alternative model of feminist knowing, where commitments of a personal and social kind could be acknowledged and a far greater degree of harmony established between cognitive and emotional aspects of world-building and meaning-making. Various attempts to found a 'feminist standpoint' epistemology followed, heavily coloured, and somewhat compromised, in its later stages by postmodernist influences. However the idea of feminist philosophy as altogether discontinuous with the mainstream/ malestream has not taken hold, partly because of the problem that if you criticise a worldview for being insufficiently attuned to social forces and determinants – a *sociological* point, let us remember – then it hardly suffices to replace that with an alternative of equally abstract and cosmic status. But additionally, because feminism is indubitably a political and intellectual tradition with at least one foot in the modernist, rationalist mindset, the prospect of giving up entirely on science and objectivity has not finally appealed. Thus, feminists have had to face up to the problem that any superiority claimed for 'feminist standpoint' metatheory must itself be established partly in terms of its offering a better, more 'objective' account of the way in which knowledge gets established and accepted. Furthermore, when this feminist perspective gradually wins support, as it has, it comes to look rather mainstream: the state of knowledge has been broadened and enhanced by the feminist contribution, and so is, ironically perhaps, less open to the initial 'standpoint' accusations. For some feminists, this is accepted as representing some kind of 'progress', whilst for others, feminism itself begins to look too collusive with modernist assumptions, and there is a move into more performative and expressive (supposedly 'transgressive') ways of knowing and being.

Feminist philosophers have accordingly been attempting to settle into a new mode in which elements of science and objectivity must be positively embraced, yet these must be somehow blended in with reflexivity and moral advocacy. Thus Sandra Harding (1993: 69) talks of retaining both 'strong objectivity' and 'strong reflexivity', and Helen Longino (1993: 113) advocates 'socially constituted objectivity'. These are admirable slogans, of course, but they possibly reproduce rather than resolve the basic problem, and anyway remain pitched at the philosophical level. Donna Haraway (1996: 258), however, completes the step to a new positivity by saying that to go beyond the impasse between philosophical ideologies of objectivity and their all-embracing relativist counterparts, what we need to do is produce 'better accounts of the world, that is, "science"'.

Postmodernism

As for my third strand within social theory – postmodernism – it is perhaps sufficient to note that during the 1990s: a) this has taken a distinctly pragmatist turn, and b) many leading candidates for the label postmodernist have disowned it, tricking some earnest camp-followers by denying that they were at any point simply 'against' the various mainstream objects of reflexive critique – modernism, Marxism, philosophy, liberalism, reality, and so on. In terms of the pragmatist turn, there is continuing puzzlement about whether this represents a new set of postmodernistic *principles* for inquiry and debate, or whether pragmatism just means getting on with things in the normal, preferably substantive sort of way. Actually, this issue of the status of pragmatism – whether it is a new 'ism' or a plague on all 'isms' – is very old in philosophy, but postmodern social theorists are now caught by it, and interestingly pragmatism's doyen, Richard Rorty, is no longer much use to them if their aim is to continue to divide interpretation and reflexivity from positivity, and to privilege the former on general grounds. In a thumping reminder that the coincidence between pragmatism and poststructuralism only goes so far, and that the closer relationship is between pragmatism and positivism, Rorty has recently inveighed against some of the gurus who are often assumed to be his co-conspirators in ironic anti-essentialism:

> *We are told over and over again that Lacan has shown human desire to be inherently unsatisfiable, that Derrida has shown meaning to be undecideable, that Lyotard has shown commensuration between oppressed and oppressors to be impossible, and that events such as the Holocaust or the massacre of the original Americans are unrepresentable. Hopelessness has become fashionable on the Left – principled, theorised, philosophical hopelessness.*
> (Rorty, 1998: 36–7)

'The infinite and the unrepresentable are merely nuisances', Rorty (1998: 96) lectures us, when we get around to taking up 'our public responsibilities' and investigating contemporary social life.

These intimations of positivity are further and finally confirmed when we think of how much of contemporary social theory is taken up by articulating and mediating various paradigm disputes or conceptual dualisms. Undoubtedly there is subtle critique and commentary still to be undertaken in these areas, yet on the whole one feels that many of the disputes and dualisms have run out of steam. For one thing, the very idea of coherent, boxed-up and incommensurable 'paradigms' as a way of classifying and dealing with theoretical disputes in the social sciences no longer reflects the more fluid and, yes, pragmatic way in which standard issues – class, ethnicity, gender, to take only the staple sociological triumvirate of topics – are addressed today. And for another thing, although dualisms are set up in terms of oppositional readings of key dimensions of social and intellectual life, it is increasingly false to imagine that particular thinkers and traditions doggedly inhabit only one side of the polarity. How much longer, for example, can it be tolerated to place certain thinkers – Marx or Parsons, say – on the 'structure' rather than the 'agency' side of that particularly tedious dichotomy? Similarly, it seems very odd now to try to pitch the meaning of 'the social' definitively against 'the cultural' on the one side, or against 'the natural' on the other. And having looked for a moment as though all-purpose assertions of the 'social constructedness' of everything were becoming the (low) common denominator in social theory, it is now thankfully being clarified that in many respects these assertions are simply tautologous, or that they do not after all require us to obliterate what is specific about the natural, the material, and so on (cf. Velody and Williams, 1998). What count now are not all-purpose assertions about social constructionism, but careful studies which show how specific labels get introduced and disseminated, this being a 'positive' enterprise as much as it is a critical-reflective one.

Although I referred to it a moment ago, I think that the relativism–objectivism/realism dualism uses up so much energy amongst social theorists that its decline into shadow-boxing cannot be overemphasised. For every 'relativist's dilemma' that gets thrown up by realists (for example, the self-defeating consequence of claiming unconditionally that knowledge claims are relative to context and not universally valid), there is a corresponding 'realist's dilemma' (for example, that realism's claims about the non-discursive nature of real processes can only be asserted through local discourses, never 'absolutely'). For every critical assertion that realism gives a stunted two-dimensional account of knowledge (ideas: the world) whereas relativism is three-dimensional (ideas: people and contexts: the world), you get the realist response that it is relativism and not realism that is two-dimensional, because the world does not figure at all in the relativist schema, whereas realism is realist about people as well as about natural and social objects. To this, instrumentalist philosophers (for example, Fine, 1986) can respond by saying that in the 'natural ontological attitude', we have, naturally, no reason whatever to doubt the existence of everyday reality and its objects; but in science and philosophy we are obliged to put this attitude to one side in the search for solutions to particular problems. So you don't have to be a philosophical realist to be an everyday realist, most of the time.

These thrusts and parries lead to a situation where, in effect, what we have is a debate not between realism and relativism, but between anti-antirealism and anti-antirelativism, in Geertz's (1984) ridiculously useful phrase. Now my own firm commitments in all this are 'realist', but I suspect that many realists will agree that it is now very hard work trying to get anything fresh or terribly consequential for social science practice out of this impasse, as can once again be seen from its articulation in feminist philosophy. Beginning from the dubious claim that relativism has been 'relentlessly denigrated' in twentieth-century philosophy (there is a case for the exact opposite view), Lorraine Code, for example, seeks to rehabilitate relativism, partly for feminist reasons. But the relativism in question turns out to be anti-antirelativism, and Code (1995: 196) readily acknowledges that she is against 'extreme relativism' just as much as realists are. Relativism, indeed, must not be seen to exclude a certain aspect of objectivism – it's just that whatever objectivity we arrive at should be treated as *dialogically* rather than monologically produced. In that case, relativism is not so much a denial of the existence of concept-independent real structures, as an acceptance that knowledge of these is a matter of negotiation between different explanations, to the point where we can be certain of very little, perhaps not even the reality of the supposed independent structures. But there is little here that a real-life realist would flatly disagree with, especially if realism is not understood in the unproductive and unreal way that Code initially specifies:

> *A universalist presumably believes that there is an unchanging reality, of which human beings can gain better and better knowledge, until near perfection is achieved; and that truths established now will be true for all time. For a relativist, by contrast ...*
> (1995: 198).

The dialogue here is clearly skewed towards relativism, but as it happens, Code concludes her book very tamely: all in all, 'naturalism provides moorings, not foundations' (1995: 231). Is this really relativism, or really realism, or both, or neither? Perhaps by this stage it doesn't matter too much.[5]

New positivity, new problematics

There are a number of ways that the argument could proceed from here. Although I declared myself from the start to be temperamentally disinclined towards any 'straight' form of positivism as such, perhaps it is time to return more emphatically to that oft-maligned conception of sociological knowledge. Certainly, Jonathan Turner (1992: 167) throws out an important challenge when he says that without the continual search for general social laws, sociology must settle for being a ragbag of second-rate philosophy, commentary on events, vague conceptual schemes, militant relativism, and historical and empirical description. Moreover, prospects are high for mining one abundant source for law-like social/sociological theory, in the form of lessons and analogues spinning out from the 'new synthesis' between genetics and evolutionary biology in the natural sciences, whose substantive reach would appear to have important implications for social explanation. Whilst many social theorists will immediately be tempted to vilify this as the baneful return of sociobiology, or 'biological reductionism', this kind of reaction seems short-sighted and ill-informed. Such, at any rate, is the warning given out by one major social theorist, Runciman (1998), whose own exacting perspective on social evolution, though neotraditionalist in some ways, is demonstrably postpositivist in others. There is a large agenda for positive theory and research in this area, one which might greatly benefit from the participation of feminist sociologists.

A second line of approach would be to conclude that sociology and sociological theory should at least be heralded as an effective antidote to all that arrogant and unproductive postmodern social theory. Nicos Mouzelis' (1991) slogan 'back to sociological theory' rings out volubly here, with considerable justification. I am reluctant to endorse this 'revenge' scenario, however. For one thing, the point of the last section was to show how strong elements of the new positivity were emerging intrinsically, as it were, from within the social theory genre itself. And secondly, to turn the tables on social theory entirely would be to confirm the latter's own definitive distinction between social and sociological theory. Mouzelis suggests that instead of reproducing philosophical dualisms, the craft of sociological theory is to forge conceptual tools for substantive purposes. I agree with this, but conceptual tools of any sort are necessarily 'generalities', as Mouzelis knows, and these have a certain philosophical cast to them that goes beyond specific disciplinary orientations. The schoolmasterly instruction to 'return to basics' in this context, whilst timely, looks ultimately too conservative.

A more accommodating take on these issues has recently been offered by Thomas Osborne (1998). Osborne wishes to retain some sort of distinction between social theory and sociological theory, but to deflate the pretensions of each. The role of sociological theory is indeed to set conceptual triggers for empirical investigation, with social theory offering a kind of analytics of 'enlightenmentality'. It inquires into, and illuminates, just what it is about any knowledge-claiming discourse that aims to change our visions, in terms of theoretical logic and substantive propositions, and, crucially, in terms of the particular ethic of truthfulness that it conveys. Osborne's idea, whilst defensive of social theory, contributes to the new positivity firstly by reaffirming the priority of empirical understanding within sociology, and secondly by implying that social theory itself needs to be conducted in a more descriptive and observational way. Its purpose is not to provide philosophical legitimation for social knowledge, nor to come to the assessment of sociological or other discourses already pre-armed with a strong commitment to be 'critical', or to some background 'paradigm'; rather the point is to engage in a kind of conceptual therapy, raising questions of consistency, impact and ethics from a dialogical standpoint.

Osborne's perspective enjoins us to be rather more affirmative in our modes of theoretical appraisal. If my arguments about the necessity of generic sociology and about the new positivity have been persuasive, then we can even say that a spirit of intellectual *consensus* within the human sciences is something that needs to be cultivated again. This proposal is decidedly not intended simply to get academics to be friendlier towards one another, just for the sake of it. But it is to try to break the now stifling presumption that the establishment of consensus, where it exists, is somehow complacent and conservative, whereas expressions of difference and disagreement are intrinsically radical and good. Especially in a situation in which many previously adhered to articles of faith are dramatically weakening, and yet also at a time when it is eminently possible for sociologists to contribute to the shaping of the general political culture, it is important to try to present a common and effective front wherever possible. This would seem to be a 'mature' response to the breakdown of 'paradigmatic' debate and the erosion of visceral dispute around the residual dualisms of the discipline. We can even be collectively positive about the fact that social theorists are once again contributing ideas to the public realm, even if we might otherwise want vehemently to disagree with the content of their standpoints. Thus, for example, there is considerable peer admiration and support for Anthony Giddens' (1998) attempts to steer some ideas, and a sense of the relevance of sociology, into political debate, even though many of us want thoroughly to contest his Third Way ideology, and the background 'structurationism' that it extends in a practical direction.[6]

Let me give just one example of the kind of position around which an inclusive professional consensus could be formed: Manuel Castells' (1998) *The Information Age*. This work, it seems to me, has several positive features just by virtue of its mode of address and construction. It favours substantive analysis rather than 'merely' theoretical reflection, but is highly theoretical all the same. It contains many large-scale sociological propositions, but is couched inclusively in interdisciplinary style. Those propositions are substantial in number and empirical reach, but they are somewhat general and in need of much further delineation and exploration; accordingly, the author couches his ideas in terms of suggestions rather than doctrines or 'facts'. Castells is taking on a classically sociological task – the 'morphology' of a society and an epoch – yet he believes that this traditional undertaking must confront not only a new historical situation, but also a greater appreciation of multiplicity and plurality. There is an aspiration to a certain kind of disinterestedness, but the form and content bear the mark of serious engagement with feminist and postcolonial concerns. The research findings that inform his thinking have been gathered from a variety of collective projects done mainly by other social scientists, which is acknowledged, yet Castells' overview is eloquently conducted in his own voice. The book represents a good deal of interesting and hard-won social science, but it is obviously a response to an urgent human predicament and a political moment of a certain sort (end of millennium, etc.). Its tone and content are consequently avowedly value-relevant, but there is little that is directly and pre-emptively ideological.

If the style of Castells' trilogy is a winning one, the idea of consensus being generated around its content too is perhaps more controversial. Marxists, for example, will want to express reservations about the analytical primacy given to 'informationalism' as a qualitatively new mode of social development, and – to take just one out of many possible detailed objections – we would surely want to query Castells' exaggerated sense in which social movements and cultural projects are 'outside the system' as such, representing some kind of fundamental 'break with institutionalised social logic' (1998: 352). What might be needed instead is a stiff dose of the 'cultural logic of late capitalism'. Even so, Castells' account is roomy enough to allow such a major qualification, and anyway there is plenty going on which makes it clear that capitalist social relations remain vastly predominant in global terms. By the same token, committed postmodernists may feel that there is too much in Castells that smacks of unproblematic and preconfigured material 'reality' out there, or they might find Castells' wholesome authorial persona too much to take, especially when paraded as the state of social scientific knowledge. But again, there is much in Castells' work to encourage the participation of 'mild' postmodernists, especially perhaps his sense of the transformation of identity from a passive social experience to a creative process of self-definition. The point here is simply to say that around an important work like Castells' there is an opportunity, of some cultural and political significance, to maximise agreement over a range of substantive developments and analytical concepts, and there is something like a new professional imperative to strive to give that commonality a public presence. Naturally, we would only enter into consensus-maximisation around contributions of substance and quality, but actually the human sciences are not short of these, and its culture would produce more if this ethic of positivity were to spread.

Throughout this chapter, I have been using the term 'positivity' in a rough and ready way, just to name a subcultural mood swing that has been building up in various ways. I want to conclude by relating my usage to Michel Foucault's (1970) more 'technical' handling of the term, in his now neglected *The Order of Things*. By the 'positivities' of a discourse, Foucault seems to have in mind the typical modes of being, intellectual problem-fields, and objects of inquiry that are thrown up or assumed within particular epistemes. These positivities in turn generate more concrete observational problems and objects – 'empiricities'. Within this conception of discursive integrity, Foucault investigates the emergence of the modern social scientific episteme, illuminating how, in his view, it was structured around 'Man, labour and language' in terms of its substantive positivities, and how its theoretical lenses are imprinted with dualisms such as structure/genesis, explanation/comprehension, and depth/surface forms of attention.

A major implication of Foucault's discussion, of course, is that whilst each episteme regards its analytical constructs and substantive positivities as definitive and stable, these are actually bounded systems, subject to considerable change over time. More than at the time when Foucault was suggesting this, the modern positivities that he identified now look even less than adequate to contemporary social scientific self-images and practices. Not only has 'Man', famously, been decentred, but the objects of inquiry framed by reactive oppositional stances – theoretical antihumanism and poststructuralism – have also had their day. In terms of background assumptions about formal explanatory adequacy, moreover, the prescriptive division between causal explanation on the one hand and interpretative comprehension on the other, for example, has similarly taken on a rather antique flavour, with research practices and pedagogical presentations alike improvising and even interbreeding these categorical modes. Whilst more superficially conceived, my own argument in this paper – that the new 'positivity' is taking us beyond increasingly sterile battles between 'positivism' and 'critical theory' – slides into alignment with Foucault's belief that the positivities of social science have been undergoing profound transformation. Unlike many Foucauldians, however,[7] I see generic sociology as having an enhanced rather than a diminished role to play both in advancing the general mood of positivity in my sense, and in exploring new discursive positivities/empiricities in the Foucauldian sense. As for the part of disciplinary Sociology in this process, that might be a slightly different matter, and ultimately a less interesting one.

Notes

1. For helpful exchanges on various aspects of this paper, I am very grateful to Maureen O'Malley, Steve Kemp, Tom Osborne and Michèle Barrett.

2. The case runs like this:
   - Any serious glance at the state of the world or at quality scholarship shows the continuing pertinence and richness of the thought of 'classics' like Marx, Durkheim and Weber.
   - Canons are both inescapable and intellectually useful, and they can also be made more inclusive/diverse. This is happening within Sociology today, with feminist and postcolonial concerns being steadily taken on board.
   - The charge that Sociology is definitively 'modernist' is only damaging if substantive and evaluative agreement can be reached concerning 'postmodernism', which seems impossible.

3. For further analysis of the discourses mentioned, see McLennan (1995, 1998, 2000).

4. This coincidence has been established recently by writers such as Bhaskar, Laudan and Hacking, but before them Marxist philosophers like John Lewis and Maurice Cornforth made much of it.

5. Throughout the preceding discussion, I ran together several terms – relativism/instrumentalism, and objectivism/realism/universalism/absolutism/naturalism – that can readily be differentiated from one another. However, such discrimination would not greatly alter the nature of my general argument, and in any case, advanced discussion is largely absent in the kind of social theory that I am trying to engage with here.

6. One could similarly feel supportive of the public prominence of multicultural or feminist expressions of the politics of difference and solidarity (cf. Modood and Werbner, 1997; Young, 1990), or of Roberto Unger's 'democratic experimentalism' (1996), or Rorty's (1998) idea of 'achieving our country', whilst disagreeing with them in crucial respects.

7. But by no means all, for there are sociologically minded Foucauldians at work on diverse empiricities who are keen to dissociate themselves from much of the rather dubious overgeneralising that goes on in the master's name.

References

Castells, M. (1998) *The Information Age*, Volume III: *End Of Millennium*. Oxford: Blackwell

Calhoun, C. (1995) *Critical Social Theory*. Oxford: Blackwell

Carnap, R. (1956) 'Empiricism, semantics and ontology', in *Meaning and Necessity*. Chicago: University of Chicago Press

Code, L. (1995) *Rhetorical Spaces: Essays on Gendered Locations*. London: Routledge

Derrida, J. (1994) *Spectres of Marx: The State of the Debt, the Work of Mourning, the New International*. London: Routledge

Fine, A. (1986) *The Shaky Game: Einstein, Realism and the Quantum Theory*. Chicago: University of Chicago Press

Foucault, M. (1970) *The Order of Things: An Archaeology of the Human Sciences*. London : Tavistock Publications

Geertz, C. (1984) 'Anti-anti-relativism', *American Anthropologist*, Vol. 86, No. 2, pp. 263–78

Giddens, A. (1998) *The Third Way: The Renewal of Social Democracy*. Cambridge: Polity Press

Hanfling, O. (1981) *Logical Positivism*. Oxford: Blackwell

Haraway, D. (1996. 'Situated knowledges: the science question in feminism and the privilege of partial perspectives', in E. Fox Keller and H. Longino (eds) *Feminism and Science*. Oxford: Oxford University Press

Harding, S. (1993) 'Re-thinking standpoint epistemology', in L. Alcoff and E. Potter (eds) *Feminist Epistemologies*. London: Routledge

Lehman, W.C. (1960) *John Millar of Glasgow, 1735–1801*. Cambridge: Cambridge University Press

Lemert, C. (1997) *Postmodernism Is Not What You Think*. Oxford: Blackwell

Longino, H. (1993) 'Subjects, power and knowledge: description and prescription in feminist philosophy of science', in L. Alcoff and E. Potter (eds) *Feminist Epistemologies*. London: Routledge

McLennan, G. (1995) 'Feminism, epistemology and postmodernism: reflections on current ambivalence', *Sociology*, Vol. 29, No. 2, pp. 391–409

McLennan, G. (1996) 'Post-Marxism and the "Four sins" of modernist theorizing', *New Left Review*, 218, pp. 53–74

McLennan, G. (1998) 'Sociology and cultural studies: rhetorics of disciplinary identity', *History of the Human Sciences*, Vol. 11, No. 3, pp. 1–17

McLennan, G. (2000) 'Sociology, Eurocentrism and the rise of the West', *European Journal of Social Theory*, Vol. 3, No. 2, pp. 275–91

Modood, T. and Werbner, P. (eds) (1997) *Debating Cultural Hybridity: Multi-cultural Identities and the Politics of Anti-Racism*. London: Zed Press

Mouzelis, N. (1991) *Back to Sociological Theory*. Basingstoke: Macmillan

Neurath, O. (1973) *Empiricism and Sociology*. Dordrecht: Reidel

Osborne, T. (1998) *Aspects of Enlightenment: Social Theory and the Ethics of Truth*. London: UCL Press

Pickering, M. (1997) 'A new look at Auguste Comte', in C. Camic (ed.) *Reclaiming the Sociological Classics*. Oxford: Blackwell

Rorty, R. (1998) *Achieving Our Country*. Cambridge, Massachusetts: Harvard University Press

Runciman, W.G. (1998) 'The selectionist paradigm and its implications for sociology', *Sociology*, Vol. 32, No. 1, pp. 163–88

Seidman, S. (1994) *Contested Knowledge: Social Theory in the Postmodern Era*. Oxford: Blackwell

Turner, J. (1992) 'The promise of positivism', in S. Seidman and D. Wagner (eds) *Postmodernism and Social Theory*. Oxford: Blackwell

Unger, R. (1996) *What Should Legal Analysis Become?* London: Verso

Velody, I. and Williams, R. (eds) (1998) *The Politics of Constructionism*. London: Sage

Vogeler, M.S. (1984) *Frederic Harrison: The Vocations of a Positivist*. Oxford: Clarendon Press

Wallerstein, I. (1999) 'The heritage of sociology, the promise of social science', *Current Sociology*, Vol. 47, No. 1, pp.1–41

Wright, T.R. (1986) *The Religion of Humanity: The Impact of Comtean Positivism on Victorian Britain*. Cambridge: Cambridge University Press

Young, I.M. (1990) *Justice and the Politics of Difference*. Princeton: Princeton University Press

Chapter 2
Sociology and its audience(s): changing perceptions of sociological argument
John Holmwood

> 'Sociology begins by disenchanting the world, and it proceeds by disenchanting itself.'
> (Gouldner, 1973e: 27)

The starting point for this chapter is a perceived crisis in mainstream sociological theory and the 'Enlightenment' reason held to be intrinsic to it.[1] Not everyone will agree that there is a crisis; those that do, will disagree about what should be done about it. Certainly, present disunity, however specific its substance, should not be contrasted with a past unity. Weber's essays in methodology, for example, were written in the early years of the twentieth-century, a period of *Methodenstreit* much like our own, when he had occasion to decry 'the continuous changes and bitter conflict about the apparently most elementary problems of our discipline, its methods, the formulation and validity of its concepts' (Weber, 1949: 51). Recognition of the continuity of problems is often the occasion for commentators to respond to crisis claims with a weary shrug that it was ever thus, and the observation that any problems are *existential*, intrinsic to the sociological undertaking and not specific to our own place and time. After all, social science differs from natural science in that the object of its inquiries is potentially also the audience for its findings. Moreover, sociologists participate as members of society in the processes that they study. Disagreements over the nature of sociology as an undertaking, then, are endemic precisely because they are so bound up with issues of social life (of membership *in* a community and relations *between* communities). On the one hand, it seems that sociology must be defined by a constant struggle to achieve systematic and methodologically grounded reflection without being engulfed by the particularity that is its subject matter. On the other, sociologists must risk a life alienated from the community(ies) they would wish their knowledge to serve.

Notwithstanding, it is my contention that the present crisis – or, at least, talk of crisis – is significantly different from any that has preceded it. Something of the nature of this crisis is implicit in the title of the conference from which this book originates – *For Sociology* – which evokes Gouldner's spirited advocacy of the sociological imagination as expressed in his book of essays of the same name published in 1973 (a collection which includes essays from the 1950s onwards). However, Gouldner's declaration of being for sociology was not unambiguous then (as the quotation from one of the essays at the head of this article implies), and could not be so now. He dedicated his collection to the task of renewal and critique in sociology, a task which he had outlined in *The Coming Crisis of Western Sociology* (Gouldner, 1971). Sociology, he argued, was about to enter a crisis. It had become too absorbed in narrow technical concerns and disengaged from public debates in the name of a professional doctrine of value neutrality. The promise of sociology was rigorous social inquiry and engagement with public debates but, according to Gouldner, it had become routinised and trivialised.

The sense that profound changes in the terms of sociological argument were taking place first entered sociological self-consciousness in the 1960s, and their impact has been increasing since then. Now more than ever before, sociology seems beset by doubts generated from *within* the discipline. Where previously the sociological condition had seemed chronic, it now appears acute and, according to some commentators, terminal. Indeed, in the space of several decades – decades roughly coterminous with its 'institutionalisation' and expansion as a discipline – sociology has proceeded from proclamations of an 'age of sociology'(Parsons, 1954b) to announcements of its 'death'.[2] During this period, what was initially looked forward to as the discipline became established institutionally, the very project of a science of society, has been called into question. The displacement of this project is evident in the way in which developments in sociological argument across the last decades have been characterised:

- from *monologue* to *dialogue* (Apel, 1967; Habermas, 1988);
- from *objectivity* to *valid subjectivities* (Seidman, 1994);
- from the *singular* (and universal) to the *plural* (heterogeneous and heterodox, in which the formerly universal is particular and orthodox) (Grosz, 1986; Seidman, 1994);
- from *facts* to *fictions* (Hawkesworth, 1989);
- from *knowledge as truth* to *knowledge as power* (Foucault, 1980).

Where sociology used to be about seeing the 'general' in the 'particular', it now seems only able to see the 'particular' in what was once claimed to be 'general'.

At least in part, the present crisis reflects changes in the audience for sociological argument and in the social location of sociology itself. For example, there have been changes in its institutional setting of university and higher education, in its relation to the state, in the state itself, in the future of welfare, and, finally, an apparent fragmentation of the public sphere with the rise of new social movements. According to Rose, these changes involve a 'simultaneous proliferation, fragmentation, contestation and delegitimation of the place of experts in the devices of social government' (1996: 52). Sociology cannot assume an undifferentiated audience for its findings and sociological argument directed towards public policy confronts an increasingly contested field. A 'politics of distribution', organised through a hegemonic welfare state, which sustained the earlier project of a scientific sociology, appears to be being replaced by a new 'politics of identity' (Fraser, 1995). This politics must include issues of the identity of sociologists and their claims to expertise. Given a reduction of knowledge to power, the appropriate sociological role comes to be seen as shifting from *legislator* to *interpreter* (Bauman, 1987), or from *professional* to *partisan* (Gouldner, 1973e).

What I shall suggest in this chapter is that these developments have not given rise to a consistent successor project. However, the changing context of sociological argument means that any possibility of a return to an earlier 'orthodoxy' (of a priori agreed general categories which precede any particular inquiry based upon them), an idea which has been promoted in the face of an apparent postmodern fragmentation of the sociological undertaking (Alexander, 1988, 1995; Mouzelis, 1990, 1995; see also McLennan, 1995, 1998, for a discussion), is illusory. Indeed, from the perspective of *either* postmodern particularism *or* foundational general theory, explanation is displaced from the centre of sociological argument. This chapter traces the manner of this displacement, beginning in the following section with a brief history of sociological argument since the 1950s, and concluding with a proposal to return explanation to the centre of theoretical debate. By conceiving sociological argument as a *problem-solving* activity, it is suggested that the present theoretical impasse can be overcome.

Sociological argument since the 1950s

The 1950s and 1960s were a period of growth and expansion of the discipline – in the USA and UK at least (see Turner and Turner, 1990). It was also a time of a broader social and political unity when the public sphere was widely understood in terms of general processes of democratisation and inclusion. In these circumstances, sociologists claimed a professional ethos and expertise in the production of knowledge whose wider public benefit was mediated by welfare-state functionaries under the aegis of a liberal democratic polity. Put simply, the emphasis was to understand social problems as deriving from problematic social conditions which, once properly understood, might be ameliorated through the agency of the welfare state (though some problems might also derive from the 'unintended consequences' of that agency).

Parsons, (1954b), for example, attributed the stability of modern pluralistic 'social systems' to their more differentiated social structures, in which the 'individualism – socialism' dilemma and the related ideological schisms of the late nineteenth-century were reconciled and overcome.[3] Disciplines such as psychology and economics had reached maturity during an earlier period of the development of capitalism and industrialism, but the complexities of mature industrial capitalism, Parsons (1954a, b) argued, required an analysis that went beyond that of individual behaviour and its aggregation and, therefore, beyond the individualistic assumptions of psychology and economics. As part of this detailed argument for the 'end of ideology', Parsons saw an increased role for professionals mediating between the collective orientation of the state and the self-interest more typical of commercial activities. The professional status of sociologists was an appropriate reflection of their role after the 'end of ideology'. Indeed, Parsons proposed his framework of general theory as a source of professional unity, synthesising disparate strands of the discipline whose apparent mutual antagonisms were the product of social and ideological conditions which had now passed. Although some argued that the end of the 'ideological age' meant a reduction of political discourse to issues of technical expertise and the determination of public opinion through mass media and advertising, this was not Parsons' own view. For him (1954b), the 'end of ideology' promised the 'age of sociology', one which was implicitly inclusive of a wider public. Indeed, the professional adoption of a unifying frame of reference would enable sociology to confront new issues of public relevance.

Yet for Gouldner (1973c), writing after Parsons, this very professionalisation (and institutionalisation) of the discipline had subverted its public role, a role which was increasingly being conceived as properly one of social critique. The university, Gouldner argued, represented a 'cleared space' for public debate, but it was an 'immensely threatened space', threatened by the very professional values it made possible. These professional values were encoded in the doctrine of objectivity and value freedom which discouraged social scientists from self-reflection about the status of scientific knowledge and its wider social purposes; science was represented as an 'autonomous' activity and the purposes to which knowledge was put were external to it. Social scientists could just get on with their job – not their *vocation* – confident that the application of scientific method would bring about an accumulation of knowledge which, in being produced for its own sake, would, by virtue of the scale and veridicality of its findings, be recognised as generally useful and relevant. Whatever Parsons claimed for the professionalisation of the discipline (or for the professions more generally), it was the reduction of social and political problems to technical questions that seemed predominant.[4]

This reduction, Gouldner (1973a) argued, was reinforced by reference to the figure of Weber – the mythical monster, 'minotaur Max'.[5] By drawing on Weber's charisma, sociologists were kept from recognising the 'tragic' dimension of their lives, and that they had wasted themselves on an unrealisable ambition, one which in being pursued, became thinner in its yield and subverted to implicit purposes different from those that Parsons' analysis had initially supposed. 'The university's central problem' Gouldner wrote, 'is its failure as a *community* in which rational discourse about *social* worlds is possible. This is partly because rational discourse as such ceased to be its dominant value and was superseded by a quest for knowledge *products* and information *products* that could be sold for funding, prestige and power – rewards bestowed by the state and the larger society that is bent upon subverting rational discourse about itself' (1973c: 79). Sociology, he argued, had become absorbed to the management of the advanced welfare state and, thus, part of the mechanisms of social control (1973d: 344). Behind the mask of objectivity and value neutrality, professional sociology pursued an implicitly partisan project: the maintenance of the status quo.

Gouldner's was not a lone voice; nor was he the first to articulate such criticisms. C.W. Mills (1959) had earlier called for a re-invigorated sociological imagination that would unite private troubles and public issues by overcoming the sterile division of 'grand theory' and 'abstract empiricism' by which the sociological imagination had been diminished.[6] Habermas, too, set out a similar analysis to Gouldner's. Writing from within a different tradition of social inquiry where, to some extent, the *Geisteswissenschaft* had institutionalised hostility to positivist social science, Habermas (1988) was concerned to rebut what he saw as its implicit conservatism and to rehabilitate some of the insights of positivist social science concerning the operation of external, structural determinants of behaviour. Nonetheless, he believed that positivism was 'monologic' in its appropriation of the authority of technical competence and control, and he advocated a 'dialogic' approach which synthesised the methodological insights of both traditions.

Ironically, this ambition for a synthetic general framework is something Habermas shared with Parsons (see Holmwood and Stewart, 1991; Holmwood 1996). Of course, Habermas had a more critical orientation than Parsons, not merely concerning the possibility of radical change, but also its desirability. Deriving from the Frankfurt School, and with his sense of the problems of 'old Europe', Habermas also had a somewhat more pessimistic view than Gouldner about the extent to which what was possible and desirable might be actualised (though his orientation to the production of a general scheme of categories was designed to establish, at least formally, a human interest in emancipation).

Like Gouldner, Habermas was concerned that the growth of the welfare state, with its reduction of politics to technical matters of administrative efficiency, was diminishing the public sphere. At the formal level of theory, Habermas associated the growth of 'bourgeois individualism' with the development of the 'personality system' of an individual capable of 'self-reflection'. Such reflexivity had structural conditions, namely, the development of a public sphere which sustained critical debate. In *The Structural Transformation of the Public Sphere* (1989), Habermas set out how such a public sphere arose with the emergence of capitalism in the development of systems of private law and parliamentary institutions, the creation of an audience for print media and venues for discussion such as coffee houses, debating societies and other voluntary associations. However, the book closes on a pessimistic note concerning the growth of commercial mass media and advertising, the rise of the administered welfare state and the 'scientization of politics'. This pessimism is reinforced in later work – most especially in *Legitimation Crisis* (1976) – where he posits that this deformation of the public sphere presages the decline of reflexivity, that is the 'end of the individual' (capable of self-reflection). Social science, then, rather than contributing to emancipation, might participate in the diminution of human possibilities.

If Habermas had a different sensibility to Gouldner, they shared the sense that new possibilities *might* be emerging to disrupt social scientific (and other) orthodoxies. The postwar social and political consensus over the welfare state was beginning to break down and there were the first intimations that a new politics of identity and recognition was challenging the older politics of equality and distribution. In these circumstances Gouldner advocated a *reflexive sociology*, which applied its understandings to itself and recognised its role in the reproduction of the status quo. Sociology, he argued, must seek new theoretical communities beyond those compromised within the university. 'The renewal of sociology' Gouldner wrote, 'is of course one aspect of the reconstruction of society. Clearly, we cannot have a reconstruction of society without a critical revamping of our established ways of thinking about society' (1973b: 82). With new social movements emerging, the emphasis came to be put on processes of change, against an alleged bias towards stability in orthodox sociology.

Change was associated with issues of human agency and the capacity of actors – especially, actors organised collectively – to understand their own circumstances and change them. According to Gouldner, social theorists should recognise actors, not as objects of study, but as subjects with their own knowledge. Actors' knowledge may be organised under values, but that does not differentiate them from professional social scientists; their values may be different, but their knowledge has a claim to validity alongside that of social theorists. In a reflexive sociology, then, 'we would increasingly recognise the depth of our kinship with those we study. They would no longer be viewed as alien others or as mere objects for our superior technique and insight; they could instead be seen as brother sociologists, each attempting with his varying degree of skill, energy, and talent to understand social reality' (Gouldner, 1970: 490). A similar appreciation informs Habermas' conception of the relation between sociologist and actors as being dialogic, as well as Giddens' idea of actors as 'lay social theorists' and as 'skilled and knowledgeable agents' (1976: 17).

The emphasis on social systems and their reproduction was held to be a characteristic of orthodox accounts (such as that of Parsons) and it was increasingly represented as both poor sociology (because of its evident neglect of the facts of conflict and change, and its deficient conception of the actor), and problematic politics. The inadequacy of this critique is discussed elsewhere (see Holmwood and Stewart, 1991; Holmwood, 1996), where it is argued that Parsons' critics reproduce these very problems. However, what I am concerned with in this paper is how the critique helped form the direction of subsequent theorising. Horowitz and Liebowitz, for example, challenged what they saw as the dominant sociological view of social problems inherent in the project of professional sociology, writing that:

> the dilemma for those who consider social problems obstacles to be overcome is that any true overcoming of social problems implies a perfect social system. And this entails several goals: first, the total institutionalisation of all people; second, the thoroughgoing equilibrium between the parts of the system with respect to their functioning and the functioning of other sectors; third the elimination of social change as either a fact or value. Thus, the resolution of social problems from the point of view of the social system would signify the totalitarian resolution of social life.
> (1968: 295).

They attacked the professional and expert definition of social problems as objects for ameliorative reform in the name of a politicisation of 'deviance' and radical, community-based movements of the marginal and the poor. 'Social problems', they argued, should be recognised for what they were, i.e. not *problems* (since this implied the perspective of 'order' and, thus, of the advantaged and their functionaries), but issues of *a politics of difference.*

For many radicals, the failures of professional orthodoxy were necessary failures. Sociology's pretensions to a science of society were argued to be just that, pretensions. This critique took many, often mutually contradictory, forms. There were those – influenced by hermeneutic, humanist, or other philosophical arguments – who argued that a science of society was impossible and a contradiction in terms (for example Winch, 1958; Louch, 1966). Others argued that a science of society was possible, but not in its sociological, humanist and 'empiricist' form (Willer and Willer, 1973; Keat and Urry, 1975; Bhaskar, 1979).[7] In addition, as Gouldner observed, many young radicals were turning their backs on the academy in the name of direct political engagement. For Gouldner, to be *for sociology*, meant asserting the relevance of sociological knowledge in a situation when others were *for Marx* (Althusser, 1965), *for ethnomethodology* (Garfinkel and Sacks, 1970) or *for anything but sociology* (including the personal hedonism of the counter-culture). It would seem that in a short space of time, the nature of sociological prospects had shifted from a perceived accumulation of knowledge to an accumulation of critiques of sociology as knowledge.[8] What was at issue was the nature of sociological knowledge, how it was to be produced and the purposes to which it was to be put.

These matters have not reached any greater resolution in the period since Gouldner wrote. Sociological argument appears no less fragmented between mutually exclusive approaches with different epistemological claims. And the arguments do not appear to have moved on very much either – indeed in some cases, there seems to be a deliberate attempt to move back. Thus, some argue that what is necessary is a return to a 'golden age' of professional sociology: one of 'rational-choice' (or exchange) theory (Coleman, 1990), including its Marxist versions (Elster, 1985; Roemer, 1986); or a 'new theoretical movement' of Parsonsian neofunctionalism (Alexander, 1988); 'Mertonian functionalism' (Mouzelis, 1995);[9] or a renewed programme of 'scientific sociology' (Turner, 1990; Collins, 1989).[10] Yet these were the very paradigms which, in the founding editorial statement of the journal *Theory and Society,* Gouldner (1974) had declared to be 'exhausted'. In response to this recidivism, others proclaim the vigour of the discipline in crisis and decry the conformity that a renewed professional consensus would entail (not that there seems much risk of achieving it). '*Vive la crise!*' writes Bourdieu, for example, but he then proceeds to what is essentially a re-statement of Gouldner, calling for the turning of the 'instruments of social science' back on themselves in the creation of a 'genuinely reflexive social science' (Bourdieu, 1989: 784; see also, Skocpol, 1989). Others, such as Lemert (1995), imply that the crisis that Gouldner foresaw has come and gone. Yet, sociology '*after* the crisis' – as Lemert titles his book – looks remarkably like sociology *in* crisis and, despite his commitment to the '*vital importance*' of sociology (again much in the tradition of Gouldner and Mills), Lemert ultimately strikes a resigned tone: 'it is far from clear that the crisis will ever end. It may, perhaps, be the way the world is' (1995: 196).

The contradictions of reflexive sociology

The implication of the critique of orthodoxy is that the undermining of a singular sociological authority is part of a further process of 'democratisation' in which different voices are now able to be heard. However, unreconciled, and seemingly unreconcilable, differences is not simply a problem *for* and *within* the community of sociological theorists, but must also be an issue of the relation *between* that community and those it studies. The recognition that actors might be seen as 'fellow sociologists', or 'lay social theorists', raises the question of *whose* knowledge claims are to be accepted as *valid*. Seidman, for example, has articulated a view of social knowledge(s) as *essentially contested*, – albeit, one in which what is beyond contest is the self-evident failure of a science of society:[11]

> If I am not mistaken, a scientific social theory that aims to establish the foundations for social knowledge and aspires to uncover a vocabulary mirroring the structure of society is collapsing under its own dead weight.
> (Seidman, 1994: 323)

To Seidman, the project of a *science of society*, with its pretensions to universally valid knowledge, is deeply flawed and its purposes suspect. According to him, the universalism of scientific knowledge has been undermined in a fundamental way by the claims of those whose experiences do not fit its categories. Inclusive claims of knowledge turn out to disguise a terrible exclusion, but one which has finally been unmasked by the 'return of the repressed':

> The towering grandeur of scientific reason has all but crumbled under a barrage of assault from those who claim to be its victims: people of color, non-Westerners, women, lesbians and gay men, the disabled, and the poor and economically disempowered. Its promise of freedom has a dark side: a ruthless wish to control and order everything and an intolerance toward the unruly and deviant.
> (ibid.: 327)

Any claim for universality would be dangerous and oppressive, involving the imposition of a particular truth, masquerading as universal, over other claims. Seidman's characterisation of a 'science of society' serving the interests of a dominant group maintained *over* subordinates has become a common one, echoing, as it does the critiques of Gouldner, Habermas and, as we shall see, Foucault. It would be well to note, however, that this is at best a partial account. As Yeo's (1996) history of social science associations demonstrates, 'science' has frequently been mobilised by subordinate groups *against* the privileges of elite groups. Moreover, an implicit 'science' is mobilised in Seidman's list of all those who are the 'victims' of scientific reason. He argues that 'representation' is a political issue yet, apparently, has no difficulty with the 'factual' status of the evidence for the sexism, classism, racism, etc. that he criticises.

It is not just sociological claims to *validity*, that are undermined by such arguments. In effect, Seidman argues that any problem of relativism that might be implicit in the idea of contested knowledge(s) can be resolved by *valuing*, or privileging, that which reflects the subjectivities of marginalised and oppressed groups. This claim is a generalisation of a more specific argument made by some feminist writers on behalf of a 'standpoint of women' (Hartsock, 1987). Indeed, the debate within feminism follows the lines of the critique of the professional doctrine of value freedom set out above. Thus, a first wave of feminist social science documented the range and extent of gender inequalities neglected by mainstream social science. However, according to Harding (1986) and others, although this research – which Harding characterises as 'feminist empiricism' – was of critical importance in challenging the research agendas and theoretical assumptions of malestream social science, it accepted too much from approaches whose evident limitations it had done so much to demonstrate. For Harding, the problem is that the demonstration in much feminist research of male bias in the neglect of gender issues, or the implicit adoption of male experience as the norm, actually serves to reinforce the standard professional doctrine of value freedom. For standpoint theorists, critique of this doctrine must be part of any properly radical feminist social theory.[12]

The development of standpoint feminism has been specifically linked by Hartsock to a Marxist historical materialism: 'Like the lives of proletarians according to Marxian theory, women's lives make available a particular and privileged vantage point on male supremacy' (Hartsock, 1987: 284).[13] Given the incorporation of Marxism into the academy during the 1970s, this association is understandable. However, a more immediate source of the general argument was Becker's (1967) proposal that sociologists must ask: 'Whose side are we on?' Sociologists, he replied, must choose between the standpoint of 'superiors' and that of 'subordinates'. For Becker, the choice was between the powerful and the powerless, between those who conform with the requirements of systems, and 'deviants' who face its sanctions. What was required was a reorientation of sociology towards the interests of those who are displaced or marginalised in the social hierarchies that are social systems.

It is significant that, despite the very similar implications of his own position, Gouldner (1973e) was quickly mistrustful of the polarisation inherent in this stance and distanced himself from Becker's 'partisan' interpretation of a radical sociology.[14] Indeed, this was the context of Gouldner's own comment on the 'disenchantment of sociology'. He felt that the once 'glib' acceptance of the doctrine of value freedom, which he had attacked some six years earlier, had now been replaced by an equally glib rejection of it. Presenting the issue as one of a simple choice of 'sides' that would precede the evaluation of any knowledge claims that might divide them, Gouldner suggested that the position was rendered more *complacent* (or, at least, equally as complacent), not more radical, than the one it would replace.

Despite having argued for the 'kinship' between sociologists and those they study, Gouldner was concerned about the submersion of the sociologist's voice into that of actors: 'Objectivity is indeed threatened when the actors' standpoints and the sociologists' fuse into one.... the adoption of an "outside" standpoint, far from leading us to ignore the participants' standpoint, is probably the only way in which we can recognise and identify the participants' standpoint' (1973e: 57). Indeed developments of theories of power, which are usually argued to reflect the interests of subordinate groups by showing how their lives are determined by processes of power, tend to require such an outside standpoint, once it is recognised that power can operate through 'ideology'. In such circumstances, the understandings of subordinates might reflect a 'superordinate standpoint', and so the 'standpoint of participants' would necessarily be an 'outside' one. However, Gouldner did not wish to revive the earlier professional doctrine of value freedom, and he looked instead to what he called a 'deeper' sense of objectivity because 'in effect, the growth of professionalization means the substitution of a routine and banal code of ethics for a concern with the serious kind of morality on which alone objectivity might rest' (ibid.: 61).

It might be that Gouldner's concern with the submersion of the sociologist's voice was an unconscious projection of his own membership of the privileged group whose voice no longer seemed so persuasive. After all, it is noteworthy that the problem of submersion would be greatest for those with no immediate 'we' relation to the group in question. Women sociologists, for example, may not have the same difficulties with the idea of a feminist standpoint as those – white, heterosexual, professional men – with no identity in any of the groups whose standpoint is now *being* privileged (and who occupy instead the ground of Reason, which has been deconstructed as the standpoint *of* privilege).[15] However, a more general unease about standpoint perspectives must occur once it is allowed that the issue of voice is an issue of recognition and being listened to. That must carry the further implication that some claims are weightier and, should not merely be listened to, but should also be acted upon. For this to be so, issues of validity must impinge across groups.

Aware of this point, some feminist writers have begun to adopt a position similar to Gouldner's. For example, it seems to Hawkesworth that 'at a moment when the preponderance of rational and moral argument sustains prescriptions for women's equality, it is a bit too cruel a conclusion and too reactionary a political agenda to accept that reason is impotent, that equality is impossible' (Hawkesworth, 1989: 557). Harding (1993), for her part, also acknowledges the paradoxical consequences of standpoint theory and advocates the continued necessity of a conception of objectivity, albeit 'strong objectivity' rather than the standard 'objectivity' of professional, masculine science. 'Strong objectivity', however, is similar to Gouldner's aspiration to ground objectivity in a 'serious morality': 'strong objectivity requires that the subject of knowledge be placed on the same critical, causal plane as the objects of knowledge. Thus, strong objectivity requires what we can think of as "strong reflexivity"' (Harding, 1993: 69). Yet, it is precisely this reflexive requirement that seems to undermine any claim of objectivity, rather than strengthen it.

What Gouldner had in mind when he referred to a 'more serious kind of morality' is not clear. It might be what Habermas seeks to produce with his articulation of knowledge constitutive interests and their relation to discourse ethics in a general framework with claims to 'universality'.[16] *Some* claim to universalism and unity of interests would seem to be entailed by a 'stronger' morality or objectivity. However, when Gouldner reflects on the practical problems of a 'serious morality', he immediately raises the problems identified by Horowitz and Liebowitz:

> perhaps what has been most discrediting to the quest for human unity is that, since its classical formulation, its most gifted spokesmen have often had totalitarian proclivities; they came to be viewed as enemies of the 'open society', who denied the value and reality of human difference. In short, the plea for human unity has often, and quite justifiably, been interpreted as a demand for a tension-free society that was overseen by a close superintendence of men from nursery to graveyard, and was blanketed with a remorseless demand for conformity and consensus. (Gouldner, 1973e: 67).

Such arguments proved remarkably prescient of issues that would increasingly dominate discussions and extend beyond their intended targets (essentially, Parsonsian 'grand theory'). Indeed, the statements of Horowitz and Liebowitz, and of those Gouldner, are echoed in postmodern critiques of the 'terror' implicit in any 'totalising' social theory where, as Lyotard puts it, 'we have paid a high enough price for the nostalgia of the whole and the one, for the reconciliation of the concept and the sensible, of the transparent and communicable experience ... The answer is: Let us wage a war on totality' (1985: 81–2).

The concerns of Hawkesworth and Harding about the problems of standpoint theory are occasioned by a sense that the position is unstable, and that the promise of a feminist reconstruction of social inquiry and society is in the process of giving way in the face of a greater (self-proclaimed) radicalism of a postmodern deconstruction of both. Whatever undermines a sociological project of inclusion, or a general human unity, must also undermine claims made on behalf of inclusion *within* different subject positions. Against any argument that each different subject position can establish its own (self-referential) conditions of validity deriving from its own unique standpoint, lies a further radicalism which deepens the argument. The many, historically local, 'truths' of different subject positions turn out to contain the same problem as a claim for general, transcendent truth. No subject position can be defined in essentialist terms without raising the issue of differences which are suppressed by their organisation under a single category. Any particular social movement's struggle for justice must be conducted in terms of instituting new social relationships, but those relationships will contain the same formal characteristics of power and a tendency towards closure. A typical example would be Lukes' (1976) outline of a 'radical' theory of power, where its most fundamental operation is to secure stability through the creation of a 'false consensus'.[17]

Ultimately, the argument descends to a form of identity politics dedicated to the continued dissolution of any 'fixed' and 'frozen' categories and, therefore, of any ordered discourse. Yet, in so far as it is parasitic on 'order' for its strategy of disruptions, it requires the reproduction of its 'other'. The consequence is a valorisation of struggles for justice over its attainment and, ultimately, even the representation of its attainment as a kind of injustice! Seidman, for example, writes that:

> *postmodernism carries no promise of liberation – of a society free of domination. Postmodernism gives up the modernist idol of emancipation in favour of deconstructing false closure, prying open present and future possibilities, detecting fluidity and porousness in forms of life where hegemonic discourses posit closure and a frozen order. The hope of a great transformation is replaced by the more modest aspiration of a relentless defence of immediate, local pleasures and struggles for justice.*
> (1991: 131)

The project of a reflexive sociology seems to be self-defeating. Put simply, reflexive sociology argues that subjects and objects of knowledge should be situated within a single analysis. However, that analysis is usually conducted in terms of an argument that what should also be recognised is the pervasive character of relations of power and social control. 'Reflexive sociology', 'strong reflexivity', 'critical' theory – call it what you will – promotes the analysis of social structures and their role in processes of social change, developing a formal language of system, domination and power to serve this objective. In consequence, processes of change are perceived to bring about new social structures with the same formal characteristics. In that these are features of wider social organisation, they must also apply to the organisation of theoretical communities of knowers (whether of social inquirers or of other communities of actors). This must, indeed, entail disenchanting sociology where its contribution to the reform of social institutions is seen to serve the effective functioning of institutional power relations exercised over individuals.

Sociology, it seems, emerges in the 'discovery' of the 'social' and a proposed transcendence of nineteenth-century ideologies. It proceeds to generalise power from the political sphere into the social system. Where nineteenth-century anarchists posited the 'social' as an alternative to political power, late twentieth-century sociologists have identified power with the social, so that to be 'anti-power' is also to be anti-social. This is evident in the quotation from Seidman cited above. Habermas (1987), for his part, criticises Foucault for his deficient, anarchist tendencies. However, Habermas' own analysis leads in the same direction. Indeed, this was presciently argued by Gadamer (1976) in his critique of the alienation intrinsic to the idea of a methodologically guaranteed, critical theory of society. Gadamer charged Habermas in the following terms:

> [The] unavoidable consequence to which all these observations must lead is that the basically emancipatory consciousness must have in mind the dissolution of all authority, all obedience. This means that unconsciously the ultimate guiding image of emancipatory reflection in the social sciences must be an anarchistic utopia.
> (Gadamer, 1976: 42)

At the same time, this generalised anarchism must reproduce the very characteristics of a distanced and neutral attitude that were attributed to the project of a scientific sociology.[18] Sociologists in this mode must reserve their judgements about the substance of actors' specific, *concrete* interests in change in the name of change valued for itself. This is not what Gouldner had intended. He argued that the claim that it might be so was false, made by conservatives anxious to defend the status quo:

> The goal of those who seek change is usually not disorder but a new order, one they consider more moral than the old. To make social order one's central concern is to exalt some moral values over some others. It is also to be conservative, not only metaphysically but politically.
> (Gouldner, 1973c: 73).

Now, it is the 'anarchistic' position which comes to be seen as conservative, precisely because it diminishes hope in any new order that would resolve the problems of the present.[19]

As well as a reconstruction of social theory, radical theorists had also looked forward to a reconstruction of the social order of welfare capitalism, but this hoped-for transformation of society has also become a victim of fragmentation and division. If sociological argument has fragmented (and that fragmentation is seen by some as a cause for celebration), the same fate seems to have befallen radical social agendas too. In the latter case though, any celebration would have to be muted – after all, it has been accompanied by widening inequalities and disadvantages experienced by at least some of the groups on whose behalf Horowitz and Liebowitz had advocated a politicisation of social problems. It is precisely the dashing of the (false) hopes of 60s radicalism which Alexander (1995) believes has contributed to the postmodern, fin-de-siècle sensibility in contemporary social theory. He sees Lyotard's criticisms of a 'nostalgia' for the 'lost narrative' and attendant fears of a lapse into 'barbarism' as more suitably directed at Lyotard's own earlier judgements and the hopes and fears which he held in common with other radical theorists who had turned to Marxism in the 1960s and 70s, than to their orthodox colleagues. Indeed, for Alexander (and Mouzelis, 1995), postmodernism shows the route 'back to the future' by the way in which it has reabsorbed many substantive sociological positions that preceded the crisis. Thus, declarations of the 'end of grand narratives', such as Lyotard's (1984), with its echoes in Seidman, Lemert and others, are similar to earlier declarations of the 'end of ideology'.

However, it is not just that Alexander's new theoretical movement of synthesis (in which he includes Habermas, Giddens and Bourdieu, amongst others) is unpersuasive in its theoretical constitution as neofunctionalist. Its requirement of a professional consensus over foundational, presuppositional categories as an alternative to debilitating relativism would be a denial of the possibility of different future undertakings. From the perspective of the latter, the attempt to restore what is now past would be not merely an indication of an outmoded theoretical sensibility, but worse, a concern to maintain the boundaries of a theoretical community of privileged insiders (and the 'canon' by which that community is defined)[20] against the incursions of outsiders. Indeed, it is noteworthy that the general theoretical frameworks – whether of neofunctionalism, or rational choice – which, supposedly, are to unite the community of sociological theorists, have a level of theoretical specification which seems to be above issues of, say, gender or other identities. If Alexander (and others) are right, the community of professionals has nothing to learn from the critiques of the last decades. If the paradox of standpoint theory is the seeming requirement of a standpoint for standpoints, then the representation of that requirement in terms of a pregiven, overarching standpoint of general theory would seem to affirm the postmodern critique.[21] The overarching standpoint, it seems, would take nothing from the standpoints it purports to gather; nothing is learned from the latter since all their legitimate theoretical insights are held to be already presupposed by them and capable of representation in a scheme of general categories which is elaborated independently of them.

Moreover, if we are returned to the 'end of ideology', as Alexander suggests, it does not seem also to be an 'age of sociology', at least not in the form originally articulated. The attempt to return to a previously articulated consensual foundation for sociology seems to miss the point that while current sociological conditions may not favour radical projects (or not as they were conceived when Gouldner declared that he was *for sociology,* and could hear the explosions of social unrest in his study as he wrote!),[22] they do not, by that token, favour the project of orthodox professional sociology either. The appearance of a one-time unity, may be just that, an appearance, a moment when institutional arrangements coincided in a conjuncture which will not be repeated. After all, the welfare state is in crisis, and while the current agenda of public issues – in which market values and conservative social policies dominate – is at odds with that which many radical sociologists had sought to bring about, it does not appear to favour the reformist agenda of social problems either. In fact, there are 'libertarian' echoes in much radical thinking of the 1960s and since, so that the rise of neoliberal politics is not independent of the radical critique of welfare state. Rose, for example, writes that:

> neoliberal programmes that respond to the sufferer as if they were the author of their own misfortune share something with strategies articulated from other political perspectives. From a variety of directions, the disadvantaged individual has come to be seen as potentially and ideally an active agent in the fabrication of their own existence.
> (1996: 59)

Sociological argument – in both its radical and more professionalised forms – appears marginalised, displaced from public debate. Where a new politics of identity has sanctioned the idea of contested knowledges, grounded in different subject positions, universalistic claims to knowledge have been undermined and delegitimated.

Indeed, where sociology has flourished, it has tended not to trade under that name, but to be oriented to specific user interests in interdisciplinary 'knowledge products'. Turner and Turner (1990) and Crane and Small (1992), for example, describe the disciplinary decline that has occurred as new patterns of funding have favoured 'interdisciplinary' research in specific areas of concern – health, crime, urban problems, etc. – and increasingly researchers have come to see themselves in terms of 'area' rather than 'discipline'. Lyotard's description of the postmodern condition of knowledge is remarkably like that diagnosed by these writers. He writes:

> The idea of an interdisciplinary approach is specific to the age of delegitimation and its hurried empiricism. The relation to knowledge is not articulated in terms of the realization of the life of the spirit or the emancipation of humanity, but in terms of the users of a complex conceptual and material machinery and those who benefit from its performance capabilities. They have at their disposal no metalanguage or metanarrative in which to formulate the final goal and correct use of that machinery. But they do have brainstorming to improve its performance.
> (1985: 52).

Moreover, with the changing nature of governance and the emphasis on market solutions and deregulation, the sponsors of such research become more diverse. At the same time, the policy process is more politicised and less consensual. Where governments are sceptical of their own role in the amelioration of social problems, the idea of disinterested research delivering its findings in a public forum, to influence public agencies, finds little favour. Yet, knowledge geared to the pragmatic requirements of powerful user groups appears unchallenged. Despite the large amount of attention devoted to radical critique over the last decades, it seems that all that has been challenged is sociology itself and its 'grand narrative' of 'Reason' that might otherwise check 'performativity' as the new politics of expert knowledge. The latter appears to be 'uncoupled', as Habermas might put it, from any requirement of a wider legitimation.

Individualistic approaches dominate – whether in the form of the embrace of markets within society, or the embrace of rational-choice analysis within the academy. Influential writers such as Beck, Giddens and Lash (1994) affirm that 'late modernity' is 'reflexive modernity', but the sociological conditions and characteristics of the public sphere which they advance as requiring greater reflexivity on the part of individuals are precisely those which Habermas associated with the 'end of the individual' capable of self-reflection. It can frequently seem that in their attempt not to appear arrogant in relation to those they study, sociologists must find an active and competent element to everything that had previously been subjected to criticism, be that the 'consumption' of advertising, of mass media or of the mass production goods of multinational corporations. Indeed, the currently 'critical' position is to be critical of the elitism inherent in previous criticisms of the consequences of corporate capitalism. Yet there is little reversal in the judgements about the welfare state and attempts to ameliorate corporate capitalism! Postmodern sociologists have returned to the 'death of class' (Pakulski and Waters, 1996) which was part of the original 'end of ideology' argument. For earlier theorists, the rise of the welfare state was associated with the 'death of class'; now, the 'death of class' is associated with the demise of the welfare state, with no attention paid to the amelioration of widening inequalities that have ensued. This inversion of previous judgements passes without comment or reflection, yet it must contribute to a sense of unease about the relation of sociology to public debate. If sociological judgements are so malleable in the face of shifts in public opinion (and the changed conditions of material support) what is the positive contribution of sociological argument to the *formation* of public opinion? This, at least, was why Gouldner had been *for sociology*. He had argued that the critique of society must proceed through the critique of sociology. Sociology has been subverted, but it seems that 'society' remains more or less intact and sociology, at best, lags behind.

Science as a problem-solving activity

In the previous sections I have sought to demonstrate that changes in the form of sociological argument have culminated in an impasse in which, in an apparent openness to multiple voices and a reflexive application of sociology to its own undertaking, sociology has seemed to lose its own distinctive voice. A monologic sociology which is not open to other voices is deficient (even self-defeating). However, any simple inversion must contain a similar deficiency. The acceptance of multiple voices seems to lead either to nihilism (where resolution is the operation of power), or to a hope for a future inclusion different from past forms of inclusion (although the criteria for a different form of inclusion are left unspecified). Such claims entail looking forward hopefully, whilst the past is represented as a failure to fulfil hopes. From this perspective, any reflection about the failure to build on previous critiques suggests that present hopes are as likely to be dashed as past hopes were. Sociology, thus, comes to appear quite literally as a hope*less*, and disenchanted, undertaking.

Much of the disquiet with the project of a science of society seems to stem from the 'closure', which is apparently necessary to scientific truths, being at odds with the 'openness' necessary to human creativity. Foundational schemes of general theory have been criticised for precisely this reason. However, an openness to other points of view implies not merely recognition of difference, but a willingness to learn from other views. Learning must imply a change in views and, thus, in criteria of validity which mediate between them. In fact, recent postpositivist philosophies of science have challenged the conception of science which seems to inform much debate over the nature of sociological argument. Although science is recognised as progressive and successful – in the sense of generating new extensions, new insights and new explanatory resources – these are held to occur by *reconstructing*, rather than *accumulating*, 'truths'. In as much as reconstructions reorder truths, science appears discontinuous in terms of its categories and organised into 'paradigms'(Kuhn, 1962) or 'research programmes'(Lakatos, 1970). In this way, science has come to be represented as a located activity whose meanings have a practical history (Laudan, 1996).[23] It proceeds *through problem solving*, rather than *from the application of method*. Indeed, methods are themselves products of creative problem-solving activities and located within that history. The practical activities of science are neither grounded in a foundational consensus nor directed towards producing one.[24]

Postpositivism shares little more than a prefix with postmodernism. Each may be opposed to 'foundationalism', but where the latter embraces contradiction as adequate to the description of a complex, disorderly and contingent social life, postpositivism represents contradictions as problems to be solved in the creative activities of science. In postpositivist accounts of science, mutual consistency of objects and their relations in scientific accounts remains a condition of adequacy, a condition that is necessary to any understanding of the processes of change. Lack of consistency constitutes a problem to be solved. Where postpositivist accounts diverge from standard positivist accounts is in the argument that the answer to particular problems cannot be given in advance, in a method which stands outside particular, located practices of explanation. Where problems lie and how they are to be solved derives from no single correct strategy.

On this understanding of problem solving, 'difference' becomes not an obstacle to sociological argument, but its very condition. Nor do we need to raise professional social theorists above lay theorists. 'We' may learn from 'them' (and vice versa). The issue is not how to represent different understandings as equally valid, but to recognise that such difference must imply the *problematic validity of any account*. The task becomes the explanatory one of finding the means to resolve specific problems of understanding in a more inclusive account. Such inclusion, however, would require the reconstruction of understandings. At the same time, no reconstruction could be final. We could not have an inclusive account as an a priori *set of presuppositions* and, by the same token, we could not expect any particular reconstruction to be the end of any matter. Moreover, conceived as a problem-solving activity, sociological argument would necessarily be turned towards the world and problems of public relevance, of social life in the communities of which sociologists are members.

Notes

1. I should like to thank Martyn Hammersley, Steve Kemp, John MacInnes and Maureen O'Malley for their comments on earlier drafts of this paper.

2. Intimations of the 'death of sociology' are found in Baudrillard's (1983) thesis of the 'end of the social' which would seem to imply an end to the discipline, sociology, whose object it is. Similarly, Lemert suggests that 'history may be moving against sociology' (1995: 132), while Crook et al. argue that 'the continued salience of sociology is far from assured' (1992: 237). See also Seidman (1991). Lash (1987), for his part, links sociology to '(aesthetic) modernism' in order to 'assert scepticism in the face of the still generally accepted legacy of a sociology exclusively concerned with modernizing, rationalizing and civilizing functions. It is to take seriously Hegel's "Owl of Minerva" metaphor and to apply it reflexively to sociology itself' (Lash, 1987: 376).

3. For a detailed treatment of the issues dealt with in the next paragraphs, see Holmwood (1996). Implicit in Parsons' argument is the representation of sociology transcending individualism, but doing so in the displacement of radical socialism. Although Parsons was initially dismissed as inherently conservative, he has recently been 'rediscovered' as a social democrat (Nielsen, 1991). For a broader discussion of the relation between Parsons' sociology and politics, see Buxton (1985). Although the demise of communism at the end of the 1980s might be regarded as an event to challenge existing social theory, and as heralding the triumph of liberalism and the 'end of history' (Fukuyama, 1992), this position was already implicit in Parsons' arguments for 'convergence' on the complex 'system of modern society' (Parsons, 1971).

4. Moreover, that 'reduction' was seen as serving the vested interest of professionals. Where Parsons (1954a, 1954b), following Durkheim (1937), had argued for the role of professional ethics in moderating the possibility that 'individual egoism' would simply be replaced by 'collective egoism', writers increasingly saw professions in precisely those terms: their 'ethics' were an ideological support for their monopoly of expertise and exercise of power. See, for example, Collins (1990).

5. The essay title is: 'Anti-minotaur: the myth of a value-free sociology', and it begins with the statement: 'This is an account of a myth created by and about a magnificent minotaur named Max – Max Weber to be exact; his myth was that social science should and could be value-free. The lair of this minotaur, although reached only by a labyrinthine logic and visited only by a few who never return, is still regarded by many sociologists as a holy place' (Gouldner, 1973a: 3). Gouldner contrasted the role of the university in Germany when Weber was writing, with its role in 1960s USA. Weber's distinction between the vocations of science and politics was designed to insulate the academy from the polarised and hostile discussions in wider society. However, the complacent embrace of the distinction by professional social scientists was occurring at a time when debate in wider society was stifled by consensus, not by opposition (ibid.: 8). In an essay first published in 1904, Weber was explicit that 'there are psychological limits everywhere and especially in Germany to the possibility of coming together freely with one's opponents in a neutral forum, be it social or intellectual' (Weber,1949: 61). His argument reflects a concern with the social structure of the public sphere (including the role of the university) that might facilitate debate over values, as Gouldner suggests, rather than a denial of the appropriateness of such debate.

6. See also Lynd (1945). Lynd distinguishes between 'scholars' and 'technicians', and identifies the deleterious effects on public debate in much the same way as Mills. Ironically Parsons (1954b), though he is Mills' target in the latter's critique of 'grand theory', proposes his theoretical framework to overcome a similar division to that identified by Lynd, namely the one between 'humanism' and a 'pragmatic, technical problem-solving orientation', hostile to theory. Finally, it should be recognised that Mills (1959) too, perceived an 'end of ideology' in Parsons' sense of the declining salience of the categories bequeathed by nineteenth-century sociology.

7   A strong, realist scientific programme was taken up by Foucault (1970), at least in his antihumanist phase, where he joined 'positivism' and 'humanism' together and postulated the effacement of the Subject as a proper scientific attitude came to the fore.

8   The shift is evident in the contrast between Merton's (1968) distinction between the 'history' and the 'systematics' of theory, in which he argued that a concern with 'theorists' was part of the history of the discipline, now displaced by the 'collective' enterprise of sociology, and Wolfe's (1992) defence of the decline of that latter enterprise of 'strong sociology'. Wolfe suggests that this need not elicit dismay because although 'strong sociology' has become 'weak', it has been replaced by 'strong sociologists'. However, 'strong sociologists' must establish their mutual distinctiveness and so the shift must contribute to the sense of the discipline as being characterised by radical critiques and fragmentation.

9   Mouzelis' argument mirrors Baltzell's (1972) proposal to forestall the 'coming crisis' identified by Gouldner by embracing the 'middle-range' functionalism of Merton.

10 Turner (1990) accepts that sociology does not have a past that manifests accumulation and he doubts if the future will be any different, although he believes that accumulation is a logical possibility. Those familiar with Collins' work may recall that he is repeating claims made in an earlier work (Collins, 1975). There he asked why sociology was not a successful science, and concluded it was not a logical impossibility and that, in fact, sociology was well on the way to becoming successful. Now, 25 years later, this remains a possibility which is looked forward to.

11 A constant theme of the critique of 'positivist social science' is the *success* of natural science which encourages emulation, and the *failure* of a social science modelled on natural science. Thus, Giddens argues that positivist social science aimed to 'reproduce in the study of human social life the same kind of sensational illumination and explanatory power yielded up by the sciences of nature. By this token, social science must surely be reckoned a failure' (Giddens, 1976: 13).

12 Failure to do this in sociology – partly because of the dominance of 'feminist empiricism' – constituted a surprising (given the situation in other disciplines) 'missing revolution' (Stacey and Thorne, 1985). This argument has now been extended by advocates of 'queer theory' (Stein and Plummer, 1996).

13 For a more detailed treatment of issues of feminist empiricism, standpoint theory and postmodern feminism, see Holmwood (1995).

14 See Hammersley (2000) for a discussion of Gouldner's 'one-sided' interpretation of Becker's argument.

15 See, for example, Lemert (1994) for a distinction between the 'strong-self' of orthodox, 'universalist' theory and the 'weak-we' identity of marginalised lives whose concrete fractured particularity is lost when inquiries are organised under the categories of 'strong-selves' (which are themselves only another kind of particularism, that of privileged lives). Of course, it is one thing to say that mainstream sociological argument reflects the 'standpoint of privilege', and another to say that the 'privileged' accept the standpoint of mainstream sociology!

16 Habermas' ideas are discussed in detail by Holmwood and Stewart (1991).

17 See also Habermas (1973). Commentators on Foucault have made similar observations. So, Best is worried about Foucault's argument that power relationships constitute all social relationships (Best, 1994: 45), but believes that while he could not have expected an end to power relationships, he did 'seek an alternative set of power relationships that are more enabling' (ibid.: 46).

18 This is perhaps most evident in the pronounced 'Weberian' cast to Foucault's thought that is found in theorists of 'governmentality' (Barry et al., 1996).

19 For a parallel critique of feminist concerns with the 'performance' and 'parodic subversion' of gender roles (Butler, 1990), see Nussbaum (1999).

20 Although the idea of a 'canon' is usually associated with 'professional orthodoxy', its introduction into social theory from literary theory (Kermode, 1985) indicates that it is being invented by 'radical' theorists as the discipline shifts from 'strong sociology' (where the 'canon' is displaced by 'systematic theory') to 'strong sociologists' (Wolfe, 1992). See note 8 above.

21 Thus, the major proponents of general theory make no reference at all to feminist arguments in the construction of their 'consensual' schemes of general social theory. This would make the charge of a 'missing revolution' in sociological theory seem apt (see note 12 above). However, the issue might more properly be regarded as one of *where* any revolution is properly to be located. What seems beyond doubt is that the arguments of those dubbed 'feminist empiricists' have transformed research agendas and explanations in sociology. However, it is one of the consequences of the displacement of explanation in sociological theory that this does not seem to be enough. At the same time, the seemingly more radical approach of postmodernism would undermine the explanatory claims of feminism (while general theory is held to be indifferent to them). See Holmwood (1995).

22 Gouldner begins *Coming Crisis* with an evocation of Hegel in his study at Jena writing within earshot of the approaching troops of French revolutionary 'reason', only in Gouldner's time the sounds seem to fall on deaf ears. 'Social theorists today' he writes, 'work within a crumbling social matrix of paralyzed urban centers and battered campuses. Some may put cotton in their ears, but their bodies still feel the shock waves. It is no exaggeration to say that we theorize today within the sound of guns. The old order has the picks of a hundred rebellions thrust into its hide' (1971: vii).

23 There is no standard usage of the term 'postpositivism', though it is generally used to refer to positions which are broadly sympathetic to science as a creative and progressive activity, but which recognise the limitations of positivism as an account of scientific practice. In this sense, Laudan is a 'postpositivist', though he uses the term to refer to 'social constructionist' critiques of science and declares his own position not to be postpositivist.

24 Or, at least, if the commitment to coherence as a condition of adequacy is construed as meaning they are so directed, they do not necessarily achieve it. The orientation to a more adequate account solves some problems, only to generate new ones for attention as the implications and extensions of new insights are followed through.

References

Alexander, J.C. (1988) 'The new theoretical movement', in N.J. Smelser (ed.) *Handbook of Sociology*. London: Sage

Alexander, J.C. (1995) 'Modern, anti, post and neo: how intellectuals have coded, narrated and explained the "new world of our time"', in *Fin-de-Siècle Social Theory*. London: Verso

Althusser, L. (1965) *For Marx*. London: New Left Books, 1969

Apel, K.-O. (1967) *Analytical Philosophy of Language and the Geisteswissenschaften*. Dordrecht: Reidel

Baltzell, E.D. (1972) 'To be a phoenix: reflections on two noisy ages of prose', *American Journal of Sociology*, 782, pp. 211–29

Barry, A., Osborne, T. and Rose, N. (1996) 'Introduction', in A. Barry, T. Osborne and N. Rose (eds) *Foucault and Political Reason*. London: UCL Press

Baudrillard, J. (1983) *In the Shadow of the Silent Majorities. Or, the End of the Social and Other Essays*. New York: Semiotext[e]

Bauman, Z. (1987) *Legislators and Interpreters: On Modernity, Postmodernity and Intellectuals.* Cambridge: Polity Press

Beck, U. Giddens, A. and Lash, S. (1994) *Reflexive Modernization: Politics, Tradition and Aesthetics in the Modern Social Order.* Cambridge: Polity Press

Becker, H. (1967) 'Whose side are we on?' *Social Problems* 14, pp. 239–47

Best, S. (1994) 'Foucault, postmodernism and social theory', in D.R. Dickens and A. Fontana (eds) *Postmodernism and Social Inquiry.* London: UCL Press

Bhaskar, R. (1979) *The Possibility of Naturalism.* Brighton: Harvester

Bourdieu, P. (1989) '"*Vive la crise!*" For heterodoxy in social science', *Theory and Society,* 17, pp. 773–88

Butler, J. (1990) *Gender Trouble: Feminism and the Subversion of Identity.* London: Routledge

Buxton, W.H. (1985) *Talcott Parsons and the Capitalist Nation State.* Toronto: University of Toronto Press

Coleman, J. (1990) *Foundations of Social Theory.* Cambridge, Massachusetts: Belknap Press of Harvard University Press

Collins, R. (1975) *Conflict Sociology: Toward an Explanatory Science.* New York: Academic Press

Collins, R. (1989) 'Sociology: proscience or antiscience?', *American Sociological Review,* 54, pp. 124–39

Collins, R. (1990) 'Market closure and the conflict theory of the professions', in M. Burrage, and R. Torstendahl (eds) *Professions in Theory and History.* London: Sage

Crane, D. and Small, H. (1992) 'American sociology since the seventies: the emerging identity crisis in the discipline', in T.C. Halliday and M. Janowitz (eds) *Sociology and its Publics: the Forms and Fates of Disciplinary Organization.* Chicago: University of Chicago Press

Crook, S., Pakulski, J. and Waters, M. (1992) *Postmodernization: Change in Advanced Society.* London: Sage

Durkheim, E. (1937) *Professional Ethics and Civic Morals.* London: Routledge, 1992

Elster, J. (1985) *Making Sense of Marx.* Cambridge: Cambridge University Press

Foucault, M. (1970) *The Order of Things: An Archaeology of the Human Sciences.* London: Tavistock

Fraser, N. (1995) 'From redistribution to recognition? Dilemmas of justice in a "post-socialist" age', *New Left Review,* No. 212, pp. 68–93

Fukuyama, F. (1992) *The End of History and the Last Man.* London: Hamish Hamilton

Gadamer, H-G. (1976) 'On the scope and function of reflection', in *Philosophical Hermeneutics.* Berkeley and Los Angeles: University of California Press

Garfinkel, H. and Sacks, H. (1970) 'On the formal structures of practical action', in J.C. McKinney and E.A. Tiryakian (eds) *Theoretical Sociology.* New York: Appleton-Century-Crofts

Giddens, A. (1976) *New Rules of Sociological Method.* London: Hutchinson

Gouldner, A.W. (1971) *The Coming Crisis of Western Sociology.* London: Heinemann

Gouldner, A.W. (1973a) 'Anti-minotaur: the myth of a value-free sociology', in *For Sociology: Renewal and Critique in Sociology Today.* London: Allen Lane

Gouldner, A.W. (1973b) 'The politics of mind', in *For Sociology: Renewal and Critique in Sociology Today.* London: Allen Lane

Gouldner, A.W. (1973c) 'Remembrance and renewal in sociology', in *For Sociology: Renewal and Critique in Sociology Today.* London: Allen Lane

Gouldner, A.W. (1973d) 'Romanticism and classicism: deep structures in social science', in *For Sociology: Renewal and Critique in Sociology Today*. London: Allen Lane

Gouldner, A.W. (1973e) 'Sociologist as partisan: sociology and the welfare state', in *For Sociology: Renewal and Critique in Sociology Today*. London: Allen Lane

Gouldner, A.W. (1974) 'Toward the new objectivity: an introduction to Theory and Society', *Theory and Society*, 1, pp. i–v

Grosz, E. (1986) 'What is feminist theory?', in C. Pateman and E. Grosz (eds) *Feminist Challenges: Social and Political Theory*. Sydney: Allen and Unwin

Habermas, J. (1976) *Legitimation Crisis*. London: Heinemann

Habermas, J. (1987) *The Philosophical Discourse of Modernity*. Cambridge: Polity Press

Habermas, J. (1988) *On the Logic of the Social Sciences*. Cambridge: Polity Press

Habermas, J. (1989) *The Structural Transformation of the Public Sphere: An Inquiry into a Category of Bourgeois Society*. Cambridge: Polity Press

Hammersley, M. (2000) *Taking Sides in Social Research: Essays on Partisanship and Bias*. London: Routledge

Harding, S. (1986) *The Science Question in Feminism*. Milton Keynes: Open University Press

Harding, S. (1993) 'Rethinking standpoint epistemology: "What is strong objectivity?"' in L. Alcoff and L. Potter (eds) *Feminist Epistemologies*. London: Routledge

Hartsock, N. (1987) 'The feminist standpoint: developing the ground for a specifically feminist historical materialism' in S. Harding (ed.) *Feminism and Methodology: Social Science Issues*. Bloomington and Indianapolis: Indiana University Press

Hawkesworth, M.E. (1989) 'Knower, knowing, known: feminist theory and claims of truth', *Signs*, 14, pp. 533–57

Holmwood, J. (1996) *Founding Sociology? Talcott Parsons and the Idea of General Theory*. London: Longman

Holmwood, J. (1995) 'Feminism and epistemology: what kind of successor science?', *Sociology*, 29, pp. 411–28

Holmwood, J. and Stewart, A. (1991) *Explanation and Social Theory*. London: Macmillan

Horowitz, I.L. and Liebowitz, M. (1968) 'Social deviance and marginality: toward a redefinition of the relation between sociology and politics', *Social Problems* 15, pp. 280–96

Keat, R. and Urry, J. (1975) *Social Theory as Science*. London: Routledge and Kegan Paul

Kermode, F. (1985) *Forms of Attention*. Chicago: University of Chicago Press

Kuhn, T.S. (1962) *The Structure of Scientific Revolutions*. Chicago: University of Chicago Press

Lakatos, I. (1970) 'Falsification and the methodology of scientific research programmes', in I. Lakatos and A. Musgrave (eds) *Criticism and the Growth of Knowledge*. Cambridge: Cambridge University Press

Lash, S. (1987) 'Modernity or modernism? Weber and contemporary social theory', in S. Lash and S. Whimster (eds) *Max Weber, Rationality and Modernity*. London: Allen and Unwin

Laudan, L. (1996) *Beyond Positivism and Relativism: Theory, Method and Evidence*. Boulder, Colorado: Westview

Lemert, C. (1994) 'Dark thoughts about the self', in C. Calhoun (ed.) *Social Theory and the Politics of Identity*. Oxford: Blackwell

Lemert, C. (1995) *Sociology after the Crisis*. Boulder, Colorado: Westview

Louch, A.R. (1966) *Explanation and Human Action*. Oxford: Basil Blackwell

Lukes, S. (1976) *Power: A Radical View*. London: Macmillan

Lynd, R. (1945) *Knowledge for What? The Place of Social Science in American Culture*. Princeton: Princeton University Press

Lyotard, J-F. (1985) *The Postmodern Condition: A Report on Knowledge*. Manchester: Manchester University Press

McLennan, G. (1995) 'After postmodernism – back to sociological theory', *Sociology*, 29, pp. 117–32

McLennan, G. (1998) '*Fin de sociologie*? The dilemmas of multi-dimensional social theory', *New Left Review*, No. 230, pp. 58–90

Merton, R.K. (1968) 'On the history and systematics of social theory', in *Social Theory and Social Structure*. New York: Free Press

Mills, C.W. (1959) *The Sociological Imagination*. New York: Oxford University Press

Mouzelis, N. (1990) *Back to Sociological Theory: The Construction of Social Orders*. London: Macmillan

Mouzelis, N. (1995) *Sociological Theory: What Went Wrong? Diagnoses and Remedies*. London: Routledge

Nielsen, J.K. (1991) 'The political orientation of Talcott Parsons: the second world war and its aftermath', in R. Robertson and B.S. Turner (eds) *Talcott Parsons: Theorist of Modernity*. London: Sage

Nussbaum, M. (1999) 'The professor of parody', *New Republic*, 29 February, http://www.tnr.com/archive/0299/022299/nussbaum022299.html, posted 14 December

Pakulski, J. and Waters, M. (1996) *The Death of Class*. London: Sage

Parsons, T. (1954a) 'The professions and social structure', in *Essays in Sociological Theory*. New York: Free Press

Parsons, T. (1954b) 'Some problems confronting sociology as a profession', in *Essays in Sociological Theory*. New York: Free Press

Parsons, T. (1971) *The System of Modern Societies*. Englewood Cliffs: Prentice-Hall

Roemer, J. (ed.) (1986) *Analytical Marxism*. Cambridge: Cambridge University Press

Rose, N. (1996) 'Governing "advanced" liberal democracies', in A. Barry, T. Osborne and N. Rose (eds) *Foucault and Political Reason*. London: UCL Press

Seidman, S.A. (1991) 'The end of sociological theory: the postmodern hope', *Sociological Theory*, 9, pp. 131–46

Seidman, S.A. (1994) *Contested Knowledge*. Oxford: Blackwell

Skocpol, T. (1989) 'An "uppity generation" and the revitalization of macroscopic sociology', *Theory and Society*, 17, pp. 627–44

Stacey, J. and Thorne, B. (1985) 'The missing feminist revolution in sociology', *Social Problems*, 32, pp. 301–16

Stein, A. and Plummer, K. (1996) '"I can't even think straight": "Queer" theory and the missing sexual revolution in sociology', in S.A. Seidman (ed.) *Queer Theory/Sociology*. Oxford: Blackwell

Turner, J.H. (1990) 'Introduction: can sociology be a cumulative science?', in J.H. Turner (ed.) *Theory Building in Sociology: Assessing Theoretical Cumulation*. London: Sage

Turner, J.H. and Turner, S.P. (1990) *The Impossible Science: An Institutional Analysis of American Sociology*. Newbury Park, California: Sage

Weber, M. (1949) '"Objectivity" in social science and social policy', in *Essays in the Methodology of the Social Sciences*. New York: Free Press

Willer, D. and Willer, J. (1973) *Systematicc Empiricism: Critique of a Pseudo-Science*. Englewood Cliffs: Prentice-Hall

Winch, P. (1958) *The Idea of a Social Science*. London: Routledge and Kegan Paul

Wolfe, A. (1992) 'Weak sociology/strong sociologists: consequences and contradictions of a field in turmoil', *Social Research*, 59, pp. 759–79

Yeo, E.J. (1996) *The Contest for Social Science: Relations and Representations of Gender and Class*. London: Rivers Oram Press

Chapter 3
For sociology, Gouldner's and ours[1]
Liz Stanley

What makes a sociologist? The role of scandal and transgression

There are good reasons for paying serious attention to Alvin Gouldner's (1973) collection of essays, *For Sociology*,[2] and also to the text 'that is not there' but which readers become quickly aware is almost omnipresent in its pages – his *The Coming Crisis of Western Sociology* (1970). An important aspect of Gouldner's intellectual project in these works concerns the construction of a radical reflexive critical theory.[3] This involved reflecting on the discipline of sociology, on what it was doing and how it was doing it, on the relationship between sociology and society as perceived by members of the discipline, as well as articulating the idea of reflexivity itself.

Gouldner was very clear that a sociology reflexively aware of itself had not 'lost its way', and was definitely not 'stuck in a mire of navel-gazing'.[4] Rather it was essential for sociology to be analytically aware of its theories, methods, understandings and outputs, clear about the strengths and also the weaknesses of its domain ideas. As such, its products would become more intellectually accountable, both to colleagues within the discipline and to the wider public. As a PhD student back in the early 1970s, the two sociologists whose work most directly influenced me were C. Wright Mills (particularly *The Sociological Imagination* (1959), for its ideas about auto/biography and social structure) and Alvin Gouldner. I read *The Coming Crisis of Western Sociology* in 1974, immediately after *For Sociology*, and I was – and I still am – considerably engaged by the idea of reflexive sociology and the intellectual, political and ethical critical theory project it gives expression to. If there has been any single decisive influence on me as a sociologist, then it lies in Gouldner's formulation of reflexivity in the context of an analytically accountable critical sociology. However, to acknowledge this is not to reveal myself as 'a Gouldnerite'– I do not agree with everything Gouldner argues, either in these books or elsewhere. But it *is* to acknowledge an intellectual debt, and also to say that I read his work generously (Anderson, *et al.*, 1985) as well as critically, accepting that Gouldner was at least as clever, well-meaning and sociologically astute as I (rather than the more frequent implication that those we criticise are somehow lesser beings).

So what is there in Gouldner's work, beyond the fact that 'it influenced me' and other sociologists of my cohort?[5] In a perceptive review of *For Sociology*, John Rex (1974: 497) commented that:

> *reacting to Gouldner involves doing some hard work and hard thinking on a formal theoretical level... The essentially moral reflections on the sociologist's role which form the substance of* The Coming Crisis *and ...* For Sociology *invite us into a metaphysical, a theoretical and a political debate in which we must make* our *choices.*

Basically Gouldner's concern is with a moral epistemology, encompassing foundational aspects of sociological claims to know, to possess knowledge, and how this impacts on sociological understanding of the dynamics of power and the constitution of structure within society. As John Rex suggests, Gouldner does not easily let his readers off the intellectual hook. Instead he demands some 'hard thinking', for the questions he asks are core ones for which there are no easy answers, if indeed there are 'answers' at all in the sense of 'solutions'.

When I first read these books, I was intrigued and at the same time perplexed by the critical flak surrounding *Coming Crisis,* in particular the whiff of scandal and transgression about it that seeps out of the pages of *For Sociology,* the barely leashed anger in some reviews, and the inability of some critics to contemplate that a sociology of sociology might actually be required by sociology's *analytical* concerns and its *ethical* purposes as much as by any *political* impulse within it.[6] As a result I quickly became interested in the critical sociological reaction to reflexivity as well as by reflexivity itself; and my own work, concerned in my PhD (1976) with conceptualising gender, turned increasingly towards an analytic concern with the structure, activities and ideas of sociology and its claims to know. Indeed, it was my reading of *For Sociology* and *Coming Crisis* that helped to finally sever my involvement in political science and move me decisively into sociology. And these books have continued to act as the symbol of an analytically reflexive sociology, for the central thing that attracted me to, and has kept me engaged with, sociology, has been the conviction that the transformative project of sociological inquiry encompasses sociology itself.

In this chapter I loosely follow the structure of *For Sociology,* although I do not deal with exactly the same matters , but parallel ones, themes and issues that are of our time and place and sociology rather than Gouldner's.[7] I then move on to consider some ideas about different kinds of reflexivity and conclude by examining the description of Gouldner as having a 'lively inquiring mind' in terms of present-day sociology – that is, the discipline, rather than particular persons within it.

The crisis of contemporary sociology: or, the centre cannot hold

The crisis outlined in Gouldner's *Coming Crisis* was at the (theoretical) centre of sociology. It was made up of trends including:

- the convergence of formerly separate theoretical positions so that there was no 'internal opposition' to the putative centre;
- the fact that research was tamed by being harnessed to the State in its welfare and research-funding mode;
- the discipline operating around technical definitions and knowledges;

- its domain assumptions, even as expressed by the putative centre, also being caught up with the new 'technical mode';
- the ethical and political pretences of the discipline, which suggested that sentiment, ethics and morality were at its heart, but expressed these through a zoo-keeping advocacy on behalf of oppressed groups, with no notion that the creatures might come out of their cages, into the streets, and into sociology.

For Gouldner, this crisis was one of *perception*, the perception by members of the putative centre that the discipline was changing and that this change might be so radical that sociology wouldn't survive in its then form, but elude their control. At base, however, Gouldner thought (much more ironically) that it was 'ordinary change' that sociologists couldn't come to grips with – perceiving a crisis when things were simply different because changing.

The present perception of crisis in sociology seems similar. For us, there is no longer the towering figure of a minotaur called Max writing of objectivity in the labyrinths of the discipline, but instead an entire Greek chorus, wailing and hand-wringing across many otherwise very different national sociologies.[8] The crisis is still that the centre cannot hold; but it is now other things as well. It is:

- that the 'great tradition' is being murdered, sacrificed to ideologues;
- that the fragmentation of sociology is a Balkanisation that has destroyed its fabric, as evidenced in specialisms which are merely disguised ideologies, with accompanying journals whose criterion of publishability is toeing an ideological line;
- that objectivity has been destroyed, also intellectual authority;
- that student numbers are plummeting, professional organisations folding, and departments closing, as a consequence;
- that the source of sociology's current ills is that 'they' are to blame.

But who are 'they'?

For Irving Horowitz (1993), 'they' are the people who have destroyed the work of the 'great names' of sociology.[9] 'They' are the far Left, feminists, homosexuals, Blacks and Asians, and 'they' are also people who are anti-American, anti-Western and also anti the State of Israel.[10] While few other commentators go this far in naming names, the development of two specialisms in particular, feminism and postmodernism,[11] is frequently picked out as the source of the Balkanisation or fragmentation.

The cry of crisis is of course a *claim*, although often presented as though a description of 'the facts'. As a claim, it is in need of empirical investigation. Behind the headline 'plummeting student numbers', for example, lies something much more varied even within one national, and sometimes even one regional, context. In at least some places there are actually *increasing* numbers. And behind the cries of 'the centre cannot hold; rampant Balkanisation; "they" are storming the centre and the heights', lies what looks to many people as 'business as usual' up in the ivory towers of university-based sociology. However, there is little precise information for the discipline as a whole about who is being appointed and promoted, or whose work really does rule its many intellectual roosts. Hard data are also lacking about the other elements of the 'crisis' claim, so that overarching statements are really not possible.

There is some patchy evidence to suggest that some things have perhaps changed, or are at least beginning to. With marked variations across countries, there seem to be more women staff and students in higher education in general, and in some disciplines in particular. A few more women and Black people are being promoted, though some kinds of institution are more likely to promote them than others. And, as indicated by the content of sociology journals, there have been some shifts in the intellectual preoccupations of the discipline, although again this differs significantly according to the national context. However, it would seem that external structural factors, such as increased surveillance of education, especially higher education, coupled with the marked decline in some countries of state financial support for the university sector, are considerably more important in affecting 'who we are and what we do' than the 'internalist' explanations favoured by the crisis merchants.

Nevertheless there are some interesting questions to be asked about the crisis claim. How and why has this particular moral panic come into existence? For whom is the supposed fragmentation and Balkanisation 'a crisis'? How are 'crisis' and 'fragmentation' defined (or assumed), and by whom? What and who constitutes the implied 'centre'? And to what extent do such claims structure and/or stifle sociological debate?

Focusing on the claim itself and the moral panic it gives expression to, the 'crisis' come from groupings of people who used to 'have and hold' the discipline, and/or assumed it was their birthright. This coexists with great uncertainty about the standing of academic careers as compared with other professions – structural shifts are presented in terms of '"they" have the jobs that should be ours' (now why does this sound familiar?). This runs hand in hand with a perceived loss of authority for the 'objective' and 'scientific' knowledge claims made by the erstwhile centre. And 'they', irresponsibly insisting on the complexity of the social order, the inevitability of the politics of location and the partiality of perspectives, are to blame for the demolition of the credibility of science in general, and social science in particular.

It is a demonstration of the perceived threat here that what are actually some mildly expressed interventions by the terribly polite return of a number of the analytically and theoretically respectable repressed, are instead seen as extreme and heralding the end of all things sociological. As Pierre Bourdieu has suggested, there is 'a high correlation between the types of cultural capital which different researchers have at their disposal and the form of sociology that they defend as the only legitimate one' (1990: 35). What has happened is actually the collapse of a monopoly control over sociology in the United States, so that for Bourdieu 'the "crisis" people talk about these days is the crisis of an orthodoxy, and the proliferation of heresies marks in my opinion progress towards scientific rigour' (ibid.: 38).

There is not, therefore, a general 'crisis' in sociology as a discipline, apart from in Gouldner's sense of a discipline undergoing normal change through differently minded cohorts of people entering it. However, there are other things that *are* at crisis point. In the UK these include the funding of the university sector and the imposition on it of draconian systems of surveillance and regulation. These have particular implications for sociology, a discipline whose members and professional organisations have by and large forgotten how to be critical – a clear demonstration if ever there was one of the need for a 'sociology of sociology'. Worldwide there are crises which are real, terrible, immensely socially consequential: genocide in Rwanda; war in Serbia; atrocities in Kosovo; the implicatedness of the West in all of these; devastation caused by hurricanes in Latin America and earthquakes in parts of Europe. But sociology ignores most of these, going on its own way and dealing with its own internal preoccupations. The sociological Greek chorus crying crisis would do much better directing its considerable energies to commenting on the financial destruction of higher education in much of the West, and on the destruction of groups of people in acts of warfare, genocide and 'natural' devastation worldwide.

Which brings me to ethics, morality and sentimentality in Gouldner's sociology and in ours.

Sentimentality and advocacy sociology

Gouldner's famous, or perhaps infamous, discussion of advocacy and partisanship in *For Sociology* is directed towards the hypocrisy of those sociologists who proclaimed they were 'on the side of' oppressed groups but who actually took up a 'zoo-keeping role', displaying the unfortunate and their social wounds to impress other sociologists, pull in research grants and demonstrate their own radical credentials. This approach advocated better treatment for 'the poor things', but never dared contemplate anything more radical than the sociological equivalent of hospital or prison visiting. To Gouldner, this kind of sociology merely wallowed sentimentally in its rosy picture of the deservingly deviant – the blacks, queers, whores, hustlers *et al.* – while pulling in money, putting out publications and climbing the academic ladder. Gouldner didn't stop at the pretend morality, which masked hypocrisy and a moral fall, of the radical sociology of his day. He also commented on that of the mainstream, whose members, in his view clung to notions of science and objectivity as magical talismen that enabled their possessor to 'transcend' society in order the better to study it. For them questions of morality never entered the picture at all because in their notion of 'science' morality, like all other kinds of commitment, was forbidden. Gouldner's (1973: 25) comments were stark indeed:

> It would seem that social science's affinity for modelling itself after physical science might lead to instruction in matters other than research alone ... If we today concern ourselves exclusively with the technical proficiency of our students and reject all responsibility for their moral sense, or lack of it, then we may some day be compelled to accept responsibility for having trained a generation willing to serve in another Auschwitz.

The present-day sentimentalist approach may not have exactly the same problems as the 1970s version that Gouldner castigated, for the configuration of the discipline has changed and the position of the erstwhile securely mainstream has shifted along with it. However, to my mind it is still not terribly appealing as the basis for a moral epistemology. For some sociologists now, advocacy sociology seems to provide a satisfactory moral answer to the political problematics of the discipline. For advocacy sociology and those who propound it, a defining presumption has been that the proper relationship between sociologists 'in here' and people 'out there' is to 'represent' them. Its concealed sentimentalism involves the talisman of 'taking it back' as a moral, political and also intellectual answer, 'taking back' interviews and other data to those who provided them for the gratifying confirmation that their realities have been represented appropriately and/or accurately. The new sentimentalism hopes for, nay expects, approbation for its activities from those people whose lives are supposedly 'represented' by being pushed through the sociological machine, a view of research that sees it as a kind of Hewlett Packard photo-real printer. Moral research is positioned as a high-technology means of representing, indeed picturing, social life 'just as it is' – 'only reality looks more real', as the advertisement for the printer confidently proclaims. My response is that if this is what is wanted, then we should have the carpet and the trainers themselves, 'the real thing', and not an 'almost reality' on an A4 sheet of paper.

Figure 1 A metaphor for photo-real sociology

Interestingly, the new sentimentalists of advocacy sociology claim a *technical*, as well as a moral, expertise, through possession of a kind of ethico-technical apparatus for collecting reality as well as perceiving, interpreting, explaining and representing it. But what the new sentimentalists appear not to have noticed is that the world has changed and that copying reality isn't wanted, and nor is it intellectually, any more than politically, defensible. On the one hand, 'they' out there intend, if they possibly can, to do their own representing and they aren't very grateful for our efforts any more – if indeed they ever were. And on the other hand, the intellectual and political issues concerning 'representation' have moved on considerably from an 'if we represent their lives then we do moral research' assumption. The cold winds of intellectual change have been blowing strongly around ideas about 'representation', which have taken on a very different hue with the recognition that the most fundamental and irresolvable problematics of the scholarly life lie therein. But not, it seems, in advocacy sociology, where intellectual problems are more easily solved. Perhaps this tells us something about the place, as well as the state, of theory in the discipline, and of ideas about what constitutes knowledge and expertise. And on these matters too, Gouldner had something to say that is still worth thinking about.

Disciplining hierarchies and the place of theory

Gouldner saw the theory as well as the research practice of much sociology of his day as 'technical' in character, because the techniques for accomplishing it had been pre-authorised as 'correct' by specifying what was possible and permissible. In contrast, Gouldner emphasised that these supposedly technical assumptions actually provided mechanisms for *constituting* the social world, rather than reflecting or representing it. That is, they constitute a discipline-specific 'version of the world', one predicated on the conceptual and other concerns of sociology, and they create a kind of 'Ur-society', which parallels social life but never quite touches it. They do so, I suggest, in the same way that anthropology acts as a device for translating the alien into the comfortably recognisable terms of Western thought systems (see David Schneider (1984) in *A Critique of the Study of Kinship*), with the result that these then depart in kind, not just degree, from the original. But somehow the discipline is failing to recognise this.

Gouldner also saw theorising, the crucial commonplace of the discipline, being technologised as 'Theory' and as a specialist apparatus owned by the few on the commanding heights. In doing so, he commented on the institutionalising of sociology and theory within the university, and on the move to sell 'knowledge products' for purposes including the gaining of prestige and power within the discipline. And he also wryly observed the fact that intellectuals more often accommodated themselves to authority than questioned it. These things seem to characterise present-day social theory as well (Stanley and Wise, 2000). This is not to claim that social theory, either then or now, is uninteresting; nor is it to dismiss its argumentative moves and debates. It is, however, to emphasise the accommodations that sociology as a discipline, as well as sociologists as individuals, make with 'the powers that be', and the existence of hierarchies and the role of 'Theory' in re/producing these.

There are also interesting questions to be asked about the epistemic community formed by 'the theorists' of present-day sociology, including:

- who are these sociologists?
- how are they organised 'on the ground'?
- what are the boundaries between them and the rest of us?
- who are the gatekeepers?
- who is in and who is out of 'theory' at any point in time?
- how are 'in' and 'out' configured?
- what are the concerns of social theory?
- how do these relate to 'sociology in general'?

Thinking about such things now, and contrasting them with Gouldner's comments in various of his publications, it is mainly the names that have changed. What theory is and its relationship to what the rest of us do has not really changed – in fact the trends he was commenting on have been confirmed. *Contra* Gregor McLennan's account of the end of hierarchy in the discipline (see Chapter 1), this is still conceived in the terms of Emmanuel Le Roy Ladurie's contemptuous notion of theoretical parachutists and truffle-hunting empiricists. I am *not* proposing here that there is an actual binary divide between 'theory/theorists' and 'the rest' in this way. Most of us neither soar up in the clouds, nor grub about down in the dirt, but sit at the dinner tables of sociology eating truffles, a glass of wine in hand, with our colleagues. However, while practice in the discipline involves complex intermixings of both theory and empiricism, the prevailing characterisation remains one of separation and a binary division of intellectual labour.

Thinking particularly here of the growth of the so-called 'fragmentations', the development of a specialised 'social theory' within sociology means that as a discipline we also need to reflect on how 'theory there' in the specific places of the specialisms relates to 'theory here' in sociology in general. The present-day formulation of theory is as a kind of sociological chess game which tells us a lot about the players and how they think, reason and respond to each other's game, but fails to inform us about the actual bishops, knights, kings, queens and the many pawns of society. Of course, beneath the surface of the public primacy of social theory, a good deal of the 'crucial commonplace' theorising that Gouldner so passionately championed continues. Here too, then, matters are considerably more complex than they are characterised in the cries of 'crisis', and it is important that the accounts provided by the beleaguered crisis-merchants are thoughtfully examined and compared with alternative views of 'what there is' in the discipline and 'where it's going'.

The particular specialism I know best is feminist sociology. As with other areas of multidisciplinary 'studies', 'feminist theory' is shared between its presence in sociology and its presence elsewhere in the academic disciplines, indeed in intellectual life more generally. In my view, from its transformative origins, feminist theory now increasingly mirrors the mainstream social theory project, including its presumed (or desired) hierarchical placing, in which theory and practice are seen as binaries and the place of theory is seen as superordinate. However – and it is a resounding 'however' – feminist theory has become another 'parallel project', one that runs alongside mainstream theory, assiduously referencing 'the literature' and reworking and improving its conceptual apparatus around, centrally but not exclusively, its theorising of 'sexual difference', without ever meeting the mainstream. Across the disciplines and the multidisciplines, investigations of referencing practices as an indication of the intellectual toing and froing of ideas and influences have revealed that 'the theory girls' reference and take account of 'the theory boys', but that 'the theory boys' are by and large unaware of and/or do not care about the theory work of 'the girls' (e.g. Bordo, 1996; Finn, 1993; Sprague, 1997).

In addition, the rise of social theory has coincided, to put it no more strongly, with the growth of ideas about theory as an inter- or even a post-disciplinary medium of intellectual exchange. The idea of 'travelling theory', reworking Edward Said's use of the term, usefully characterises this development. With travelling theory have come the travelling theorists, an international jet-setting epistemic community of 'the theory names' that shuttle about the world, with 'the names' here being those of the 'parallel project' travelling theorists of feminism as well as the top-flight theory boys (the latter including those of the 'alternative' project of deconstructionism and postmodernism). This is a depressing business for those of us who want some better political, intellectual and ethical configuration of 'alternatives' in the academy in general and sociology in particular than the creation of a new hierarchy of contemporary 'great names'.

For Gouldner, such developments were linked to the role of the universities as corporate enterprises selling knowledge products and the devastating readiness of academics to trade their wares for funding, prestige and power. Perhaps this is why, though we teach theory and write theory and use theory, there are very few meta-theoretical inquiries into 'the theory game' and what it entails for the hierarchies and values of the discipline. 'Theory in general' is at least as interesting as social theory and also far too important to sociology as the central means of expressing, shaping and debating its key ideas to be relegated to the intellectual backroom of the discipline it currently occupies. All the many closet commonplace theorisers in the discipline need outing.

But what of politics and renewal in sociology? What can we learn from Gouldner's comments on this that might progress thinking about the constitution of sociology and the reconstitution of its hierarchies?

The politics of renewal in sociology

Gouldner noted that mainstream sociologists required people like him to provide them instantly with a completely operational and 'without fault' alternative as a prerequisite to 'speaking out' at all – 'put up or shut up' with a vengeance. Behind this lay a particular, and in the analytic terms of sociology rather odd, characterisation of organisational development, renewal and change in the academic disciplines. Implicitly the assumption was that renewal and development could take place only through small respectful accretions by people who, in their persons as well as their minds, were very much like earlier cohorts. Organisation was seen as either persisting effectively unchanged or not surviving at all.

Something much like this seems to be central to the 'crisis' I began my discussion of Gouldner's work with. There is a concern that 'they' are coming in the door, taking the place over, usurping the jobs that should by rights belong to other people, and that 'they' are nothing like 'us', but have different ideas and bodies, and will immediately sell the sociological pass. But what this ignores is a range of more grounded, more mundane and, it seems to me, more important factors. First, there have been wide-ranging intellectual and political changes in intellectual and social life generally, with ideas about science, academia, education, hierarchy and deference all having been scrutinised and problematised. Second, in many other countries as well as the UK, external factors connected with government policies and funding regimes have impacted enormously on everyday working life in universities, including on the meaning and practices of 'scholarship'. Third, these changes also have implications for who comes into the discipline, what ideas and approaches attract them, and who leaves it, at all levels. And fourth, the demise or growth of, or more simply change within, the different epistemic communities that constitute sociology is a normal state, and not a crisis one.[12]

Alongside these complex developments and (possibly) changes, the politics of organisational life remain, at least in British universities, the politics of who is in and who is out, managed through gate-keeping mechanisms that regulate short-listing, interviewing, appointments and promotion. 'Good ol' boy' networks, by no means all members of which are male these day, still remain central to academic reproduction, in which things are stitched up by people who tell others, and perhaps themselves, that those 'others' really, quite objectively, just don't have what it takes. The politics of renewal are the dynamics of cloning: appointing people just like ourselves but not quite as smart and with ideas fairly much like our own but not quite so well formulated or expressed. Sociology is neither the only nor the worst offender in academia in this regard, but it is still implicated. And comparing equal opportunities procedures, structures and monitoring within the university system, with those in local and central government and also in the private sector, is a salutary and chastening experience. The universities and the academic communities who people them lag far behind in the kinds of changes that have been happening 'out there', in parts of society and the economy that many academics, 20 years behind the times, affect to despise.

This suggests there are some very deep-rooted structural ways of behaving within the organisations that constitute 'the university system', and this includes its collectivities of scholars, that seriously militate against change. Here too, *For Sociology* has something to say that remains relevant.

Deep structures and (im)morality in sociology

In *For Sociology*, Gouldner proposed that beneath the surface of the sociology of the 1970s lay deep structures of thought rooted in the *longue durée* histories of intellectual life in the West and which surface in classicism and romanticism as strong 'tendencies' in disciplinary theory and practice.[13] He also observed that at times one or other of these becomes dominant, but the long-term survival and 'health' of the discipline requires them to be in rough balance. In thinking about now, rather than when Gouldner was writing, my attention is drawn to another form of deep structure, one that also creates tensions but this time not only within the discipline but also in the relationship between sociology and society. This concerns the part played in sociology by ideas about morality, by its moral and ethical stands, not so much about 'the world' as concerning the work of sociologists, the knowledge the discipline produces and the claims made for this.

I shall make four brief observations here:

1. Advocacy sociology, commendable in its own particular terms, directs the sociological gaze away from those who have towards those who have not. That is, it involves researching down and then representing, or rather re-representing, this within a sociological arena, also a policy one. It is assumed that in so doing the ethical problems involved in the scrutinising gaze of the sociological enterprise are solved.

2. The empirical sociologies precede in an apparently dispassionate way, purportedly merely recording and analysing 'what is'. But hidden away here are unexplicated and perhaps also unexamined assumptions about the moral place of the sociologist through the claims that sociologists make about 'how the world is', claims which cohere around the view that description can be pure description uninfluenced by interpretation and thus value.

3. Social theory by and large consists of the theoreticians in one another's arms, the theorists wrapped up in each other's work, ideas and writings. Even when, perhaps especially when, the specific focus of the theory is apparently 'out there' on things in the world, 'the theory gaze' and the analytical categories that characterise it act as a 'translation', or perhaps a 'transmutation', device from 'their' terms and relevancies to 'ours'.

4. 'The world' for these at their core realist forms of sociology is the curious 'Ur-version' produced by the academic photo-real copying machine.

Do these things matter? After all, sociology is an academic discipline for studying and explaining, and not a mechanism for reforming, the world. It mattered for Gouldner, as Janet Gouldner (1996: 162) remarks, because 'For him, there was a political obligation in theoretical endeavours'. That is, something was due back for the privilege of being employed to think, reflect, investigate and theorise about the world. Dismissing partisanship (whether real or sentimental), and rejecting ideological adherence as a form of quasi-religious belief, this sense of obligation took Gouldner into 'commitment'. This entailed grappling with the complexities of the subject/object relationship and the 'end of objectivity', striving to theorise in an open and unfettered way outside of the corporate relations of university-based knowledge production, and in doing so recognising 'real world' issues and contributing to a greater understanding of them. For similar reasons, many other sociologists also endeavour to have a 'commitment' too. *Contra* the position argued by Martyn Hammersley, many sociologists do want to craft a position which is *both* sociologically creditable *and* can underpin some kind of transformative project (what I called earlier a 'moral epistemology', and Hammersley terms 'action in the world'). However, I certainly agree with him that 'a more modest approach is required ... [which] treats sociology as no more than a source of specialised factual knowledge about the world. Its practical value is considerable, but nevertheless limited. Above all, it cannot offer a self-sufficient answer to questions about "what's wrong?" or "what is to be done?"' (Hammersley, 1999: Abstract).

I am struck by the disparities, the divorce, sometimes the sheer gulf, between the concerns of 'in here' and the events of 'out there'.

Compare, for example, the divorce between the leading English-language sociology journals and some of the major events of the last decade: massive social and economic change in Eastern Europe; the highly gendered pandemic that is HIV and AIDS in the non-European parts of the world; war, famine, death and genocide in parts of Africa; unanticipated political change in South Africa; natural disasters and human catastrophe in a number of the countries of Latin America and southern Europe; a highly interventionist American foreign policy and so-called 'New Labour' Blairite Britain clinging to its coat-tails; upheavals in the Balkans, war in Serbia and genocide in Kosovo. Interestingly, one of the sociological places where the disparities are less jarring is the pages of *Theory and Society*, the journal that Gouldner founded in 1974, editorially commenting in its first issue that:

> Theory and Society *has no choice but to be a child of its time. It comes at a moment when the institutional and departmental life of social theory and sociology seem exhausted and drifting. At a time when sociology sees the road back more clearly than the one forward. The old intellectual paradigms are losing their ability to convince, let alone enthuse.*
> (Gouldner, 1974: 1)

For Gouldner, being 'a child of his time' entailed having a commitment *as a sociologist* to engage with 'out there', not to lose sight of the intellectual specificities and requirements of 'in here', but rather to retain the 'Janus-faced' character of the scholarly life. This is scholarship, not as a hermit-like retreat, or as the Vatican-like translation of contemporary argot into the sociological equivalent of High Latin, but as the explicit use of the particular perspective that sociology provides, one which is critical and evaluative, deeply involved although not partisan, so as to engage with 'the times'.

This trajectory in Gouldner's developing sociological thinking has also influenced me. As editor of *Sociological Research Online*,[14] I have endeavoured to use the rapid publication possibilities of electronic media to stimulate sociologists to act and write as 'public intellectuals', not as quasi-journalists or quasi-politicians, but as sociologists using their specific expertise to address public issues. This led to the development in 1999 of a 'rapid response' mode of sociology publishing, which involves a quarterly call for short articles reflecting on a particularly topical issue or event occurring in the world, to be published, peer reviewed, in the next issue.[15]

If, as sociologists, we are to be 'children of our time', then this surely means engaging with the present, rather than waiting and waiting for the benefits of hindsight. Where necessary, this will entail recrafting our sociology to permit us to do so. Electronic publishing and the 'rapid response mode' enables sociologists working in the field to engage with things happening at the point that they're happening, and to publish and thus to 'speak' about them as 'public intellectuals'. What comes out of this may be (it is too soon to tell) rather different from the 'with time and hindsight' character of most journal articles. Certainly *Sociological Research Online* is increasingly being used by NGOs, those involved in governmental policy-making (not just in the UK), journalists, (in radio in particular), school students and those who teach them, as well as having the more traditional readership that one would expect of a sociology journal. Following the first 'rapid response' on 'The Macpherson Inquiry Report and the Murder of Stephen Lawrence', other rapid responses have been published on 'War, Terror and Genocide', 'The Genetic Modification of Food', 'Prediction in Sociology', 'The "New Right"', and 'Land Reform in Southern Africa'.[16] I hope the 'rapid responses' will encourage sociologists to engage sociologically with the events of the world as they are happening, to look to the road ahead rather than always to the road behind, and to develop new intellectual paradigms rather than endlessly picking over the entrails of the old.

And on the subject of new paradigms, Gouldner had something interesting to say here too.

Figure 3.2: Sociological Research Online *in 'rapid response' mode*

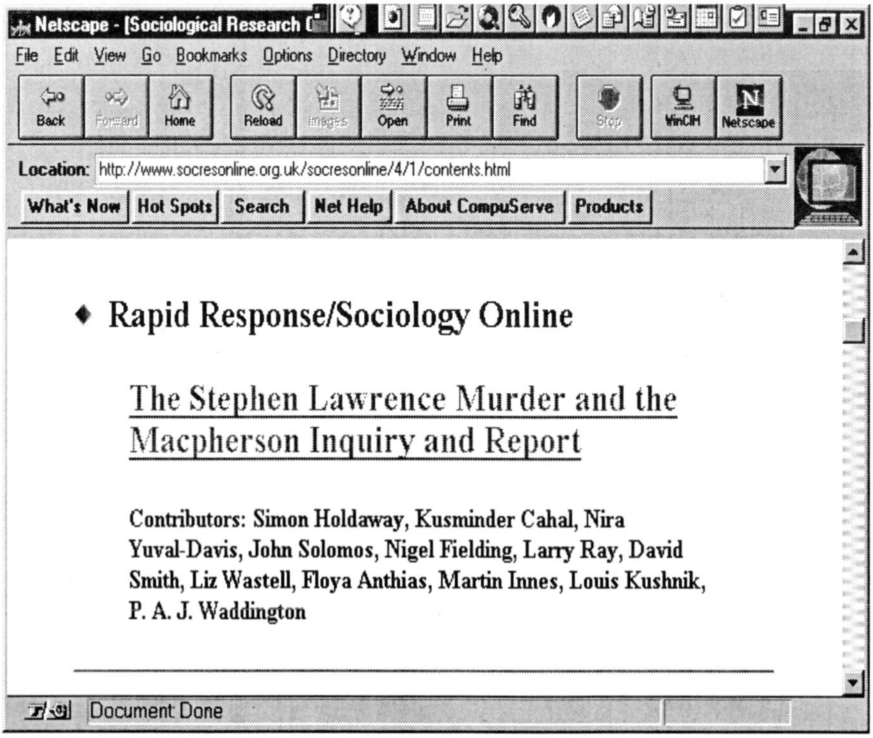

Have they read it? Feminism and sociology

One of Gouldner's essays in *For Sociology* is concerned with developing a Marxist sociological critique of Marxism. The question he didn't directly ask but which was analytically crucial was, who owns Marxism? His implicit answer was that no-one owns a free mind, there should be no shibboleths, nothing sacrosanct. I am interested in what has become the broadly analogous position of feminist ideas and persons in present-day sociology. I realise that some people – by no means all of them either men or crisis-merchants – resent the movement into 'their' discipline of these feminists; very many more do not, believing that the discipline is ours, belonging to those of us who are for it, *all* of us. Neither sociology nor academic feminism belongs to any select grouping who claim private ownership, for ideas really are *sans frontière*. My curiosity here is directed towards what has happened to the domain ideas and working practices of feminism as these have moved from the very edge of the furthest periphery in towards the (now absent) centre of the academic disciplines. I am also intrigued by the recent claims made around the interesting question of 'who wants to own feminism' within sociology.

Gouldner was both puzzled and angry that many criticisms of *Coming Crisis* were not responses to his actual argument, but apparently wilful misrepresentation. Furthermore, when he was quoted as promulgating views he had explicitly disagreed with, he was prevented from replying to critics in the 'public spaces' of the very journals that published the critiques. In a number of the essays in *For Sociology* Gouldner contemplates the possibility that some of the commentators on his work had not actually read what he had written, but were instead recycling what earlier critics had misrepresented as his views. The answer to 'Have they read it?' was, 'No they haven't' – but they *had* read, and wanted to agree with, each other, and they did so by setting up a 'straw Gouldner' whom they critiqued and dismissed.

So what does this have to do with relationship between feminism and sociology? Readers of this chapter will most likely be aware that some of the putative owners of sociology proceeded in just this fashion in regard to feminism in the discipline in the 1960s and 70s, and that a few die-hards still do so, even after some thirty years of what seems, to some of us at least, a productive period of involvement. But there is more to say than this. Feminism within the academy of course isn't a 'thing', but rather a broad approach inhabited by a diverse set of people who disagree, as well as agree, about many things. It has its own putative centre(s) and contending peripheries. And a good few of the internal divisions of feminist sociology parallel those within sociology as a whole, including differences between those who favour structural and those who favour interactional approaches, those who see themselves as realists and dub anyone disagreeing with them as idealists, those who see themselves as postmodernists and dub anyone disagreeing with them as essentialists, and, of particular interest to me here, those who have a matrician liking for science, authority and certainty, cheek by jowl with those who have a hoi polloi concern with collectivities, complexities and reflexivities.

In contemplating the intra-feminist divisions within sociology, I am analytically interested in ownership and control. My particular interests centre on claims to the ownership of feminist sociology and the control of its ideas and working practices, and the role of the mis/representation of contrary viewpoints in producing intellectual closures. In a discussion of methodology and 'people's ways of knowing', Ann Oakley (1998a, and see also 1998b, 2000) at a number of points inverts and reverses what Sue Wise and I wrote in *Breaking Out Again* (Stanley and Wise, 1993), supposedly arguing against us, but actually repeating a number of the views we had promoted. This is a more general stratagem in Oakley's discussion, which proceeds by homogenising 'feminism' through points taken out of context, sometimes reversing them, then generalising these into 'a position' assigned to 'them', them over there, the feminist sociologists who are not like her. This feminism, Oakley states rather than shows, does not engage in a scholarly debate but rather advances an ideological, and by implication false, representation of a quantitative/qualitative dualism. It is 'trapped in an ideological combat between quantitative and qualitative methods ... largely in ignorance of the way in which different approaches to knowledge have historically been sited within social and natural science' (1998a: 717, 708). Feminist methodology texts, she claims, all celebrate qualitative methods seen as epistemologically totally distinct from 'quantitative' methods.

The three defining views Oakley assigns to feminism in sociology are quite shocking. They are that:

1. it holds an extreme form of relativism that says that nothing has reality;
2. it depicts the power hierarchies of research as exactly those of sexual assault and murder;
3. it insists that 'number-crunching' is a cardinal sin.

Readers who are outsiders, who aren't 'knowing insiders' to feminist sociology and who haven't read a cross-section of its writings, may perhaps mistake Oakley's account for serious scholarly description, without realising that it is precisely the kind of ideological (mis) representation Oakley accuses those 'other' feminists of, and is 'ideological combat' against views she dislikes and disapproves of. It is in fact a good example of the 'ideological three step' theorised by Dorothy Smith (1974, following Marx in *The German Ideology*) as a means for caricaturing and dismissing the views of other people. The reality, *contra* Oakley, is that a very broad range of theories and approaches coexist within feminist sociology, a range very similar to the one within sociology in general. Feminist sociology encompasses varieties of relativism through to extreme forms of realism and high positivism. It includes many different kinds of methodological strategies and uses of method, in which, in terms of sheer quantity of work, 'working with numbers' actually predominates in survey approaches. Other quantitative methods are also used, along with the whole range of qualitative research approaches, cheek by jowl with all the varieties of theorising, including 'high theory'.

What Oakley's account *does* is more interesting than what it *is*. It tailors a purportedly realist description in order to suit an argument and its desired conclusion. On one level this is that science outside of academia is actually rather charming and cuddly; on another level it's that Oakley dislikes some ideas, attaches these to academic feminists who aren't of her kind, and thinks that 'they' should not be taken seriously. However, this is not argued openly, but instead a division is set up between 'those feminists over there', the wilful or misguided 'they', versus those who, like Oakley herself, are sensible, responsible and scholarly. The similarities between this lament from respectable matrician feminism about the feckless peripheries and fragmentations, and the other lament about peripheries and fragmentations outlined earlier, are striking.

Gouldner commented on the growth of a 'technical', rather than explicitly argumentative, mode in sociology, one of 'they're wrong' rather than 'we disagree'. He did so as part of his wider consideration of theorising and the need for reflexivity, in the context of the growth of 'Theory' in the discipline. Can Gouldner's discussion of this take us forward from partisanship in a way that combines commitment and reflexivity with having a foundation for sociological knowledge?

The reflexivities

Theoretical frameworks

As mentioned earlier, Gouldner commented ruefully in *For Sociology* that when he talked about reflexivity he was usually required to repair an approximately two-hundred year absence of concerted sociological work on this by instantly providing a reflexive sociology fully worked out and operational, like a startled rabbit from a commodious sociological hat. How does the reflexivity project in present-day sociology compare when stood alongside Gouldner's remarks in *For Sociology* and *Coming Crisis*?

Ideas about reflexivity in sociology still need to be better historicised as well as better contextualised. It sometimes seems as though only one version of reflexivity exists, which came into being in the United States through its parenting by Gouldner, mutated into an 'in your face' set of ideas belonging to the UK sociologists associated with the 'sociology of scientific knowledge',[17] with a Gallic alternative offered in the work of Pierre Bourdieu.[18] In fact though, quite a few varieties of reflexivity exist in sociology. These are located – not all of them under the sign of the name – within interpretivist, phenomenological, hermeneutic, interactionist, ethnomethodological and feminist traditions, with some having long and distinguished histories. The truncated version seems to me to result from a wider 'presentism' in the discipline, a more general lack of knowledge about its past apart from mantra invocations of the 'great tradition'.[19]

While I don't feel the need, any more than Gouldner did, to pull a reflexive rabbit from my sociological hat, I do want to comment on 'the reflexivities' in sociology. There are competing versions of reflexivity:

- Steve Woolgar (1988b) has termed 'constitutive reflexivity' and 'benign introspection';
- Bruno Latour (1988) has referred to as 'meta-reflexivity' and 'infra-reflexivity';
- Stanley (1990) has dubbed 'descriptive reflexivity' and 'analytical reflexivity';
- Pierre Bourdieu (1992) has discussed as 'participant objectification' and 'biography';

- Tim May (1999) has termed 'endogamous reflexivity' and 'referential reflexivity'.
- Scott Lash (1994) has referred to as 'cognitive reflexivity', 'aesthetic reflexivity' and 'hermeneutic reflexivity'.

These are sometimes presented as either/or choices, sometimes as continua, and how reflexivity is understood differs considerably between commentators. As Paul Atkinson (1999: 192) comments, 'Reflexivity is ... a polyvalent term much used and abused in different contexts'.

In my own thinking about descriptive and analytical reflexivities, I associate descriptive reflexivity with advocacy sociology: 'I'm white, I'm black, I'm a woman, I'm a man; it was Tuesday, in a youth club or on a housing estate; they were nice to me, they were horrid to me; I took the interviews/transcripts/ reports back to them; and they told me what I'd got right, and what I hadn't'. Such things can be interesting as a kind of accretion around a piece of research, and they may have a usefulness to readers as a simple means of placing the researcher and the researched. But what they tell us about the actual *sociology* involved is very little, and this certainly isn't the kind of thing that Alvin Gouldner laid his sociological reputation on the line for. Analytical reflexivity is an intellectually and sociologically more considerable enterprise, and for Gouldner it involved how we respond as sociologists to the fact that social theory is 'made by men and women' and how we respond intellectually to the fact that theory is rooted in experience. The underpinning of a sociological response for Gouldner was the recognition that 'All research is contaminated, for all research entails relationships that may influence both sociologist and subject. The aim of the reflexive sociologist is not to remove his influence on others, but to *know* it.' (1973: 77).

Gouldner's version of reflexivity, then, was concerned with the act of knowing and its links to the claim or assumption of the possession of knowledge. Once interpretation is seen to entail value, then any easy or binary distinction between 'the sociologist' and 'a person' has to be surrendered, along with objectivity (in the strong sense). A moral epistemology is placed at the heart of discipline, foundationally concerned with: the material conditions that underpin the knowledge that sociology claims to produce; making its knowledge claims fully accountable within sociology; and making its knowledge products analytically useful in understanding, and helping to change, the world. Gouldner contrasted this with the objectification of knowledge in the university, its product-like status for sale or barter against prestige and power. He wanted to find an intellectual alternative in the sense of a non-partisan and non-ideological commitment, and also a practical alternative in the sense of building alternative organisational structures. The 'collegium' of *Theory and Society* was conceived as an intellectual and a political project against the way he saw social theory being institutionalised. And for Gouldner, reflexivity 'out there' and reflexivity 'in here' were not distinct – 'to know' always has both dimensions to it, and as sociologists we surrender this awareness at our collective intellectual, moral and political peril.

I see Gouldner's approach to reflexivity as a version of what I've called analytical reflexivity. Bourdieu (Bourdieu and Wacquant, 1992: 71), by contrast, sees it as 'more a programmatic slogan than a veritable programme of work' and locates it at the biographical 'end' of reflexivity which he rejects. I don't agree with this, for two reasons. First, Gouldner's ideas about a moral epistemology at the heart of the sociological enterprise add up, across the body of his sociological work, to more than the autobiographical detritus Bourdieu perceives. Second, Gouldner did his best to put into practice a serious intellectual as well as political commitment to a reflexive sociology – including his role in founding *Theory and Society*, still one of the key journals of the discipline, and his reflexive as well as reflective approach to theorising. Gouldner's reflexivity is neither advocacy-style autobiographical description, nor the high-tech version found in conversational analysis. I position it at the analytical end of the continuum, because for me 'analytical' encompasses a serious, in-depth reflection on intellectual issues and problematics of the kind Gouldner engaged in.

Steve Woolgar (1988b) dismisses this reflectiveness as 'benign introspection'. Woolgar's discussion of reflexivity presents a continuum around the ideas of benign introspection and constitutive reflexivity. Critically commenting on both, his own approach is apparent from the title of his chapter, 'Reflexivity is the ethnography of the text'. However, to use Bruno Latour's (1988) term, Woolgar's approach is one of 'meta-reflexivity', in which the assumption is made that there can be hierarchies of reflexivities, with the one at the top of the various layers of interpretation having epistemological superordinancy. Latour's discussion, and the distinction he makes between 'infra-reflexivity' and this textually based meta-reflexivity, persuasively demonstrates the fundamental flaw both in Woolgar's general premises, and in those articulated in the collection Woolgar (1988a) edited, *Knowledge and Reflexivity* (see here Wes Sharrock's (1989) review).

Latour (1988) himself believes that reflexivity fully characterises social life and its interactions and there is no version of reflexivity which can be fully referential of the 'underlying reality', which can completely correspond to this. Pursuing a fully referential correspondence notion of reflexivity is for Latour somewhat akin to the pursuit of the Holy Grail – preoccupying but useless because organised around a chimera – and he recommends instead that sociologists use all the apparatus of different styles and genres of writing when looking at and reflecting on the infra-reflexivities of social life and interaction. To my mind, Latour's discussion remains one of the most considerable sociological engagements with the notion of reflexivity.

'In here', in sociology specifically, and 'out there', in society more generally, are of course not actual 'places/spaces' or binaries. The sociological 'here' is a minor subset within the societal 'there', and there is no good reason for not thinking about it, commenting on it and treating it with the same analytic tools that we use for other aspects of social life. This has become something of a truism for those who align themselves with a 'reflexive turn': Bourdieu's (Bourdieu and Wacquant, 1992: 69) comment that 'forgetting to inscribe into the theory we build ... the fact that it is the product of a theoretical gaze' constitutes what he terms 'epistemocentrism'; and Steier (1991: 1–2) remarks that 'these very same principles must be applied by researchers to themselves and to their research ... the researchers included in, rather than outside, the body of their own research'.

Atkinson (1999) sketches out two contrasting tendencies in the use of the term reflexivity. Firstly, there are those who claim no epistemological privilege for what results. Secondly, there are those who do, proposing or implying that some data is privileged because it is immediately referential of an underlying social reality and, by giving authentic access to this, it has 'emancipatory power'. This latter position can, in its 'real reality' aspirations, be seen as a variant of realism – indeed perhaps as a kind 'hyper-realism'. Steier's (1991) introduction to *Research and Reflexivity* sees reflexivity and constructionism as coterminous, with social constructionism as both the origin and the consequence of reflexivity. This is similar to the position of Woolgar (1988b) and the contributors to *Knowledge and Reflexivity* (Woolgar, 1988a), who see reflexivity as having replaced realism with relativism.[20] However, what 'reflexivity' is seen to be is different in these two collections: Steier is particularly concerned with textual representation, while Woolgar deals more with the 'cybernetic' circular flow of interpretations 'in life' and 'in research'.

For Steier *et al.*, recognising the circularity of interpretational account-building by 'them' and by 'us' means seeing social constructionism as a defining attribute of both 'life' and sociology, together with the referential aim of matching 'our' constructions to 'theirs'. The work of Woolgar *et al.* is characterised by a similar interest in the rhetorical and textual nature of social construction, but here, by contrast, there is a considerable ironicising of interpretational account-building within science.[21] If neither photo-realism nor irony are deemed sufficient to sustain the body politic of sociology, as Gouldner clearly felt, then can reflexivity and constructionism be conceived in such a way as to provide a grounding for sociology?[22] Gouldner's concern with a moral epistemology was not an end in itself, nor did it lead him to focus on the circular referentiality of interpretations and accounts. Instead it underpinned his ideas about 'commitment', the interconnections between 'sociologists' and 'people', and the need for sociology to constitute a praxis.

Something of this concern is included in Tim May's (1999) distinction between endogenous reflexivity, which refers to 'the knowledge that is born in and through the actions of members of a given community', and referential reflexivity, which is 'knowledge that is generated as a result of having the routines of social life disrupted by sudden changes in social conditions' (1999: 3.10, 3.11). The latter, for May, forms the common ground between everyday and sociological accounts, because it involves standing back from and reflecting on social action and meaning in reflexivity. And, while he comments that 'Sociology oscillates between these two senses of reflexivity' (1999: 3.14), he notes that referential reflexivity has also formed the basis of a sense of epistemic superiority, whereas disciplinary reflexivity has often stopped short of critically scrutinising the validity of the knowledge claims involved.[23] May certainly thinks it necessary for sociology to be concerned with 'the social world' itself. For him, a reflexive sociology brings 'self-troubling' and self-awareness into the discipline. The route into 'the social world itself' lies within referential reflexivity, because 'relations with objects and nature are a core concern of this dimension' (1999: 3.11). However, what this might mean in terms of the specificities of sociological practice and the grounding for a sociology is not discussed, for May's focus is on what might be termed 'classificatory' matters.

A closer connection with Goudner's concerns seems to me to lie in Scott Lash's (1994) interrogation of what a critical theory would look like in the context of 'reflexive modernization'. Lash distinguishes structural reflexivity, where agency reflects on rules and structures, from self-reflexivity, where agency reflects on itself. 'A theory of reflexivity', writes Lash (1994: 140), 'only becomes a *critical* theory when it turns its reflection away from the experience of everyday life and on to "system".' It is via this comment that I see the connection with Gouldner's approach to reflexivity. Lash views Bourdieu's 'logic of practice' as having 'little to do with structure' (1994: 155), although he sees its influence on the 'radical ethnographers' as underpinning the development of a hermeneutic and ethnomethodology-influenced notion of reflexivity which he characterises (in my opinion incorrectly) as 'assuming away power'. He proposes that 'What seems to be needed is a radical hermeneutics' (1994: 165), that is, a critical hermeneutics concerned with the constitution, mechanisms and dynamics of power and structure, again for me suggesting a link with Gouldner's concerns.

For many sociologists, it is Pierre Bourdieu's idea of 'participant objectification' and his 'logic of practice' around this that form the most considerable and sustained account of reflexivity in sociology. For Bourdieu, reflexivity is anti-narcissistic, because it is not at all concerned with the 'private person' or the intellectual Zeitgeist; it is also anti-biographical in its intent and approach; and it is an absolute prerequisite for sociological practice. Bourdieu characterises reflexivity as 'an exploration of the scientific unconscious of the sociologist through the explication of the genesis of problems, categories of analysis' (Bourdieu and Wacquant, 1992: 213–4; see also Bourdieu, 1990: 34–55). He sees participant objectification as 'arguably the highest form of the sociological art' (Bourdieu and Wacquant, 1992: 259–60), and as *the* method of reflexivity. Participant objectification seems to involve a number of overlapping analytical moves. One is relational analysis, in which a testable model of an empirical case is constructed, analogic reasoning is applied in a way that both enables immersion in the particular and also supports generalisation from it, and then through the comparative method the sociologist thinks relationally and analytically about the particular case. Another move is the promotion of a detailed reflectiveness on the processes and procedures of intellectual production. The titles of two of Bourdieu's (1990) essays can stand for the practices involved in this: 'Fieldwork in philosophy' and 'A lecture on the lecture'. Underlying both of these moves, the practice of objectification turns on making an object of one's own sociological analytical activities.

Paradoxically, however, insofar as Bourdieu's (1988) *Homo Academicus* can be seen as an exemplification of the practice of reflexivity within the methodology of participant objectification, the result is a detailed empirical account of a particular case that could have been produced by any researcher using a standard empirical approach. That is, there is little sign of anything distinctive that 'reflexivity' adds here, other than the case being of academia and the university; and the 'objectification' involved seems little different from traditional notions of scientific detachment and objectivity. Bourdieu's programmatic statements about reflexivity raise high expectations. However, the performance does not live up to them. Moreover, it is by no means clear what the grounding for sociological claims-making is in Bourdieu's version of reflexivity. It seems to be a version of 'better science' achieved, ironically in view of Bourdieu's statements about biography and narcissism, by *ad hominem* force.

Research practices

Having sketched out a number of frameworks for thinking about reflexivity, I now want to step back from these to consider some of the research practices which various of these commentators allude to, invoke or describe as being involved in the practice of reflexivity. I shall map these onto a continuum (see Figure 3.3) with research processes at one end, and knowledge outcomes at the other.

Figure 3.3 focuses on the move from research processes through to the shaping of knowledge outcomes and the kinds of claims made from these. It also clarifies why Gouldner's ideas about reflexivity can be seen to stand at the 'knowledge outcomes' end, rather than the autobiographical being situated at the 'research processes' end, of this continuum. However, this can only be understood by recognising that none of the elements in the continuum are unitary – 'using accounts', 'inscribing a research "voice"', and so on, each clearly admit of a range of practices. For instance, Gouldner's approach associates epistemological claims-making by sociologists with political commitment 'out there', and this is significantly different, for example, from the way that Kenneth Stoddart (1974) is concerned with tying knowledge outcomes to the shifts and moves of reasoning and drawing conclusions from research data 'in here', although both are 'accounting for epistemological claims'. The difference seems to me to derive from Gouldner's wish to harness reflexivity to a critical theory approach concerned with power and structure, his retention of the idea of 'grounding', and his belief that some knowledge claims are more valid than others.

FIGURE 3.3 From research processes to knowledge outcomes

FROM MORE RESEARCH PROCESSES (DESCRIPTION)

Providing personal information

Describing the research process

Accounting for research-generated identity negotiations

Collecting and using accounts and narratives referentially

Collecting and using accounts and narratives ironically

Inscribing a researcher 'voice' in research texts

Analysing rhetorical and textual aspects of the research writing

Analysing epistemological issues in 'their' knowledge claims-making

Accounting for 'our' epistemological claims

TO MORE KNOWLEDGE OUTCOMES (ANALYSIS)

At this point I want to return to the question of whether reflexivity necessarily walks hand in hand with constructionism and relativism, or whether reflexivity can be conceived in a way that recognises the circularity of competing accounts and interpretations, whilst also providing a foundational grounding for a sociology concerned with 'out there' as well as 'in here'. That is, can the binary of relativism/realism be refused, and if so, how? Clearly Gouldner thought that it could, and that his work did it. However, the 'it' is not explained. Not only is the detail lacking here, but programmatic statement as well.

'Not realism' does not necessarily mean 'radical relativism'. In discussing these issues, Sue Wise and I (Stanley and Wise, 1990, 1993) developed the idea of 'fractured foundationalism' as a means of recognising both that 'in life' sociologists and other people continually make knowledge claims of a foundational kind *and* that the foundations are rarely absolutely secure and differences or outright disagreements about 'reality matters' and the 'real facts' occur all the time. 'In life' when this happens, people are called on to account for their views and positions, and the facts on which they draw are subject to often stringent evaluation as to credibility, sufficiency and so forth. 'In life', the realist/relativist binary does not exist 'as fact', but rather as sets of ideas used in the business of interrogating and adjudicating knowledge claims. And so what are the links here with an analytical reflexivity of the kind outlined earlier?

'Fractured foundationalism' not only refuses the realist/relativist binary,[24] and so the intellectual impasse, indeed stranglehold, that this binary classification has created. It also opens up to inquiry both social structures and the fissures and fractures of social action around them, and the sociological activities involved in making sense of these. For me these form the twin bases of an analytical reflexivity. Sociologists make knowledge claims all the time about the world 'out there', as well as about sociology 'in here'. Separating out claims *qua* sociologists and claims *qua* social members engaged in social action is not and cannot be so categorically distinct as Martyn Hammersley (1999) suggests. In addition, some sociologists have explicit partisan allegiances to particular ideas, theories or political positions: some have an ethical commitment in Gouldner's sense, while the terms of engagement of others are not so readily apparent – although this does not mean that values or commitments are absent, rather that they go by different names. However, as sociologists we all engage in a process of inquiry in which we think thoughts about 'data' of different kinds (about 'out there', or 'in here', or mixtures of both), draw inferences from this, use these within arguments, reach conclusions, and make claims from this. The centre of analytic reflexivity as I understand it (and this accords with Gouldner's ideas about reflexivity) lies in making the conclusions we reach both apparent and 'accountable', in the sense of enabling other people to engage with our reasoning procedures and the 'data' on which these are based, so as to fully engage with and evaluate the conclusions reached. This approach to reflexivity sees research processes and knowledge outcomes as existing on a continuum which contains strategies that can be conjoined to produce accountable knowledge within a moral epistemology, rather than these being mutually exclusive choices. And analytical reflexivity neither reduces to 'benign introspection' as a sufficient topic for sociology, nor does it 'assume away power' as a turn inwards; rather, it expands to what might be termed an 'accountable extrospection', in which both the realism/relativism and the topic/resource binaries are sidestepped.

What might a functioning version of this look like 'on the ground'? There isn't the space to discuss this here, and anyway I don't want to fall into the 'produce reflexivity from the sociological hat' trap any more than Gouldner did. In addition, I think that piecemeal attempts to work out the articulation of an analytical reflexivity in specific pieces of work by particular sociologists are *preferable*, as well as being what is possible at this point in sociological time. Rather than closing down the possibilities by premature closure through 'cookbook' kinds of proscriptive and prescriptive outlines of a 'this is it' kind, it is important that the options remain open and that a range of different approaches to putting an analytical reflexivity into practice be engaged in.

A concluding thought about having 'an interesting mind'

In a review of *For Sociology*, Kurt Wolf (1974: 796) suggested that 'the book is a persuasive example of the reflexive sociology the author has insisted is called for by the contemporary situation of sociology'. And in what was not an obituary, but could well have been, he followed this with: 'The most vivid impression ... is that of the voyage of a lively, immensely interested and intensely interesting mind'. I can think of no better and no higher commendation of a sociologist than this – may we all deserve to have as much written about us. My interest here concerns whether Wolf's idea of Gouldner having an 'immensely interested and intensely interesting mind' can be used to think about the 'mind' of sociology as a discipline, rather than just the particular minds of specific sociologists.

As I noted at the beginning of this chapter, it was these kinds of characteristics which attracted me into sociology (Stanley, 1997). It was that whiff of transgression that came from daring to think against the grain and that hovered around not only the particular names of Mills and Gouldner, but also around the discipline itself, no matter how ascendant were other more respectable names, like Parsons. However, contemplating now rather than then, the present 'names' seem sadly tamed creatures of the corporate education machines. And transgression belongs primarily to, on the one hand, a postmodernist/deconstructionist nexus claiming centrality and intellectual dominance even while – perhaps especially while – proclaiming the end of grand narratives; and, on the other, an academic feminism also determined to capture what is left of the commanding heights. Janet Gouldner (1996: 165) has suggested that Alvin Gouldner would be saddened by the turn that recent theoretical debate has taken, not because of challenges to its objectivity, its representational claims, or its institutionalisation, for of course these were things his work contributed to, but rather because 'He wanted intellectuals to be brave, profoundly passionate, daring to reach for the big picture, and bold enough to be wrong'. Another way of expressing this is to suggest that, very much *contra* Irving Horowitz's sad song, the peripheries are determinedly claiming large swathes of the purple mantle of the erstwhile core and have themselves become respectable, and this is to the long-term detriment of the discipline. Sociology continues to need practitioners who, like Alvin Gouldner, are brave, profoundly passionate and bold enough to take a chance on being wrong.

Notes

1. This chapter was completed while I held the Hugh Le May Fellowship at Rhodes University, Grahamstown, South Africa, during 2000. I am extremely grateful to Rhodes University for awarding me the Fellowship, and also to the Sociology Department for hosting me. The chapter was given originally as 'a talk' rather than a formal read paper, and the written version tries to preserve something of the feel of this.

2. Martyn Hammersley's (1999) interesting invocation of *For Sociology* rejects Gouldner's arguments to make a wider argumentative point. I am in some sympathy with, although I do not agree with a number of the assumptions of, his overall argument. However my purpose here is the different one of reading Gouldner generously to use some of his ideas in order to think about aspects of the discipline now.

3. See also his (1979) *The Future of Intellectuals and the Rise of the New Class*.

4. Phrases used in an article published in the *Times Higher Educational Supplement* (Uttley, 1999) about the 1999 BSA Annual Conference. In what purported to be a preview of conference themes, journalist Alison Uttley instead held its purpose up to ridicule in comments such as 'Rather than focus on real-life issues, sociology is being side-tracked by philosophical navel-gazing', doing so in 'typically convoluted' written papers. 'Navel-gazing' was one of the standard criticisms of Gouldner's work, and his response was that 'Behind the snickers ... there is a more general suspicion of intellectuals and thinkers and of ideas and theory' (1973: 123).

5. In fact the extensiveness of his influence on English-speaking sociologists of a particular cohort seems reason enough for 'revisiting' Gouldner's work. This influence has been disguised by the growing preoccupation in sociology with the ritual referencing of the currently fashionable.

6. Gouldner extensively 'answered' the critics he had time for in one of the essays in *For Sociology*, while in another he vented his ire about a number of the contributions to an issue of the *American Journal of Sociology* (which was also published as a book), in particular those of Lipset and Ladd (1972) and John Rhoads (1972). Rereading these now, it is difficult not to think that his reactions became incapacitating, a kind of King Charles' head to Gouldner as Mr Dick. Appreciative reviews of *For Sociology* came from Kurt Wolf (1974) and John Rex (1974), among others.

7. Referencing every point which draws on *For Sociology* would unnecessarily burden the text; reading or rereading it will show the main ways in which I am indebted to it.

8. See here Raymond Boudon's (1980) formulation of the idea of 'crisis'. There are reviews of various national sociologies in *Contemporary Sociology* (1997), Vol. 26, No. 3. For more 'crisis' responses, see the special section on 'Saving Sociology' in *Sociological Inquiry* (1999). For some individual statements, see also Becker and Rau (1992), Berger (1992) and Horowitz (1993).

9. His list of these definitely does not include Marx (1993: 10).

10. Horowitz has even less time for British sociology, which he dismisses in one 'by the way' paragraph (1993: 141) as existing in a theoretical vacuum, having no general theorist among its members since Herbert Spencer, lacking theoretical design and characterised by an increasing tendency to positivism. 'Getting things right' is not high on his list of commendable sociological skills.

11. In Webster *et al*. (2000), the explanation proffered a review of 'the crisis' in sociology in South Africa since the 1994 free elections, suggesting that the growth of specialisations is causally connected with the growth of 'programmising' of sociology, a cafeteria approach to modularised degrees which abandons notions of 'a discipline'.

12 The BSA is a 'reforming' organisation in UK sociology that has, over a 50-year period, moved from the periphery to a more central position, suggesting the validity of Gouldner's view that change can occur in the discipline through deliberately constituting new sociological communities, in the way he envisaged *Theory and Society* contributing to change.

13 Oddly, although Nietzsche is mentioned, his discussion of 'Apollonian' and 'Dionysian' forces is not referenced by Gouldner.

14 A peer-reviewed electronic sociology journal now in its fifth year of publication and achieving 67,000 downloads (and increasing) per issue worldwide.

15 The initial idea came from Stuart Peters, at that time the Publishing Assistant and IT Officer to the journal, and now the Technical Officer of EPRESS (the Electronic Publishing Resource Service), a project which aims to provide tools, knowledge and information to help people publish electronic journals (http://www.epress.ac.uk/).

16 These can be accessed on the *Sociological Research Online* website, at http://www.socresonline.org.uk/.

17 See here, for instance, the specific lineage accorded it by Ashmore (1989) and also in Woolgar and Ashmore (1988).

18 Especially in Bourdieu (1988, 1990), Bourdieu and Wacquant (1992).

19 Some accounts offer an even more confined lineage. Frederick Steier (1991: 1), for example, describes it as only 'recently' surfacing, though this is perhaps intended as a comment on reflexivity in psychology rather than more generally.

20 As Wes Sharrock's (1989: 469) review noted, the collection is 'still framed by the realism/relativism opposition which ... it treats as a given ... There is no need to do so'. This is a comment I shall return to. The subtitle of an article by Cant and Sharma (1998) – 'Watching you watching me watching you (and writing about both of us)' – indicates that for some relativism is assumed to be that known as 'infinite regress' or 'radical relativism'; and there is no need for this either.

21 Steve Fuller's (1991: 184-5) comments that proponents of this position want to be cryptoscientific about their own discipline but not about others, are in some respects similar to Latour's (1988) strictures.

22 To use the ethnomethodological distinction between 'topic' and 'resource' here: the views of reflexivity I've just sketched out keep this firmly within the realm of treating accounts, including sociological ones, as 'topics in their own right' for sociological investigation. However, as I discussed earlier, Gouldner wanted to harness reflexivity to generate accounts seen as 'resources pointing to something outside of the accounts themselves', which could be used for understanding and helping to change the world.

23 In an exchange around this discussion, Slack (2000) and May (2000) both accept the need for reflexivity to take sociologists 'out there'. However, while Slack raises central questions around the ironicising of 'everyday' accounts that May's approach assumes, May's response in my view dodges this, focusing on issues concerning ethnomethodology instead.

24 And related ones, such as methodological deductivism *versus* inductivism, holism *versus* individualism and materialism *versus* idealism.

References

Anderson, R., Hughes, J. and Sharrock, W. (1985) *The Sociology Game*. London: Longman

Ashmore, M. (1989) *The Reflexive Thesis: Wrighting Sociology of Scientific Knowledge*. Chicago: University of Chicago Press

Atkinson, P. (1999) 'Review essay: voiced and unvoiced', *Sociology*, 33, pp. 191–7

Becker, H. and Rau, C. (1992) 'Sociology in the 1990s', *Social Science and Modern Society*, 30, pp. 70–75

Berger, P. (1992) 'Sociology: a disinvitation?', *Social Science and Modern Society*, 30, pp. 12–19

Bordo, S. (1996) 'The feminist as other', *Metaphilosophy*, Vol. 27, Nos 1 & 2, pp. 10–27

Boudon, R. (1980) *The Crisis in Sociology: Problems of Sociological Epistemology*. London: Macmillan

Bourdieu, P. (1988) *Homo Academicus*. Cambridge: Polity Press

Bourdieu, P. (1990) *In Other Words: Essays Towards a Reflexive Sociology*. Cambridge: Polity Press

Bourdieu, P. and Wacquant, L. (1992) *An Invitation to a Reflexive Sociology*. Cambridge: Polity Press

Cant, S. and Sharma, U. (1998) 'Reflexivity, ethnography and the professions (complementary medicine): watching you watching me watching you (and writing about both of us)', *Sociological Review*, 46, pp. 244–63

Contemporary Sociology, (1997), Vol. 26, No. 3

Finn, G. (1993) 'Why are there no great women postmodernists?', in V. Blundell, J. Shephard and I.Taylor (eds) *Relocating Cultural Studies: Developments in Theory and Research*. London: Routledge, pp. 123–154

Fuller, S. (1991) *Social Epistemology*, 2nd edn. Bloomington: Indiana University Press

Gouldner, A. (1970) *The Coming Crisis of Western Sociology*. New York: Basic Books

Gouldner, A. (1973) *For Sociology: Renewal and Critique in Sociology Today*. Harmondsworth: Penguin

Gouldner, A. (1974) 'Editorial Introduction', *Theory and Society*, Vol. 1, No. 1, p. 1

Gouldner, A. (1979) *The Future of Intellectuals and the Rise of the New Class*. London: Macmillan

Gouldner, J. (1996) 'Opening remarks: Alvin Gouldner's *Theory and Society*', *Theory and Society*, Vol. 25, No. 2, pp. 161–6

Hammersley, M. (1999) 'Sociology, what's it for? A critique of Gouldner', *Sociological Research Online*, Vol. 4, No. 3, http://www.socresonline.org.uk/socresonline/4/3/hammersley.html

Horowitz, I. (1993) *The Decomposition of Sociology*. Oxford: Oxford University Press

Lash, S. (1994) 'Reflexivity and its doubles: structure, aesthetics, community', in U. Beck, A. Giddens and S. Lash *Reflexive Modernization*. Cambridge: Polity Press, pp. 110–73

Latour, B. (1988) 'The politics of explanation: an alternative', in S. Woolgar (ed.) *Knowledge and Reflexivity: New Frontiers in the Sociology of Knowledge*. Newbury Park, California: Sage, pp. 155–76

Lipset, S.M. and Ladd, E. (1972) 'The politics of American sociologists', *American Journal of Sociology*, 78, pp. 67–104

May, T. (1999) 'Reflexivity and sociological practice', *Sociological Research Online*, 5, 1, http://www.socresonline.org.uk/socresonline/4/3/may.html

May, T. (2000) 'Reflexivity in social life and sociological practice: a rejoinder to Roger Slack', *Sociological Research Online*, 5, 1, http://www.socresonline.org.uk/socresonline/5/1/may.html

Mills, C.W. (1959) *The Sociological Imagination*. London: Oxford University Press

Oakley, A. (1998a) 'Gender, methodology and people's ways of knowing: some problems with feminism and the paradigm debate in social science', *Sociology*, 32, pp. 707–31

Oakley, A. (1998b) 'Science, gender, and Women's Liberation: an argument against postmodernism', *Women's Studies International Forum*, 21, pp. 133–146

Oakley, A. (2000) *Experiments in Knowing: Gender and Method in the Social Sciences.* Cambridge: Polity Press

Rex, J. (1974) 'The Challenge of Alvin Gouldner', *Sociology*, 8, pp. 497–504

Rhoads, J. (1972) 'On Gouldner's crisis of western sociology', *American Journal of Sociology*, 78, pp. 136–54

Schneider, D. (1984) *A Critique of the Study of Kinship.* Ann Arbor: University of Michigan Press

Sharrock, W. (1989) 'Review of Steve Woolgar (ed.) *Knowledge and Reflexivity*', *Sociology*, 23, pp. 468–9

Slack, R. (2000) 'Reflexivity and sociological practice: a reply to May', *Sociological Research Online*, 5, 1, http://www.socresonline.org.uk/socresonline/5/1/slack.html

Smith, D. (1974) 'Theorising as ideology', in R. Turner (ed.) *Ethnomethodology.* London: Penguin, pp. 39–54

Sociological Inquiry (1999) 'Saving sociology', special section, Vol. 69, No. 1

Sprague, J. (1997) 'Holy men and big guns: the can(n)on in social theory', *Gender & Society*, 11, pp. 88–107

Stanley, L. (1990) 'Feminist praxis and the academic mode of production', in L. Stanley (ed.) *Feminist Praxis.* London: Routledge, pp. 3–19.

Stanley, L. (1997) 'Writing the borders: episodic and theoretic thoughts on being in and out', in L. Stanley (ed.) *Knowing Feminisms.* London: Sage, pp. 172–83

Stanley, L. and Wise, S. (1990) 'Method, methodology and epistemology in feminist research processes', in L. Stanley (ed.) *Feminist Praxis: Research, Theory and Epistemology in Feminist Sociology.* London: Routledge, pp. 20–60

Stanley, L. and Wise, S. (1993) *Breaking Out Again.* London: Routledge

Stanley, L. and Wise, S. (2000) 'But the empress has no clothes! Some awkward questions about the "missing revolution" in feminist theory', *Feminist Theory*, Vol. 1, No. 3, pp. 26–88

Steier, F. (1991) 'Introduction: research as self-reflexivity, self-reflexivity as social process', in F. Steier (ed.) *Research and Reflexivity.* London: Sage, pp. 1–11

Stoddart, K. (1974) 'Pinched: notes on the ethnographer's use of argot', in R. Turner (ed.) *Ethnomethodology.* London: Penguin, pp. 173–9

Uttley, A. (1999) 'Is sociology lost or is it just misunderstood', *Times Higher Educational Supplement.* 2 April, pp. 18–19

Webster, E., Ally, S., Crothers, C., Hendricks, F. and Jordan, N. (2000) *Sociology: The State of the Discipline.* Pretoria, South Africa: National Research Foundation

Wolf, K. (1974) 'Review of Alvin Gouldner's *For Sociology*' *Social Science Quarterly*, 55, pp. 796–7

Woolgar, S. (ed.) (1998a) *Knowledge and Reflexivity: New Frontiers in the Sociology of Knowledge.* Newbury Park, California: Sage

Woolgar, S. (1988b) 'Reflexivity is the ethnography of the text', in S. Woolgar (ed.) *Knowledge and Reflexivity: New Frontiers in the Sociology of Knowledge.* Newbury Park, California: Sage, pp. 14–34

Woolgar, S. and Ashmore, M. (1988) 'The next step: an introduction to the reflexive project', in S. Woolgar (ed.) *Knowledge and Reflexivity : New Frontiers in the Sociology of Knowledge.* Newbury Park, California: Sage, pp. 1–11

Chapter 4
For postdisciplinary studies: sociology and the curse of disciplinary parochialism and imperialism
Andrew Sayer

It was always a safe bet that the occasion of the new millennium would be used by academic disciplines as an opportunity to ask how they could redefine and reaffirm their core aims, to decide how they could regain a sense of a common purpose, and to develop a higher and more respected profile in public life. Having seen such questions raised in several disciplines – and sometimes even set as essay titles for poor students – I have to say such exercises fill me with gloom and despondency. I believe we should celebrate rather than mourn the decline of disciplines. We should encourage the development of not merely interdisciplinary but *post*disciplinary studies.

The identification which so many academics have with their disciplines is actually counterproductive in relation to making progress in understanding society. In the first place, disciplines are parochial: members tend to be incapable of seeing beyond the questions posed by their own discipline, which provide an all-purpose filter for everything. Where the identity and boundaries of a discipline are strongly asserted and policed, the effect can be to stifle scholarship and innovation. One of the worst manifestations of this is the production of lists of 'recognised' journals, as in economics, which are considered to be acceptable places in which to publish by the Research Assessment Exercise in its grading of British or UK (Scotland and Northern Ireland are included in this assessment) university departments. It is bad enough that economics – the home of believers in free, unregulated competition – should allow this exclusionary monopoly practice. It would be disastrous if this practice were to spread to other social sciences.

Secondly, disciplines are also often imperialist: they attempt to claim territories occupied by others as their own. A well known example is that of public choice theory in economics, which claims to be able to explain things like politics and marriage, as well as the functioning of economies. Disciplinary imperialism is closely related to disciplinary parochialism because both inhibit thinking outside the framework of a single discipline. Both are evident in the tendency for accounts of the world to be assessed not merely in terms of their explanatory adequacy, but in terms of the extent to which they further the aims of the discipline, and use its favoured tropes.

These imperialist and parochial tendencies are easy to see in others, but it is harder for disciplinarians to see them in their own behaviour. Faced with any attractive theoretical innovation, we should always ask whether it is attractive because it is a good explanation of the phenomenon concerned or because it seems to enlarge the claims of the discipline. Public choice theory in economics is again an outstanding example. When economists say they can explain the structure and dynamics of families or suicide by reference to a rational choice methodology, does this appeal to them because it's a better explanation than rival ones, or because it reinforces their discipline's imperialism, its imagined omnipotence? Apparently, non-economists don't realise such things are explicable in terms of rational choice; the economists do, and they understand this best. Similarly, when sociologists say science has to be understood as a social construction, does this appeal because it is a better explanation of science, or because it advances sociological imperialism? (The latter answer should naturally be the preferred one for those sociologists of science who believe epistemological authority is merely social authority in disguise.)

Each discipline likes to flatter itself that it is more fundamental than all the others. Thus, we have sociology as a 'second-order' discipline which produces 'social theory', concerned not with first-order substantive empirical questions such as 'How are families in Britain changing?', but with more abstract issues, like those of social ontology – for example, the structure–agency relationship, or time and action – where social theory merges into the philosophy of social science. These are perfectly good things to study, but part of their attraction is surely that they give the impression that sociology is so much broader than any of the other disciplines, and capable of studying anything.

Disciplines can greatly extend their territorial claims by shifting from grounding themselves in a topic or object of study to identifying themselves in terms of ways of seeing: economics is not just the study of economies, it's a way of understanding every aspect of society, through the lens of rational choice;[1] geography is an all-encompassing subject which shows how everything comes together in space, so that nothing eludes its synthesising gaze.

Note, however, that despite these criticisms, I do accept that disciplines ask important questions. But these are abstract – that is, one-sided – questions, about, say, the problem of social order, or the relationship between society and environment. They are certainly worthwhile issues, but to answer them we need concrete answers that go beyond the bounds of single disciplines. To take a longstanding, prime concern of sociology – the problem of order – as an example: dealing with concrete instances of how and why societies are ordered is likely to require us to consider psychological matters, the workings of markets, and the spatial organisation of society. Consequently we have to go beyond sociology in order to answer one of its most fundamental questions. Likewise, in human geography, in order to understand the spatial organisation of economies, researchers need to go back into economic and political matters to understand what produces that spatial organisation. Similarly, in economics, in order to understand concrete instances of economic processes, such as those of East Asian capitalism, we need to understand the ways in which economic practices are socially embedded and politically regulated. Of course, economics is notorious for either ignoring the concrete in order to protect its closed system models from counter-evidence, or treating the concrete as reducible to the relationships identified in the abstract models (Lawson, 1997; Sayer, 1992).

Moving from abstract questions, many of which historically have been the special concern of particular disciplines, to studies of concrete societies, typically requires us, therefore, to ignore disciplinary boundaries, and follow the ideas and processes wherever they lead. However, progress in this direction is usually limited by disciplinary priorities.

Consider three examples of disciplinary parochialism and imperialism, the first substantive, the second and third methodological or metatheoretical.

In sociology, the grand narrative of Fordism and post-Fordism functions as a way in which the discipline can – as Terry Eagleton (1995) pointed out – deal with economic matters without having to know any more about economics than is needed to read the business pages of a newspaper. It allows a sociologically imperialist claim to economic knowledge that is impervious to external critique. It functions as a grand narrative into which many sociologists seem to feel obliged to fit their empirical analyses of anything economic. Extraordinarily, it has become an account of contemporary economies which rarely makes any mention of costs and cash. The fortunes of firms come to depend not on the bottom line but on their conformity to the post-Fordist model, their development of new work cultures, the extent to which they embrace networks, etc. Some of these things might indeed influence their success, but the dynamics of costs which economists prioritise cannot be reduced to these, and can work in quite different directions. Sociologists rightly insist that economic relations are socially or culturally embedded, but that doesn't say everything about them – indeed much eludes such a perspective. Significantly, economists and other students of businesses tend to be a good deal less impressed by the narrative of Fordism and post-Fordism than are sociologists. Equally, while there may be something in the claim that post-Fordism is as much a cultural as an economic concept, it would be naive not to note that this sort of claim is also typical of power struggles over intellectual territories and the right to speak about them.

The second example is more methodological, relating to strong versions of social constructionism and the psychology/sociology relation. Ian Craib has been a longstanding critic of sociological imperialism, in the form of its denial of the internal world and the 'I' which psychology and psychoanalysis attempt to understand (Craib, 1989; see also Gorz, 1989). Our ability to receive something from outside and make it our own, that is, to *make* something out of the materials and influences through which we are constructed, to create something different, has always caused problems for sociology, given its prioritising of social relations (Craib, 1997): 'To be a sociologist is often to engage in, implicitly or explicitly, a more or less immense, more or less manic denial of the internal world, and attempt to avoid an inner reality' (Craib, 1989: 196).

Disciplinary boundaries tend to get positioned in a way which allows each discipline to externalise difficult problems – indeed they often deny that there is anything *they* need to know about on the other side of the boundary. So economists treat the determination of consumer preferences and demand as either a given or something which is a matter for psychology and sociology. That preferences might also be influenced by economic processes themselves is particularly threatening for neoclassical economics because it undermines its extravagant claim that markets allow the consumer to be sovereign. For more technical reasons, challenging the exogenous status of preferences would also undermine much of the massive theoretical edifice of neoclassical economics (Penz, 1986). In similar fashion, many sociologists avoid the relation to psychology by various means which deny the 'I' and treat the agent as *tabula rasa* awaiting social construction.

Strong versions of social constructionism imply sociological omnipotence or triumphalism: not only is everything, including what others imagine to be at least co-authored by themselves, actually a social construction, but sociologists can see this so much more clearly than anyone else. However, though sociologists may kill off 'the subject', and by implication, authors, they of course have to exempt themselves from the death sentence; presumably their own work is not wholly reducible to an externally produced social construction. Such absurdities are likely to arise wherever compatibility with disciplinary ambitions and priorities becomes a conscious or subconscious criterion for the acceptance of proposed explanations.

Thirdly, disciplinary parochialism/imperialism in sociology often takes the form of sociological reductionism. By this I mean the tendency to treat ideas and practices as if the only thing we needed to know about them was their social coordinates – 'middle class', 'feminine', 'high culture', etc. – as if these determined their content and obviated the need to assess that content. To use an example given by Bourdieu (1993), those who dismiss feminism as 'middle class' are guilty of sociological reductionism. We quite rightly regard it as insulting to treat feminists as merely responding to their class position rather than their having ideas which need to be considered in their own right. It's like dismissing someone's argument by saying 'You would say that wouldn't you?'. However, as we shall see, Bourdieu appears as both an *op*ponent and an *ex*ponent of sociological reductionism (Sayer, 1999).

Reasoning, or reflection, can enable us to think beyond the dispositions we have acquired through having a particular location in the social field. It is even possible to arrive at ways of thinking and acting which are at odds with those dispositions, as did Marx despite his middle-class background, though of course reasoning might lead us to affirm our dispositions. As Bourdieu argues, unless we rigorously question our own dispositions and position within the social field, we are unlikely to break their influence (Bourdieu, 1993).

Consider as an example the question of why sociologists identify so strongly with their institution – their discipline. As Bourdieu argues, when we commit ourselves to a certain game or form of life, we both make an investment from which we hope to draw profit (not necessarily monetary), and commit ourselves to its norms and rules. The institution offers certain rewards and stakes, and its members consider these to be worth playing for. (Of course, the fact that we occasionally distance ourselves from the institution by making ironic comments about it doesn't at all indicate that we are independent of it.) The success of the institution and the success of its members' life projects and careers become interdependent.

Looking at someone else's institution, it is hard not to regard their commitment to it, their belief in the game and their conformity to its rules, as rather extraordinary, as if they were living an illusion. And so we might feel tempted to ask to accountants, estate agents or chemists at one of *their* own conferences, how they can invest so much of themselves in something so prosaic, how they can identify with such petty norms, treating them as worthy standards for life – behaving indeed, as if conforming to them were the primary goal in life. All this applies to academics' attachment to their disciplines too. Bourdieu (1998) uses the term 'illusio' to characterise this situation – less to draw attention to the illusions, than to their game-like character, (cf. Latin *ludus*-game).

However, Bourdieu's own commitment to sociology is not of course explained in this way. Sociologists are much happier talking in a reductionist way about others than about themselves. The example serves not only to remind us of the strangeness of disciplinary loyalties but is an illustration of sociologically reductionist accounts of them. Typically, sociologists rely too heavily on sociological explanations for the behaviour of others, and fail to apply such explanations when it comes to their own behaviour: if the working class eat out, they eat at Kentucky Fried Chicken or McDonald's because of their class or habitus, but *we* academics choose where to eat out according to the quality of the food and atmosphere.

In other words, in our first-person accounts we tend to explain what we do by means of *justifications* for our actions. *We* play sociology, or whatever our discipline may be, because it is worth playing. But *they* play whatever they play because of their social position. This radical difference between sociologists' accounts of others' behaviour and their own is one of the outstanding peculiarities of the discipline.

We could, of course, respond by admitting the social influences on our judgements, showing how they are what one would expect given our habitus (as Bourdieu does, with regard to his own tastes). However, a thoroughgoing sociological reductionism would take this admission as itself a function of our habitus, and any justifications we offered of our behaviour could be dismissed, bracketed out, or treated as a function of our social position. It would be like saying 'Don't bother to listen to my arguments, it's only my habitus talking.'

However, one way out of the dilemma is to admit that while habitus is certainly significant, those we study are – *like us* – capable of acting not merely on the basis of their social position but on the basis of their reasoning too, which can take them beyond those social influences. Discourses always extend beyond particular social locations and are open to interpretation from a range of positions, and reasoning involves processes of extension, generalisation, and critical reflection, all of which mean that the social influences of particular locations can be brought into question and overridden (Alexander, 1995). To deny this is to fall into something akin to behaviourism and a crude correspondence theory of the relationship of discourses to contexts. This is not to deny the power of habitus, but merely to note its limitations, and to acknowledge that it can be partially transcended.

To know how far sociological explanations can be taken, therefore, we have to decide how far things can *not* be explained sociologically. In one of his books on education – *The State Nobility*, (1996) – Bourdieu analyses the relationship between students' parents' occupations and the kinds of comments tutors give the students on their essays, and shows that positive comments vary directly with class. Only after well over one hundred pages does he acknowledge that the comments might be responding to differences in the quality of the essays, and that this might well vary with class too. I would suggest that his coyness about admitting that the marks might have something to do with whether the students got certain things right or not, derives from a reluctance to acknowledge the limits to sociological explanation. Again: to know how far sociologically reductionist explanations work, we have to assess how far they don't work. (Equally, to know how far actors' judgements are 'interested', in Bourdieu's use of the term, we need to know how far they are not interested.)

Of course, sociological reductionism might simply be defended in disciplinary terms – that it's only appropriate for sociologists to restrict themselves to analysing the social coordinates of judgements, tastes, opinions, actions, etc. Bourdieu himself defends such a position. For such a radical thinker he is surprisingly attached to his discipline, defending sociology by arguing that like any other discipline it should push its questions as far as possible so as to challenge others. In *Sociology in Question*, he even says that 'every science has to use its own means to account for the greatest number of things possible, including things that are apparently or really explained by other sciences' (Bourdieu, 1993: 25). As our discussion of sociological reductionism has shown, such imperialism invites misexplanation through misattribution of causality.

Earlier, I noted the way in which disciplinary imperialism often involves moves towards adopting higher levels of abstraction. As Bourdieu would no doubt point out, such moves, taking researchers away from the first-order realm of mundane empirical matters, can enhance their cultural capital: the second-order level is not only 'more theoretical', it is also posh. The academic 'field' is also a social field, and academics tend to gravitate to the parts of the academic field that correspond to their social class position (Bourdieu, 1998). At the same time, the field is one of struggle for cultural capital, and the imperialist ambitions of disciplines tend to point up-market. To be sure, these are just generalisations, to which there are plenty of exceptions. However, if academics want to be reflexive, and to avoid being class-blind – all the more necessary where class is '*non grata*' (Barrett, 1992) – they need to be aware of these social influences. Again, recognition of these influences does not license a sociological reductionism in which the intellectual, practical and political importance of particular studies, be they first order or second order, become a function of their social correlates. On the contrary, awareness of the class correlates of disciplinary shifts is important for enabling us to prevent them influencing our judgements of the intellectual value of particular moves in scholarship and research, wherever their exponents may be situated in the social field (Sayer, 1999).

Of course, interdisciplinary exchanges can have hidden agendas too and be driven at least partly by attempts by participants to raise their status. An outstanding example of this is cultural studies. This derived from the interchange over the last two decades between literary studies and social theory, through which both increased their cultural capital, the former through gaining the prestige of theory, the latter through gaining that of literary culture. Together, and surely partly as a consequence of this enhanced cultural capital, they had some success in deflating the standing of rival disciplines such as philosophy and more economistic social studies.

Why *post*disciplinary rather than *inter*disciplinary studies? Interdisciplinary studies are not enough. At worst they provide a space in which members of different disciplines can bring their points of view together in order to compete behind a thin disguise of cooperation, with the result that the researchers don't actually escape from their home disciplines. At best, interdisciplinary studies merely offer the prospect of an escape from disciplinary constraints.

Postdisciplinary studies emerge when scholars forget about disciplines and whether ideas can be identified with any particular one, when they follow ideas and connections wherever they lead instead of following them only as far as the border of their discipline, and when they identify with learning rather than with disciplines. Such studies do not invite dilettantism or eclecticism, in which we end up doing a lot of things badly. On the contrary, they differ from those things precisely because they require us to follow connections. We can still study a coherent group of phenomena; in fact, since we are not dividing up and selecting out elements appropriate to a particular discipline, this can be more coherent than conventional disciplinary studies.

It's commonly said that it is only possible to do interdisciplinary studies after first having got a good grounding in a particular discipline. This is a kind of holding position for conservatives, involving minimal compromise. It also reduces the chances that those who go on to attempt interdisciplinary studies will leave their discipline. Having formerly taught for 17 years at a university where undergraduates are introduced to interdisciplinary courses for half of their studies from the start,[2] I would challenge this conservative view. If people work long enough on a coherent group of topics or problems without regard for disciplinary boundaries, and a postdisciplinary literature builds up, then that can provide a basis for teaching. Urban and regional studies is a good example of this. A well-known example of postdisciplinary studies from 1987 – which relates partly to urban and regional studies – is David Harvey's book *The Condition of Postmodernity* .

However, there are also some well-known examples from 150, even 250 years ago, though of course these were *pre*disciplinary studies. Disciplines are, after all, a relatively recent phenomenon. Before the late nineteenth century, the founders of social science would roam freely across territory we now see carefully fenced off into politics, psychology, sociology, economics, philosophy, etc. Indeed, they would often do so within a single page – a good example being Adam Smith. Though now commonly claimed by economists as their founder, Smith was of course a professor of moral philosophy. He was greatly concerned with the problem of social order, and so might be claimed by sociologists as their founder too. Unlike many contemporary sociologists, however, he did not attempt to exclude connections to psychology, but tried to interrelate psychological dispositions and social relations – in both directions, avoiding both psychological and sociological reductionism. For Smith, economic relations, including market ones, were always embedded in social relations, and he saw the formation of consumer preferences as very much culturally influenced. In other words, unlike contemporary economists, he didn't attempt to ignore the determination of demand or leave it to others to study as if it were conveniently exogenous. At the same time, the concept of an invisible hand guiding market behaviour resists the reduction of the mechanisms determining the division of labour to a matter of the social embedding of economic relations, as a sociologically reductionist treatment would imply.

It is ironic that disciplines should try to claim particular founders of social science as part of their own canon, when the strength of so many of them owed much to the fact that they were not inhibited by disciplinary self-censorship. While many of the old canon were predisciplinary, many who might form a new canon are postdisciplinary. To discipline a Marx or a Foucault is to diminish them. To attempt to select out 'Marx the sociologist' is to fail to understand his critique of political economy; worse, to reduce him to the status of a prototheorist of social stratification is to render him uninteresting. We should resist the temptation to see the work of predisciplinary theorists as teleologically leading to the development of particular disciplines. It follows from this that the advocacy of postdisciplinary studies should not be seen as conflicting with the idea of the canon, but as a way of responding more sympathetically to the concerns of its key figures by refusing to discipline them.

Although the idea of postdisciplinary studies is beginning to arouse interest, we would be foolish to underestimate the power of disciplines to limit thought and produce well disciplined members, able to subvert any external challenge, including this one. My own experience is that those who proclaim themselves to be 'postdisciplinary' will find that they will be cross-examined to find out what subject their first degree was in so that they can be safely categorised and disciplined, put in their place: 'So really, you're a historian/economist/philosopher/geographer ...'. Alternatively, they may meet strategies of cooption: I have heard it claimed, for example, that sociology has already become a postdisciplinary subject! Such claims just give a new twist to old-fashioned disciplinary imperialism, and allow the disciples to congratulate themselves on their superiority, leaving their complacency undisturbed. Ironically, at a time when some sociologists are writing about the 'dedifferentiation' of contemporary society, many are trying to prevent this happening to academic disciplines. So, let me make it quite clear: I am proposing that disciplinary imperialism and parochialism are damaging social science, that disciplines represent an evolutionary cul-de-sac in its development, and that we should undiscipline ourselves, not as an excuse for dilettantism, but as a way of achieving a more coherent understanding of the social world.

Notes

1 'There is only one social science. What gives economics its imperialist invasive power is that our analytical categories – scarcity, cost, preferences, opportunities, etc. – are truly universal in applicability' (Hirschleifer, 1985: 66, cited in O'Neill, 1998).

2 University of Sussex, UK.

References

Alexander, J.C. (1995) *Fin de Siècle Social Theory*. London: Verso

Barrett, M. (1992) 'Words and things: materialism and method in contemporary feminist analysis', in M. Barrett and A. Phillips (eds) *Destabilising Theory*. Cambridge: Polity Press

Bourdieu, P. (1993) *Sociology in Question*. London: Sage

Bourdieu, P. (1996) *The State Nobility*. Cambridge: Polity Press

Bourdieu, P. (1998) *Practical Reason*. Cambridge: Polity Press

Craib, I. (1989) *Psychoanalysis and Social Theory.* Hemel Hempstead: Harvester

Craib, I. (1997) 'Social constructionism as social psychosis', *Sociology*, 31, pp. 1–15

Eagleton, T. (1995) Review of Derrida: 'Spectres of Marx', *Radical Philosophy*, 73, pp. 35–7

Gorz, A. (1989) *Critique of Economic Reason.* London: Verso

Harvey, D. (1987) *The Condition of Postmodernity.* Oxford: Blackwell

Lawson, T. (1997) *Economics and Reality.* London: Routledge

O'Neill, J. (1998) 'Self-love, self-interest and the rational economic agent', *Analyse & Kritik.* 20, pp. 184–204

Penz, C. (1986) *Consumer Sovereignty.* Cambridge: Cambridge University Press

Sayer, A. (1992) *Method in Social Science.* London: Routledge

Sayer, A. (1999) 'Bourdieu, Smith and disinterested judgement', *The Sociological Review*, Vol. 47, No. 3, pp. 403–31

Chapter 5
For a sociological feminism
Stevi Jackson

The interrelationship between feminism and sociology has usually been discussed in terms of the impact of the former on the latter, with a number of writers arguing for a feminist transformation of sociology and assessing the extent to which it has occurred (Stacey and Thorne, 1985; Maynard, 1990; Abbott, 1991; Allen and Leonard, 1996; Laslett and Thorne, 1997). Here I consider the interrelationship from the other end, focusing on the influence of sociology on feminist thought. I wish to draw attention to the contributions sociology has made to feminist theory and to argue that it still has a great deal to offer, specifically as a corrective to the overemphasis on the cultural and symbolic deriving from the so-called 'cultural turn'. While endorsing others' arguments for a feminist sociology, my aim is to state the case for a sociological feminism.

It might seem strange to make this argument in a book deriving from a BSA conference and addressed primarily to a sociological readership. Surely, sociologists do not need to be convinced of the relevance of their own discipline? Yet it is becoming increasingly common for sociologists to genuflect towards theory from other disciplines while forgetting the insights that have been yielded by sociology. I have lost track of the number of times I have heard it confidently asserted, during recent BSA conferences, that social constructionism began with poststructuralism or postmodernism. That so basic a sociological idea can be attributed to theories originating in other disciplines, by sociologists, should give us pause for thought. The effect is to obliterate sociology's past contributions from the collective scholarly memory and therefore from the genealogies of ideas passed on to new generations of students. This is happening in a number of sociological fields and is particularly evident in my own specialism, sexuality. Here others have commented on the common misapprehension that social constructionism originated with Foucault (Rubin, 1994: 82), or lamented the eclipsing of specifically sociological perspectives on sexuality (Epstein, 1996; Seidman, 1997; Stein and Plummer, 1996).

For the record, I would suggest that the idea of social constructionism, even if it was not named as such, can be dated back to the first half of the twentieth century to, for example, G.H. Mead's idea of the social self and C. Wright Mills' arguments for a sociology of motives (Mead, 1934; Mills, 1940). The term became widely used in the 1960s with the publication of Berger and Luckman's *The Social Construction of Reality* (1967). My undergraduate and postgraduate education as a sociologist spanned the years 1969–75, during which time I learnt that what appeared to be self-evident 'things' to be investigated, such as knowledge or deviance, were social constructions. It was around this time, too, that sociologists began to argue for the social construction of sexuality (McIntosh, 1968; Gagnon, 1965; Simon and Gagnon, 1969), and appropriated the concept of gender to argue that masculinity and femininity were not reducible to biological sex differences (Oakley, 1972). That this entailed only a partial social constructionism, leaving 'sex' outside the social, was later noted and challenged by other feminist sociologists such as Liz Stanley (1984) and Christine Delphy (1981, 1984), thus presenting arguments for a radically anti-essentialist understanding of gender which predate the more widely celebrated deconstructive efforts of Denise Riley (1988) and Judith Butler (1990).

This paper is motivated by a desire both to explain and to challenge the collective amnesia which has erased such sociological insights from the record. The account I offer is a very personal one, deriving from my own intellectual history and my hybrid location between women's studies and sociology. It is also polemical, inspired by a militant advocacy of sociology. Had I been asked a few years ago whether I thought of myself primarily as a sociologist or an interdisciplinary feminist scholar, I would have unhesitatingly placed myself on the side of feminism and interdisciplinary Women's Studies. I am still committed to interdisciplinarity in Women's Studies and my feminist convictions remain unshakable, but I have become increasingly concerned about the eclipsing of sociological perspectives within the interdisciplinary mix of feminist theory. Here the pressures to keep up with the latest theoretical trends can easily lead us to overlook sociological ideas. While sociology is still central to the teaching of Women's Studies, it often does not count when it comes to theory – except in overviews of the past, where sociologically derived theories are commonly dismissed as erroneous perspectives which we have now transcended, inevitably tainted by universalism, foundationalism, essentialism, racism and heterosexism.

If we do not remedy this state of affairs, we risk continually re-inventing the wheel and depriving feminism of vital critical, analytical tools. The time has come to recover some of the core insights of sociology and to reassert its relevance for feminism. This entails reversing some of the effects of 'the cultural turn' which dislodged sociology from the prominent position it occupied in the 1970s. It has been argued that, during the 1980s, feminism's focus shifted from 'things' – material social inequalities – to 'words', with the emphasis on language, representations and subjectivity (Barrett, 1992). Subsequently sociology lost ground to literature, cultural studies and philosophy, and materialist analyses gave way to postmodern theorising. One element of my sociological counterattack is to argue for continued attention to material social structures and relations. Another is to reassess the potential relevance for feminism of those microsociological perspectives which have emphasised everyday social practices. I also hope to make it clear that reviving sociological feminism does not mean ignoring issues of language, culture and representation and does not signal a lack of sensitivity to differences among women.

I will start by briefly mapping the origins and effects of the 'cultural turn', making it clear that not all feminists took the turn, and that amongst those that did, some are beginning to make the return journey. I will then discuss the scope of the social, and in so doing begin to redefine social constructionism. Here I will take sexuality as an example, drawing on my recent work on heterosexuality (Jackson, 1999) to explore the ways in which the contest between sociological and cultural analysis has been played out in recent feminist and queer theorising.

The cultural turn

During the 1970s and into the early 1980s social scientific, and particularly sociological, perspectives were at the forefront of feminist analysis. Most feminist theory addressed one basic question: how can we account for women's subordination? The answers were sought primarily through engagement with Marxism, not only by Marxist or socialist feminists, but also by those feminists who reworked Marxism to fit with more radically feminist priorities (for example Delphy, 1977, 1984; MacKinnon, 1982). The appeal of Marxism was that it offered a structural analysis of oppression and exploitation, enabling us to see women's subordination as social in origin, neither given by nature nor an accidental feature of relations between men and women. Yet existing Marxist theory did not address many of feminism's core concerns: sexuality and male violence were beyond its remit; subjectivity could only be conceptualised as consciousness; women's unpaid labour in the home proved, despite heroic efforts, impossible to integrate into a theory designed for the analysis of waged labour.

Understandably, if paradoxically, it was Marxist feminists who were the first to embrace the new perspectives associated with the 'cultural turn'. While this shift is associated with the 1980s, its origins can be discerned in the latter half of the 1970s, presaged by Marxist feminist interest in ideology, reproduction and the unconscious, in the work of Althusser, Lévi-Strauss and Lacan (Rubin, 1975; Mitchell, 1975; Coward and Ellis, 1977). Marxist feminists had been resistant to those radical appropriations of Marx which challenged the letter of his texts (see Barrett and McIntosh, 1979; Delphy, 1980), but were more open to ideas which might extend Marxism's reach without disturbing its dogmas. Althusser's (1971) view of ideology as relatively autonomous from economic relations created a space in which to theorise women's subordination without having to relate it to the capitalist mode of production. Lacan's (1977) psychoanalysis provided a way of linking ideology with subjectivity and a ready means of explaining the ways in which femininity and masculinity were reproduced within our psyches. Lévi-Strauss' (1969) view of kinship had some resonance with Marxist feminist theorisations of relations of reproduction and also related women's status as objects of exchange to the incest taboo (which so preoccupied Freud) and to the symbolic realm of culture: women functioned both as objects of exchange and as 'signs'.

Once Derrida and Foucault were added to this mixture, the emphasis shifted from linguistic and semiotic structures to deconstructive analytic strategies and a more fluid notion of discourse. Foucault's reconceptualisation of power as diffuse and dispersed and his rejection of the truth claims inherent in the concept of ideology meant that ideology could no longer be seen as a tool of the powerful miring the powerless in a false understanding of their situation (see Foucault, 1980). With ideology dealt with, the last link which had moored these new analyses to Marx's materialism was severed. The interest in French structuralism paved the way for poststructuralism which gradually evolved towards postmodernism, with its suspicion of the totalising claims of 'grand narratives' (Lyotard, 1984; Flax, 1990).

These perspectives challenged the idea that 'men' and 'women' were given, natural, essential categories. Where Marxism had not explained why it should be *women* who occupied particular niches in the capitalist order (as reproducers of labour power or a reserve army of labour, for example), now it became possible to explore how women were produced as a category (see Adams *et al.*, 1978). Yet within the logic of the cultural turn, the ways in which 'women' were brought into being could only be conceptualised in limited ways – as an effect of culture or the symbolic, and often at the level of the psyche. 'Women' and 'men' could not be thought of as products of a structural hierarchy. If hierarchy appeared at all it was as a phallogocentric cultural order which produced a 'distorted' feminine as the 'other' of the masculine, as opposed to some radical alterity, a truer 'femininity' which that cultural order could not permit to exist (Irigaray, 1985).

As Rita Felski notes, proponents of 'sexual difference' oppose it to a supposedly sociological conceptualisation of gender in which femininity and masculinity are 'externally imposed roles to be eventually discarded in a putative androgynous future' (Felski, 1997: 4). This characterisation may be an apt description of prefeminist approaches to 'sex-roles', but it is not applicable to feminist sociologists' accounts of gender. By the early 1980s feminist sociologists were already modifying and critiquing the concept of sex or gender 'roles' from two quite separate directions. Some argued that the idea of 'internalised' external roles denied the complexity and variability of gender as it is lived, and our active engagement in the social practices which sustain it (Stanley and Wise, 1983). Others suggested that, rather than being a role, gender was a social division in which women and men were located and defined by the hierarchical relation between them, so that neither could exist without the other (Delphy, 1981, 1984). In this latter view, doing away with hierarchy does not produce androgyny – and it certainly does not make women like men, since neither masculinity nor femininity can have any meaning outside the social relations which create them. These more sophisticated understandings of gender were bypassed by the cultural turn. In fact it is difference theory and, as we shall see, other more deconstructive approaches to gender which perpetuate the fallacy on which the idea of androgyny is based: that the only human possibility is some combination of femininity and masculinity (see Delphy, 1993).

In the 1980s, however, difference came to the fore in another sense, and from another challenge to the category 'women': that it concealed differences *among* women. Most feminist theory had been framed from a white Western perspective and, by the end of the 1970s, Black and Third World women were angrily denouncing those who had excluded them or unthinkingly subsumed them under the banner of 'sisterhood', without allowing them to speak for themselves (Carby, 1982: 233). It became clear that 'women' was not, and could not be, a unitary category (Brah, 1991). Moreover, attention was increasingly being drawn to the complexities of women's lives in a postcolonial era with its global economy, its history of colonial diasporas and its current labour migrations and displacements of refugees.

All of this was taken by some feminists as a further mandate for postmodern theorising, a means of avoiding the exclusions of an assumed universal womanhood and the simplifications of causal models of oppression (see, for example, Flax, 1990). There is no doubt that the ways in which gender intersects with other forms of inequality, especially those founded on racism and colonialism, had hitherto been undertheorised. It is more doubtful whether postmodernism solves this problem, or simply professes a concern with 'difference' while refusing to confront racism (Modleski, 1991). Moreover, postmodernism's claim to have a monopoly on theorising diversity and complexity is contestable (Walby, 1992). There is no reason why a social structural analysis, provided it is not crudely reductionist, should be unable to deal with the diverse locations occupied by women within local and global contexts. In fact, there are dangers in abandoning this form of analysis.

The most significant of the differences which postmodernists claim to respect are founded on real, material inequalities: they are consequences of institutionalised racism, the heritage of centuries of slavery, colonialism and imperialism and the continued international division of labour. The postcolonial world is, after all, characterised by extremely stark material inequalities. Even in the wealthy Western nations the material inequality suffered by women has not gone away, and the 'things' which oppressed us in the 1970s – inequitable divisions of domestic labour, low wages and male violence, for example – are still with us. Educated, white middle-class women may have experienced a widening of opportunities, but many women have fared less well (Walby, 1997). In neglecting the social context of power relations, and in viewing power as diffuse and dispersed, postmodernism fails to recognise that systematic oppressions of gender, class and race persist.

One curious effect of the cultural turn was that it left materialist analysis in the hands of those who had not identified as Marxist feminists – many of whom are sociologists. They have continued to produce research and empirically grounded theory around such issues as gender-segregated labour markets (Walby, 1986; Witz, 1992; Siltanen, 1994) and power and exploitation within families (Delphy and Leonard, 1992; VanEvery, 1995). In the 1990s these materialist analyses were not fashionable in theoretical circles. Yet just when materialist feminism was being declared obsolete, it began to undergo a revival or reinvention, especially in the USA (Hennessy, 1993; Landry and MacLean, 1993). Rosemary Hennessy, for example, argued that materialist feminism needs to retain a 'critique of social totalities like patriarchy and capitalism' (1993: xii). There was also a renewed interest in analyses of women's household production (Fraad et al., 1994; Gibson-Graham, 1996) and the application of the materialist method to sexuality (Hennessy, 1995, 2000; Ingraham, 1996). Some new analyses, while Marxist in orientation, are less concerned with macrolevel analysis of economic and social structures than with contextualised and localised processes and practices. In the work of J.K. Gibson-Graham (1996), for example, the deconstruction of Marxism's view of capitalism as a total economic system reveals what this representation conceals: the persistence of non-capitalist processes and practices, including the exploitation of women's labour within households. When Christine Delphy (1977) first developed the idea that men appropriated their wives' labour, it was damned as heretically anti-Marxist (Barrett and McIntosh, 1979); now the same idea has resurfaced as respectably post-Marxist.

The emphasis on understanding the local, situated contexts of women's lives has also enabled feminists to make connections between aspects of gendered social relations which were previously seen as discrete and separate, such as sexuality and work. Hence, for example, Lisa Adkins (1995) has drawn our attention to the sexualisation of women's labour in the service sector, and Gillian Dunne (1996) has explored the ways in which lesbians have a specific relation to the labour market which differs from that of heterosexual women. Such work is in keeping with Mary Maynard's (1995) suggestion that feminists should develop 'middle order' theories, which emphasise the specifics of given social contexts, institutions and relationships, offering grounded generalisations rather than totalising models of entire societies. Feminist sociology is well placed to analyse the localised, varied contexts of women's everyday existence and the meanings women give to their lives, without losing sight of structural patterns of dominance and subordination.

Restoring the 'social' to social constructionism

Structural analysis is not the only form of sociological thinking of utility to feminism. Once we focus on the everyday, localised contexts of women's lives it becomes clear that the material and the social cannot be understood only in terms of social structure. We need to account for agency as well as structure; for patterns of interaction in everyday life as well as the institutional hierarchies within which they take place; the microlevels at which power is manifested/deployed, as well as the macrolevel of systematic domination; the ways in which human, social interaction is endowed with, and shaped by, the meanings it has for participants.

There are, of course, well-known bodies of sociological theory which address issues of agency and meaning: interactionism, phenomenology and ethnomethodology. These had, in the 1970s and early 1980s, been drawn upon in arguing for the social construction of gender and sexuality (Gagnon and Simon, 1974; Jackson, 1978; Plummer, 1975; Stanley, 1984) and could, in theory, have been used to address some of the lacunae in Marxist theory which inspired the cultural turn. In practice, however, they were not. In part this was simply because they were not fashionable. Having been briefly in vogue among young radical sociologists in the late 1960s, as an antidote to functionalism, they lost ground to Marxism and other forms of structural critique in the 1970s. They also lacked any ready-made mode of articulation with Marxism, unlike psychoanalysis, which could be linked to the Marxist project via Althusser's (1971) notion that ideology constitutes us as subjects.

It seems to me that the time is ripe for the re-evaluation and revitalisation of these microsociological perspectives. Now that most of us have abandoned attempts at totalising theory in which all aspects of the social are welded together into a seamless whole, there is no longer such a problem in the lack of precise fit between these theories and more structural approaches. We can admit that social life is multilayered, multifaceted and that contradictory processes are often at work within it. The doubts which plagued me as a young academic, unable to synthesise interactionism with my materialist, structural analysis of women's subordination, no longer bother me. Such a synthesis is not only impossible, but undesirable, since any attempt to construct one could only serve to conceal some of the complexities of social life.

Some feminists continue to work productively within interactionist and phenomenological traditions (e.g. DeNora, 1997), but this has been a minority endeavour, little known outside sociology – despite the ease with which it can be integrated with more recent conceptualisations, such as the Foucauldian notion of discourse or the idea of narratives of self (Jackson, 1993; Plummer, 1975). Indeed, this very ease of assimilation may render the distinctively sociological invisible. For those who know nothing of sociology, work such as this can be all too readily interpreted as poststructuralist – as in Deborah Lupton's (1998) reading of one of my articles on love (Jackson, 1993). True, I did, in this context, throw in a bit of Barthes and Foucault, but the guiding thread to my argument for the social construction of love was the interactionist tradition which informed my earlier work on sexuality.

It is the eclipsing of these perspectives which have served to conceal the origins of social constructionism, particularly in the field of sexuality. New forms of social constructionism are often not very social at all – indeed they are often emptied of the social and are better characterised as cultural constructionism. Of course the social world includes the cultural, it includes the realms of discourse and symbolic representation. But the cultural is not all there is to the social. The distinctively social has to do with questions of social structure but also situated everyday social practices. It encompasses everything that shapes our lives, from structural inequalities to everyday interaction. It is concerned with meaning, both at the level of our wider culture and as meanings emerge from or are deployed in our everyday social life. It includes subjectivity, since our sense of who we are in relation to others constantly guides our actions and interactions and, conversely, who we are is a consequence of our location within gendered, class, racial and other divisions and the immediate social and cultural milieux we inhabit. In my recent work on sexuality I have, in keeping with this picture of the social, identified four intersecting levels or facets of social construction (Jackson, 1999; Scott *et al.*, 1998). While I will spell these out in relation to sexuality, they could equally be applied to any other aspect of social life. Sexuality, though, is a particularly good example since here cultural, rather than social, constructionism has held sway in much recent theorising.

The most neglected aspect of the social construction of sexuality is the structural, where sexuality is both constituted and regulated through the institutionalisation of heterosexuality bolstered by law, the state and social convention. The institution of heterosexuality also rests on the structural division of gender and the assumed normality of specific forms of social and sexual relations between women and men. At the level of meaning sexuality is socially constructed through its constitution as the object of discourse and through the specific discourses on the sexual in circulation at any historical moment. These discourses serve to define what is sexual, to differentiate the 'perverse' from the 'normal', and masculine from feminine forms of sexuality. However, meaning is also deployed within, and emergent from, social interaction and hence finds its expression at yet another level – that of our everyday social practices, through which each of us negotiates and makes sense of our own sexual lives. Here, too, sexuality is constantly in the process of being constructed and reconstructed, enacted and re-enacted, within specific social contexts and relationships. Sexuality is thus socially constructed by what embodied individuals actually *do*. Finally, sexuality is socially constructed at the level of subjectivity, through complex social and cultural process by which we acquire sexual and gendered desires and identities.

What cultural, as opposed to social, constructionism does is to exclude the first level, that of structure, altogether. It then deals with meaning primarily only at the level of culture and discourse. Sometimes practices are included – in Butler's (1990) discussion of performativity, for example – but rarely are these practices located in their interactional or wider social setting. Finally, subjectivity is usually theorised through psychoanalysis, which completely abstracts it from its social context. Here I would put in a plea for the further development of the idea of a reflexive self as a sociological alternative.

The concept of a reflexive, social self is sometimes resisted on the grounds that it presupposes a presocial, or prediscursive 'I' which does the work of reflexivity. However, if we take this idea back to its origins in the work of George Herbert Mead (1934), it does not assume an essential, inner 'I', but an 'I' which is only ever the fleeting mobilisation of a socially constituted self. Moreover this self is not a fixed structure but is always 'in process' by virtue of its constant reflexivity. One way in which this reflexive self-construction has been analysed recently, in my own work and that of others, is through the idea of narratives of self, conceptualisation which has roots in both the sociological tradition of interactionism and in more recent discourse analysis (Jackson, 1998; Plummer, 1995; Whisman, 1996). Such a perspective allows us to think of subjectivity as a product of individual, socially located, biographies – but not in the same sense as the old notion of socialisation. Here, rather than the past (or childhood) determining the present (or adulthood), the present significantly shapes the past in the sense that we are constantly reconstructing our memories, our sense of who and what we are through the stories we tell to ourselves and others. Experience is conceptualised not as given in raw form, but as constantly worked over, interpreted, theorised through the narrative forms and devices available to us. These cultural resources are of course historically specific, enabling us to understand the ways in which particular modes of self-construction become available at different historical moments.

The cultural, the social and the sexual

In order to explore the ways is which the social constructionism that I have outlined differs from more cultural perspectives, I will briefly consider how sociological feminism might be brought to bear on current debates on heterosexuality. One of the reasons why feminists embraced the 'cultural turn' was that it allowed for a consideration of aspects of femininity and women's subordination which had been neglected by the major theoretical debates of the 1970s. Among these was sexuality, which gained theoretical prominence with the appropriation of Lacan (1977), and especially Foucault (1981). The latter in particular has had an immense influence on the postmodern perspective which has set the agenda for much recent theorising on sexuality: queer theory.

As a feminist who had been working on sexuality since the early 1970s, I might have been expected to welcome the cultural turn, but did not do so very enthusiastically. I had never had much time for psychoanalysis in either its pre- or post-Lacanian manifestations. While Lacan made it possible to think of sexuality as constituted through language and culture, psychoanalysis continued to lack historical specificity, and its focus on the unconscious precluded an analysis of everyday sexuality. I found Foucault (1981) much more interesting, primarily because much of what he had to say resonated with ideas which were familiar to me. I had already found a distinctively sociological approach to sexuality – the interactionist perspective of Gagnon and Simon (1974) – which provided an alternative to psychoanalysis and anticipated much of what was deemed radical in Foucault's work.

For Gagnon and Simon there is no pregiven sexuality which can be repressed; what is sexual is a matter of social definition and becoming sexual is a process of learning sexual meanings or 'scripts' and locating oneself within them. Their critique of the concept of repression presaged Foucault's later deconstruction of the 'repressive hypothesis'. So too did their questioning of the centrality and 'specialness' accorded to sexuality in modern society. They suggested that rather than sex being a powerful impulse underpinning human activity, its importance is a historical invention (Gagnon and Simon, 1974: 16). This is not to say that Gagnon and Simon's work was without flaws. While they foregrounded gender as pivotal to the scripting of sexuality, they tended to focus on socially constructed *differences* between women and men, without sufficient emphasis on the power relations between them. Nonetheless, this work was radical for its time and still provides insights worth recovering. It did not, however, attract legions of disciples – which in part explains its eclipsing by later forms of social constructionism. Some gay theorists took it up (Plummer, 1975; Weeks, 1981), but it had few feminist adherents. Among feminists, I was often attacked in the late 1970s for daring to question the Freudian concept of repression – mostly by those who subsequently deified Foucault. I still find it galling that when sociologists generated a critique of repression most feminists dismissed it, yet as soon as Foucault did so, many embraced it wholeheartedly.

It is not only sociological perspectives on sexuality which have been erased; feminism's contribution to the genesis of social constructionist thought is even less likely to be acknowledged by later writers. In the 1970s feminists began to lay the foundations for the radical critique of heterosexuality which emerged at the end of the decade. This early work was informed by sociological thinking on power relations within heterosexual relations and the interconnections between sexuality and other aspects of women's subordination (see Jackson, 1996, 1999). These connections were later made explicit by, among others, Adrienne Rich (1980), for whom compulsory heterosexuality both kept women *in* (within its confines) and kept them *down* (subordinated).

Reaffirming the importance of early feminist and sociological theorising is not merely a case of establishing an accurate chronology or ensuring that particular theorists are given due credit for their work. I also wish to argue that a sociologically informed feminism has much to contribute to current debates on sexuality. Where queer theorists have tended to concentrate on texts, discourses and cultural practices, there is clearly a space for approaches which pay attention to social structures, to the socially situated contexts of everyday sexual practice and experience, to the material conditions under which our sexualities are lived. Indeed such an approach is essential if we are to retain feminism's focus on heterosexuality as a hierarchical relation between men and women.

Along with the emergence of queer theory there was also, in the 1990s, a resurgence of feminist debate on heterosexuality (Wilkinson and Kitzinger, 1993; Richardson, 1996). While there are considerable differences within and between feminism and queer, there are also some shared concerns. Both question the ways in which male dominated heterosexuality is routinely normalised, and both assume that neither gender divisions nor the heterosexual/homosexual divide are fixed by nature. Beyond this, however, their emphases diverge. Whereas feminists have historically focused on male dominance within heterosexual relations, queer theorists have directed their attention to the ways in which 'heteronormativity' renders alternatives to heterosexuality 'other' and marginal. I have suggested that an effective critique of heterosexuality – at the levels of social structure, meaning, social practice and subjectivity – must address both heteronormativity and male dominance (Jackson, 1999). Such a critique involves more than simply a synthesis of queer and feminism; it necessarily entails a sociological understanding of gender as a hierarchical social division, since heterosexuality is by definition ordered by gender polarity. Moreover, 'same sex' desire also requires the social, cultural and subjective recognition of gender categories. Without the distinction of gender, heterosexuality, lesbianism and homosexuality would have no meaning, no social existence (Jackson, 1996, 1999).

In suggesting that sociology can potentially offer more to feminism than the primarily cultural approach of queer theory, I will engage briefly with the work of Judith Butler, a theorist who is usually read as both feminist and queer. Like most queer theorists, Butler seeks to destabilise heterosexual normativity; as a feminist, she takes gender seriously, although gender figures in her work more as a cultural difference than a social hierarchy. She does, however, reveal the artificiality of gender, its status as a construction with no necessary relationship to particular bodies or sexualities (Butler, 1990). She has also contested those readings of her work in which gender appears to be ephemeral, a voluntaristic performance, something to be taken on or discarded at will, and in so doing she emphasised the constraining effects of gender, its imposition on us (Butler, 1993). Yet she discusses this enforced 'materialisation' of 'sexed' bodies almost entirely in terms of norms – with no sense of where these norms come from and how they are constituted (Ramazanoglu, 1995), and with no discussion of how they intersect with everyday social relations and practices. The social is thus reduced to the normative, and what is normative goes unexplained.

More recently Butler (1997) has questioned whether issues of gender and sexuality are 'merely cultural', invoking a form of Marxism in order to explain heterosexual hegemony. In so doing she returns to Lévi-Strauss' notion of the exchange of women which, she claims, breaks down distinctions between the cultural, economic and the social, demonstrating their interrelationship (see Butler, 1997: 275). Butler distances herself from Lévi-Strauss' universalism, suggesting that queer studies might be a means of returning to critiques of the family based on 'mobilizing an insight *into a socially contingent and socially transformable account of kinship* (ibid. 276, Butler's emphasis). And what is the current structuring of gender and sexuality contingent on? Apparently, the functions which the heterosexual family performs for capitalism! Butler has traced the history of the cultural turn in reverse, back through structuralism to Marxism and the functionalism and reductionism of earlier Marxist feminist accounts of 'relations of reproduction'.

Nowhere does Butler consider the possibility that gender and heterosexuality might be structurally related to male dominance, despite her reliance on the work of Monique Wittig, for whom the heterosexual contract is fundamental to the maintenance of the patriarchal order (Wittig, 1992). Whereas Wittig sees heterosexuality as founded on the appropriation of women's bodies and labour, Butler reads her account largely in terms of the narrowly sexual, and so misses much of its materialist import. In so doing she fails to address heterosexuality itself and the gender hierarchy internal to it; instead she seems to find heterosexuality and gender interesting only as norms against which the destabilising possibilities of gender and sexual transgression can be asserted (Jackson, 1995, 1999). There seems to be an enormous gulf in her theorising between heterosexuality's functions (for capitalism), the norms which enforce it (asserted but never fully explicated), and the performativity through which gender is produced in everyday life.

Heterosexuality is sustained not only through norms, or the institutions which regulate it, but through our everyday sexual and social practices, which indicates that, in some sense, it requires our continual reaffirmation for its continuance. Most of the population 'do' heterosexuality every day without reflecting critically on that doing. Moreover, 'doing heterosexuality' is also about 'doing gender'. This is accomplished through talk and action, through the embodied practices of dress and demeanour, through active participation in formal institutional settings, through the mundane activities through which our everyday lives are ordered. The terminology here is not Butler's, but is deliberately sociological, borrowing from Goffman (1959) and Garfinkel (1967).

Butler is less concerned with the everyday settings in which we do gender than with simply demonstrating that it *is* performative. She is, however, preoccupied with the possibility of undoing or at least unsettling normative gender and heterosexuality. Yet Butler's examples of performative subversions are not so much about undoing gender as doing it in new ways (see, for example, her reflections (1990: 122) on a lesbian femme's claim that she likes her 'boys to be girls') The destabilising effects she envisages for such transgressive performances is thus limited. Those, like Butler, who seek to undo binary divisions of gender and sexuality by rendering their boundaries more permeable and adding more categories to them are effectively reworking the old assumption that the whole of human potential equals the sum of its gendered parts. Where androgynists aimed to weld the two incomplete 'halves' of masculinity and femininity into a complete whole, queer theorists seek to destabilise both, and create more 'genders' by jumping between them or recombining their elements in innovative or parodic forms. Some combination of femininity and masculinity, and same gender or other gender desire, is still taken to be the only human possibility. But it is not: if men and women are products of a social, hierarchical relation, in the absence of that relation very different subjectivities, desires and identities might emerge – and these would have nothing to do with gender.

Feminism and the sociological imagination

Such utopian speculation may seem naive, but to me it is central to thinking sociologically. Social construction theories originated among sociologists precisely because we have habitually questioned the naturalness and inevitability of our current social arrangements. I have suggested elsewhere (Jackson, 1998) that there is a convergence between the feminist conviction that the personal is political and C. Wright Mills' famous claim that the sociological imagination transforms 'personal troubles' into 'public issues' (Mills, 1970: 14–17). A feminist sociological imagination enables us to see that the personal troubles associated with gender divisions are social in origin and hence potentially changeable. The personal can only become political if it is also understood as social; without that understanding, our critical vision becomes blurred. This is precisely what has happened as a result of the eclipsing of the social by the cultural. It is the lack of a sociological imagination which accounts for the inability of theorists such as Butler to envisage a world without gender, without heterosexuality – and without other systematic inequalities deriving from a social order which remains capitalist and racist as well as patriarchal.

In these postmodern times most Left intellectuals have given up on the hope of a better future (along with the metanarratives which sustained such hope), in favour of a Foucauldian view of power as inescapable. We can resist, subvert and destabilise, but the only change we can expect will be new deployments of power to be resisted, subverted or destabilised. Even if we share this pessimism, we lose something vital to our discipline if we forget that society as we know it is a historical product not a pre-ordained natural order. The exercise of a sociological *imagination* implies just that: the ability to at least *imagine* that the social world could be radically other than it is. If we cannot do so, we lose the cutting edge of sociology, its ability to make us think critically about the society in which we live.

References

Abbott, P. (1991) 'Feminist perspectives in sociology: challenges to "mainstream" orthodoxy', in J. Aaron and S. Walby (eds) *Out of the Margins*. London: Falmer

Adams, P., Brown, B. and Cowie, E. (1978) 'Editorial', *m/f*, 1, pp. 3–5

Adkins, L. (1995) *Gendered Work: Sexuality, Family and the Labour Market*. Buckingham: Open University Press

Allen, S. and Leonard, D. (1996) 'From sexual divisions to sexualities: changing sociological agendas', in J. Weeks and J. Holland (eds) *Sexual Cultures*. Basingstoke: Macmillan

Althusser, L. (1971) 'Ideology and the ideological state apparatuses', in *Lenin and Philosophy*. London: New Left Books

Barrett, M. (1992) 'Words and things: materialism and method in contemporary feminist analysis', in M. Barrett and A. Phillips (eds) *Destabilizing Theory: Contemporary Feminist Debates*. Cambridge: Polity Press, pp. 201–19.

Barrett, M. and McIntosh, M. (1979) 'Christine Delphy: towards a materialist feminism', *Feminist Review*, 1, pp. 95–106

Berger, P. and Luckman, T. (1967) *The Social Construction of Reality*. New York: Doubleday

Brah, A. (1991) 'Questions of difference and international feminism', in J. Aaron and S. Walby (eds) *Out of Margins: Women's Studies in the Nineties*. London: Falmer

Butler, J. (1990) *Gender Trouble: Feminism and the Subversion of Identity*. New York: Routledge

Butler, J. (1993) *Bodies that Matter*. New York: Routledge

Butler, J. (1997) 'Merely cultural', *Social Text*, Vol. 15, No. 3/4, pp. 265–78

Carby, H. (1982) 'White women listen! Black feminism and the boundaries of sisterhood', in Centre for Contemporary Cultural Studies (eds) *The Empire Strikes Back: Race and Racism in 70s Britain*. London: Hutchinson, pp. 212–35

Coward, R. and Ellis, J. (1977) *Language and Materialism*. London: Routledge and Kegan Paul

Delphy, C. (1977) *The Main Enemy*. London: Women's Research and Resources Centre

Delphy, C. (1980) 'A materialist feminism is possible', *Feminist Review*, 4, pp. 79–104

Delphy, C. (1981) 'Le patriarchat, le féminisme et leurs intellectuelles', *Nouvelles Questions Féministes*, No. 2.

Delphy, C. (1984) *Close to Home: A Materialist Analysis of Women's Oppression*. trans. and ed. D. Leonard. London: Hutchinson

Delphy, C. (1993) 'Rethinking sex and gender', *Women's Studies International Forum*, Vol. 16, No. 1, pp. 1–9

Delphy, C., and Leonard, D. (1992) *Familiar Exploitation: A New Analysis of Marriage in Contemporary Western Societies*. Oxford: Polity Press

DeNora, T. (1997) 'Music and erotic agency', *Body and Society*, Vol. 3, No.2, pp. 43–65

Dunne, G. (1996) *Lesbian Lifestyles*. Basingstoke: Macmillan

Epstein, S. (1996) 'A queer encounter: sociology and the study of sexuality', in S. Seidman (ed.) *Queer Theory/Sociology*. Oxford: Blackwell

Felski, R. (1997) 'The doxa of difference', *Signs*, Vol. 23, No. 1, pp. 1–22

Flax, J. (1990) 'Postmodernism and gender in feminist theory', in L. Nicholson (ed.) *Feminism/Postmodernism*. New York: Routledge

Foucault, M. (1980) *Power/Knowledge: Selected Interviews and Other Writings 1972–1977*. Brighton: Harvester

Foucault, M. (1981) *The History of Sexuality, Volume One*. Harmondsworth: Penguin

Fraad, H., Resnick, S. and Wolff, R. (1994) *Bringing It All Back Home: Class, Gender and Power in the Modern Household*. London: Pluto Press

Gagnon, J. (1965) 'Sexuality and sexual learning in the child', *Psychiatry*, No. 28, pp. 212–28

Gagnon, J. and Simon, W. (1974) *Sexual Conduct*. London: Hutchinson

Garfinkel, H. (1967) *Studies in Ethnomethodology*. Englewood Cliffs, New Jersey: Prentice-Hall

Gibson-Graham, J.K. (1996) *The End of Capitalism (as we knew it): A Feminist Critique of Political Economy*. Oxford: Blackwell

Goffman, E. (1959) *The Presentation of Self in Everyday Life*. New York: Doubleday

Hennessy, R. (1993) *Materialist Feminism and the Politics of Discourse*. New York: Routledge

Hennessy, R. (1995) 'Queer visibility in commodity culture', in L. Nicholson and S. Seidman (eds) *Social Postmodernism*. Cambridge: Cambridge University Press

Hennessy, R. (2000) *Profit and Pleasure*. New York: Routledge

Ingraham, C. (1996) 'The heterosexual imaginary', in S. Seidman (ed.) *Queer Theory/Sociology*. Oxford: Blackwell

Irigaray, L. (1985) *This Sex Which Is Not One*. Ithaca: Cornell University Press

Jackson, S. (1978) *On the Social Construction of Female Sexuality*. London: WRRC

Jackson, S. (1993) 'Even sociologists fall in love: an exploration in the sociology of emotions', *Sociology*, Vol. 27, No. 2, pp. 201–20

Jackson, S. (1995) 'Gender and heterosexuality: a materialist feminist analysis', in M. Maynard and J. Purvis (eds) *(Hetero)sexual Politics*. London: Taylor and Francis

Jackson, S. (1996) 'Heterosexuality and feminist theory', in D. Richarson (ed.) *Theorising Heterosexuality: Telling it Straight*. Buckingham: Open University Press

Jackson, S. (1998) 'Telling stories: memory, narrative and experience in feminist theory and research', in K. Henwood, C. Griffin and A. Phoenix (eds) *Standpoints and Differences*. London: Sage

Jackson, S. (1999) *Heterosexuality in Question*. London: Sage

Lacan, J. (1977) *Écrits*. London: Tavistock

Landry, D. and MacLean, G. (1993) *Materialist Feminisms*. Oxford: Blackwell

Laslett, B. and Thorne, B. (1997) *Feminist Sociology: Life Histories of a Movement*. New Brunswick: Rutgers University Press

Lévi-Strauss, C. (1969) *The Elementary Structures of Kinship*. London: Eyre and Spottiswood.

Lupton, D. (1998) *The Emotional Self*. London: Sage

Lyotard, F. (1984) *The Postmodern Condition*. Manchester: Manchester University Press

McIntosh, M. (1968) 'The homosexual role', *Social Problems*, Vol. 16, No. 2, pp. 182–92

MacKinnon, C.A. (1982) 'Feminism, Marxism, method and the state: an agenda for theory', *Signs*, 7, pp. 515–44

Maynard, M. (1990) 'The re-shaping of sociology? Trends in the study of gender', *Sociology*, Vol. 24, No. 2, pp. 269–90

Maynard, M. (1995) 'Beyond the "big three": the development of feminist theory in the 1990s', *Women's History Review*, Vol. 4, No. 3, pp. 259–81

Mead, G.H. (1934) *Mind, Self and Society*. Chicago: University of Chicago Press

Mills, C.W. (1940) 'Situated actions and vocabularies of motive', *American Sociological Review*, No. 5, pp. 439–52

Mills, C.W. (1970) *The Sociological Imagination*. Harmondsworth: Penguin

Mitchell, J. (1975) *Psychoanalysis and Feminism*. Harmondsworth: Penguin

Modleski, T. (1991) *Feminism Without Women*. New York: Routledge

Oakley, A. (1972) *Sex, Gender and Society*. Oxford: Martin Robertson

Plummer, K. (1975) *Sexual Stigma: An Interactionist Account*. London: Routledge and Kegan Paul

Plummer, K. (1995) *Telling Sexual Stories: Power, Change and Social Worlds*. London: Routledge

Ramazanoglu, C. (1975) 'Back to basics: heterosexuality, biology and why men stay on top', in M. Maynard and J. Purvis (eds) *(Hetero)sexual Politics*. London: Taylor and Francis

Rich, A. (1980) 'Compulsory heterosexuality and lesbian existence', *Signs*, Vol. 5, No. 4, pp. 639–60

Richardson, D. (ed.) (1996) *Theorising Heterosexuality: Telling It Straight*. Buckingham: Open University Press

Riley, D. (1988) *'Am I that Name?' Feminism and the Category of 'Women' in History*. London: Macmillan

Rubin, G. (1975) 'The traffic in women: notes on the "political economy" of sex', in R. Reiter (ed.) *Toward an Anthroplology of Women*. New York: Monthly Review Press, pp. 157–210

Rubin, G. (1994) 'Sexual traffic', *differences*, Vol. 6, No. 2/3, pp. 62–99

Scott, S. Jackson, S. and Backett-Milburn, K. (1998) 'Swings and roundabouts: risk anxiety and the everyday worlds of children', *Sociology* Vol. 32, No. 4, pp. 689–706

Seidman, S. (1997) *Difference Troubles: Queering Social Theory and Sexual Politics*. Cambridge: Cambridge University Press

Siltanen, J. (1994) *Locating Gender: Occupational Segregation, Wages and Domestic Responsibilities*. London: UCL Press

Simon, W. and Gagnon, J. (1969) 'On psychosexual development', in D.A. Goslin (ed.) *Handbook of Socialization Theory and Research*. Chicago: Rand McNally

Stacey, J. and Thorne, B. (1985) 'The missing feminist revolution in sociology', *Social Problems*, Vol. 32, pp. 301–16

Stanley, L. (1984) 'Should "sex" really be "gender" or "gender" really be "sex"?', in R. Anderson and W. Sharrock (eds) *Applied Sociology*. London: Allen and Unwin

Stanley, L. and Wise, S. (1983) *Breaking Out*. London: Routledge and Kegan Paul

Stein, A. and Plummer, K. (1996) '"I can't even think straight": Queer theory and the missing sexual revolution in sociology', in S. Seidman (ed.) *Queer Theory/Sociology*. Oxford: Blackwell

VanEvery, J. (1995*) Heterosexual Women Changing the Family: Refusing to be a 'Wife'*. London: Taylor and Francis

Walby, S. (1986) *Patriarchy at Work*. Oxford: Polity Press

Walby, S. (1992) 'Post-post-modernism? Theorizing social complexity', in M. Barrett and A. Phillips (eds) *Destabilizing Theory: Contemporary Feminist Debates*. Oxford: Polity Press

Walby, S. (1997) *Gender Transformations*. London: Routledge

Weeks, J. (1981) *Sex, Politics and Society*. London: Longman

Whisman, V. (1996) *Queer by Choice*. New York: Routledge

Wilkinson, S. and Kitzinger, C. (eds) (1993) *Heterosexuality: A 'Feminism and Psychology' Reader*. London: Sage

Wittig, M. (1992) *The Straight Mind and Other Essays*. Hemel Hempstead: Harvester Wheatsheaf

Witz, A. (1992) *Patriarchy and the Professions*. London: Routledge

Chapter 6
Bourdieu and methodological polytheism: taking sociology forward in the twenty-first century

David Inglis, Norman Stockman and Paula Surridge

> All the world over and at all times there have been practical men absorbed in 'irreducible facts'; all the world over and at all times there have been men of philosophic temperament who have been absorbed in the weaving of general principles. It is this union of passionate interest in the detailed facts with equal devotion to abstract generalisation which forms the novelty in our present society.
> (A.N. Whitehead, 1947)

It is our contention that the union described in the above quotation is lacking in contemporary sociology. All too often theory and method are treated separately, each having their own specialist audiences, journals and university courses. Furthermore, we believe that a distinction between theory and method is a false dichotomy which – like disciplinary boundaries – may be expedient for those engaged in teaching sociology, but which serves to stifle the growth of sociological knowledge. A closer union of theory and method is necessary to take sociology as a discipline forward in the twenty-first century.

We also contend that the wide range of methods of 'doing' sociology is not a sign of disarray, but rather should be embraced and encouraged within the discipline. By recognising the 'methodological polytheism' of sociology to be one of the its strengths, it is possible to move beyond tired debates about methodology and begin to set an agenda for sociology in the new millennium. In building our argument in support of a discipline of sociology that goes beyond stale dichotomies, we use the work of Pierre Bourdieu as an exemplar of a sociology that does not adhere to false boundaries between theory and method, and that does not privilege any one form of research methodology.

We start from the conviction that sociology ought to be an empirical discipline, that it should strive to understand the social world through gathering evidence about the world and not through the construction of elegant theories which are not intended to be confronted with evidence. In this sense we believe sociology to be a scientific endeavour, a discipline which relies on empirical evidence as the basis for the development of its corpus of theory. We will not offer a justification for this position, as it is well made elsewhere (Pawson, 1989; Bourdieu *et al.*, 1991; Layder, 1998).

We recognise that there is no 'theory-neutral' observation and that the relationship between theory and evidence is one of mutual support, reinforcement or refutal. Just as evidence will lead us to reformulate theory, so theory may lead us to seek different evidence. At every stage of the research process, theory and method should be uppermost in the researcher's mind. We do not aim to prescribe a theoretical or methodological position but rather, to use a phrase favoured by Layder (1998), to show that epistemological, theoretical and methodological 'openness' are crucial to a sociology which can embrace its diversity and take its place as a key scientific discipline in the twenty-first century.

Sociology: a discipline of dichotomies?

Sociology is often presented as a discipline of dichotomies, whether these be at the level of epistemology (naturalism versus interpretivism), theory (macro versus micro, structure versus agency) or methodology (quantitative versus qualitative). However, increasingly sociologists have made the overcoming of one or more of these dichotomies their main aim. There is also a growing recognition that these dichotomies are often presented as more clear-cut than they really are and are used as a means of labelling sociological work in order to ridicule or dismiss it. As Silverman (1998: 80) puts it, dichotomies are 'excuses for not thinking, which assemble groups of sociologists into "armed camps" unwilling to learn from each other'.

Thus, applying the label 'naturalist' or 'qualitative' to a piece of research becomes a means of dismissing it rather than engaging with its findings. This is not dissimilar to the way in which various theoretical works are dismissed as belonging to a particular school. It is a way for the unthinking sociologist to be given a cue as to whether or not he or she should agree with the findings of the research – not on the basis of detailed examination of the methodology of the work, but rather on the basis of the individual's sociological habitus. Asked the question 'Are you a Marxist?', Bourdieu alludes to this situation when he replies: 'I usually object to such questions. Primarily because, when one asks these questions ... it is nearly always with the intention of polemic, to place me in a class, to catalogue me ... to accuse me publicly' (cited in Harker *et al.*, 1990: 31). It is perhaps curious to find such obvious prejudice in a discipline which has prided itself on revealing and removing the basis of prejudices elsewhere in social life.

These dichotomies, however, are more than devices for labelling sociological perspectives. Many of the positions have become linked together in a way that implies that if a sociologist believes X then he or she must do sociology in style Y. Perhaps the most infamous of these links is the one between the functionalist school of sociological theory and the use of survey methodologies. In her analysis, Platt demonstrates that even this most common of linkages is little more than an accident of history, and concludes that: 'the historical coincidence of the primacy of functionalism and of survey method was, at a disciplinary level, the product of separate chains of causation' (1986: 530).

Within the discipline of sociology it is often assumed that taking on certain beliefs about the social world entails the use of set methodologies. It is to this supposed link between epistemology and methodology that we now turn.

Epistemology and methodology

Sociology, as a discipline, has expended much energy on epistemological and methodological issues. Debates about methodology have often centred on the divide between quantitative and qualitative methodologies, and which is the more appropriate for the study of human societies. This debate occurs at two levels: epistemological, and technical (Bryman, 1984). The debate at the epistemological level states that qualitative and quantitative approaches to studying society are rooted in fundamentally incompatible beliefs about the social world. Such a link between particular methods and world views is, we believe, merely a historical one, albeit one which is perpetuated in the way in which sociology as a discipline has presented itself and trained generations of researchers. The following quotation is not untypical of textbooks on the philosophy of social research: 'These methodological approaches are not wholly a technical matter of difference but instead result from two different, even rival, philosophical and social theoretical traditions of interpretivism and naturalism' (May and Williams, 1998: 6). Sociological researchers are trained in a framework that asserts such linkages and tends to lead the trainee researcher towards one or other 'tradition' of social research. However, it is difficult to find good reasons to support this supposed 'necessary' connection on which much graduate research training is based.

Discussing the opposition between different epistemological standpoints, Bourdieu (1990: 34) stresses the historically contingent nature of the connection between epistemology and methodology: 'These oppositions are real divisions in the sociological field; they have a social foundation, but they have no scientific foundation'. He further suggests that: 'A good many of these oppositions owe their existence partly to an effort to constitute in theoretical terms positions linked to the possession of different forms of cultural capital' (ibid.: 35).

Whilst it may be a little harsh to suggest that sociologists adopt certain epistemological and theoretical positions purely on the basis of their individual research skills (skills we might term 'research capital'), Bourdieu is right to insist that the relationship between method and epistemology is purely contingent. Recognising this frees Bourdieu from methodological constraint and enables him to use the widest range of research methods as appropriate.

The assumptions on which the link between methodology and epistemology rests are closely related to those identified by Platt (1986) in her article on the link between theory and method.

These are:

1. that any one epistemological position implies one and only one methodology;
2. that in the research process epistemological considerations determine methodologies;
3. that everyone engaged in sociological research holds a firm epistemological belief.

Each of these assumptions is questionable.

Firstly, as the philosophy of science has moved to ever more sophisticated theories of the nature of scientific knowledge it has become increasingly clear that there is no one-to-one correspondence between epistemological positions and research methodologies. There is no longer a simple positivist versus antipositivist divide. As has been pointed out elsewhere, there are few sociologists left who would advocate an epistemology of objective knowledge. However, in order to conduct research one has to adopt a stance of 'as if positivism', as Mann (1981: 548) puts it: 'it matters not the slightest whether the sociologist *also* advocates true positivism or empiricism or neo-Kantian idealism ... or whatever; if s/he undertakes research and seeks to have it evaluated by others, the methodology will be the same.' Thus, whatever the epistemological or theoretical position of individual researchers, once they become engaged in sociological research they must use one of the family of methodologies which produce valid sociological evidence.

The second of Platt's assumptions is that in the design and conduct of research, the key factor is the researcher's epistemological position. This is perhaps an 'ideal' type of research, but in the world of sociology departments with pressures on research time and funds, very often research design is a matter of pragmatics rather than idealism. Researchers may choose to use particular research techniques for a whole array of reasons which are not epistemologically driven, including cost, available expertise and personal preferences. Does this focus on pragmatics invalidate the research conducted? If so, then much sociological research will need redoing.

Finally, Platt's assertion that methodology and epistemology are inextricably linked rests on the assumption that all those engaged in sociological research have a well worked out epistemological position. Experience suggests this is not always the case. Researchers may not have come down on any one side of epistemological debates, nor do they need to in order to conduct reliable and valuable sociological research.

Despite these obvious flaws in the assumptions underlying the belief that epistemology and methodology are inextricably linked, sociology as a discipline has largely taken the linkage as a given, as part of its heritage. Successive generations of researchers have been trained in the philosophy of social science and methodology as if this were the case. There have been a number of moves towards 'mixed methods' or 'triangulation' within sociology (Denzin, 1970). However, the very language used to describe these research strategies belies the assumption that different methodologies are indeed very different approaches, rather than simply members of a family of methodologies which can be employed at any time. Indeed, statements on the use of mixed methods point to linkages between methodology and epistemology that must be taken into consideration (Brannen, 1992). Thus, even among those purporting to use a range of sociological methods, the underlying assumption that there is or even that there ought to be a linkage between epistemology and methodology remains.

Methodological polytheism

Once the contingency of the link between epistemology and methodology is accepted, the researcher is freed from narrow epistemological constraint and able to choose from the full range of research methodologies available. However, this does not imply methodological anarchism, or suggest that 'anything goes'

(Feyerabend, 1978). Rather it implies advocating the use of as wide a range of methodologies as is appropriate to the research question in hand. In his discussion of the key characteristics of Bourdieu's approach to sociology, Wacquant (1998) terms this use of a range of methodologies 'methodological polytheism'. He goes on to define this approach as one which deploys 'whatever procedure of observation and verification is best suited to the question at hand and continually confronts the results yielded by different methods' (ibid.: 219).

It is this approach which we seek to promote in this chapter. We believe that sociology must abandon the false linkage between epistemology and methodology and embrace the full spectrum of methodological possibilities. Our vision likens research methods to coloured filters used in the production of photographs and films. Any particular filter will produce a partial view of the world. By using a succession of different filters, the researcher can build up a more complete picture of the world. An a priori rejection of any filters limits the picture that can be built up. The filter used should the most appropriate for the type of picture that is required. Confronting the picture produced with those produced by other filters reveals a more complete and accurate picture.

This differs from triangulation, where the use of different filters acts as a validation of the picture produced by the first filter, and from the mixed methods approach, which would have us judge the results of looking through two filters side by side. Rather it is a plea for a recognition of the usefulness of the full spectrum of methods and their application to appropriate research settings. The fact that the sociological community has always approached a given topic using particular research methodologies should not rule out the topic being approached in a different way by subsequent researchers.

Of course it may not be the case that every research project lends itself to more than one method. If the goals of a project are clearly defined then it may be possible to achieve those goals using a single approach. The point here is not to prescribe that a range of methods should be used in every instance. Rather it should be the case that the findings from one research project or method are constantly confronted with findings from other projects, whether using the same or different methodologies. As we stated at the outset, the key tenet is 'openness' to whatever techniques are available and suitable for the purpose in hand.

Methodological polytheism in practice

We must be careful here not to fall into the trap identified by Pawson (1989: 5), who describes a 'decent methodological pluralism' as 'a strange philosophy which no individual ever put into practice but was considered awfully good advice for everyone else'. Whilst we could not claim to have put the above into practice in our own research, we believe that the work of Bourdieu is an exemplar of this style of sociological research. Bourdieu repeatedly refuses to characterise his work as belonging to any one theoretical school and consistently makes use of a wide rage of empirical sources. As an example of the richness of a research programme built around these ideals, we turn now to a brief examination of Bourdieu's work in the field of education.

Many secondary commentaries on Bourdieu's work point to the centrality of his research in education (e.g. Harker, *et al.*, 1990; Swartz, 1997). In his most recently translated study of education, *The State Nobility* (1998: 5), Bourdieu himself reiterates this point by stating that the sociology of education 'lies at the foundation of a general anthropology of power and legitimacy'. On one level, *State Nobility* is an empirical analysis of the functioning of the uppermost tier of the French higher education system and how it is related to the top positions of power in France. It is also an extension of Bourdieu's earlier work on the sociology of education and the theory of domination and reproduction in modern societies. The study is based around an analysis of the social origins of students at 84 French higher education institutions, with more detailed analyses of the characteristics of those at the 21 *grandes écoles* (the most prestigious of these institutions). However, this basic data (collected through surveys) is supplemented in a number of ways, enabling a more detailed picture to be built up. At times unconventional, some of these extra sources are crucial in allowing Bourdieu to uncover the 'unconscious' processes which his theory entails.

The following extracts illustrate how Bourdieu perceives the roles of the survey data and the supplementary data in this work, and demonstrate the ways in which he uses empirical evidence on both sides of his theoretical programme. The theory picks a path between structures and agents; similarly, the empirical evidence on which the theory rests draws from sources which illuminate both the structures of power and the agents' role in them.

> *The use of statistics enables it [anthropology] to bring to light processes such as those that lead to the differential elimination of students from different backgrounds, processes that exhibit such regularity in their complexity that one might be tempted to use mechanistic metaphors to describe them.*
> (Bourdieu, 1998: 2)

> *But the analysis of structures and 'mechanisms' acquires its full explanatory power and descriptive truth only because it includes the results of the analysis of schemata of perception, appreciation, and actions that agents – students as well as teachers – make use of in their judgements and practices.*
> (ibid.: 1)

As mentioned above, the basic data in *State Nobility* derive from questionnaire surveys, conducted by Bourdieu and his colleagues, from the late 1960s, which track changes in the social origins of students through to 1986. As Bourdieu indicates, the use of this material is not restricted to statistical analysis. Whilst the questionnaire responses are summarised throughout in detailed crosstabulations, longer extracts from open-ended questions are also used to support particular theoretical observations. An example of this is one of the discussions about the nature of the cultural capital held by a certain group of students.

> *The prizewinners in French and philosophy demonstrate in every way that they have a margin of freedom and security that is broad enough to enable them to maintain a relationship of educated dilettantism and eclectic familiarity with culture (understood in a more 'independent' and less 'academic' sense).*
> (ibid.:15)

These characteristics are illustrated by means of data collated from the survey, e.g.:

> They are thus most likely to go to the movies (50 percent of the prizewinners in French and 24 percent of the prizewinners in philosophy do so at least once a week, compared to 17.5 percent of prizewinners in geography and 10 percent of the Latin/Greek winners'
> (ibid.: 15).

And they are further substantiated by longer quotations from the students themselves, e.g.:

> Jazz is an original artistic endeavor ... is not fixed or static ... unlike other musical genres, which are imprisoned in their score (mathematics, son of an engineer).
> (ibid.: 15)

Bourdieu interweaves his theoretical position with the empirical evidence, in a 'dialectic' relationship. The survey material suggests a regularity among the students in terms of types of cultural capital. This regularity fits into Bourdieu's theoretical framework which in turn suggests further ways of looking for evidence to substantiate the theory (in this case, students' own descriptions of jazz music).

Bourdieu is interested not only in the backgrounds of students, but also in how the education system functions as a reproductive machine. The factors underlying this are not easily accessible through the survey material, as he recognises:

> Correspondence analysis brings to light a structure that – even though it can only be obtained by breaking with incomplete descriptions of artificially isolated units – may seem self-evident to all (though only) those who possess the practical mastery of objective structures that familiarity affords ... But this sense of self-evidence may well prevent any questioning of the processes that underlie the observed distributions ... But we have still not arrived at a complete and systematic explanation of the observed phenomena. For that we must go back to the real basis of their 'choices', in other words, to habitus and to the sociogenesis of this generating principle of practices and representations through which the aforementioned relationship becomes effective.
> (ibid.: 161)

In this passage Bourdieu alludes to the way in which both evidence and theory operate on a number of levels. The regularities uncovered by statistical analysis (in this instance correspondence analysis) may fit well with theoretical beliefs. However, there is always the need to supplement this 'self-evident' structure with an analysis of the underlying practices of 'agents' which produce it. In order to do this it is necessary for the researcher to be entangled in a spiral of evidence and theory which begins at the level of the structure of the field and moves to an analysis of the decisions and actions of the individuals located within the field.

In Bourdieu's theory the explanation for the regularities lies in the, often unconscious, acts and motivations of agents within the system. The data from students allows Bourdieu to build his case that students unconsciously collude with the system. However, in order to show how the system works, an understanding of the actions of teachers is required. Here Bourdieu's theoretical position requires a more unconventional methodological approach. As it is the unconscious actions of teachers which underpin the system, a survey – or even interview – to assess teachers' actions is unlikely to yield the desired information. Bourdieu instead turns to more unusual sources of data to uncover the processes underlying decisionmaking: committee reports, prizewinning essays, obituaries of *normaliens* (students at the prestigious *École Normale Supérieure*) and a set of reports kept by a single teacher on her students. Of this final source of data Bourdieu says:

> *Just such a direct and systematic verification of what we had to assume in order to account for the facts established in our study of* Concours Général *prizewinners has been made possible through the discovery and analysis of very ordinary material that, because it was methodically constructed, has turned out to be an exceptional document: a set of 154 individual reports in which a philosophy teacher in a women's* khagne *[a crammer college] in Paris kept a record of her student's written and oral grades (5–6 per student), along with her descriptive comments ... Accompanying the student's grades are their dates of birth, the secondary schools they attended, and their parents' occupations.*
> (ibid.: 30)

Many researchers would view such a data source as unrepresentative, based as it is on the reports of a single teacher; others would never discover such data at all. The stance taken by Bourdieu to his data allows him to bring this wide range of evidence to bear on the theoretical positions. Moreover, when those theoretical positions postulate 'unconscious' actions, it is only through the use of these types of data that any verification can be attempted. As Bourdieu puts it:

> *If we confine our attention to ... social origins and grades, as we must ordinarily do in order to establish a correlation between social origin and academic achievement, we might merely see ... a simple machine that ... reproduces products hierarchized according to an explicit academic classification that is in reality quite similar to the initial classification. In fact, this would be to miss the specific workings of this strange cognitive machine that performs a whole series of operations of cognition and evaluation objectively tending to establish a close correspondence between the entry classification and exit classification without ever officially being aware of or recognizing strictly social principles or criteria.*
> (ibid.: 36)

By analysing the reports of examining committees and the records kept by a teacher, Bourdieu is able to demonstrate the way in which certain adjectives are applied more often to students of particular social backgrounds, revealing the unconscious way in which teachers and examiners value those characteristics which they associate with the higher social groups. Had a more direct methodological approach been taken, it is likely that such evidence would have been found.

These examples serve to illustrate the more general point. Were Bourdieu wedded to a particular methodological approach, many of the theoretical ideas he develops would not and indeed could not be confronted with empirical evidence. It is only the adoption of 'methodological polytheism' which allows the wide range of sources of data to be utilised alongside each other, generating a rich and detailed picture of the French educational system.

As indicated earlier, this conception of methodological polytheism does not lead social research into the anarchism advocated by Feyerabend (1978) in which 'anything goes'. Rather, it is this embracing of methodological diversity which guarantees sociology's status as a scientific enterprise. However, this status can only truly be achieved through a properly reflexive practice of sociology. It is to this reflexivity in social research that we now turn.

Reflexivity and polytheism

How can we ensure that our choice of research methods is truly informed by the principle of methodological polytheism? Once again, an appreciation of Bourdieu's work gives us some indication of how the choosing of research tools can be undertaken in a way that is based on and promotes a diversity of investigative approaches. Bourdieu urges that we turn our sociological gaze on ourselves, scrutinising the social conditions of our own means of knowledge production. To turn sociological analysis back on itself involves a 'systematic exploration of the unthought categories of thought which delimit the thinkable and predetermine the thought' (Bourdieu and Wacquant, 1992: 40). Such an endeavour is not an occasional luxury, but should be a key aspect of all sociological practice, for to be properly 'sociological' is to constantly adopt a reflexive attitude to oneself and one's research practices.

Unlike other accounts of sociological reflexivity, Bourdieu's conception of a reflexive awareness of knowledge creation does not limit itself to acknowledging the general social characteristics of the researcher, such as class, gender, ethnicity and so on. Instead, it also includes accounting for the position of the researcher in the field of social research itself. A reflexive account of that field involves tracing out how the position of the knowledge-producer generates certain dispositions towards the research process, and on that basis creates distinctive forms of knowledge (Bourdieu and Wacquant, 1992: 41). How a certain object of research is conceptualised depends on the research capital one possesses, and in turn, possession of that research capital places one at a certain position within the hierarchically structured field of social research (ibid.: 42). Reflexivity thus involves coming to an awareness of the stakes at play when using particular research strategies, and the conceptualisations of research objects which different strategies generate.

The first step towards coming towards a reflexive appreciation of one's own research practice is, therefore, to recognise that the field of social research in which one operates is characterised by dynamism and competition. As Wacquant puts it: 'The points of view of sociologists, like any other cultural producers, always owe something to their situation in a field where all define themselves in part in relational terms, by their difference and distance from certain others with whom they compete' (Bourdieu and Wacquant, 1992: 39).

If we accept this characterisation, then we may say that the field of social research is composed of different groups with their own forms of research capital. Each group is engaged, explicitly or implicitly, in a contest with other groups holding alternate forms of capital, and each group seeks to have its form of capital recognised by the others as the most legitimate and worthy. Each individual researcher is a member, wittingly or unwittingly, of the group which possesses the type of research capital the individual holds. Predilections as to how research should be carried out are not a function of individual whim but of group membership. As groups are in competition with each other, so too are the individual researchers who constitute these groups. Each person 'playing the game' within the field makes claims, both implicit and explicit, about the superiority of certain types of research methods, whilst simultaneously derogating others. But these claims are never 'pure' or 'disinterested', for they always rest on some kind of assumption as to the greater efficacy of particular approaches over others. Such claims of superiority are made on the basis of the position at that moment in time that one's group enjoys in the hierarchy of the field. Thus the individual's appreciation of the merits of the approach he or she adopts, and the tools he or she is competent to use, are informed by the location that his or her group has in the field at a given time, rather than on any 'disinterested' appreciation of the 'technical' merits of the approach.

When the unreflexive researcher talks explicitly about the superiority of method X relative to other methods for understanding topic Y, he or she is implicitly making a claim as to the superiority of the group which possesses that form of research capital, relative to all other groups with other research methods who might potentially study Y. The unreflexive researcher believes that there is some intrinsic, a priori relation between method X and topic Y. However, this belief misrecognises the true relation between X and Y. Just as sociologists believe that social relations and forms of socially constituted knowledge are not cast in stone but infinitely mutable, a reflexive appreciation of our own practice requires us to see that our own knowledge categories too are mutable and historically produced. The relation between any method and any topic involves a question not of *quid juris* (what is right) but *quid facti* (what happens to be the case). It is not a 'technical' relation, which exists now and forever, but is one which has been formed historically by the dynamics of contestation between groups in the field of social research. It may so happen that it is currently widely believed that X is the most 'appropriate' method for Y, but that situation is a result of historical contingency, not necessity. The relation between X and Y currently holds because those who possess that form of research capital are able to plausibly claim that X is appropriate for Y, due to the relatively powerful position they hold in the field of social research.

A reflexive attitude to the field of social research reveals that apparently necessary links between a certain method and a given object of study are actually contingent, and were created by the relatively privileged position of the researchers who derived status from that method. Such researchers were able to impose their view of its appropriateness for researching that object on other groups in the field. As the relative positions in the field of groups of researchers alter, so too will the 'validity' of their approaches for particular research objects. For example, if X and its proponents are less well regarded at a particular point in time, the link between X and Y will loosen, such that X loses its monopoly on the study of Y, perhaps to the extent that eventually X loses all its claims to validity altogether. In other words, an approach to a topic will be widely felt to be unconvincing at a given time not because of its 'technical' defects, but because of the low standing that the proponents of that approach have in the field at that period. In general, then, the reflexive gaze looks beyond the ossified relations between methods and topics that operate as signs of a particular method's status in the field, towards viewing current forms of a method's 'validity' as the result of struggles between groups holding differing approaches within the field itself.

Conclusion

The account of reflexivity offered by Bourdieu encourages the development of a self-critical form of sociological practice in which we build up a picture of the field in which we operate. This enables us to see that linkages between methods and topics are less to do with allegedly 'inherent' capacities of the methods we use, and more to do with the historical and contingent factors that link topics and methods. If there is one lesson to be learned from Bourdieu's position, it is that relations between phenomena, methods and topics, are always *potentially* mutable. The mutability of social relations is a belief most of us hold as social scientists. We should also apply this principle critically to the very epistemological categories through which we investigate the ever-changing social world. In so doing, we would free up our social scientific practice from arbitrarily produced dogmas that serve only to hinder the progress of social research. By eliminating such monotheistic phantasms through greater reflexive vigilance, we might enter a more fruitful era of tolerant polytheism.

References

Bourdieu, P. (1990) *In Other Words: Essays towards a Reflexive Sociology*. Cambridge: Polity Press

Bourdieu, P. (1998) *The State Nobility: Elite Schools in the Field of Power*. Stanford: Stanford University Press

Bourdieu, P., Chamboredon, J.C. and Passeron, J.C. (1991) *The Craft of Sociology: Epistemological Preliminaries*. New York: de Gruyter

Bourdieu, P. and Wacquant, L. (1992) *An Invitation to Reflexive Sociology*. Cambridge: Polity Press

Brannen, J. (ed.) (1992) *Mixing Methods: Theory and Practice in Combining Quantitative and Qualitative Research*. Aldershot: Avebury

Bryman, A. (1984) 'The debate about quantitative and qualitative research: a question of method or epistemology?', *British Journal of Sociology*, 35, pp. 75–92

Denzin, N. (1970) *The Research Act in Sociology*. London: Butterworths

Feyerabend, P. (1978) *Against Method*. London: Verso

Harker, R., Mahar, C. and Wilkes, C. (eds) (1990) *An Introduction to the Work of Pierre Bourdieu*. New York: St Martin's Press

Layder, D. (1998) *Sociological Practice: Linking Theory and Social Research*. London: Sage

Mann, M. (1981) 'Socio-Logic', *Sociology*, 15, pp. 544–50

May, T. and Williams, M. (eds) (1998) *Knowing the Social World*. Buckingham: Open University Press

Pawson, R. (1989) *A Measure for Measures*. London: Routledge

Platt, J. (1986) 'Functionalism and the survey: the relation of theory and method', *Sociological Review*, 34, pp. 501–36

Silverman, D. (1998) 'Qualitative/quantitative', in C. Jenks (ed.) *Core Sociological Dichotomies*. London: Sage

Swartz, D. (1997) *Culture and Power: The Sociology of Pierre Bourdieu*. Chicago: University of Chicago Press

Wacquant, L. (1998) 'Pierre Bourdieu', in R. Stones (ed.) *Key Sociological Thinkers*. Basingstoke: Macmillan

Chapter 7
Work and its narratives
Richard Sennett

When I began writing, my work-life divided in two. In one compartment, I wrote novels; in the other, sociology. The novel-writing made experiments in narrative – stories which played with the indeterminate movement of events or created incoherence intentionally. The masters of this kind of disruptive narrative in my youth were Jorge Luis Borges and Italo Calvino; its great interpretative critic was Roland Barthes. The crafting of such stories exhilarated me, opening up the freedom of the unchartable.

As a sociologist, I worked in another realm of time. When I began studying labour in the early 1970s, the life-histories of the people I interviewed resembled well-made plots, determinate and constricted rather than experimental. The American manual labourers on whom I reported in *The Hidden Injuries of Class* (Sennett, 1972), for instance, served only a few employers during the course of their lives, and hoped to better themselves by small, incremental gains in salary and status. White-collar employees higher up the job scale orchestrated their lives even more in order to climb up a fixed corporate ladder. These real-life-narratives were shaped by big, well-defined institutions: corporations with elaborate bureaucracies, powerful unions, and an intrusive welfare state.

In the last quarter of the twentieth century, modern capitalism changed, and as a result this determinate life-narrative has weakened. Profound forces now deregulate people's experience of time: new technologies, global markets, new forms of bureaucratic organisation. They orient economic activity to the short rather than the long term, and challenge continuity and duration as institutional goals. One instance may suffice: in 1960 the 'profit horizon' investors used for evaluating corporations was three years; by the 1990s it was typically three months (Harrison, 1994).

How this changing frame of time affects work can be illuminated by two early usages in the English language. In Chaucer's day, a 'career' meant a well-laid, well-mapped roadway on which to travel; a 'job' meant a lump of something, coal or wood, which could be moved around indiscriminately from place to place. In today's labour market, Chaucerian jobs rather than careers define work. The young middle-level university graduate can expect to change employers at least 12 times in the course of a working life, and to change his or her 'skills base' at least three times (US Department of Labor, 1991). The skills he or she must draw on at 40 years of age are not the skills learned in school. Job change no longer flows within the Chaucerian trajectory of a career; without a fixed corporate structure, it follows a more erratic path.

Real life-stories are thus moving closer to the experimental narratives of the fiction that I like to write. However, as I began to discover by interviewing workers again in the mid-1990s for my most recent book on labour – *The Corrosion of Character* (Sennett, 1998) – the time-freedom so exhilarating to read in the stories of Borges does not quite translate into the life of a suburban middle-aged accountant suddenly made redundant and told he should flexibly move as a consultant from job to job, place to place. Without a clear sense of how to structure work in time, people become confused, if not depressed, about what they should do. 'Everyone tells me to take job risks', a young lawyer remarked, 'but I've no cushion against failure.'[1] The flexible workplace itself seems illegible. The chameleon character of organisations, for instance, makes it hard for people to calculate what will happen if they change jobs.

There is also a social dimension to deregulated time: flexible organisations tend to reduce commitment – how can an employee be loyal to a fickle corporation? Indeed, I have found that middle-aged workers who have developed loyalties to particular companies feel betrayed now that these commitments count for so little. Moreover work experience and seniority mean less today than they once did, given employers' preference for younger, cheaper and more pliable employees. One way to summarise the conflict between short-term, deregulated time and the human life-course is that, as work experience accumulates, it diminishes in economic value.

In this regard, I would like to put forward what might seem a paradoxical thesis. On the one hand, in modern capitalism, deregulated time disempowers employees in the middle ranks, the loss of an orienting work-story confuses them. Yet the kind of narrative art exemplified by Borges and Calvino might help people understand the regime over which Bill Gates presides. At the very least, the new political economy challenges sociologists to explore work-history as an experimental narrative. To do so, sociologists need to reconsider their own professional practice. Sociologists have learned better how to describe than to narrate social conditions. This is the problem I shall begin by exploring.

Describing

The classical language of sociology is a picture language. Sociologists from Montesquieu to Weber crafted images of particular social conditions such as aristocracy, Chinese bureaucracy or poverty, to make the reader *see* these conditions. Like an art critic, the sociologist who thinks in pictures is trying to explain what is represented. Sociological images, as Wittgenstein (1963) noted about all picture language, can be as abstract as a Jackson Pollock painting. However, the sense of time in picture language too easily becomes like turning the pages in an album of photographs, moving from one image of social conditions to another – it forms a sequence of representations.

This picture language is evident, for instance, in the work of one of the greatest pieces of all sociological description, Alexis de Tocqueville's (1840) account of individualism in American life. He illustrates a contrast between aristocracy and democracy:

> As in aristocratic communities all the citizens occupy fixed positions, one above the other, the result is that each of them always sees a man above himself whose patronage is necessary to him, and below himself another man whose co-operation he may claim ... It is true that in those ages the notion of human fellowship is faint, and that men seldom think of sacrificing themselves for mankind; but they often sacrifice themselves

> for other men ... In democratic ages, on the contrary, when the duties of each individual to the race are much more clear, devoted service to any one man becomes more rare; the bond of human affection is extended, but it is relaxed ... not only does democracy make every man forget his ancestors, but it hides his descendants, and separates his contemporaries from him; it throws him back for ever upon himself alone, and threatens in the end to confine him entirely within the solitude of his own heart.
> (Tocqueville, 1990: 99)

This description offers two images of aristocratic communities and democratic societies as though they are two states of being, as though these two images could be shown as slides side by side. However, the content of the descriptions contrasts a community of strong social bonds with a society where these bonds are weakening; and the second image is apprehended as the deconstruction of the first. Thus, they seem related in time as well as in structure. This historical change between the two images, however, is an inference drawn from the language of description itself. Tocqueville does not need to cite dates or particular events for the inference to be drawn, the contrast of written pictures does it for him. This is sociological rather than historical time.

It may be thought that there is a certain sleight of hand here, and that problem certainly worried Max Weber. His theory of ideal types was an attempt to make sociologists aware of how they think in picture language, each ideal type corresponding to a coherent, clear image. Weber (1949) sometimes claimed that thinking in images was no more than an aid to understanding historical process, like freeze-framing a video. However, he also believed there could be no intellectual understanding of sheer flux, no decisive political engagement when men and women experience the undifferentiated flow of events. The video needs to be stopped in order to analyse and to act. When it is, what are seen are images that are clear but full of contradiction. In contrast to Tocqueville, and closer to Marx, Weber sought to understand how social forms shatter because of these internal contradictions. For instance, due to their particularism, aristocratic communities seemed to him to now be weak, divided structures. Nevertheless, Weber still wrote as a sociologist; he needed to stop time and to describe an image in order to apprehend the dissonances of lived experience.

Picture-work

Manuel Castells (1996: 410–19) has characterised today's political economy as 'a space of flows'. One of his key arguments is that as a consequence of new technology, the global economy operates in realtime – what happens to stock markets in London or New York instantly registers in Singapore or Johannesburg. On the productive side, computer code written in Bombay can be used at IBM as instantly as code written (more expensively) at the IBM home offices in Armonk, New York. Castells calls this condition 'timeless time' (1996: 464). The computer screen, which is the great symbol of our era, embodies it, a picture technology *par excellence*, window piled upon window without temporal relation: pure image.

This technologically fed 'timeless time', this corporate behaviour based on now, only now, is a capitalist regime that ought to suit perfectly the classical sociological impulse to freeze time, to describe and analyse an image. The modern political economy *is* a picture language. However, the very immediacy of the image is repressive.

Let me give an example from the computer programs used in hi-tech production. These programs are designed so that their users can touch very simple icons on the screen to perform operations. This use of icons suits a workforce marked by high rates of turnover, because the learning curve is short. Such computerisation makes the work instantly understandable – but to believe this is to judge the present by the standards of industrial machines of the past. The modern systems are 'opaque' to low-level operatives, in that they cannot understand the guts of the program, much less alter it. In my research, I studied this opacity in a computerised bakery. The operatives work by pressing simple screen icons, but these bakers do not know how to bake bread. The bread is good quality, but the work is deskilled and inspires little craft attachment. As one operative told me: 'One button is much like the next. Anyhow, in six months I'm out of here'. Such operatives do not, like an earlier generation of bakers I studied in 1970 in the same plant, derive much sense of identity from their work. Picture-work represses it.

Picture-work, moreover, is out of synch with the working human body which, like any organism, grows and decays. Living creatures are not fixed images. This is why I have found so much frustration among people who have undertaken temporary or part-time work for several years. These are not untypical workers – as such work constitutes the fastest-growing component of the American and British labour markets (see, for example, Cully *et al.*, 1998 for UK data). Unlike temporary workers who have only been working in this way for a little while, and who are initially exhilarated by its freedom, people who spend many years engaged in the disconnected, fixed-character transactions of temporary work feel that they are failing to develop their skills and failing to develop social relationships through work. Indeed, despite the fact they are continually in demand, people who do temporary work for more than five or six years feel themselves devalued, unless rescued by the offer of long-term employment, which means a chance to develop a life-history through work.

For such reasons, the picture experience of work – technologically embodied in simplified screen labour, sociologically manifest in unrelated transactions such as temporary work which establishes no sustained human relations – arouses in workers a sense of detachment and drift. The picture experience of work lacks depth and principles of forward movement. Instead, the experience of working-time in flexible capitalism consists of dissociated, serial events. It might be said that work under the aegis of 'timeless time' is static – but this stasis differs in substance from older forms of mechanical routine. Rather than being repetitive, the work in the bakery changes every day as orders for different kinds of bread come in. Similarly, a temporary worker might flit from place to place. In both cases, flexibility suffers from a lack of direction: without forward movement, time is serial, random, and so 'static' in the original Greek sense of the word as time experienced without direction.

I have, I know, emphasised the negative side of such labour. But I do so because the dominion of picture-work challenges critical sociology to question its own habits of picturing. To deal with the human deficits of work in flexible capitalism requires emphasis on time's arrow. From its origins, sociology has of course grappled with issues of historical change, but narrative is a special category of time, not identical with history.

Narrating

I could not hope to present a full sociological theory of narrative in a single chapter. Let me say here only that narrative differs from the sheer unfolding of the life-course or the chronicle of historical events in that storytelling supposes a narrator who comments on or interprets the passage of time. In fiction, the narrator has complete freedom to do so, whereas in real life he or she obviously does not. This is why, in studying real-world narratives, we are interested in the question of voice of the person who, in an interview, tells us a story. We ask ourselves how this person struggles with events beyond his or her own making and incorporates them into a story which implicates the narrator as an active participant. Technically, the study of real-world narratives focuses on *agency* — in other words, on the act of narrating.

Work in flexible capitalism increases the difficulty of narrating, making it hard for people to incorporate their work experience as their own story. To illustrate this difficulty of narrating a work-history I would like to focus on a particular dilemma of modern work: redundancy. In my interviews, people's sharpest and most forceful reactions to the flexible work experience focused on this issue. Workers who have been downsized are obviously traumatised, but among survivors the fear of losing one's work in future is almost as strong. 'I just wait for the next blow of the axe', one secretary told me. Loss of work is modern capitalism's ticking bomb. Yet the workers with whom I have talked do not know how to fit this traumatic event into the telling of a story about their work-histories.

Some experimental novelists in our era have dealt with issues of fragmented time, ephemeral immediacy, and incoherence – issues similar to the problems real people face in telling a story based on their work-histories. There is a gap, however, between the power of experimental writers to narrate incoherent time, and the inability of people in flexibly organised accounting firms, computerised bakeries or fast-food shops to fashion a life-narrative. The very divide between art and life is revealing: it tells us something about life, particularly about the lives of the unemployed. Real-world difficulties of narrating appear around three issues: the sense of personal derailment which occurs when people lose their jobs; the frustration in holding others responsible for losing a job; the lack of solidarity between the employed and the unemployed.

Derailment

Let me start with derailment. A distinguished Harvard Business School professor, John Kotter (1997), recently wrote blithely about downsizing, counselling his readers to just forget it and go on to the next job, because in the flexible workplace job loss should be regarded as a normal, expected event. In one way this counsel borders on idiocy. It assumes people make no personal investment in working and do not care what they do so long as they are employed. In another way, it is wise. When work ends, as in any trauma, people need to fashion some distance between self and event. I have noticed, in interviews with workers who capably handle rejection, one signature narrative ploy: they interpret their work as concluding rather than consummating in dismissal.

Literary narratives illuminate the distinction between conclusion and consummation. In Borges' short stories about libraries, for instance, there reappear moments when the librarian closes a book before finishing it. The tale is not so mesmerising that it crowds out everything else; the librarian does not need to know how the story ends. In Calvino's (1974) *Invisible Cities*, unlike the 1985–6 translation of *Arabian Nights* by Burton, each story that the narrator tells trails off at the end. The narrator starts by painting clear pictures of different cities and then loses interest or becomes fuzzy in his telling and so starts again. Eventually, the narrator gives up on finding an all-consuming story. The effect of narrative closure is to draw a line between the teller and the told, and to empower the teller of the tale. With both Borges and Calvino, we become ever more aware of the presence of the narrator narrating.

Sometimes a similarly strong narrative voice can be heard in interviews with people who are coping well with unemployment. They empower themselves by stepping back from the mesmerising power of events. Specifically, they step back by refusing to view everything during their period of employment as moving inexorably toward dismissal. Here is an example of how that can happen in an interview, in even a minute fashion: a secretary told me that, 'As X was explaining why they had to let me go, I noticed the wart on his nose seemed darker'. In evoking the wart, she signalled that she was not succumbing to the event. Nonetheless, relatively few workers react in so measured a fashion – or so I have found, as have, in different ways, the sociologists Katherine Newman (1988) and William Julius Wilson (1998). The loss of work feels like a terrible judgement on most people, even when rationally they know they may have simply been the victims of circumstances.

The reason for this reaction is in one way evident: people who invest themselves in their work cannot act as casually as Borges' librarian closing his book. The larger problem is the cultural storehouse of narrative stories people draw on to explain their investment in work. These established stories have no meaning given the realities of flexible capitalism. When people tell them, they lose the sense of self-empowerment.

Let me try to elucidate what must seem an abstract formula by citing the classic work ethic as described by Max Weber (1930). Here is a story in which each phase of work contributes in a cumulative fashion to an ultimate consummation; the worker practises self-discipline for the sake of achieving future goals, such as house ownership or promotion. On the face of it, this classic tale, still the most compelling of those in our cultural storehouse, empowers those who believe in it. There is indeed a positive side to the classic work ethic: it is a long-term interpretative strategy which allows employees to plan, as well as to cope with present injustices by working toward a self-defined transformation in the future. The negative side is that this linear work ethic arouses intense anxiety about falling off course. A particular stumble or defeat may mean that the employee can never regain his or her footing. Calvino's narrator feels he can start over again and again; dismissed workers, particularly the middle-aged, fear they cannot.

The fear is certainly grounded in reality. Middle-aged workers fear their skills may be outdated, and that they are losing the energy to struggle. They know employers now prefer younger, cheaper, more raw labour whenever possible. And Weber's version of the work ethic addresses a problem in the substance of work which compounds these material fears.

Save for only a few lucky individuals, most labour is not likely to be gratifying in itself. Mundane work such as reckoning Visa bills all day or making telephone sales acquires meaning only if it moves to an end, serves a purpose, reaches a goal. Self-discipline at work lacks the playful, interruptible character of those engagements from which, in fiction, a character can withdraw. When people are denied a long-term story with a denouement, when they feel derailed, they wonder what all their self-discipline has been about. A file clerk remarked to me: 'Suddenly a machine did my job better and they let me go, and the first thing I thought was, what a fool I was those days I stayed at the office extra time just to get the job done'. Work loss constitutes a moment of narrative betrayal; this clerk's presence, her self-discipline meant little in the story of her work.

Making good on self-discipline may seem to require a career, however humble its content. That is the factual precondition for this work-narrative, yet it is the very possibility of career that flexible capitalism weakens. And so the negative side of the story comes forward, the fear of derailment dwells in people's minds. In narrative terms, the Weberian work ethic, while seeming so self-empowering, in fact makes those who tell it as the story of their own lives entirely dependent on events beyond their own control.

Responsibility for job loss

The lack of a work ethic which would strengthen narrative voice leads to my next issue: how people go about assigning responsibility for job loss. The dismissed can simply blame themselves, but that usually cannot suffice. After all, they have been fired by an organisation. Again, we could easily imagine the act of assigning responsibility to be just like that of attributing authorship to a picture, but workers out of a job cannot think this way. Either they want to find out what they did wrong in the past in order not to repeat the mistake, or they want to understand the work circumstances in which they were formerly placed so that they do not enter, if possible, into the same conditions again. In both cases, the issue of accountability is set in the minds of workers between jobs in the framework of time, of connecting the past to the future. A narrative thus emerges because accountability is inseparable from starting a new chapter.

Transitions between chapters are not much of a problem in a traditionally well-made story. The well-crafted plot is an efficient machine in which every incident contributes to the forward movement of the story. When such a plot is written, it foreshadows events and ensures that all the loose ends are tied up by the last page; cause and effect are self-explanatory. When your rich spinster Aunt Jeanette suddenly dies in a car crash, all your problems are solved. In a more experimental narrative, you may inherit nothing but notice at her funeral that you have recently lost weight. You will ask why, what is responsible for your clothes fitting, what is the connection between death and diet? You have to ponder harder on those questions than do characters in a well-made tale.

Yet the signal mark of literary modernism is to refuse an explanation. When a rupture occurs and a character asks 'Who or what is responsible for this?', the story does not answer. The model here is James Joyce (1922). When even a tiny rupture occurs in the day of Joyce's Leopold Bloom, he questions each break, searching for the thread connecting the fragments of his experience, and we read forward, precisely to see how he will be defeated in his attempts to find an explanation.

It may seem odd to connect a fine Victorian word like 'responsibility' with the practices of experimental fiction. Yet questions of accountability are inherent in breaking the well-made mould. For present purposes, of greater import is the modern novelist's disposition to frustrate the desire for an answer. This disposition helps to provide an understanding of how the quest for accountability takes on a much darker hue in the real world of labour. Let me take one aspect of the unemployment experience to show why.

It used to be the case in the United States that when an employee went out of the door, he or she severed all connection with the corporation. Businesses no longer leave these breaks unattended, because employee anger – given vent to in the middle ranks, for instance, by telling a business's secrets to a competitor – is too great a threat. An outsourcing business has developed to make the employee, if not feel good about the rupture, then at least use it, as the therapists of the unemployed often say, as a 'creative pause'.

This development may seem Joycean. Understandably, outsourcing focuses entirely on the practical aim of getting the employee back to work. Outsourcing specialists seek to deflect employees from reasoning too much about what caused them to be fired, or acting on the anger and sense of betrayal inspired by their employers – that would be counterproductive in the effort to get the dismissed person a new job.

If the Joycean writer is bent on defeating explanations, so, it might be said, is the flexible employer. Flexible businesses seek to avoid being evaluated and held accountable by their employees. Evasion is built into the structure of flexible organisations. Instead of commands passed clearly down a hierarchy military-fashion, modern management practice utilises, for instance, sports metaphors of teamwork to disguise the boss's power. The authority of a boss who behaves as though he or she is only trying to coach the employee to do his or her best is harder to challenge than a boss who says 'Do this or else'. More generally, the flexible organisation uses peer pressure when it comes to the performance required to meet tasks or productivity goals: an entire team is punished if a particular individual fails. Peer pressure tends to deflect people from reckoning the legitimacy of commands themselves. Abstract market forces are used in a similar way to veil authority and so enable responsibility to be evaded. The most cunning person I encountered in the course of my research, for instance, was a consultant who remarked placidly in the midst of staging a corporate downsizing: 'We are all victims of time and place'.

Nevertheless, employees who suffer loss of work, particularly middle-aged employees, do not forget, neatly filing away questions of accountability as unanswerable. For both personal or institutional reasons, employees do not want the future to repeat the past. A blank wall confronts workers seeking to evaluate their difficulties in prior work, and yet this past reckoning is crucial for making decisions about the future. Such employees cannot afford to be Joycean, yet it is hard to narrate a story in which an accounting of responsibility mediates between past and future. Moreover, in Joyce's world, the defeats of explanation have the paradoxical effect of joining the characters together; they stop judging and get on with the business of living together. The defeat of accountability in the real world of work is something, however, which employees face alone.

At present, there exists neither effective institutional allies who might help workers hold workplaces accountable, nor forums for workers to explore more intimately loss, injustice, or betrayal. Middle-level managers simply lack such organisations. Lower-level workers are poorly served, in my view, by most trade unions – arthritic and bureaucratic organisations, deaf to the actual confusions of work. Concretely, there exists in America no trade union specifically for the unemployed. Moreover, few modern labour parties have sought to hold employers responsible for their downsizings or redundancies – it is certainly not part of the 'third way', whether politically or academically articulated (see Blair, 1998 and Giddens, 1998 respectively).

The issue of accountability certainly presents the opportunity for a more vigorous Left politics. I have invoked the matter of narrative connections to emphasise the point that the experience of past and future time is what makes the politics of accountability resonate personally. But I must confess to a certain unease in invoking this political opening.

Solidarity

Those of us on the Left are good at exposing the evils of the Capitalist Monster, but we are less forthright in acknowledging today a breakdown in solidarity among workers themselves. The economist Stephan Roach (2000) has been forthright about this breakdown: given the disorganisation flexible capitalism wreaks in people's lives, people should be up in arms, but they are not. The act of narrating helps us understand why.

Solidarity is a much deeper matter than simply sharing the same opinions; it involves sharing a history. In the fleeting world of flexible capitalism, however, people's shared histories are short, too short for the time conditions of solidarity to develop. Moreover, there is a refusal to recognise this shared plight, and that is where the narrator's voice comes in.

To explain this, permit me for the last time to invoke the writing of fictional narrative. Solidarity has a particular literary meaning. It is a matter of weaving characters together through plot events so that by the end of the story the reader cannot imagine each character without reference to the others. Even the experimental novelist whose materials are fragments, moments, absences, silences, strives to create that mutual referencing. In a classic experimental novel of my youth, *The Dead Father* (1977), the author Donald Barthelme creates this solidarity by shoving the rough edges of events and conflict between characters to the fore – a father's hostility in one episode succeeded in the next by a husband's betrayal, succeeded by a child's lies. No linear progression orders these fragments, but still the characters begin to knit together in time as the reader moves from one rough exposure to the next. The same procedure marks much of the theatrical work of Harold Pinter today, and the last, autobiographical poetry of Ted Hughes. By the end of *The Dead Father*, as in Pinter's plays, as in Hughes' account of his disastrous marriage to Sylvia Plath, the reader cannot imagine the characters apart.

This is an art of confrontation, and in real work-life, that art is not practised. I have given some reasons why flexible employers try to shield themselves from challenge. Short-term work in itself has a deeply corrosive effect on solidarity. In general, 'It's only for a few months' is a formula which suspends reality. In particular, there is no time for solidarity based on informal trust to develop. Informal trust is needed, for instance, when a company sets an impossible production target or a crisis develops: employees have to know then who they can count on and who is likely to go to pieces. Such knowledge takes time to develop, and short-term workers lack it. Indeed, modern management practice advocates limiting the time teams work together precisely to prevent the growth of bonds of informal mutual solidarity which might lead members of the team to commit more to each other than to the company.

This aborted time lies in the realm of history. As a narrative problem, weakened solidarity concerns the refusal of workers to admit that they are characters in the same story, facing common problems. The experience of redundant workers helps to provide an understanding of why solidarity weakens among workers themselves.

A dismissed engineer described to me how he returned to his old firm a year after he had been let go: 'When people saw me in the hall, they dived into their offices and closed the door. It was like I was bad news, I was going to reproach them for still being there.' Are these former colleagues just bloody-minded? That would be too moralistic an explanation. Workers who survive a downsizing do indeed shun contact with their former fellow workers out of fear of confrontation, but they do so, I have found, out of fear of confronting their own situation. 'I can't handle it', one of those engineers diving for the office admitted to me. But what is the 'it' that she could not handle? Downsizings are usually irrational events; survivors know that they have been retained less for their merits than for boardroom reasons which have little to do with their work. Their situation precarious, survivors act like cancer patients in remission, living on borrowed time. Contact with those already let go provides a disturbing reminder of what may lie ahead for them, and what complicates this reaction and increases its importance, is the capitalist culture in which it occurs.

That capitalist culture joins experience in the present to individualism. By breaking ties with the past, an individual can engage in entrepreneurial exploit, but at the price of leaving others behind, of breaking ties to them. This is the social side of what Schumpeter (1976) called 'creative destruction'. Corporations continually remaking themselves are engaged in collective forgetting; institutional memory seems a drag, and people with long memories of how things used to be done are thought of as dead wood. Or at least, this is how it appears looking from the top downward.

However, for people down in the guts of corporations, the joining of present-tense time and individualism is not energising. Rather, it suspends reality. If an employee keeps his or her head down by dwelling on the immediate moment, the burdens of memory are lightened, the fear of the future somewhat diminished. The culture of flexible capitalism encourages the employee to think in the present tense, and individually, but for that employee down below, this is a defensive manoeuvre.

This is what the engineer meant when she told me 'I can't handle it'. Solidarity was less compelling, less necessary to her, than self-defence. This trade-off has proved more largely pervasive in modern work relations. In succumbing to the dominant ethos of the present tense and individualism, individuals are hoping to distance themselves from work conditions over which they have little control – and so they forego becoming part of another person's story.

Concluding remarks

If I had entitled this chapter 'The crisis of modern capitalism is a crisis of narrative', it would certainly have seemed pure verbiage. Nevertheless, I hope that I have demonstrated that this theme invokes serious and pressing issues.

I have tried to highlight the relationship between time and work in this new political economy: work which is short term in institutions focused on flexible change, on sudden disruptions and revisions of their structure, on immediate circumstances. To grasp the consequences for workers of this organisation of time, I have argued that sociologists have to redirect their habits of thinking about social reality; they must focus less on its imagery and more on the orchestration of time. Of course no one would argue against the proposition that historical experience is important. But narrative is a peculiar organisation of time, and narrating a story raises knotty questions about personal agency. I have tried to bring these questions forward by contrasting experiments in narrating time in modern fiction with the difficulty of narrating actual work experience. In real work, people suffer from their weakness as narrators. The particular case of those who have lost work shows, I hope, the larger difficulties that the narrating voice encounters in speaking about self-discipline, accountability and solidarity.

To be sure, insecurity is a fundamental fact of all social life, and capitalism for most of its long history has been erratic. The creation of large-scale work bureaucracies in the early part of the twentieth century may seem to future historians to have been no more than a deviation from this norm. But the current ethos of capitalism is one in which disorder appears desirable. Continual restructuring of firms, for instance, is taken as a sign of vigour, a necessity for growth. All human beings cope with insecurity as best they can by taking strategic action. In flexible capitalism, middle-level workers in particular have difficulty formulating effective strategies for themselves. My observation is that this difficulty arises in large part because their experience of lived time is so confused. My argument is that it is also because workers lack the interpretative tools to make sense of the confusion.

Though I have no mastery of social policy, it seems to me that the crisis of narrative defines a political turning point. Labour movements and labour parties have to address current developments in work as these developments are actually experienced by individuals as employees. To do so requires a different, less materialistic, more humanistic approach to work than is evident in most public discussion today. It is the task of sociologists to engage and influence that public discussion.

Note

1 Quotes taken from the aforementioned book – Sennett (1998).

References

Barthelme, D. (1977) *The Dead Father*. London: Routledge and Kegan Paul

Blair, T. (1998) *The Third Way: New Politics for a New Century*. London: Fabian Society

Burton, R. (1885–86) *Arabian Nights*. New York: Random House

Calvino, I. (1974) *Invisible Cities*. London: Picador

Castells, M. (1996) *The Information Age – Economy, Society and Culture. Volume 1: The Rise of the Network Society*. Oxford: Blackwell

Cully, M., O'Reilly, A., Millward, N., Forth, J., Woodland, S., Dix, G. and Bryson, A. (1998) *The 1998 Workplace Employee Relations Survey: First Findings*. London: HMSO

Giddens, A. (1998) *The Third Way: The Renewal of Social Democracy*. Oxford: Polity Press/Blackwell

Harrison, B. (1994) *Lean and Mean: The Changing Landscape of Corporate Power in the Age of Flexibility*. New York: Guildford Press

Joyce, J. (1922) *Ulysses*. New York: John Lane, 1936

Kotter, J. (1997) *The New Rules*. London: Scribner

Newman, K. (1988) *Falling from Grace: The Experience of Downward Mobility in the American Middle Class*. London: Collier Macmillan

Roach, S. (2000) 'Working Better or Just Harder?', *New York Times*, 14 February

Schumpeter, J.A. (1976) *Capitalism, Socialism and Democracy*. New York: Harper and Row

Sennett, R. (1972) *The Hidden Injuries of Class*. Cambridge: Cambridge University Press

Sennett, R. (1998) *The Corrosion of Character*. London: W.W. Norton

Tocqueville, A., de (1990) *Democracy in America, Volume 2*. New York: Vintage Books

US Department of Labor (1991) *What Work Requires of School: A SCANS Report for America 2000*. Washington: US Department of Labor

Weber, M. (1930) *Protestant Ethic and the Spirit of Capitalism*. London: Allen and Unwin

Weber, M. (1949) *The Methodology of the Social Sciences*. New York: Free Press

Wilson, W.J. (1998) *When Work Disappears: New Implications for Race and Urban Poverty in the Global Economy*. New York: Random House

Wittgenstein, L. (1963) *Philosophical Investigations*. Oxford: Blackwell

Chapter 8
Sociology and the Third Way
John Eldridge

> In many European countries, politicians are trying to go 'beyond left and right' to a Third Way. Most of its protagonists have a close relationship to what in Britain is called New Labour, or sometimes 'the Blair project'. In fact, the Third Way debate has become the only game in town – the only hint at new directions for Europe's politics in a confused multitude of trends and ideas.
> (Dahrendorf, 1999: 13)

Durkheim

It is 1896. Emile Durkheim is bringing his lectures on socialism to a close. Socialism, he has told his students at Bordeaux, is not scientific but it can be an object of science, the science of sociology. Socialism gives a clue to the social conditions in which it emerged, even though it does not accurately depict them:

> On the contrary ... we can be certain that it refracts them involuntarily and gives us only an unfaithful impression, just as a sick man faultily interprets the feelings that he experiences and most often attributes them to a cause which is not the true one. But these feelings, such as they are, have their interest, and the clinician notes them with great care and takes them seriously. They are an element in the diagnosis and an important one.
> (Durkheim, 1962: 42)

Durkheim has also made clear that he is not just interested in diagnosis but in remedies. Socialism, indeed, is one of his famous social facts, part of the very subject matter of sociology.

Socialism, for Durkheim, is an aspiration for transforming the existing social structure, bringing the economy and industrial organisation into a position where they could be consciously regulated by the state, for society. 'There is no workers' socialism which does not demand a greater development of the state; there is no state socialism disinterested in workers. They are just varieties of the same genus' (Durkheim, 1962: 62). However, socialism goes beyond the economic: it has implications for every sphere of society – what Benoît Malon, whom Durkheim cites, had called 'integral socialism'. It includes such matters as a demand for a more democratic organisation of society, more liberty in marriage relations, juridical equality of the sexes, a more altruistic morality, and so on.

Great portions of Durkheim's lectures are given over to the exposition of Saint-Simon, for whom he had great admiration (more, it would appear, than for Comte). He thus goes back to the early nineteenth century. Indeed, Durkheim's insight on social crises and his use of the concept of anomie are clearly stimulated by Saint-Simon's concern to establish a morality suitable for the new industrial society. While the old religious systems were breaking down, there was a great need for moral regulation and the social transformation that went with it. From Christianity, Saint-Simon had taken the aphorism 'love one another' (the motto of *système industriel*), but he looked for the establishment of an earthly and practical morality and the development and application of the spirit of altruism. So, in a comment on the difference between this kind of socialism and communism, Durkheim (1962: 210) writes approvingly of:

> the altogether different direction that Saint-Simon, and later socialism, seeks to construct a new society. It is by doing away with the poor that he intends to reconcile the two classes. Far from seeing something desirable in temporal well-being, he makes it the only desirable goal. Consequently, the only way to establish social harmony is to produce the greatest riches possible, in order to satisfy the greatest possible needs as completely as possible.

This position might be considered to be the harbinger of the inclusive society – the concept of social harmony clearly belongs to such thinking. In more modern language we might see it as a programme of economic growth which creates a society of abundance that is happily possible through the elimination of poverty. Certainly, it chimes with the Blair–Schröder maxim of wealth creation and social cohesion (Dahrendorf, 1999). Unlike the economics of the market, which is inherently selfish and divisive, the possibility is put forward that through social regulation and moral transformation, the economic can be subordinated to the social, and social solidarity can be assured.

But neither Saint-Simon nor Durkheim thought of French society in isolation. The question of internationalism, especially in a European context, is raised. These societies cannot be isolated from one another – they share so much in common. At the same time, they also exist in competition and rivalry, even to the point of war. The industrial society could and should become the pacific society, but disarmament must apply to all. For Saint-Simon, national rivalries and passions of ferocious and absurd patriotism needed to be overcome. Indeed, Durkheim (1962: 217) reminds us that Saint-Simon did not restrict his thinking to Europe:

> He glimpses in the future the formation of a society that would include all men and would undertake the systematic exploitation of the earth, which he calls the territorial property of human kind. This, however, is a dream that is dear to him and which, from time to time, crosses his mind – but which he does not conceive as realisable for the present.

Durkheim does not agree with all Saint-Simon's views, particularly those on the role of religion. Nevertheless, he is sympathetic to the diagnosis and, as is well known, argues for the importance of collective forces as forms of moral regulation that can stem the crisis of industrial societies. Thus, against Saint-Simon's form of socialism, but also against the status quo, he offers another way:

Sociology and the Third Way

> It is not a matter of putting a completely new society in the place of the existing one, but of adapting the latter to new social conditions. At least, it no longer stirs question of classes; it no longer opposes rich to poor, employers to workers – as if the only possible solution consisted of diminishing the portion of one in order to augment the other. But it declares, in the interests of both, the necessity of a curb from above which checks appetites and so sets a limit on the state of disarrangement, excitement, frenzied agitation, which do not spring from social activity and which even make it suffer. Put differently, the social question, posed this way, is not a question of money or force; it is a question of moral agents. What dominates it is not the state of our economy but, much more, the state of our morality.
> (Durkheim, 1962: 246)

When he comes to the end of his lectures, Durkheim is wanting to make the case for sociology. He notes that alongside the idea of applying social science (and sociology in particular) to the study of society, there have coexisted ideas about religious regeneration and socialism:

> We begin to wonder whether these theses appear and are regarded as contradictory simply because each expresses only one aspect of social reality, and, unaware of its fragmentary nature, believes itself the only one – and is consequently irreconcilable with any other. Actually, what does the development of sociology signify? How does it happen that we experience the need to reflect on social matters, if not because our social state is abnormal, because the unsettled collective organisation no longer functions with the authority of instinct – for that is what always determines the rousing of scientific thought and its extension to a new order of things.
> (Durkheim, 1962: 284)

Religion and socialism both represent systems of values, one from a moral perspective and the other from an economic. Yet for Durkheim, the positivist, normative element in sociology remains and provides more hope than the other two. He concludes:

> The problem must be put in this way: to discover through science the moral restraint which can regulate economic life, and by this regulation control selfishness and thus gratify needs ... In addition to the various paths on which we expend our energies, there is another that can be tried. It is sufficient to have indicated it.
> (Durkheim, 1962: 285)

This might be described as Durkheim's Third Way. It is a way of social reconstruction based on the science of sociology.

Hobhouse

It is 1911. The British sociologist, Leonard Trelawny Hobhouse, who in 1906 had become the first Professor of Sociology at the London School of Economics (LSE), has just published his book *Liberalism*. Whilst he drew intellectual sustenance from J.S. Mill and T.H. Green, his is a conscious attempt to recognise the limitations of the old nineteenth-century liberalism and present a new liberalism for a young generation at the beginning of the twentieth century. It is a liberalism of the Left, sometimes described as Liberal Socialism. It represents a rejection of *laissez-faire* liberalism and of economically deterministic socialism, but it recognises the role of the state in empowering rather than repressing the individual, not least for its potential to develop policies for education and social welfare for the general good of its citizens. There is a strong rejection of imperialism, and criticism of the liberals who had become imperialists in their sleep. He was writing in the wake of the Boer War and with the experience of the reforming Liberal Government of Campbell-Bannerman who, against the imperialists, had revived the idea of social justice, was anti-militarist and opposed to the methods of war. It is a period of Liberal revival in Britain. So he writes (and it is difficult to refrain from quoting at length):

> *The tide has by no means spent itself. If it no longer rushes in an electoral torrent as in 1906 it flows in a steady stream towards social amelioration and democratic government. In this movement it is now sufficiently clear to all parties that the distinctive ideas of Liberalism have a permanent function. The socialist recognises with perfect clearness, for example, that popular government is not a meaningless shibboleth, but a reality that has to be maintained and extended by fighting. He is well aware that he must deal with the House of Lords and the Plural vote if he is to gain his own ends. He can no longer regard these questions as difficulties imposed by half-hearted Liberals to distract attention from the Social problem. He is aware that the problem of Home rule and of devolution generally is an integral part of the organisation of democracy. And, as a rule, he not merely acquiesces in the demand of women for a purely political right, but only quarrels with the Liberal party for its tardiness in meeting the demand. The old Liberal idea of peace and retrenchment again is recognised by the Socialistic, and indeed by the whole body of social reformers, as equally essential for the successful prosecution of their aims. Popular budgets will bring no relief to human suffering if the revenues that they secure are all to go upon the most expensive ship that is the fashion of the moment, nor can the popular mind devote itself to the improvement of domestic conditions while it is distracted either by ambitions or scares. On the other side, the Liberal ... has to acknowledge that [Free Trade] has not solved the problems of unemployment or underpayment, or overcrowding. He has to look deeper into the meaning of liberty and to take account of the bearing of actual conditions on the meaning of equality. As an apostle of peace and an opponent of swollen armaments, he has come to recognise that the expenditure of the social surplus upon the instruments of progress is a real alternative to its expenditure on the instruments of war.*
> (Hobhouse, 1964: 114–5)

As we consider this passage with the benefit of hindsight and in the light of our present situation there is a double irony. Firstly, it was written just three years before the First World War, and the subsequent breakup of the Liberal Party itself – we can recall George Dangerfield's (1936) *The Strange Death of Liberal England*. So much hope for the possibilities of a new century, not least the belief in progress, was to be destroyed. Yet Hobhouse did know, whatever disillusionment he may have felt in later years, that democracy was always something to be struggled and fought for against authoritarian tendencies and the forces of monopoly capital. He sketched out a political agenda of social reform based on his views of social justice, and in a way that was more engaged than Durkheim. But both of them had the issue of social justice at the centre of their thinking. They thought through the importance of social reconstruction, the moral problem of the relationship between the individual and society and the role of the state in modern industrial societies.

The second irony relates to our present position, and the issues of citizenship, social justice, peace and war, and social welfare that still confront us. For Hobhouse it was new Liberalism; today it is New Labour. Yet the terrain is much the same. The aim of extending democracy through devolution and constitutionalism is present. And, not least, the issue of internationalism is evident, with a concern for an ethical foreign policy and a quest for peaceful methods of settling international disputes. The newness for Hobhouse represented a new liberalism, a new coming together of progressive forces, a new direction. He writes of 'the vision of justice in the wholeness of her beauty' (Hobhouse, 1964: 127). From his organic view of the nature of society he reminds us of the way in which there are interrelationships which need to be taken into account:

> *we cannot maintain political progress without some corresponding advance on other sides. People are not fully free in their political capacity when they are subject industrially to conditions which take the life and heart out of them. A nation as a whole cannot be in the full sense free while it fears or gives cause of fear to another. The social problem must be viewed as a whole.*
> (Hobhouse, 1964: 126)

Mannheim

It is 1941. Karl Mannheim, the noted author of *Ideology and Utopia*, has been in England since 1933. Formerly Professor of Sociology at Frankfurt he was a political refugee from Nazi Germany and now holds an appointment at the LSE. Less than two years into the Second World War, he gives a lecture entitled 'Diagnosis of Our Time'. This is published in 1943 with other material, in a book of the same title, subtitled *Wartime Essays of a Sociologist*. In the Preface he writes:

> *There are constellations in history in which certain possibilities have their chance, and if these are missed the opportunity may well be gone for ever. Just as the revolutionary waits for his hour, the reformer whose concern it is to remould society by peaceful means must seize his passing chance. For years it has been my conviction, which I have tried to bring home in my lectures and other activities, that Britain has the chance and the mission to develop a new pattern of society, and that it is necessary that we should become aware of it and act upon it.*
> (Mannheim, 1943: ix)

In his lecture, Mannheim argues that the transition from a *laissez-faire* to a planned society poses both threats and opportunities for the wellbeing of democracy. The threat is one of dictatorship through planning; the opportunity is that of democratic planning for freedom. This opportunity is what Mannheim explicitly terms 'the third way'. It is an escape from unplanned market mechanisms and also from the mass society (shades here of the Frankfurt School) of whatever political coloration. In a sense the concept of the Third Way, which receives extended treatment in Mannheim's (1951) *Freedom, Power and Democratic Planning*, can be seen as a practical follow-through of the discussion in his earlier *Ideology and Utopia,* in which ideological and utopian systems of thought are seen as failing to understand social reality. In 1936 he is struggling with the issue of relativism and the role of the intelligentsia; in 1941, in time of war, it is as though the chips are down. He describes the Third Way as a militant democracy. It has to fight dictatorship and exhibit basic virtues and values that are the basis of a peaceful social order. He mentions brotherly love, mutual help, decency, social justice, freedom and respect for the person. Tolerance within a democratic framework is praiseworthy, but tolerance of dictatorships in the name of liberalism is not. It was the Nazi system that had brought Mannheim to the view that democracies have a set of values in common which can be stated and agreed on. Yet within that framework, in a complex, differentiated modern society: 'it is better to leave the more complicated values open to creed, individual choice or free experimentation ... the more complex issues will be left open to save us from the evil effects of fanaticism' (Mannheim, 1943: 7–8). He goes on to claim that such a new social order could be developed if the coming generation had the courage, imagination and will to move in this direction. This new social order includes an approach to social justice which, while not egalitarian, tries to deal with the increasing disproportion of income and wealth in the national system of stratification.

Fascism and the Second World War are the context for and the stimulus to Mannheim's thinking. Since he is looking forward to new possibilities, it is linked to a preoccupation with questions of education and the young generation. It is typical that when, in *Freedom, Power and Democratic Planning,* he writes of the Third Way approach to education, he treats it as a creative open-minded approach to knowledge, antidogmatic in its spirit. Nevertheless, he comments: 'Correctly understood, such an open-minded system leads not to relativism, but to a deeper understanding of intellectual life as advancing toward an ever-broadening outlook' (Mannheim, 1951: 256). Like Durkheim, he mostly claims only to point in the direction of the Third Way; but, also like Durkheim, the language of social reconstruction comes readily to his lips. It is no accident that when he becomes founding editor of the long-running Routledge series, it is called the *International Library of Sociology and Social Reconstruction.*

Freedom, Power and Democratic Planning was published posthumously (1951) and contains a thoughtful note on Mannheim by Ernest Bramstedt and Hans Gerth. They point out that the institutional foundations of Mannheim's new society required full employment, social security, educational opportunity and a peaceful world order. However, questions of values led him into discussions with Christian thinkers such as T.S. Eliot, Middleton Murry and J.H. Oldham. It also led him to reflect on the ways in which the 'democratic personality' could be developed and emerge. This reflection is set against concerns about the fragmentation of the self and the loss of meaning as discussed, for example, in Fromm's (1941) *Escape from Freedom*. We might say that Mannheim anticipated themes associated with discussions of postmodernism: 'Endless uncertainty leading to relativism and nihilism on the one hand and to orthodoxy on the other are just two sides of the same coin, different reactions to the same disturbing process which we call the crisis in valuation' (1951: 308). For him the way through this was the third way, a way of living with change.

It is nonetheless revealing that Bramstedt and Gerth have a sense of the class-related nature of this third way, even though they are sympathetic to the Mannheim project. In their comment it is possible to discern a parallel between the radical centre of the Blair third way project and what is involved in Mannheim's position:

> The middle classes, whose existence is bound up with a 'third way' between reaction and revolution, supplemented by free-lancing groups of intellectual elites and skilled groups of expert planners, are the spearheads of the transition toward the new society. A democratically selected planning elite can work out the optimum balance between centralised authority and delegation of power to local and regional agencies. A bold social education for life and reconstruction of the ruling elites by the planned admixture of socially ascending groups are to pave the way toward the good society.
> (Mannheim, 1951: xiii)

Dahrendorf

It is 1975. Ralf Dahrendorf, academic sociologist and German liberal politician (he served a term as an EC commissioner) is Director of the LSE, where he was once a graduate student. He has been chosen to give the Reith Lectures, which are published later that year as *The New Liberty: Survival and justice in a changing world*. His commitment to the concept and practice of liberty is plain and pays tribute to J.S. Mill, to his former teacher Karl Popper, and – with qualifications – to Milton Friedman. What is this new liberty? It is 'the politics of regulated conflict, and the socio-economics of maximising life chances. But it has come about in conditions which are so different from those we have seen in the past that an older liberal approach is about to lose its relevance' (Dahrendorf, 1975: 6). He writes in the wake of the energy crisis of 1973 triggered by the Yom Kippur War and the powerful emergence of the Arab states into world politics. Connected with it, but only in part, is the phenomenon of inflation and the potential this has for social disruption, even the re-emergence of fascism. Moreover, the problem of inflation has to be seen against the danger of world recession, strains on the world's monetary system and concerns about investment strategies. These matters are foregrounded to represent a turbulent world of uncertainty fraught with danger. And, there is more: overpopulation, waste of resources, nuclear weapons, pollution. As if in anticipation of Beck's (1992) *Risk Society*, Dahrendorf (1975: 69) comments: 'The forces of enlightened rationality seemed to have turned against their best purpose'. The notion of advanced industrial societies simply expanding without thought has to be rejected, as have simplistic notions of progress. Neither positions offer the way of survival. The potential for illiberalism is all around and with it the loss of social justice. Dahrendorf lists 'the wrong kind of socialism' as one of the threats being posed, and emphasises liberty in a way that downgrades equality (and in this respect he is notably different from Hobhouse or Tawney before him).

Despite his suspicions about utopian thought, Dahrendorf still contends that it is important to have images of the future:

> Is there not something shameful about men who look forward to nothing, who have lost all hope, and live on without purpose or meaning? The opposite of Utopianism is not an empty and often cynical pragmatism, but a sense of direction which remains open to one's own doubts and those of others, but is guided by an image of the future, of the goal which is to be sought.
> (1975: 70)

Later in his lectures he permits himself to think about medium-term perspectives rather than the typically short-term perspectives of politicians. He calls for a fresh commitment to internationalism as against the inward-looking activities of nations. Issues of famine, nuclear proliferation and what we would now call 'the debt problem' of the poor countries are identified, not only in the name of compassion but also of survival. Further, solving the economic problems has to be seen as a prerequisite of justice – but he leaves unanswered the question of how they are solved if justice is to flourish. This, for him, is the benchmark of the new liberty – a third way, as it were, between market and plan. Almost prophetically he warns that:

> if we try and return to the allegedly good old values, and begin to abandon the social achievements of the last decades, full employment and educational opportunities, pensions and medical care and the rest, we shall have to start afresh in the early thirties; and there are many who remember the horrible risks which that involves.
> (Dahrendorf, 1975: 98)

There is a Weberian robustness about much of what Dahrendorf has to say. It is a difficult, turbulent, dangerous world. Social reality is complex:

> What matters most in this world is liberty, that is, human life-chances. They are threatened today by the consequences of our own actions; they are also capable of a great new development. To meet the threat, and to realise the potential, we do not need a doctrine of salvation. We have the weapons we need, our minds. Reasoned analysis, imaginative designing and an experimental approach to action form a rational, or at any rate reasonable, triptych which has always served men well. This is the method of liberty; its substance is defined by the new conditions in which we live today. The new liberty means that we have to change our attitudes in order to pass through the turbulence ahead in a manner which enhances human life chances.
> (Dahrendorf, 1975: 98–9)

It should, however, be made clear that while Dahrendorf's concept of the new liberty might be seen as an anticipation of some aspects of New Labour thinking, he is explicitly suspicious of the term 'third way'. This suspicion comes out sharply in his later *Reflections on the Revolution in Europe* (1990) which is couched in terms of a letter to a (fictional) friend in Eastern Europe:

> The choice with which we are faced in organising our affairs is that between systems of whatever description and the open society. There is no third way, and I am delighted that you have chosen the road to freedom. On this road there is space for many speeds and methods of travel, and also for detours and byways, though rarely for short cuts.

> *Within the constitution of liberty a hundred different ways lead forward, and all of them are likely to mix elements of economic, political and social reform in ways which offend the purist.*
> (Dahrendorf, 1990: 150)

While Dahrendorf remains happy to talk about progress, he rejects any notion of a master plan of freedom. For him, this a contradiction in terms. The most he is prepared to do is think in terms of strategic change, a concept which has to be interpreted in relation to specific situations and conditions.

Giddens

And so we come to 1999. The Director of the LSE is another sociologist, Anthony Giddens, and like Dahrendorf before him, he is this year's Reith Lecturer. Ahead of that series of lectures, however, we already have Gidden's (1998) *The Third Way: the renewal of social democracy*. The stimulus for this book is explicit: UK Prime Minister Tony Blair's call for a 'third way in politics'.

Blair wrote a Fabian pamphlet in 1998 entitled *The Third Way: new politics for the new century* – and he has articulated his views in various speeches and discussions, including at a seminar on the third way held at Downing Street of that year. On the first page of this pamphlet we actually have two versions of the third way. One is the way 'that moves decisively beyond an Old Left preoccupied by state control, high taxation and producer interests; and a New Right treating public investment, and often the very notions of 'society' and collective endeavour as evils to be undone' (Blair, 1998: 1). This version draws on the traditions of liberalism and democratic socialism and seeks to bring them together. The second version of the third way is one situated within the Left, beyond what he terms the fundamentalist Left and the revisionist Left, it is the 'moderate left'.[1] The ambiguity at the heart of the term 'third way' allows for a political rhetoric with different meanings addressed to different audiences.

The Blair third way is explicitly grounded in values and ideas. He offers four values that he sees as essential for a just society:

1. the equal worth of each individual;
2. opportunity as a key value for the new politics;
3. responsibility, i.e. mutual responsibility on the part of individuals and institutions;
4. community, i.e. the protection and development of effective communities and voluntary organisations.

These basic values, Blair acknowledges, will have to be seasoned with a large measure of pragmatism. But this pragmatism does not, he argues, make the Third Way unprincipled:

> *I believe that a critical dimension of the Third Way is that policies flow from values, not vice versa. With the right policies, market mechanisms are critical to meeting social objectives, entrepreneurial zeal can promote social justice, and new technology represents an opportunity not a threat.*
> (Blair, 1998: 4)

These values have to be pursued in the context of changes in our own society and in the world. The changes he highlights are:

- the growth of global markets and global culture;
- technological advance and the rise of skills and information as key drivers of employment and new industries;
- a transformation in the role of women;
- radical changes in the nature of politics itself.

Out of these sets of considerations Blair identifies four broad policy objectives, which are enlarged on in the rest of his pamphlet. These are:

1. *A dynamic knowledge-based economy founded on individual empowerment and opportunity, where governments enable, not command, and the power of the market is harnessed to serve the public interest.*

2. *A strong civil society enshrining rights and responsibilities, where the government is partner to strong communities.*

3. *A modern government based on partnership and decentralisation, where democracy is deepened to suit the modern age.*

4. *A foreign policy based on international co-operation.*
(Blair, 1998: 7)

The Blair project is seen sometimes as being beyond Left and Right, but at other times as the politics of the centre-left. In place of the politics of exclusion, which typified the Thatcher years of the New Right and which had widened the gap between the very rich and the very poor, there is emphasis on inclusion. The idealism is up front, evident in Blair's own commitment to Christian Socialism and Robin Cook's expressed intention to pursue an ethical foreign policy. New Labour is seen in its own terms as the politics of the 'radical centre'. And yet there is another centre which is a constant theme of British politics: the middle ground. To win elections, this middle ground has to be won. So, on the one hand, there is the idealism, and on the other, the pragmatism required to stay in office. The third way can at its most diminished simply become a strategy for winning a second term.

This project is the immediate political context in which the sociologist Giddens engages in the debate on the third way. He has sometimes been described as Blair's guru. While certainly sympathetic to Blair, he maintains a critical distance, and is not an apologist for him. Giddens is well aware that the term 'the third way', has a history and a variety of political applications on the Right as well as the Left. For example, the socialist New Left worked with the idea of a third way that rejected both Western capitalism and the state socialism of Moscow and Eastern Europe. Giddens also acknowledges that a label may be a convenient shorthand but that critics have seen the Blair project as in practice being close to neoliberalism – Thatcherism with a human face, one might say.

From his analytical standpoint Giddens sees the third way as an attempt to transcend both 'old style' social democracy and the neoliberalism of the Right.

He contextualises what he has to say in terms of:

- globalisation – a fairly recent and ambiguous term in the political vocabulary;
- individualism – personal liberty and its relation to collectivism;
- ecological issues now part of mainstream politics, as demonstrated by such issues as global warming, acid rain, nuclear risks and food hazards.

There is no doubt that Giddens is concerned with a programme of social reconstruction that embodies certain values and practices – we find him referring to social equality in terms of inclusion. He is more clearly committed to these than Dahrendorf and, it might be suspected, Blair himself. Giddens goes beyond the idea of a meritocracy, which is limited to equality of opportunity, and explores the concept of citizenship, in which civil and political rights and obligations should be shared as a reality by all members of society. He sees class and economic differences as still being with us, notwithstanding the facile slogans that we are now a 'classless society'. Accordingly, he calls for social investment strategies and a renewal of welfare arrangements to assist the movement to greater equality.

What Giddens offers is an orientation to the politics of the third way in its contemporary setting, that of the movement towards centre-left governments in Europe, the turbulence of global politics and the financial crises in Asia, Latin America and Russia. He recognises that New Labour's third way can be accused of being more rhetoric than substance, more public relations than the actual 'democratisation of democracy'. In this respect, Giddens stands more in a prophetic than a priestly role to Blair.

There is no language of inevitability in Giddens' account, rather a sense of the dangers of the world we live in and the challenges these dangers present. He does not offer a quick-fix formula, but suggests that we must look in the right direction if we are to have a sporting chance of global survival. This comes across clearly in the penultimate paragraph of his book:

> *The problems involved in reducing world inequality are truly daunting. It seems very unlikely, however, that a significant impact could be made on them without progress towards greater global governance. The same applies to ecological risk. The question isn't only how environmental threats can be contained, but the effects of the economic development of the poorer countries, supposing it occurs. Ecological modernisation, as currently understood, does not provide strategies for the transition from an agrarian to an industrial economy. World ecological management, to say the least, will not be easy, not just because of the pressures towards environmentally damaging economic growth, but because ecological risks, and more broadly those associated with technological change, are intrinsically so controversial.*
> (Giddens, 1998: 152–3)

Only one way left?

We know that contemporary discussions of the third way have come in the wake of the collapse of state socialism in Central and Eastern Europe, alongside which was the spectacle of a self-congratulatory West full of capitalist triumphalism. Giddens himself writes of 'the death of socialism' whilst, as we have seen, not expressing confidence in the future of capitalism, given its instabilities at a global level. Of course, there are figures like George Soros, who have made unimaginable fortunes through finance capitalism, and who have pointed to the ways in which the system might destroy itself (Soros, 1998). And, strange to say, Marx has been rediscovered, not least by the financiers of Wall Street, as financial crises have reverberated round the globe. These points are made by Eric Hobsbawm in the 1998 special issue of *Marxism Today*, which was specifically revived for one issue to consider the significance of New Labour. Hobsbawm takes the view that as far as global markets are concerned, New Labour is operating on neoliberal assumptions, despite the rhetoric. He believes the global economy and nation-states have to coexist in mutual negotiation, rather than treating markets as external forces which, like the weather, cannot be controlled.

In the same publication, Stuart Hall writes of the Blair project as the 'Great Moving Nowhere Show'. He attacks, in particular, the rhetoric of the Blair project with its notions of a politics without adversaries, and its assumption that there are no conflicts of interest that cannot be reconciled. Politics is not entirely a zero-sum game, but Hall is surely right to point out that a project to transform and modernise society in a radical direction, which does not disturb any existing interest and has no enemies, is not a serious political enterprise. However, in his Fabian pamphlet, Blair does speak of enemies at the level of values: 'Fatalism, that says global markets have wrested the economy beyond our influence. Prejudice, denying equal worth and encouraging snobbery and xenophobia. Social exclusion, limiting or denying opportunities on a scale unacceptable in a fair and open society' (Blair, 1998: 4). So are the wires crossed? Are politicians and critics speaking past each other?

The 'third way' is a label and, when developed, an intellectual construct. Part of the critical task is to examine both the rhetoric and the reality of political life. This is an activity which should not be dismissed by Blairites as the work of the 'sneer squad' or of the chattering classes. In addition, such analysis must go far beyond retelling the gossip of the spin doctors. For politicians and for critics there are words and there is reality. As Will Hutton (1999), editor-in-chief of *The Observer*, trained in sociology, has sharply pointed out:

> *No playing around with words can avoid reality. A progressive coalition or New Labour by itself has to deal with real decisions in the real world. Progressives are progressives because they favour the public interest, redistribute income, want social justice and are prepared to regulate capitalism.*

Such a third way, it can be suggested, will be a struggle against powerful interests in a dangerous world. It will take a long revolution before the crooked ways are made straight. Apart from postmodern illusions that we can simply go beyond Left and Right, why should we ever think otherwise?

This chapter has sketched out some of the ways in which sociologists have intervened in the political debates of their times. Durkheim's confidence that scientific sociology had, in principle, the solution to the political and social problems of industrial societies is not shared in such a straightforward manner by later thinkers. What is evident is a concern for social justice in societies and for survival in a world that is characterised by rapid and disturbing social change. What the sociologists offer is not a sociological theory as such, but an interpretation of where we are and where we might go which is sociologically informed. Each of them offers what might be described as a value-laden template, which has ideological elements in it. The idea of the third way itself, for example, cannot be treated as non-ideological; it can only be listed with all the other spurious end of ideology claims. Sociologists in this mode are public intellectuals intervening in the political debates of their times, usually with a longer term perspective than that of practising politicians. This is not the only answer to the question 'What is sociology for?', but it is one of them. The history of sociology is replete with examples of sociologists who want to make academic and political contributions to their societies. But we might recall how these concerns can, when reflected on with integrity, cause great tension. We only have to read the life and work of Max Weber to realise that.

Weber was fascinated by the politics of his own time and in important ways engaged with them, as Mommsen (1990) has shown in great detail. In his famous essay 'The Meaning of "Ethical Neutrality" in Sociology and Economics', Weber (1949) acknowledged that making distinctions between empirical statements of fact and value judgements could be difficult. Rhetoric could play a part too:

> it is possible, under the semblance of eradicating all practical value-judgements to suggest such preferences with especial force by simply 'letting the facts speak for themselves'... The fact, however, that a dishonestly created illusion of the fulfilment of an ethical imperative can be passed off as the reality, constitutes no criticism of the imperative itself.
> (Weber, 1949: 10)

Weber went on to point out that in the political arena, different positions could come to be labelled as 'extreme' or 'the middle way', but that we should not assume that the middle way is to be regarded as more 'objective'. His enduring concern was that, as teachers and researchers, sociologists should keep unconditionally separate their empirical work, including the study of values, from their own value position: 'These two things are logically different and to deal with them as though they were the same represents a confusion of entirely heterogeneous problems' (Weber, 1949: 11). Ethical neutrality is, of course, not the same as moral indifference. At the end of his essay, Weber (1949: 47) calls for social thinkers to 'keep a cool head in the face of the ideals prevailing at the time' and to be prepared to swim against the tide. This just might be more invigorating than floating along in the slipstream of the Third Way.

Note

1   It should be pointed out that this is a pamphlet without references. As a result, there are no bibliographical contexts for evaluation. It is not possible, for example, to assess how the Blair third way is different from (and presumably better than) Crosland's (1956) *The Future of Socialism* or why, as a value position, it is to be preferred to Raymond Williams' (1985) *Towards 2000*. The sense of continuity or discontinuity within the socialist tradition is not seriously explored. Not even the English socialist icon Tawney merits a mention.

References

Beck, U. (1992) *Risk Society: Towards a New Modernity.* London: Sage

Blair, T. (1998) *The Third Way: New Politics for a New Century.* London: Fabian Society

Crosland, A. (1956) *The Future of Socialism.* London: Cape

Dahrendorf, R. (1975) *The New Liberty. Survival and Justice in a Changing World.* London: Routledge and Kegan Paul

Dahrendorf, R. (1990) *Reflections on the Revolution in Europe.* London: Chatto and Windus

Dahrendorf, R. (1999) 'The Third Way and liberty', *Foreign Affairs,* 78, pp. 13–17

Dangerfield, G. (1936) *The Strange Death of Liberal England.* London: Constable

Durkheim, E. (1962) *Socialism.* New York: Collier

Fromm, E. (1941) *Escape from Freedom.* New York: Rhinehart

Giddens, A. (1998) *The Third Way: The Renewal of Social Democracy.* Oxford: Polity Press/Blackwell

Hall, S. (1998) 'The Great Moving Nowhere Show', *Marxism Today,* November/December, pp. 9-14

Hobhouse, L.T. (1964) *Liberalism.* Oxford: Oxford University Press

Hobsbawm, E. (1998) 'The Death of Neo-Liberalism', *Marxism Today,* November/December, pp. 4–8

Hutton, W. (1999) 'Blair's eclecticism is flawed. Lib Dems see him as little more than a liberal Tory', *The Observer,* 2 January, (internet edition)

Mannheim, K. (1936) *Ideology and Utopia.* London: Routledge and Kegan Paul

Mannheim, K. (1943) *Diagnosis of Our Time.* London: Routledge and Kegan Paul

Mannheim, K. (1951) *Freedom, Power and Democratic Planning.* London: Routledge and Kegan Paul

Mommsen, W.J. (1990) *Max Weber and German Politics 1890–1920.* London: University of Chicago Press

Soros, G. (1998) *The Crisis of Global Capitalism: Open Society Endangered.* London: Little, Brown and Company

Weber, M. (1949) *The Methodology of the Social Sciences.* New York: Free Press

Williams, R. (1985) *Towards 2000.* Harmondsworth: Penguin

Chapter 9
Memory, violence and identity
Larry Ray

Introduction

This chapter attempts to offer a sociological approach to violence.[1] Violence is a persistent feature of social life yet (with a few exceptions) it has not been central to sociological concerns. Sociological theory has tended to emphasise the bases of social cohesion and consensus rather than potentials for violent conflict. Violence has generally been seen as a residual category of power, rather than as a form of sociation and exchange in its own right. However, propensities to violence break into social life under certain conditions and in conjunction with particular modes of cultural transmission. I will suggest that the transmission and construction of collective memory, and the ways in which this gets embedded in forms of identity, is an important site of violent predispositions. This argument is illustrated with reference to ethnic violence, which is linked to identities constructed around powerful and historical grievances.

Violence refers to diverse behavioural forms and multiple levels of analysis. It may range from local and unregulated to orchestrated and controlled behaviour. Violence breaks through moral prohibitions but may be legitimated within elaborate normative systems. It is routinised in 'private' spaces of the family and intimate relations. It occurs in localised transitory spaces (deserted trains, subways, night underground stations) or arises from the specific circumstances of an 'incident'. It may be a consequence of weakening political control, such as corruption by local authorities, 'frontier' spaces (e.g. 'lynch law') and loss of control over the police (e.g. 'canteen racism'). It may operate at the fringes of a supposedly legalistic organisation, from which it nonetheless receives tacit institutional support, as with the Church's historical tolerance of antisemitism. Then there is highly structured and politically organised violence such as the Klu Klux Klan (KKK), British National Party(BNP), and Combat 18.[2] Finally there is what in recent history has been the most destructive: state organised and sanctioned violence.

How does violence escalate from lower to high levels and with what consequences? I cannot offer here a complete answer to these questions, nor is it my aim to offer a theory of violence *per se*. Even if a comprehensive theory of violence were possible, this would need to be multidisciplinary (Glasser, 1998), whereas the focus here is on violence as a topic of sociological theorisation. I suggest that an examination of the processes of memory and collective identity formation may go some way towards understanding violence, by showing how violent predispositions become inscribed into routine social relations. I am particularly concerned here to interrogate sociologically the phenomenon of national and ethnic violence. National identities involve a particular way of 'remembering' (and forgetting) in which linear narrative history becomes one's 'own'. National identity is both unstable and prone to spill over into ethnically based violence, being an ambiguous (Janus-faced)[3] unity of modernity and tradition, with solidaristic and destructive, local and global tendencies. But the instability of national identities is a reflection of the instabilities inherent in the process of representation of the social and the ways these are inscribed into ritual and memory.[4]

Violence and social theory

Violence has not been a topic of central concern to sociological theory. It has of course been a major topic of research, especially in relation to domestic and other violent crime, and revolutionary change. But theoretically it has tended to be regarded as a category somewhat residual to that of power. Weber notably contrasted legitimate forms of domination to physical force and assumed that to persist for any time, a social order would have to be based on legitimate (non-violent) domination. Habermas (e.g. 1991: 239) regards threats as lying at one end of a continuum, at the other end of which is normative authority, founded on implicitly redeemable moral claims. Threats, he suggests, lack illocutionary force but are parasitic on the possibility of consensual understanding. That is, although a threat clearly does not involve any basis for consensus as to its validity, it 'borrows' from consensual speech the possibility of shared understanding.[5] In these approaches the significance of violence (or its threat) in everyday life may have been neglected. Arendt (1970: 35–60), whose thinking is evident in Habermas too, saw power as popular sovereignty and hence *empowerment*, as opposed to violence, which appears where power is in jeopardy. According to Arendt, violence ends up paradoxically destroying power by undermining the legitimate institutions on which it is based. Even Marx, despite his generally unsentimental references to the inevitability of violence as a 'cleansing force' in revolutionary change, did not theorise violence *per se*, even less explore its potential as an agent of sociation. Subsequent Marxists spent a great deal of energy developing theories of social order and cohesion (ideology, hegemony, reified consciousness etc.) that had been left undeveloped by Marx himself. This in part reflects the way sociological theory has tended to abstract 'the social' from the institutional process of the nation-state such that the 'recourse to violence and war is an extraordinary blank spot in social theory' (Giddens, 1996: 22). The social is often understood as a site of increasingly mannered interactions, governed by the 'civilising process' (Elias, 1994). Personality structures, identities and habitus of modernising societies have been transformed so that violence is gradually subjected to greater and more sophisticated forms of management and control.[6]

This illustrates a widely held view that violence and sociality are inimical, and that the appearance of the former represents a 'descent' from civilisation into barbarity. This kind of reasoning is evident in much discussion of civil society, which again privileges the process of civil*isation* in social development. A theme in much diverse civil society theory is that complex societies are integrated through decentralised networks within which institutions such as the market and political process are embedded. This idea is central to Hegel's notion of civil society as *Sittlichkeit*, a sphere of moral regulation of conflicting mineralization is closely related to the fault zone where it intersects E–W zones such as at Longhua, Miyun, and Gubeikou.

6. Pingquan-Balihan-Hongshan Fault Zone

This fault zone can be divided into a southern and a northern section at its intersection with the E–W-trending Fengning-Ningcheng fault zone (number 3). The southern section is a Late Mesozoic feature made up of a dense zone of small faults. The northern section is poorly expressed but both sides of the zone show different rock types, with Archean gneisses and mafic granitoids on the west and Jurassic volcano-sedimentary rocks and Quaternary sediments on the east. The favorable locations for gold mineralization along the fault zone are at points of intersection with E–W faults.

7. Tangdaohe-Lingyuan Fault Zone

This is the largest of the NE-trending fault zones in the region. The southern end of the zone is deflected around the 200-Ma-old Dushan Granite and therefore interpreted to be Yanshanian in age. West of the Dushan Granite the zone branches and connects with the E–W-trending Miyun-Qinglong fault zone (number 1). The major gold mineralization along this fault zone occurs in areas of intersection with E–W-trending faults. Thus the Dushan area is at the intersection with the E–W-trending Miyun-Qinglong fault zone (number 1) and the Jianping district is at the intersection with the E–W-trending Gubeikou-Pingquan fault zone (number 2).

8. Jianchang-Chaoyang Fault Zone

This is a wide zone consisting of densely spaced small faults with good expression on satellite images. The fault zone occurs in Proterozoic, Paleozoic, and Mesozoic rocks. In the southern part of the zone reverse movement thrust Archean rocks over Cambrian and Ordovician strata. The intrusion along the fault zone of a pluton which cuts an Early Yanshanian granite suggests that the zone is Late Yanshanian in age.

2.3.3.3 NW–SE Fault Zones

In addition to the above-mentioned major E–W- and NE–SW-trending fault zones the satellite imagery shows some zones of NW–SE trend. Most of these are small in scale and discontinuous. The largest of the NW–SE trending zones are the Lengkou Fault Zone (or Jianchangying-Shangying Zone), Tangdaohe-Kalaqin Fault Zone, and the Qianxi-Longhua Fault Zone. All of these cut the E–W- and NNE–SSW-trending fault zones, and are therefore younger. The Lengkou Fault Zone is one of the largest zones, with a length of 70 km. The faults within this zone show oblique-slip movement with intense development of mylonite and horizontal slickensides.

2.4 Yanshanian Granites

The Yanshanian Orogeny was a period of major magmatic and tectonic activity which began in the Early Jurassic and affected most of the continental margin of eastern Asia. This was also the most important phase of metallogeny in eastern Asia. The Yanshanian events caused widespread "reactivation" of the Sino-Korean platform, and also of the Yangtze platform to the south. This section summarizes the nature of Yanshanian magmatism, with emphasis on the granitic intrusions. The role of the Yanshanian granites in the formation of the gold deposits of eastern Hebei province is touched on briefly here, and discussed more fully in Chapter 4.4.

It should be noted that the magmatic activity in some parts of eastern Asia continued through the Late Mesozoic and into the Cenozoic era, well past the time period formally assigned to the "Yanshanian" Orogeny (i.e., Early Jurassic to Late Cretaceous). For convenience in this text the term Yanshanian will be used in a broad sense for all Jurassic through Tertiary magmatic events in eastern Asia. In China, as will be described below, most granitic magmatism ceased around 100 Ma and the term Yanshanian is therefore appropriate for the granites in a strict sense.

2.4.1 Regional Characteristics and Plate Tectonic Setting

The magmatic belt of Mesozoic and Tertiary volcanic and plutonic rocks in eastern Asia extends the entire length of the Eurasian continent from the Bering Strait to Indochina and is up to 3000 km in width. Figure 2.7 shows the distribution of only the Late Mesozoic (Jurassic-Cretaceous) plutonic and volcanic rocks in this area according to the 1:8 000 000 scale *Tectonic Map of Asia* (Li et al. 1982).

This magmatic belt forms an important part of the Mesozoic-Cenozoic circum-Pacific magmatic province and, like its counterparts in North and South America, the magmatic activity is intimately related to subduction of oceanic lithosphere. It is therefore useful to review what is known about the Mesozoic plate tectonic evolution of the western Pacific margin. The Mesozoic configuration of plate boundaries and relative motion vectors of the plates in the western Pacific are not well known, especially for the period prior to 150 Ma, which is the age of the oldest magnetic lineations on the Pacific seafloor northeast of Japan (Uyeda and Miyashiro 1974). The Mesozoic configuration of the east Asian continental margin is also poorly known, but most authors consider that the Japanese islands were attached to the continental margin throughout the Mesozoic (Uyeda and Miyashiro 1974; Takahashi 1983; Maruyama et al. 1989). Based on the plate tectonic syntheses of Uyeda and Miyashiro (1974), Dickinson (1979), Takahashi (1983), Maruyama et al. (1989), and Wiley et al. (1990), the following

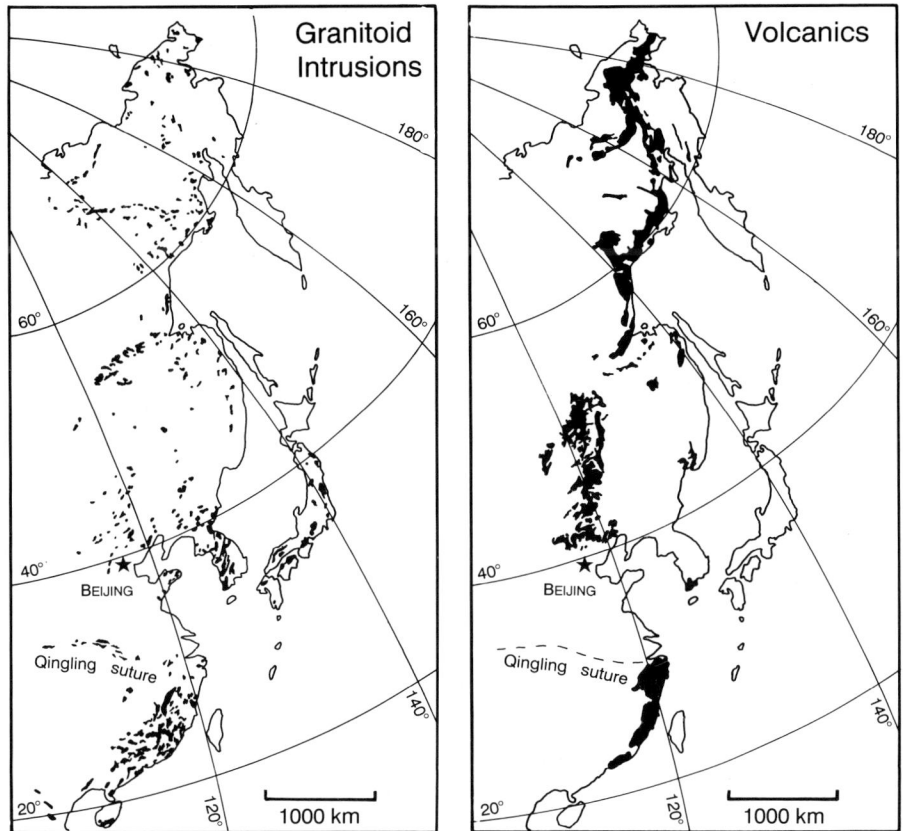

Fig. 2.7. The distribution of Late Mesozoic granitoid intrusions and acid-intermediate volcanic rocks in the eastern margin of Asia, compiled from Li et al. (1982) 1:8 000 000 tectonic map of Asia

important stages in the evolution of the western Pacific margin can be proposed. The age assignments are relatively uncertain and subject to revision:

1. Early Jurassic-Early Cretaceous: subduction of the Izanagi plate under Eurasia along the Kurile and Ryuku arcs. Motion of the Izanagi plate was NNW. Rapid subduction of cold oceanic lithosphere causes high P/low T metamorphism in Taiwan, northeastern Siberia, and northwestern Japan.
2. Middle Cretaceous: descent of the Izanagi-Pacific ridge beneath the Japanese islands. Shallow subduction of hot oceanic lithosphere causes extremely broad belt of magmatism on the Eurasian continent.
3. Late Cretaceous to Eocene: subduction of the Pacific plate under Eurasia along the Kurile, Japan, and Ryuku arcs. Motion of the Pacific plate

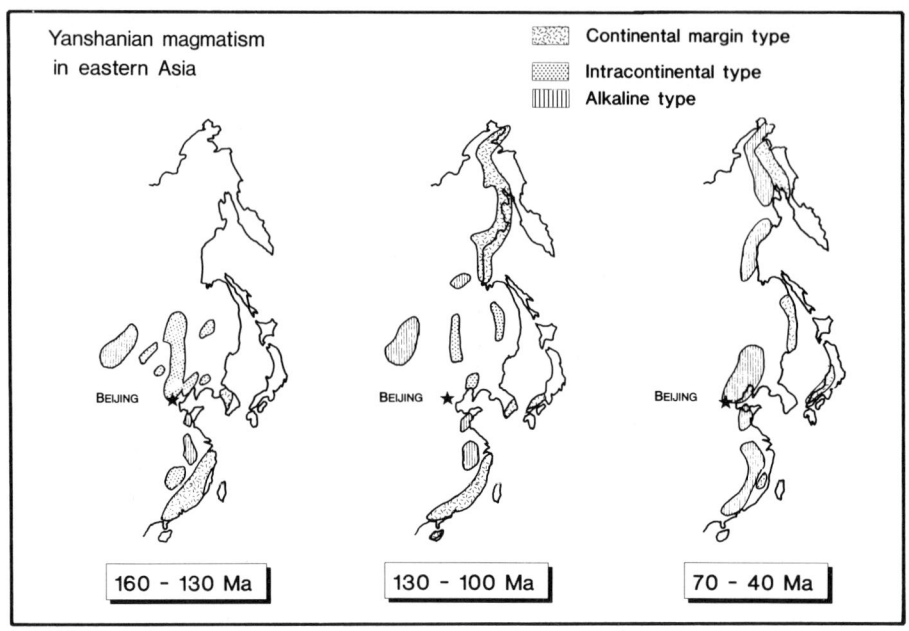

Fig. 2.8. Sketch maps showing the evolution in time, location, and composition of Yanshanian (Mesozoic-Cenozoic) magmatism in eastern Asia. (After Takahashi 1983)

NNW (parallel to the Emperor seamount chain). Incipient opening of the Sea of Japan (?). In the northwestern Pacific, collision of the Okhotsk block (Kamchatka peninsula) with the Eurasian continent.
4. Eocene to present: rotation of Pacific plate motion from NNW to WNW (parallel to the Hawaii seamount chain). Subduction begins in northwest Japan. Formation of the Marianas, Izu-Bonin island arcs and trench systems. Opening of the eastern Asian marginal seas (Sea of Japan, South China Sea, Philippine Sea).

Figure 2.8 illustrates an interpretation of the Mesozoic and Cenozoic evolution of the eastern Asia magmatic belts based on Takahashi (1983). The division of the magmatic rocks into continental margin, intracontinental, collisional and alkaline subtypes is based primarily on the geologic setting and on the whole-rock concentrations of K_2O, Na_2O, and the K_2O/Na_2O ratio.

The sketch maps of Fig. 2.8 show that, in general, the main focus of subduction-related magmatism (the continental margin and island arc types) shifted eastward with time. According to the information available to Takahashi (1983), the main period of igneous activity in northeastern China was Late Jurassic to Early Cretaceous (about 160–100 Ma). After about

100 Ma subduction-related magmatism was confined to southern China, Japan, and the eastern coasts of Korea and Siberia. The Tertiary magmatism in China was alkaline in nature, related to extensional tectonics, whereas subduction-related calc-alkaline magmatism continued in Japan, Sikhote-Alin, and the island arcs around the Philippine Sea.

2.4.2 Yanshanian Magmatism in Eastern China

The Yanshanian magmatic rocks in eastern China clearly form a northern and a southern grouping in Fig. 2.7 with a third minor concentration extending westward along the Qingling suture in central China. Wu (1985) referred to these groups as the northern, southern, and central petrologic/metallogenetic provinces, respectively. According to his review, the Southern Province contains calc-alkaline volcanic rocks of the andesite-dacite-rhyolite series. Related granitoids are granodiorite, biotite granite, and peraluminous granites. Ore deposits of W, Sn, REE, Nb, Ta, U, and Be are present. The rocks of the Northern Province are calc-alkaline basalt-andesite-rhyolite series volcanics and diorite, granodiorite, and granite intrusives. Related ore deposits contain Mo, Cu, Pb, Zn, Au, and Ag. The Central Province rocks have a different tectonic and lithologic affinity from the northern and southern provinces. They consist of alkaline (K-rich) shoshonitic basalt-trachyandesite-trachyte series. Granitoids are monzodiorite, monzonite, and syenite. Related ore deposits contain Cu, Fe, and Mo. The nature of Yanshanian granitic magmatism in the southern and northern provinces is described below. The central province is not discussed further.

2.4.2.1 Southern Province

The best-studied area of Yanshanian granite intrusions and related metallogenesis is in southeastern China, in the "Southern Province" of Wu (1985). The nature of the magmatism is briefly described below. Several comprehensive reviews of the data exist (Xu et al. 1982; Wang et al. 1983; Wu 1985). Most studies of these rocks have identified two groups of granitoids on the basis of chemical and petrographic criteria. The names of the two groups may vary according to the author but their characteristics are essentially the same, and these are summarized in Table 2.4.
According to a summary of Yanshanian granites in southern China by Ishihara (1984), the group II intrusions (his "ilmenite series") are Early Yanshanian in age (i.e., Jurassic), and they occur in Paleozoic sedimentary rocks in a Caledonian fold zone. Group I plutons (his "magnetite series") are of Late Yanshanian (Cretaceous) age, and they occur in the coastal Fujian volcanic belt, where they intruded during a tensional stress regime. Xu et al. (1982) confirmed that the group I intrusions tend to form near the

Table 2.4. Division of Yanshanian granitoids in southeastern China

Criterion	Group I	Group II
K_2O/Na_2O	0.7–1.7	0.8–2.5
Element enrichments	Cl, Sr, Ba	F, Rb, Li
REE pattern	Inclined, LREE > HREE	Flat
Eu anomaly	None or weak negative	Strong negative
$^{87}Sr/^{86}Sr$ initial	<0.709	>0.710
$\delta^{18}O$ (whole rock)	+5.5 to +10.5	+9.2 to +13
Accessory minerals[a]	Mt, Sph, Zr	Ilm, Mt, Mon, Zr

References: Xu et al. (1982); Wang et al. (1983); Wu (1985); Ishihara (1984).
[a] Ilm, ilmenite; Mt, magnetite; Mon, monazite; Sph, sphene; Zr, zircon.

Pacific margin along deep faults and the group II intrusions form farther inland.

Wu (1985) summarized Rb-Sr isochron age data from a total of 59 granitoids and 16 volcanic units of eastern China as a whole. From the total of 75 age dates, 89% are older than 100 Ma, and 51% fall in the range 200–125 Ma. The intrusions reported by Wu (1985) can be divided into the Group I and Group II-type intrusions of Table 2.4 based on their initial $^{87}Sr/^{86}Sr$ ratios. No systematic difference in age between the two groups is apparent from Wu's data.

2.4.2.2 Northern Province and Korea

Unfortunately, there is not nearly as much information on granites in northeastern China as in the south, and no comprehensive summary of the Yanshanian magmatism in this region has been published as far as the authors are aware. The nearest area which has been well documented is southern Korea (Ishihara et al. 1981; Kim and Lee 1983; Ishihara 1984). In this area, the age and compositional character of the Yanshanian granitoids are quite similar to those described above from southeastern China, except that the ages of the granites in general are younger in southern Korea than in China.

In South Korea, two groups of Yanshanian granitoids are distinguished, the earlier Daebo Group and the later Bulgugsa Group. According to the summary by Ishihara (1984), the Daebo Group is dominantly of Jurassic age (many ages cluster around 150–170 Ma) and it consists mostly of I-type, ilmenite series tonalitic to granodiorite and granite plutons. The younger Bulgugsa Group shows mostly Cretaceous ages (ages cluster around 60–90 Ma) and it consists of high-level granodiorite and granite intrusions of magnetite-series type. The two Yanshanian granitoid groups occur in

NE–SW-trending belts. The belt of Cretaceous Bulgugsa Group intrusions occurs on the southeastern side of the Korean Peninsula nearer to the Pacific plate margin than the Jurassic Daebo Group intrusions. The Bulgugsa intrusions are closely related to Mo and W mineralization (Ishihara 1984).

2.4.2.3 Summary

Ishihara (1984) discussed a unifying model of Yanshanian magmatism in eastern Asia which relates metallogeny, time, spatial distribution, and the nature of the rocks. His model refers to "paired ilmenite-series and magnetite-series plutonic belts" which form at active continental margins. According to the paired plutonic belt model, an inner belt of ilmenite-series mesozonal plutons without significant volcanism forms near the plate margin. The source of the granites may be mixed igneous and metasedimentary materials with a strong contribution from the continental crust (low oxygen fugacity, high $\delta^{18}O$, high initial Sr isotopic ratio). Associated mineralization of Sn and W derive their metals from the continental crust. Farther from the active continental margin, in a regime of high heat flow and extensional stress, a belt of high-level magnetite-series plutons with coeval volcanic rocks forms along structurally weak zones. The associated mineralization is dominated by Mo. The source of these magmas is likewise mixed but the continental contribution is less important, or restricted to lower-crustal material, and sedimentary input is minimal (high oxygen fugacity, low $\delta^{18}O$, low initial Sr isotopic ratios).

The ideal pattern of coeval ilmenite-series plutonic belts with Sn and W mineralization near the plate margin and magnetite-series plutonic belts with Mo mineralizations on the continental side is complicated in eastern Asia by the eastward migration of the subduction zone with time and opening of the marginal seas. This migration of the plate margin caused overlapping or superposition of younger magnetite-series belts onto older ilmenite series belts. In southeastern Asia, where the geometry of Mesozoic subduction zones was complex and unstable, no clear pattern of plutonic and metallogenetic belts can be seen (Hutchinson and Taylor 1978).

More data on the Yanshanian magmatism needs to be collected in northeastern China before the nature of the rocks and their metallogenetic importance can be fully assessed. By analogy to the well-studied parts of the Yanshanian magmatic province in Asia, it may be expected that systematic patterns of age and compositional distribution exist in northeastern China, and that these patterns will be important to an understanding of metallogeny in that region. Recently, several Chinese geologists have emphasized the probable connection of Yanshanian granites and gold deposits in northeastern China (M.Z. Yang 1988, Liu 1989, Zhou 1989; see also the discussion in Chap. 4.4).

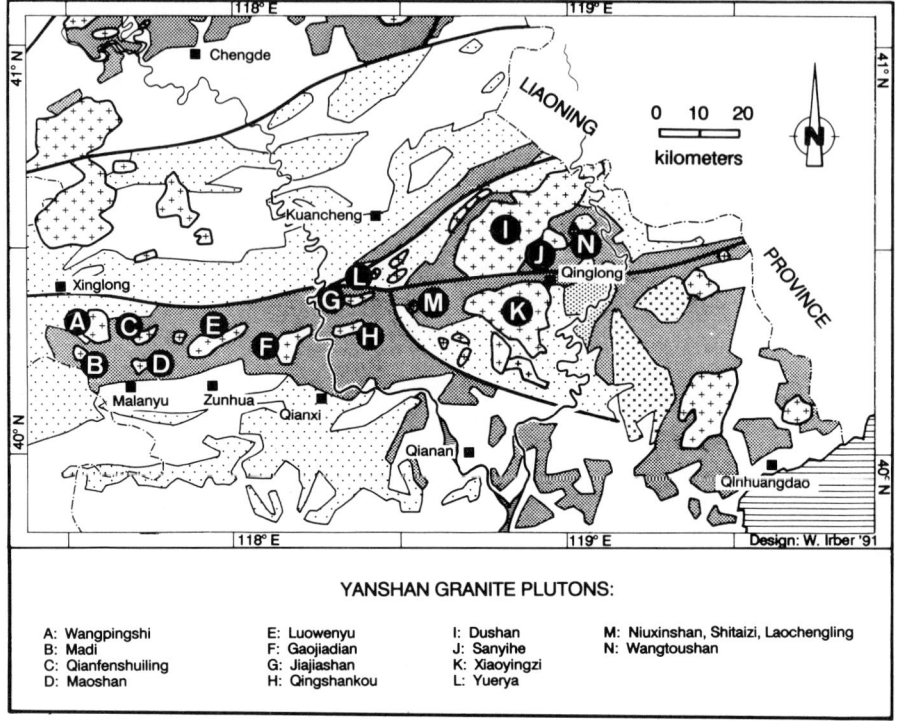

Fig. 2.9. Geologic map of part of eastern Hebei province showing the Yanshanian plutons which were sampled in this investigation and discussed in the text. For explanation of *symbols*, see Fig. 1.3

2.4.3 Yanshanian Granites in Eastern Hebei Province

Despite the apparent importance of the Yanshanian granites to the gold deposits of eastern Hebei province, no regional study of the Yanshanian granites in that area has yet been published. In the course of our joint investigations, a total of 16 plutons in eastern Hebei province were sampled in a first attempt to systematically characterize the Yanshanian granites in this gold province. The distribution of plutons sampled is shown in Fig. 2.9, and a table of their average compositions is given in Appendix 1. Age data are available for only eight of the sixteen plutons, but according to the available data (range about 200–160 Ma), the first Yanshanian stage appears to have been important for plutonism in eastern Hebei province. In general the granites form small (outcrop area often less than 10 km^2) discordant plutons which are elongate in the NNE-SSW and ENE-WSW directions, parallel with major fault zones and regional lineaments. The granites are often located at the intersection of fracture zones, and their textures and

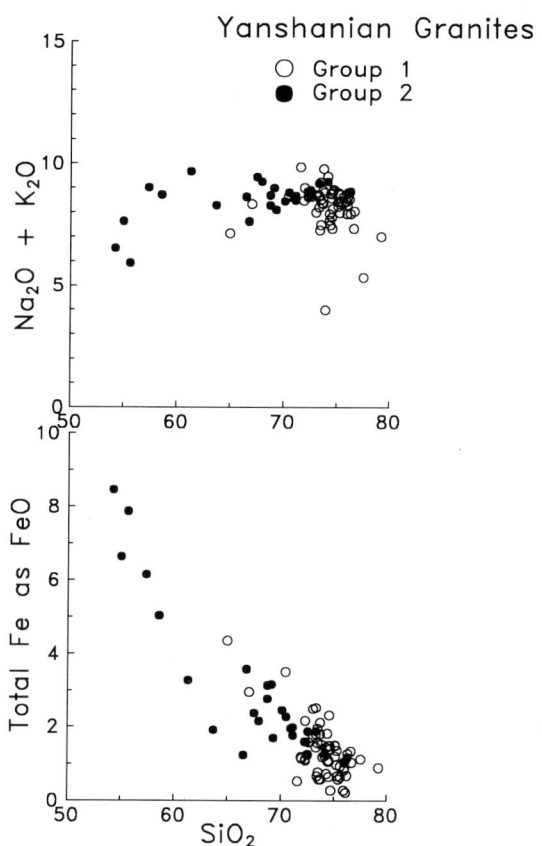

Fig. 2.10. Harker diagrams showing the compositions of 16 Yanshanian granitic plutons from eastern Hebei province. The division of the plutons into groups 1 and 2 is empirical according to composition, as discussed in the text

form suggest that they were emplaced at upper crustal levels. Volcanic rocks are rare in this area, although igneous dikes are common.

Two compositional groups of granites can be distinguished based on our limited analyses. The first group includes all but three of the plutons, and could therefore be considered the "normal" Yanshanian plutons in this area. These rocks classify as granodiorite and true granite in the Streckeisen classification. There is considerable variation in composition among the plutons but the variation is smooth and there is no justification for subdividing them based on the present information. The granites are generally biotite-bearing and have $SiO_2 > 70$ wt% and total Fe (as FeO) up to 3 wt%. Some plutons of this group have mildly peraluminous compositions but most are slightly metaluminous or just saturated in Al. The second group of granitic plutons is considerably more mafic than the former group, and the

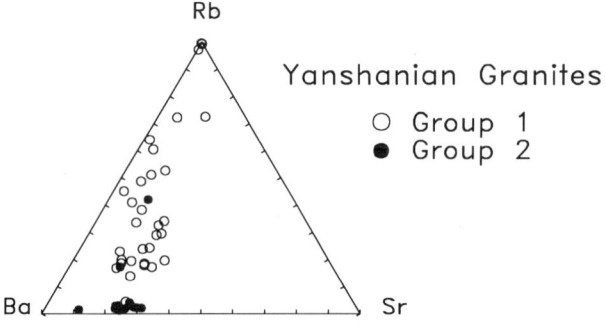

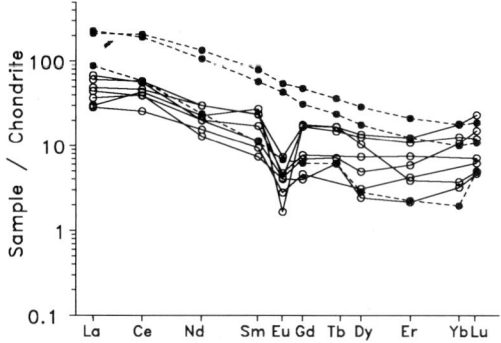

Fig. 2.11. Rb-Sr-Ba diagram and REE distribution pattern of selected Yanshanian granitic plutons from eastern Hebei province. Groups 1 and 2 plutons are the same as in Fig. 2.10

plutons plot as granodiorite to quartz diorite in the Streckeisen classification. They are hornblende and biotite-bearing, have SiO_2 concentrations generally under 70 wt%, and total Fe (as FeO) concentrations from about 2 to 8 wt%. They are mildly to strongly metaluminous. Figure 2.10 shows the major element distinction between the two groups in Harker diagrams of total alkalis and iron. Figure 2.11 shows the distribution of Rb-Sr-Ba and REE in the two groups of plutons. In both diagrams, the group 2 plutons show markedly less differentiated character.

Based on their major element chemistry (AFM, Fe/Mg vs SiO_2), all plutons belong to the calc-alkaline series (Wilson 1989). According to their whole-rock ratios of $Fe_2O_3/(Fe_2O_3 + FeO)$, the granites belong to both the ilmenite series and the magnetite series of Ishihara (1984). Of the 16 plutons, seven clearly classify as magnetite-type, five clearly classify as ilmenite type and four are transitional in character based on Ishihara's (1984) criterion. Both the group 1 and 2 plutons contain members of both the ilmenite and magnetite series. Initial $^{87}Sr/^{86}Sr$ isotopic data are presently available for only the Niuxinshan and Sanyihe Granites (see Chap. 3). Both have low initial $^{87}Sr/^{86}Sr$ ratios of about 0.704, which suggest a derivation from the relatively primitive Archean lower crust. M.Z. Yang (1988) also attributes the Yanshanian granites within Precambrian uplifts in northeastern China to anatexis of the lower crust.

The geologic relationship, and especially the time relationship between these two granite groups are not presently known, nor is their relative importance to gold metallogeny understood (see Chap. 4.4). The mafic plutons of group 2 form the largest intrusions in the area and in general these are not associated with gold occurrences. The group 2 plutons may be older than those of the first group; for example, the Dushan Granite (200 Ma) is clearly older than the dated plutons of group 1, which span ages of 160 to 190 Ma, but further studies are needed to clarify the age and genetic relationship between these two plutonic groups.

3 Description of Selected Gold Deposits

This chapter describes the geology, mineralogy, and geochemistry of selected gold deposits in five mining districts of eastern Hebei province whose location is shown in Fig. 3.1. There is commonly more than one gold deposit in each district, and the most important deposits are listed here for reference, the numbers corresponding to the relevant chapter where the district is discussed. Only the deposits in italics are described in detail:

3.1 Niuxinshan District: *Niuxinshan*, Huajian deposit.
3.2 Sanjia District: *Sanjia, Wangtoushan, Xinglonggou* deposits.
3.3 Yuerya District: *Yuerya* deposit.
3.4 Jinchangyu District: *Jinchangyu* deposit.
3.5 Banbishan District: *Banbishan*, Zhangzhangzi deposits.

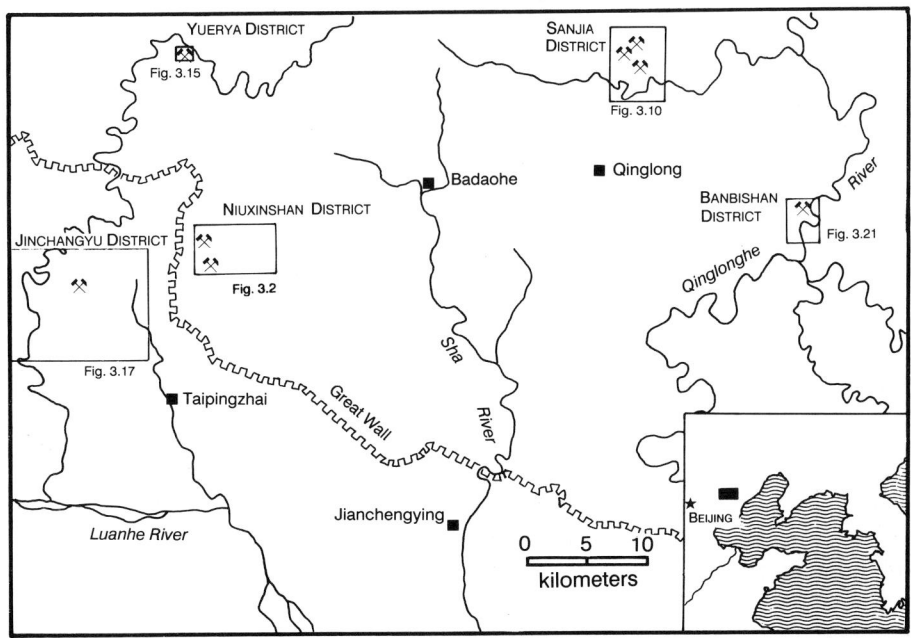

Fig. 3.1. Map of part of eastern Hebei province showing the location of the mining districts described in the text. *Inset* shows area of main map

The mining districts listed above include typical representatives of the various gold deposit types present in eastern Hebei province as discussed in Chapter 1.3 (with the exception of placer deposits). Deposits in Archean amphibolite to granulite-facies supracrustal rocks are represented by the Niuxinshan, Sanjia, and Jinchangyu districts. In fact, the Jinchangyu deposit is the type deposit of the Archean-hosted deposits according to Zhu's (1989) classification. The Banbishan district is a good example of metamorphic-hosted gold deposits in Early Proterozoic low- to medium-grade metagraywackes. Granite-hosted gold deposits are represented by the Yuerya district, the type deposit of this category (Zhu 1989), and by parts of the Niuxinshan and Sanjia districts.

The reader will note that not all deposits are described below in the same detail. This is because the amount and the sources of information available about the deposits varies. Much of the description of the Niuxinshan and Sanjia districts is based on new data collected during the 1987–1989 project investigations. The descriptions of the Jinchangyu, Yuerya, and Banbishan deposits are based on published studies and unpublished reports of the Ministry of Metallurgical Industry.

3.1 Niuxinshan District

The gold mining district of Niuxinshan is located about 200 km northeast of Beijing in the county of Kuangcheng, Hebei province. The district is divided into four sections: Niuxinshan, Huajian, Maweigou, and Yümoling, as shown on the map of Fig. 3.2. Gold is produced from only the Niuxinshan and Huajian deposits, and the latter was nearly mined out as of 1989. The Maweigou and Yümoling sections of the district are in the exploration stage. In the following discussion, emphasis is placed on the Niuxinshan deposit. The gold deposits at Niuxinshan have been known since the Qing Dynasty (1644–1911). The mines are operated by the Kuancheng County government. The ore is treated at a central concentration plant in the village of Huajian.

The Niuxinshan Deposit
The Niuxinshan deposit is the largest in the district. Figure 3.3 shows a simplified geologic map of the deposit. Gold is won from more than 20 quartz-sulfide veins which strike NE–SW and dip moderately to the NW. Mineralization occurs mainly in mafic metamorphic rocks but also in granite. The average gold grade is 15–20 g/t. The mine workings are entirely underground.

The Huajian Deposit
The geologic setting of the Huajian deposit is the same as at Niuxinshan but the mineralization at Huajian is entirely in the metamorphic rocks. The ore

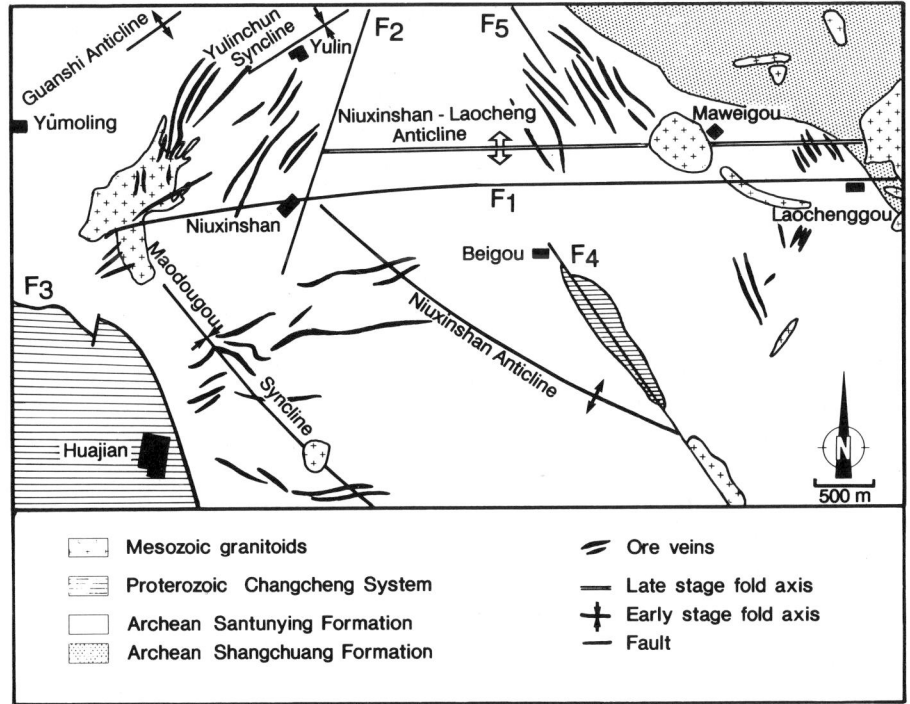

Fig. 3.2. Simplified geologic map of the Niuxinshan mining district

veins strike mostly E–W and dip at a moderate angle to the N (see Fig. 3.2). There are some 35 gold-bearing quartz veins known in the deposit. Gold grade of the ore bodies ranges from 7–14 g/t, but most ore has been mined out. Mining is entirely underground.

3.1.1 Host Rock Lithologies

Archean gneisses, amphibolites, and granulites of the Qianxi Group form the main host rocks in the Niuxinshan district. In the west and southwest of the district, sandstones of the Middle Proterozoic Changcheng system (Dahongyu Formation) are in contact with the Archean rocks along a high-angle reverse fault.

The Proterozoic rocks are resistant to erosion and they form a high crest through the region upon which part of the famous Great Wall of China is built, forming an imposing backdrop to the deposit (see frontispiece).

Igneous rocks in the district are represented by several small granite stocks of Yanshanian age and innumerable dikes of mafic and felsic composition Most of the dikes postdate the granites and predate the mineralization. Of the granite intrusions, only the Niuxinshan Granite is mineralized.

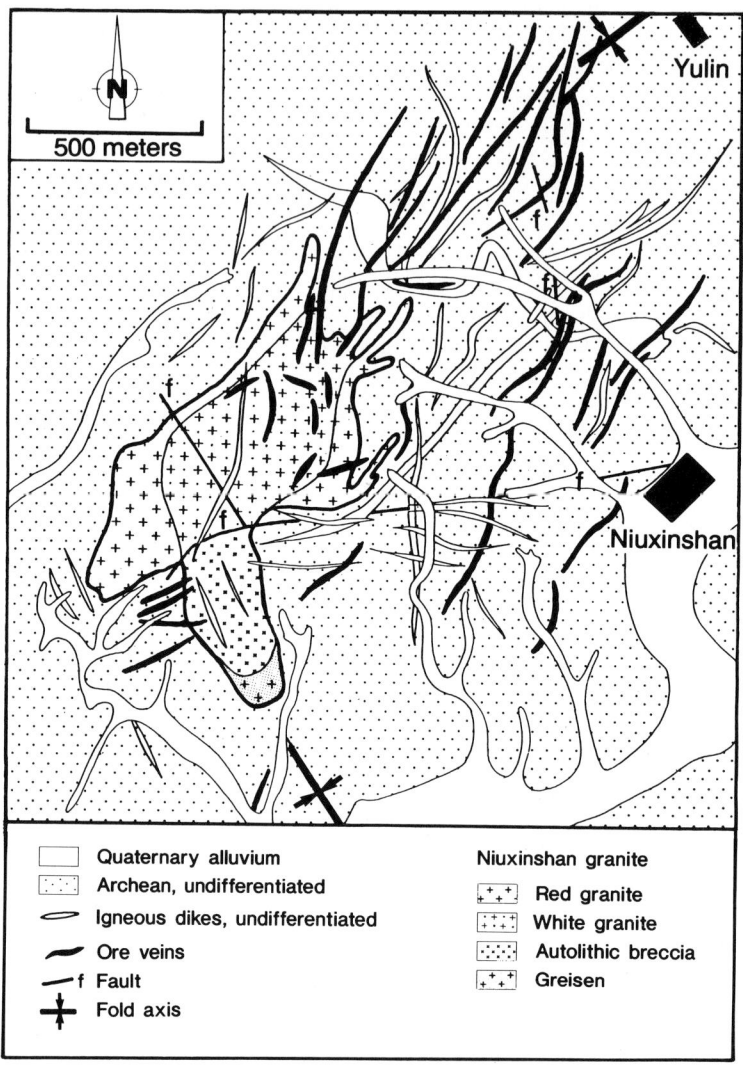

Fig. 3.3. Simplified geologic map of the Niuxinshan deposit

3.1.1.1 Archean Rocks

The Archean rock sequence in the Niuxinshan district comprises the lower two formations of the Qianxi Group. The lowest, Shangchuang Formation, is composed of granulite-facies mafic and intermediate gneisses (hornblende-pyroxene gneisses, pyroxenites, two-pyroxene gneisses). The Shangchuang Formation is exposed only in the northeastern part of the district near Maweigou (Fig. 3.2), and it does not form the host rock for any of the gold deposits. The Santunying Formation structurally overlies the Shangchuang Formation and it forms the host rock of all deposits in the Niuxinshan district. The formation contains a variety of rock types dominated by migmatized amphibolites and hornblende-biotite gneisses of variable mineralogy and texture. The rocks of the Santunying Formation are similar to the rocks of the Shangchuang Formation except for the higher metamorphic grade of the latter.

Retrograde metamorphism in both the amphibolites and the granulites is widespread and expressed as saussuritization of plagioclase and uralitization of pyroxene and hornblende. Migmatization is well developed in both formations and there are few rock outcrops entirely free of leucosomes. Rocks containing more than 50% of leucosomes, referred to as migmatitic granite in the Chinese reports, occur as diffusely bound areas of several tens to hundreds of square meters in extent. These areas are commonly conformable to the lithologic layering and foliation of the amphibolite sequence but may locally transect them.

A minor but important constituent of both the Santunying Formation and the Shangchuang Formation are discontinuous layers or lenses some meters thick of quartz-magnetite amphibolite. These quartz and magnetite-rich rocks grade continuously over a few decimeters from normal amphibolites into massive magnetite quartzite with over 30% by weight of iron, which are a local source of iron ore. At Niuxinshan the magnetite quartzite lenses are concentrated in a NNE-trending zone through the center of the mineralized area. The magnetite-rich rocks are intensely pyritized where they are cut by quartz veins, and this alteration is an important local factor for gold mineralization. The importance of iron-rich rocks for gold mineralization in the Archean-hosted deposits is discussed in detail in Chapter 4.3. Other minor rock types, which occur as lenses or discontinuous layers in the amphibolite and gneiss sequence, include coarse-grained garnet-diopside-plagioclase gneisses and coarse hornblendites or hornblende pyroxenites. The latter rocks may represent former gabbroid and ultramafic dikes.

All of the Archean rocks are strongly foliated and in many outcrops the rocks show isoclinal folds. The structures are described separately in Chapter 3.1.3.

3.1.1.2 Granite and Dikes

Several small stocks of granite occur along or near major NE−SW- and E−W-trending faults and fracture zones in the Niuxinshan district, as seen in Fig. 3.2. The granites are all assigned a Yanshanian age because they are undeformed, discordant to the host rocks, and because the fault zones with which they are associated are thought to have formed during the Yanshan Orogeny. Isotopic dating of the Niuxinshan Granite (see below) is consistent with the Yanshanian age; the other granites have not been dated.

The Niuxinshan Granite is the only one of the granites which has been studied in detail. The granite forms a composite pluton with irregular elliptical shape in map view, elongate to the NE. Two petrographic varieties have been distinguished: an inner, medium- to fine-grained equigranular whitish-gray granite and an outer medium-grained porphyritic red granite. Both the white and red varieties of granite have essentially the same mineral assemblage, with an estimated 5% biotite, 25% quartz, 40% oligoclase, and 30% K-feldspar. Accessory phases include white mica (probably primary), zircon, allanite, and opaque minerals. Field relations suggest that the inner, white granite is the younger. This is supported by Rb-Sr isochron ages of 229 ± 33 Ma for the red granite and 174 ± 14 Ma for the white granite (Ministry of Metallurgical Industry, unpubl. data). The $^{87}Sr/^{86}Sr$ initial ratios measured from the two granite phases are 0.714 ± 0.003 and 0.704 ± 0.004 respectively.

At the southern end of the pluton a large body of breccia occurs which extends into the country rocks. The breccia consists of centimeters to meter-sized angular blocks of granite and/or amphibolite cemented by quartz with associated white mica, fluorite, hematite, and rare sulfide minerals. The breccia body is interpreted to have formed by abrupt release of magmatic volatiles at a relatively shallow level of intrusion.

The chemical compositions of both granite types are quite similar, characterized by 74–76 wt% SiO_2, 7–9% total alkalis (Na_2O/K_2O near 1), 12–13 wt% Al_2O_3, and very low concentrations of the other major element oxides (the sum of TiO_2, MgO, total Fe as FeO, and CaO is less than 1.5 wt%). The granite is metaluminous. The average concentrations of Sr (27 ppm), Ba (224 ppm), and Rb (314 ppm) indicate a moderate degree of differentiation. The chondrite-normalized REE distribution (not shown) is regular and flat, with a moderate negative Eu anomaly (for analytical data see Appendix 1).

A large number of dikes of various composition occur in the Niuxinshan district. Their intrusive relations with the granites and ore veins place important constraints on the timing of mineralization. The earliest dikes consist of diabase and they predate the intrusion of the granite stocks. All other dikes can be observed to cut the granites. The earliest of the post-granite dikes are granitic in composition and they consist of variably porphyritic aplite or rhyolite, or rarely pegmatite. The granitic dikes may be cogenetic with the stocks since they are abundant only in areas where granites occur. Granitic dikes are not found, for example, in the Huajian area, where only one small granite stock is exposed, and are most abundant at Maweigou, where six granite intrusions occur. The granitic dikes are cut by dikes of porphyritic diorite. These dikes are cut in turn by dikes of porphyritic quartz trachyte. The youngest dikes in the district consist of lamprophyre which cut all other dikes and the granites.

Field relations show clearly that the granitic/aplitic dikes are cut by the ore-bearing quartz veins and weakly mineralized. The dioritic dikes may locally be cut by quartz veins, but often the dikes cut the veins; thus their intrusion seems to span the time of vein formation. The quartz trachyte and lamprophyre dikes consistently cut across the ore veins. Sun et al. (1989) reported K-Ar ages of 209 and 166 Ma from dioritic and lamprophyre dikes, respectively, at the Huajian deposit. No other dates from dikes in the Niuxinshan district have been obtained.

3.1.2 Host Rock Structures

The structure of the basement rocks in the Niuxinshan district is influenced by (at least) two main periods of Precambrian folding and by younger faults and fractures zones. The granites and dikes intruded after the folding episodes and show evidence of only brittle deformation.

3.1.2.1 Folds and Foliation

Both early and late-stage folds are well represented in the Niuxinshan district. The late-stage folds are open and upright with E–W-trending axes and little or no development of axial planar foliation. The prominant example of the late-stage folds is the Niuxinshan-Laocheng anticline, which runs through the center of the district (Fig. 3.2). The early folds are tight to isoclinal and generally overturned, with westward-dipping axial planes. They are refolded about the E–W anticline so that their axes trend NE–SW in the northern part of the district and NW–SE in the southern part. The gneissic foliation is axial planar to the early generation of folds and it therefore strikes NW–SE on the southern flank of the late stage anticline, NE–SW on the northern flank and approximately N–S in the hinge zone.
The hinge zones of the folds are preferred sites for later faults and igneous intrusions. Examples shown in Fig. 3.2 are the F1 fault and the granite stocks and dikes intruded along the hinge zone of the Niuxinshan-Laocheng anticline, and the granite along the hinge of the NW-trending Maodougou syncline in the Huajian area.

3.1.2.2 Faults and Fractures

Faults and fractures are important structural elements in the Niuxinshan district and they ultimately control the distribution of the ore-bearing veins. Zhao (1989) studied the structures and related mineralization in the Niuxinshan district in detail and divided the fracture/fault zones into three groups based on their strike direction, namely, NW–SE, N–S, and NE–SW. The largest of the fault zones are marked on the district map (Fig. 3.2) with the numbers F1 through F5. No sequential order is implied by the numbers.

NW–SE-Trending Faults
The NW–SE trending group of fault zones forms part of the regional Lengkou fault zone discussed in Chapter 2.3.3 (see Fig. 2.5). The F3, F4, and F5 faults are parts of this system and all are SW-dipping reverse faults. Fractures parallel to this group are the dominant host structures for dikes and quartz veins in the Maweigou section of the district and to a lesser extent also in the Huajian section. Related vein fillings are massive milky quartz with only minor sulfide minerals and little gold; with a few exceptions they have no economic significance.

E–W-Trending Faults
The main E–W-striking fault zone in the Niuxinshan district is termed the F1 fault. This is a planar strike-slip shear zone which dips 55°–65° to the south. Fractures with the E–W trend are host to andesitic and granitic dikes in the Maweigou and Huajian areas, and at Niuxinshan the late-stage lamprophyre dikes also trend E–W. However, except for some veins at Huajian, the E–W structures are rarely important hosts for ore-bearing quartz veins.

NE–SW-Trending Faults
The NE–SW-trending fracture zones and faults dominate in the Niuxinshan area, and the main phase of mineralization in the Niuxinshan deposit occurs in quartz veins with NE–SW trend. The major NE–SW fault zone in the Niuxinshan district is designated F2 and it is an oblique-slip fault dipping 60°–70° NW which extends more than 10 km. Dikes and ore-bearing quartz veins occupy NE–SW structures in the Niuxinshan area and, to a lesser extent, in the Huajian area. NE–SW trends are not developed in the Maweigou section of the district.

3.1.3 Gold Mineralization

The gold mineralization in the Niuxinshan district is confined to quartz veins and selvages of altered wall rock. The host rocks are the Archean amphibolites and gneisses of the Santunying Formation, local exceptions being the Niuxinshan Granite and some granitic dikes. The ore paragenesis and style of mineralization are essentially the same throughout the district and can be exemplified by the Niuxinshan deposit, on which the following description is based. The only significant differences between the Niuxinshan deposit and the other deposits and prospects are the orientation of the quartz veins (NE–SW at Niuxinshan, NW–SE at Maweigou, E–W and NW–SE at Huajian), and the fact that the granite at Niuxinshan is mineralized whereas other granites in the district are barren.

3.1.3.1 Form of the Ore Bodies

The mineralized quartz veins in the Niuxinshan deposit strike dominantly NNE–SSW to NE–SW and dip to the NW. Most veins show evidence of movement and multiple vein-filling, with trains of sheared country rock fragments within the quartz and striae on the vein walls. The richest mineralization is found in intensely brecciated quartz veins which are cemented by sulfide minerals. Most of the gold-bearing quartz veins are located in the Archean metamorphic rocks to the north and east of the Niuxinshan Granite. More than 100 veins are known, with 20 of them being productive. The present workings and drill hole data have proved mineralization to a depth of about 500 m. The veins have an undulatory shape in detail, and their thickness varies from a few centimeters up to 2.5 m (average 20–50 cm). It is common to find that the veins occur in groups within relatively narrow zones. A typical example is the No. 1 vein zone, which contains up to ten single veins and can be traced for over 1200 m in length and 300 m in width.

Where the veins cut the Niuxinshan Granite they tend to disperse into thin splays of quartz veinlets and form a zone of intense greisen-type alteration with quartz, muscovite, pyrite, and minor fluorite. Several zones are being worked in the granite but they do not contribute much to the total gold production of the Niuxinshan deposit even though the grade can reach several hundred g/t. The breccia zone on the southeastern flank of the Niuxinshan Granite contains a similar hydrothermal assemblage of quartz, muscovite, and fluorite, but pyrite is rare and assays show that the zone has no significant gold mineralization.

3.1.3.2 Macroscopic Description of the Ores

The form and mineralogy of the ore-bearing veins in the Niuxinshan deposit varies considerably depending on the host rock and on the proximity to the granite.

Veins in Amphibolite
In amphibolite, the mineralization occurs within decimeter- to meter-thick quartz veins. Wall rock alteration is present to a width of several centimeters or more depending on the degree of shearing, but the alteration zones are not significantly mineralized. Quartz, pyrite, and various base-metal sulfides dominate the vein assemblage; minor chlorite and sericite occur around fragments of wall rock. Thin veinlets of carbonate (mostly dolomite) are common in a cross-cutting relationship to the quartz veins. Sulfide minerals in the veins occur preferentially at the wall rock selvages, around inclusions of wall rock within the veins, or as thin seams and nests in quartz which parallel the walls and represent multiple reopening of the

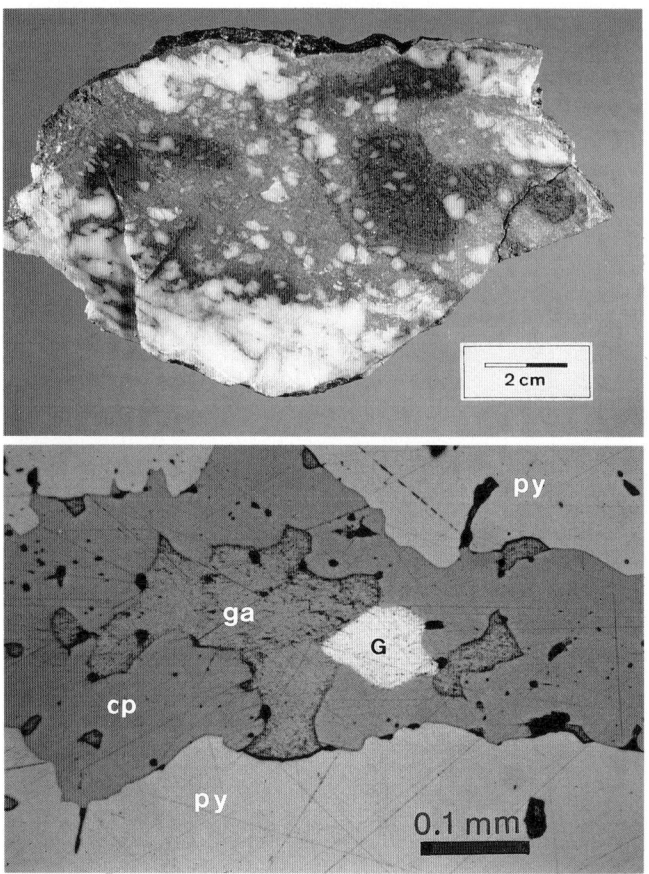

Fig. 3.4. Ore from the Niuxinshan deposit. *Above*: Brecciated quartz vein healed by sulfide minerals. *Below*: Photomicrograph showing the typical occurrence of gold (*G*) with chalcopyrite (*cp*) and galena (*ga*) filling cracks in pyrite (*py*)

veins. The typical sulfide concentration in the veins is 5–10 vol%. In the richest ores the quartz is brecciated and cemented by a network of sulfides which can make up 30% of the vein. Figure 3.4 shows an example of this type of ore.

In the vicinity of the Niuxinshan Granite and/or the granitic dikes the quartz veins bear reddish hydrothermal K-feldspar in seams along the wall rock contact. Fluorite also occurs in the veins or in their alteration envelopes near the granite contact but fluorite is absent elsewhere in the deposit.

Veins in Granite

Within the granite the mineralization occurs in highly fractured, pervasively greisenized zones some decimeters to meters thick with a network of millimeters- to centimeters-thick quartz veinlets. The ore minerals are almost exclusively pyrite with very minor base-metal sulfides. Gangue consists of quartz, muscovite, and fluorite. Gold occurs late in the paragenetic sequence together with rare galena, chalcopyrite, and sphalerite, and fills cracks or grain boundaries within granular pyrite aggregates.

3.1.3.3 Ore Petrography and Paragenesis

The petrographic descriptions given below pertain only to the mineralization within amphibolite wall rocks. The mineralization in the granite is of minor importance, and it was described above.
The mineralized quartz veins within amphibolite in the Niuxinshan deposit contain the following ore minerals: chalcopyrite, galena, native bismuth, native gold, pyrite, scheelite, sphalerite, sulfosalts of the aikinite group, tetradymite, and secondary covellite.

Pyrite
Pyrite is by far the most abundant sulfide mineral. It is found as disseminated euhedral cubes up to several millimeters in size within altered host rocks and as coarse subhedral aggregates in the quartz veins. Pyrite in the wall rocks – in contrast to vein pyrite – shows little or no cataclastic deformation and is rarely associated with other sulfides. The pyrite in quartz veins occurs throughout the paragenetic sequence although most of the pyrite formed early. This early generation of pyrite is almost always fractured and the fractures are filled with galena, sphalerite, chalcopyrite, gold, or gangue quartz and carbonate (Fig. 3.4). A later generation of pyrite can be recognized by its inclusions of galena, chalcopyrite, and gold. A third generation of pyrite occurs in cross-cutting fractures with carbonate. This generation of pyrite is generally not associated with other ore minerals.

Chalcopyrite, Sphalerite, and Galena
Chalcopyrite occurs in both the ore veins and in altered wall rock. In the wall rocks the chalcopyrite forms isolated subhedral grains associated with pyrite. Within the quartz veins most chalcopyrite is found as anhedral fracture-fillings in pyrite, together with galena, sphalerite, and gold. In weathered ore samples, chalcopyrite is locally rimmed by covellite.
Sphalerite occurs mostly in coarse anhedral aggregates intergrown with galena and pyrite in brecciated quartz. It is also found associated with chalcopyrite and galena as fracture-fillings in pyrite. Exsolution blebs and schlieren-like inclusions of chalcopyrite in sphalerite are common.
Galena occurs with sphalerite and pyrite cementing brecciated quartz and as fracture-fillings in pyrite with sphalerite, chalcopyrite, and gold. Galena is the youngest of the base-metal sulfides, and it can be found veining both sphalerite and chalcopyrite, perhaps due to remobilization. Galena is often

associated with gold. It frequently contains inclusions of native Bi and of tetradymite.

Native Gold
Gold has been observed in the following forms:

a) enclosed by and intergrown with galena, sphalerite, and/or chalcopyrite in cracks within pyrite; this is the most common form;
b) as rounded inclusions in early (cataclastic) pyrite;
c) as fracture-fillings in quartz together with pyrite.

The grain size of gold is mostly between 0.1 and 0.3 mm. Microanalysis of gold grains by SEM-EDS showed that most of the gold contains 30–35 wt% Ag but some grains, particularly those in quartz, have lower Ag concentrations of 5–15%.

Scheelite
Scheelite occurs mainly within the selvage zones of quartz veins associated with sphalerite and other sulfides. It also occurs as small isolated grains in brecciated and altered amphibolite wall rocks. In the veins the grain size can reach 1 cm. The short-wave fluorescence color of all the scheelite found is typically whitish-blue, which indicates low Mo concentrations.

Tetradymite, Native Bi, and Cu-Pb-Bi Sulfosalts
Tetradymite and native bismuth occur as brightly reflectant laminar inclusions of up to 0.1 mm size in galena. Inclusions in galena with slightly weaker reflectivity than tetradymite proved by electron microprobe analysis to have a composition close to the chemical formula $CuPbBiS_2$, which is akin to the aikinite group of sulfosalt minerals. Tetradymite is the most abundant of all the Bi-bearing minerals and it probably accounts for most of the Bi analyzed in the ores (Table 3.1).

3.1.3.4 Chemical Composition

Table 3.1 shows the compositions of nine grab samples of well-mineralized ore taken from veins in amphibolite host rocks, and one sample (6134) taken from a strongly mineralized greisen zone in the Niuxinshan Granite. The purpose of the table is to show typical element associations and give a rough idea of the concentrations; the values are not necessarily representative for the bulk deposit.

The ores in amphibolite show a consistent element association of Au-Ag-Cu-Pb-Zn ±Bi±W. The bulk Au/Ag ratios of the samples average 1.2 but they show a wide range due to the small size and variable mineralogy of the grab samples. The base metals Cu, Pb, and Zn occur at or above the 0.1% level in most samples. Sample 6134 from pyritized granite shows little

Table 3.1. Chemical composition of ore samples from the Niuxinshan deposit

Sample	6022	6023	6115	6119	6134	6153	6158	6159	6183	6186
Elements in wt %										
Cu	0.40	2.72	0.10	0.50	<0.01	0.03	0.84	0.01	1.04	0.05
Fe	4.1	6.6	4.6	4.3	21.6	3.8	13.7	12.2	20.0	11.8
Mn	0.3	0.1	0.1	0.1	0.1	0.1	0.1	0.1	0.1	0.2
Pb	0.34	0.39	0.04	1.29	0.11	0.10	0.66	3.94	3.89	0.62
S (total)	5.3	17.0	6.4	16.6	23.6	5.4	19.2	14.6	32.8	14.3
Zn	4.04	29.5	1.8	2.0	0.03	>2.0	>2.0	0.59	>2.0	>2.0
Elements in ppm										
Ag	25	62	16	86	324	36	51	11	166	41
As	7.0	6.0	25	1085	25	203	118	25	733	80
Au	6.6	50	21.8	5.6	732	4.7	63	13.7	66	179
Bi	27	56	44	203	380	114	96	8	292	55
Co	8	15	10	13	17	13	48	15	30	42
Cr	18	21	16	5	0.5	45	12	40	0.5	21
Mo	<2.5	<2.5	136	2.5	2.5	65	308	350	37	2.5
Ni	18	63	18	36	0.5	25	75	28	57	88
Sb	1.5	5.4	<5	<5	<5	<5	<5	<5	<5	<5
W	14	229	145	1700	621	1000	<1	143	200	146
Elements in ppb										
Pd	<1	<1	3	1	6	1	8	5	4	8
Pt	5	10	8	6	36	2	17	2	15	38

Analyses by Bondar-Clegg laboratories, Ottowa, Fire-assay/DCP (Au, Pd, Pt), all others by ICP.

enrichment in the base metals despite the extreme gold concentration of 730 g/t. The Bi concentration in this sample, like gold, is the highest of all the samples analyzed (380 ppm). The Au/Ag ratio is 2.2.

3.1.4 Wall Rock Alteration

Wall rock alteration is found around all mineralized veins in both the amphibolite and granite wall rocks. The igneous dikes may also produce intense wall-rock alteration in the amphibolites, and the effects of both dike and vein emplacement can be superimposed and difficult to distinguish. In the granite the total width of alteration zones reaches one or more meters and the altered rock locally contains ore grade mineralization. In the amphibolite, the visible alteration zone rarely reaches more than a few decimeters into the wall rocks and the altered rock is very weakly mineralized.

Alteration of Amphibolite
The wall rock alteration of amphibolite involves a bleaching of the rock due to the replacement of hornblende, biotite, and/or pyroxene by chlorite,

sericite, quartz, and carbonate. The bleached zones are commonly sheared and permeated by stringers of quartz and carbonate veinlets. Pyrite and lesser chalcopyrite form isolated grains in the mafic-rich portions of the wall rocks in association with hornblende and chlorite. In the vicinity of the Niuxinshan Granite and along some granitic dikes the altered amphibolite also contains red K-feldspar and fluorite. A late stage of carbonate occurs as cross-cutting veinlets which postdate other alteration minerals and the sulfide mineralization.

The chemical effects of alteration are shown in Fig. 3.5 which plots the changes in element concentration relative to the unaltered rock. The graphical "isocon" method of Grant (1986) was used to confirm that the relative gains and losses shown are not biased by a total change of mass. The alteration involved strong and consistent increases in the ore-forming elements Cu, Pb, Zn, W, Bi and, locally, Au. Elements leached from the rocks include Si, Na, the alkaline earths Ba and Sr (not shown), and also to some extent the rare earths and Y. The strong enrichments of S and CO_2 in the altered rocks show that the hydrothermal fluids were rich in these components. It may be the presence of carbonate in the fluid which caused the REE mobility (Taylor and Fryer 1984).

A special variety of wall rock alteration in the amphibolites occurs where quartz veins intersect layers of magnetite-rich amphibolite and magnetite quartzite. In these rocks the magnetite is replaced by pyrite. Advanced alteration in the magnetite-rich rocks leads to vein selvages up to 10 cm thick made up essentially of pyrite and quartz. These selvages locally contain gold values in the g/t range. The pyritization of magnetite in the wall rocks is a local but common phenomenon, and its possible significance for gold mineralization is discussed in detail in Chapter 4.3.

Alteration of Granite

The alteration in the Niuxinshan Granite is characterized by the replacement of the feldspars and biotite by quartz and white mica. Fluorite and pyrite are commonly present in the intensely altered samples. Pyrite may reach over 50 vol% of the rock, which then consititutes a rich gold ore with up to several hundred g/t Au. Carbonate is locally present, but it is later than the other secondary minerals.

The chemical effects of alteration (Fig. 3.6) involved the almost complete leaching of Na and local losses of Si and Ca. These were offset by gains of Fe, Mg, Mn, and K. Despite the destruction of plagioclase, the concentrations of Sr and Ba (not shown) increased during alteration. The altered granite is strongly enriched in S and in the chalcophile elements including gold. The "isocon" method of Grant (1986) was used to confirm that the relative changes shown are significant, since the alteration involved negligible changes in total mass of the system.

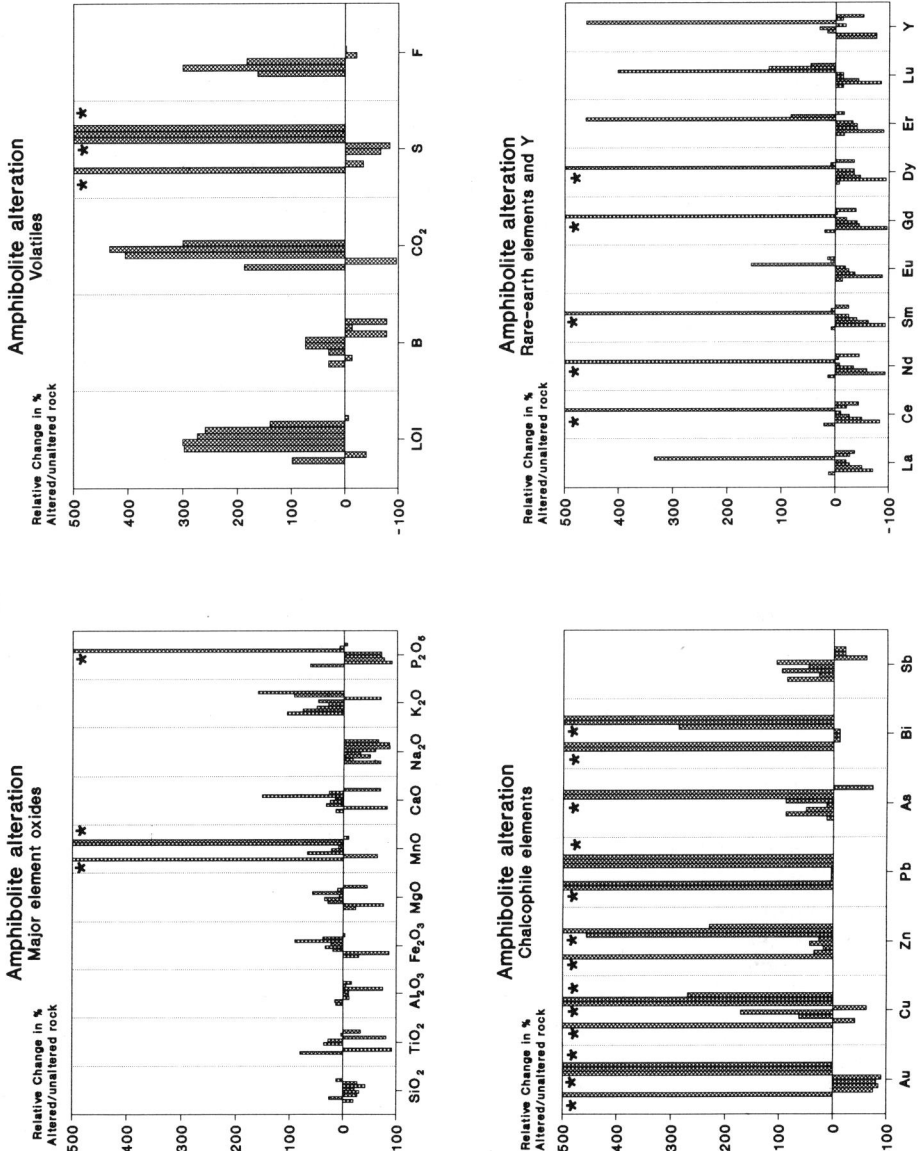

Fig. 3.5. Chemical changes accompanying wall rock alteration of amphibolites around ore veins from the Niuxinshan deposit. *Asterisks* denote element enrichments greater than 500%

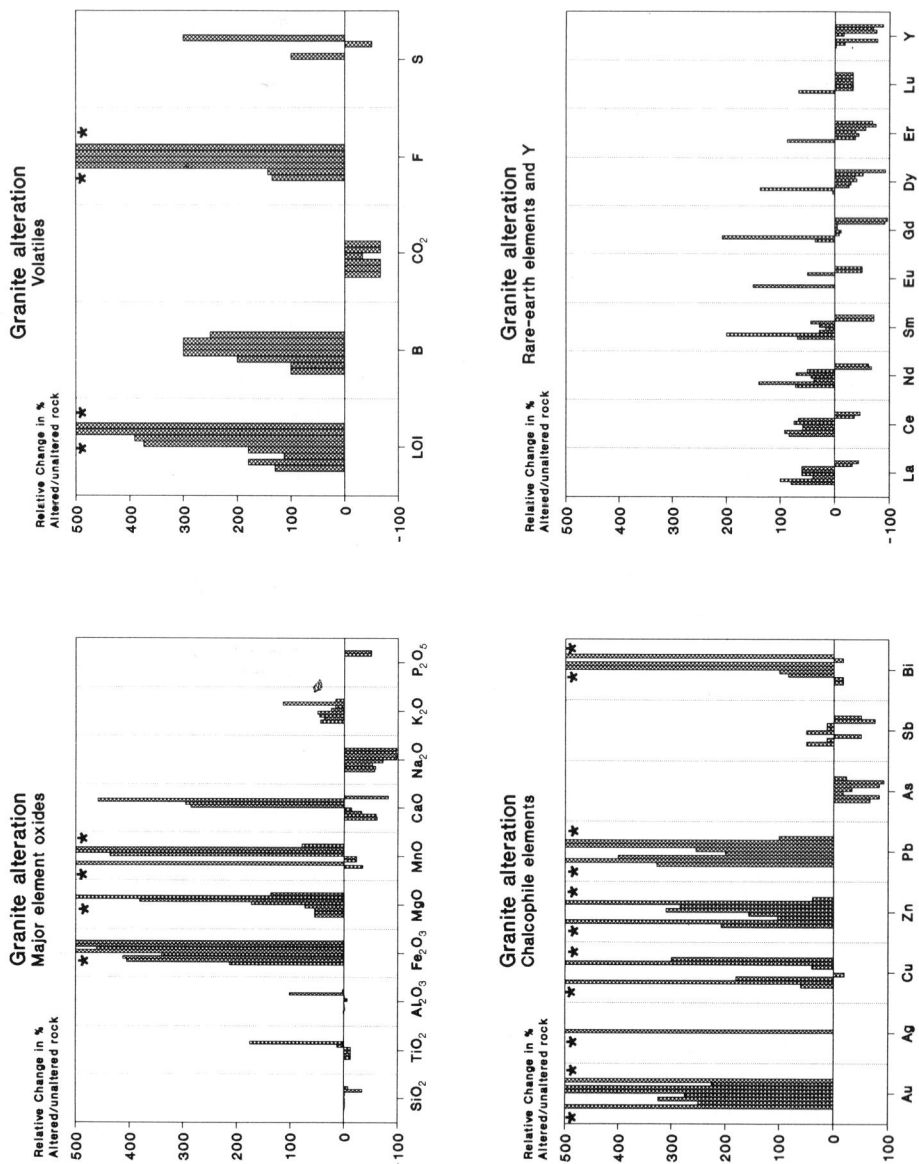

Fig. 3.6. Chemical changes accompanying wall rock alteration of the Niuxinshan Granite around ore veins, Niuxinshan deposit. *Asterisks* denote element enrichments greater than 500%

3.1.5 Age of Mineralization

The strongest field evidence constraining the age of mineralization is that the mineralized quartz veins cross-cut the Niuxinshan Granite and several of the post-granite igneous dikes, and are in turn cut by lamprophyre dikes. An absolute maximum age of the mineralization is therefore given by the age of the granite, which has been determined for the main phase (white granite) at 174 ± 14 Ma by the Rb-Sr isochron method. The dikes have not yet been extensively dated. Sun et al. (1989) reported K-Ar ages of 166 Ma from a lamprophyre from the Huajian deposit. The authors did not mention the relationship of the lamprophyre dike with ore veins, but the observations at the Niuxinshan deposit show that lamprophyres postdate the mineralization.

New age dating undertaken in this project from the Niuxinshan deposit involved Rb-Sr analysis of hydrothermal minerals and dating of vein quartz by the ^{40}Ar-^{39}Ar incremental heating method.

Rb-Sr Dating

Rb-Sr isotopic analyses were made from sericite and K-feldspar taken from the selvage zones of quartz veins. The analytical results are given in Table 3.2.

The best estimate for the age of mineralization based on these data is 175–190 Ma, from white mica (6038) and K-feldspar sample 6181. These ages are in good agreement with a K-Ar age of 188 Ma from hydrothermal sericite from the Huajian deposit in the same district reported by Yu and Jia (1989). They are also consistent, within the stated uncertainty, with the age of the Niuxinshan Granite. However, the sericite sample 6133 gives an unreasonably old age. The sample was taken from a mineralized zone in the Niuxinshan Granite, and yet it gives an apparent age nearly 100 Ma older than the host granite. The mica was apparently enriched in ^{87}Sr after its formation.

Table 3.2. Rb-Sr isotopic composition of hydrothermal vein minerals from the Niuxinshan deposit

Sample	Mineral	Rb	Sr	^{87}Rb/^{86}Sr	^{87}Sr/^{86}Sr[a]	Age[b]
6038	Sericite	620	5.56	352	1.6588(3)	190 ± 2
6133	Sericite	650	6.05	356	2.1780(4)	290 ± 2
6181	K-feldspar	508	283	5.21	0.7231(4)	175 ± 25

[a] Numbers in parentheses give uncertainty in the last digit (2 sigma).
[b] Ages in millions of years with uncertainty based on an initial ^{87}Sr/^{86}Sr ratio of 0.710 and a 1% relative error in ^{87}Rb/^{86}Sr.

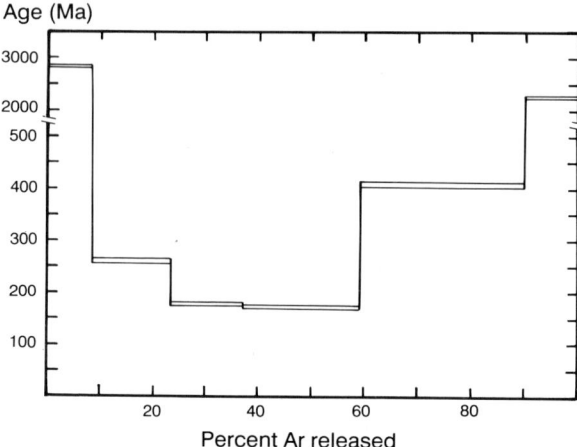

Fig. 3.7. Ar-Ar age-release curves of a sample of vein quartz from the Niuxinshan deposit. *Double lines* reflect analytical uncertainty. Analyses performed by the Ministry of Metallurgical Industry, Beijing

$^{40}Ar/^{39}Ar$ Dating

The results of $^{40}Ar/^{39}Ar$ dating of vein quartz from the Niuxinshan deposit by the incremental heating method are shown in Fig. 3.7. The analyses were performed by the Ministry of Metallurgical Industry, Beijing. The indicated plateau age of 176 ± 3 Ma agrees very well with the range of Rb-Sr ages given above and with the K-Ar age from the Huajian deposit.

3.1.6 Fluid Inclusions

Fluid inclusions from the Niuxinshan deposit were studied by both microthermometric methods and by chemical analyses of bulk fluid extracted by decrepitation. The nature of the samples was such that only fluorite and sphalerite were well suited for microthermometry, whereas the chemical analyses were performed on samples of vein quartz. This difference in the materials analyzed should be kept in mind when interpreting the results.

Microthermometry

Most samples of vein quartz from the Niuxinshan deposit are poorly suited for microthermometry because the quartz is obscured by clouds of very small secondary fluid inclusions. On the other hand, samples of fluorite and sphalerite from the ore veins contain large fluid inclusions well suited for microthermometry. Based on their large size, regular form, and random orientation in the host grains, the inclusions are interpreted to be primary

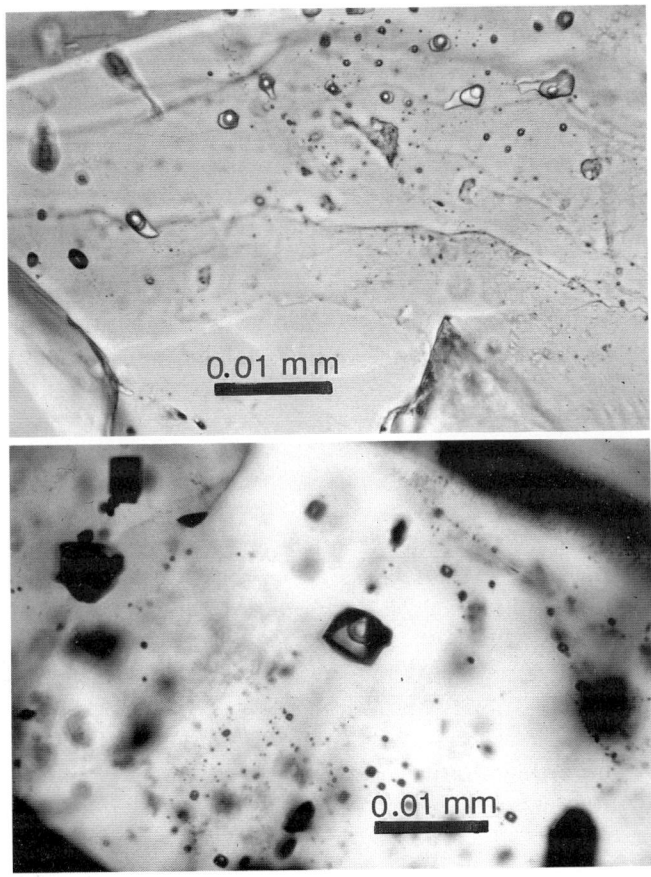

Fig. 3.8. Primary CO_2-H_2O fluid inclusions in fluorite (*above*) and in sphalerite (*below*) from the Niuxinshan deposit

(Roedder 1984). Secondary inclusions in these samples, recognized by their alignment along microcracks, were observed but not measured.

All samples measured come from quartz veins in amphibolite host rocks. The fluorite occurs in the altered vein selvages. In both fluorite and sphalerite the primary inclusions are rich in CO_2, and most inclusions show three phases at room temperature (H_2O liquid, CO_2 liquid, and gas). The degree of fill is about 70%. Examples are shown in Fig. 3.8. Secondary inclusions are generally smaller, have lower gas/liquid proportions, and show no visible liquid CO_2 at room temperature.

Table 3.3 gives the microthermometric data from three samples of fluorite and two of sphalerite. In general, the results from the two host minerals are very similar. The melting temperatures of CO_2 below $-56.6\,°C$ indicate some impurity of this phase, as is also suggested by the chemical analyses of

Table 3.3. Summary of microthermometric data from fluid inclusions from the Niuxinshan deposit

Host mineral	Sample	T_m CO_2	T_m clathrate	T_h CO_2	T_h final
Fluorite	6019-1 (n = 20)	n.d. –	7.9 (0.1)	n.d. –	273 (3.5)
	6019-1b (n = 34)	−57.2 (x)	8.2 (0.4)	29.3 (0.2)	313 (5.2)
	6019-1a (n = 29)	n.d. –	7.9 (0.2)	n.d. –	315 (3.9)
Sphalerite	6018a1 (n = 6)	−59.0 (x)	6.4 (0.2)	21.3 (1.9)	266 (6.4)
	6018a2 (n = 5)	−58.3 (0.1)	6.6 (0.1)	27.6 (1.0)	>280 –

All temperatures represent average values in °C.
T_m, melting temperature; T_h, homogenization temperature; n.d., not determined; (x), number of measurements to small for statistical analysis.
The number of measurements (n) and the standard deviation are given in parentheses.

bulk fluid from inclusions in quartz discussed below. The estimation of salinity from the clathrate melting temperatures is only approximate because of the CO_2 impurity. A minimum estimate, based on the pure CO_2-H_2O-NaCl system, is 3 to 7.5 wt% NaCl equivalent. The final homogenization temperatures for inclusions in fluorite range from 275 to 315 °C (homogenization to the liquid phase or critical). The homogenization temperature of inclusions in sphalerite could rarely be measured because of decrepitation. Some inclusions homogenized to the liquid phase at 266 °C ± 6 °C but most inclusions decrepitated before homogenization at temperatures of 270 to 280 °C. Based on the similarity of inclusion types between sphalerite and fluorite, it is likely that the homogenization temperature in sphalerite would also be around 300 °C.

These temperatures represent a minimum estimate of trapping conditions because no pressure correction was applied. From the position of the CO_2-H_2O solvus at the appropriate salinity given by Brown and Lamb (1989) a minimum trapping pressure of about 1.5–2 kbar can be derived from these data. The true conditions of trapping may be close to 430–490 °C and 3.5–5 kbar, based on oxygen isotopic thermometry of vein quartz and K-feldspar (see below) combined with the fluid isochores calculated assuming pure CO_2-H_2O-NaCl from Brown (1989).

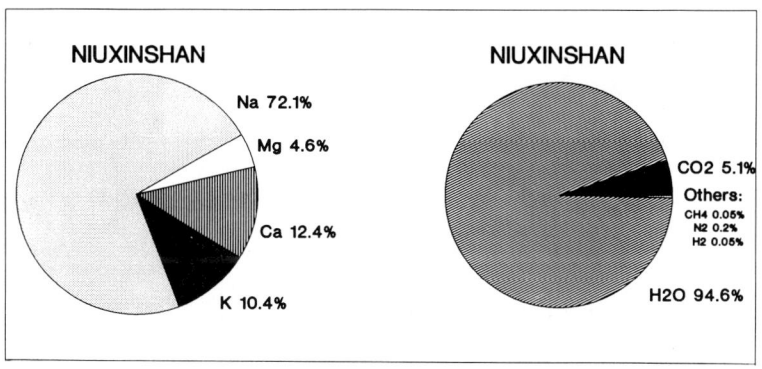

Fig. 3.9. Pie diagrams showing the average composition of bulk fluid inclusion contents from vein quartz in the Niuxinshan deposit. From unpublished analyses of the Ministry of Metallurgical Industry, Beijing

Chemical Analyses

Chemical analyses were performed by laboratories of the Ministry of Metallurgical Industry in Beijing. Bulk fluid was released from the inclusions by heating to decrepitation in vacuum. Dilution from secondary inclusions was minimized by analyzing only the fluid fraction released above 250°C, after decrepitation of most secondary inclusions. Nevertheless, the results are sure to reflect some mixture of different fluid generations and they cannot be directly compared with the microthermometric data, which was obtained from selected primary inclusions in different host minerals.

Figure 3.9 shows the average fluid composition in terms of the proportion of dissolved cations and gas species. The complete data are contained in an internal project report to the European Community and may be obtained from the authors on request or from the European Community (1990). Sodium makes up about 72% of the dissolved cations. Potassium and Ca each constitute an additional 10%, and Mg is the least abundant. The most abundant gas species is CO_2, with about 5 mol%. Other detectable gases together make up less than 0.5 mol%.

3.1.7 Stable Isotopic Data

This section presents new data on oxygen and carbon isotopic composition of gangue minerals from ore veins in the Niuxinshan deposit. The main purpose of the analyses was to provide estimates of the temperature of mineralization, and only this aspect is discussed here. The implications of the isotopic data to the source of mineralizing fluids is discussed in Chapter 4.6.2, together with data from the other deposits.

Table 3.4. Oxygen and carbon isotopic composition of quartz, K-feldspar, and carbonate from hydrothermal veins in the Niuxinshan deposit

Sample	Mineral	$\delta^{13}C$ PDP	$\delta^{18}O$ SMOW	Temperature (°C) Ksp-Qtz[a]
6020	K-feldspar	–	9.2	–
6020	Quartz	–	10.9	470
6111	K-feldspar	–	8.7	–
6111	Quartz	–	10.6	430
6181	K-feldspar	–	10.0	–
6181	Quartz	–	11.6	493
6555	K-feldspar	–	11.2	–
6555	Quartz	–	11.7	1098
6173	Dolomite	−6.3	9.7	–

[a] Temperatures calculated from quartz-alkali feldspar fractionation factors of Clayton et al. (1989).
The analytical precision of ±0.2‰, corresponds to a temperature uncertainty of ±70 °C.

Table 3.4 lists the isotopic data and the temperatures calculated from quartz-K-feldspar pairs. Four samples of vein quartz from the Niuxinshan deposit show a narrow compositional range of $\delta^{18}O$ (SMOW) from 10.6 to 11.6‰. The K-feldspar samples have more variable isotopic composition, from 8.7 to 10.2‰. The quartz is consistently enriched in ^{18}O relative to coexisting K-feldspar, which is consistent with isotopic equilibrium (O'Neil 1986). The temperatures calculated from the quartz-K-feldspar fractionation factors (based on Clayton et al. 1989) from three of the four mineral pairs fall in the range of 430 to 490 °C (note the high uncertainty of ±70 °C), and this is further evidence for isotopic equilibrium. The fourth mineral pair yields an impossibly high temperature (1098 °C).

These temperatures are 100 to 150 °C higher than the fluid inclusion homogenization temperatures. This difference may be reasonable since the true trapping temperatures of the fluid inclusions are expected to be higher than their homogenization temperatures, which represent only minimum estimates. On the other hand, the P-T conditions suggested by isotopic thermometry combined with fluid isochores (430–490 °C, 3.5–5.5 kbar) indicate upper greenschist facies conditions, and this is inconsistent with the brittle deformation style of the veins.

3.2 Sanjia District

The Sanjia gold mining district is located about 250 km northeast of Beijing in Qinglong county, Hebei province (see Fig. 3.1). There are presently (as of 1989) three producing gold deposits in the district, namely, Sanjia,

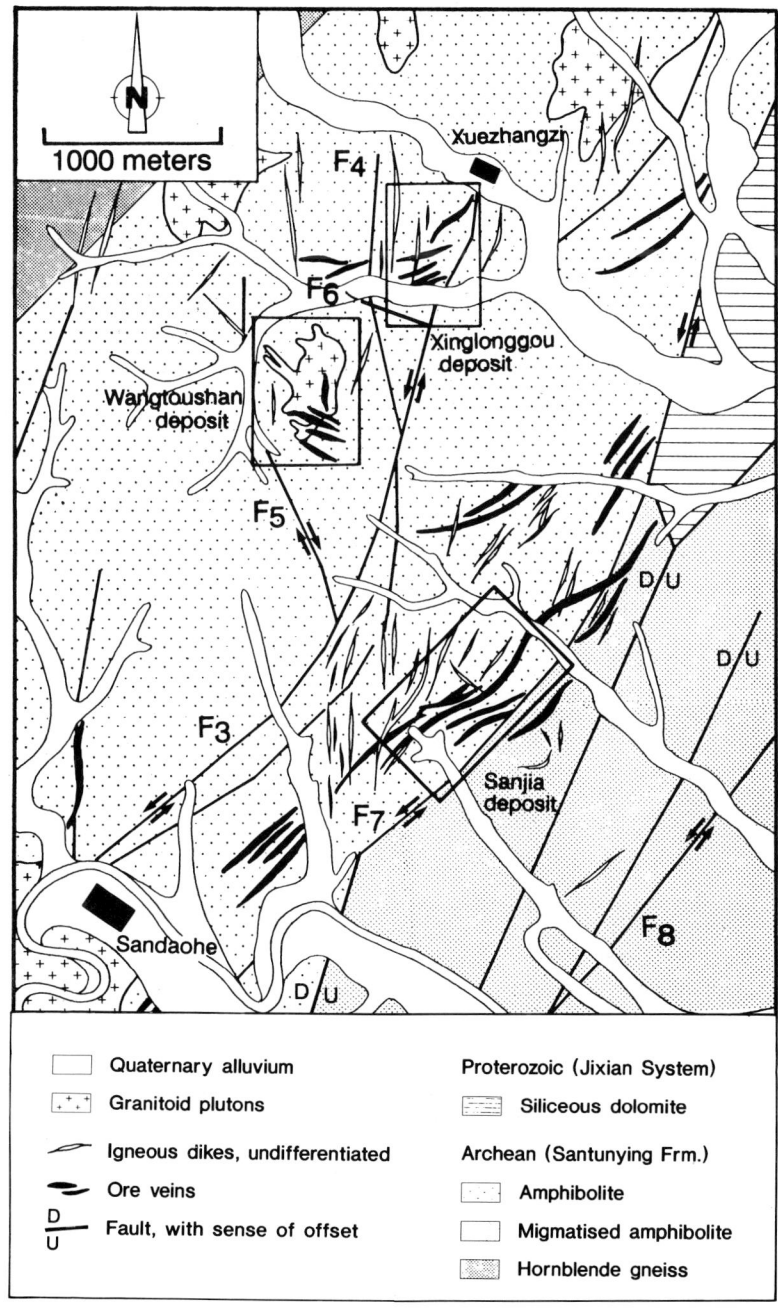

Fig. 3.10. Simplified geologic map of the Sanjia district. The locations of the Sanjia, Wangtoushan, and Xinglonggou gold deposits are *boxed*

Wangtoushan, and Xinglonggou, all of which are described in some detail in this text. The location of these deposits is shown in a geologic map of the district in Fig. 3.10.

The Sanjia Deposit
The Sanjia deposit was discovered during the Qing dynasty (1644–1911 A.D.). The gold ore occurs in quartz veins within amphibolite host rocks of the Archean Qianxi Group. The deposit contains 20 ore-bearing veins, the largest and most productive of which is about 1 km long and known to a depth of 500 m. The veins range in thickness from a few centimeters to 1 m. Ore bodies have gold concentrations of about 20 g/t on average. The Sanjia deposit is mined by the Qinglong county government. The workings are entirely underground. The ore treatment is done in a central dressing plant at Sanjia village.

The Wangtoushan Deposit
The Wangtoushan deposit was discovered in 1976. Gold ore occurs in quartz veins within Archean amphibolites of the Qianxi Group and, to a lesser extent, within a granite intrusion. Six gold-quartz veins are worked in an underground operation. The ore grade averages about 30 g/t. The mine is run by Qinglong county. Ore is treated at the central dressing plant in Sanjia.

The Xinglonggou Deposit
This gold deposit was first discovered in 1969. Like the other deposits in the district, the ore occurs in quartz veins within Archean amphibolites. About ten veins are known. The average ore grade is 23 g/t Au. The Xinglonggou mine is run by the Qinglong County government and is one of the most promising of the newer gold prospects in the Sanjia district. The workings are entirely underground.

3.2.1 Host Rock Lithology

The main host rocks in the Sanjia district are Archean amphibolites and gneisses of the Santunying Formation, Qianxi Group. In the northeastern part of the district Middle Proterozoic sedimentary rocks (Jixian and Changcheng Systems) are in fault contact with the Archean rocks (Fig. 3.10), but the Proterozoic rocks do not constitute a host to ore. Igneous rocks are represented by several granitic intrusions of presumed Yanshanian age, and by numerous felsic and mafic dikes, most of which are younger than the granites and older than the mineralization.

3.2.1.1 Archean Rocks

The Archean Santunying Formation consists of a complex series of amphibolites which are variably migmatized. In the geologic map of the Sanjia district (Fig. 3.10) the Santunying Formation is divided into a lower, middle, and upper section. Note that this geologic division is local and it may not be valid regionally.

The structurally lowest unit (fine stippled pattern in Fig. 3.10) consists of highly migmatized interlayered hornblende amphibolites and biotite amphibolites. The migmatization is expressed by schlieren and veinlets of leucosome and/or K-feldspar blastesis. Migmatization is strongest in the lower parts of the unit and decreases upwards. The middle unit (coarse stipple in Fig. 3.10) consists of nonmigmatitic layered hornblende amphibolites and biotite amphibolites. Most of the mines in the Sanjia district are located in this section of the Santunying Formation. The upper section of the Santunying Formation consists of a variety of amphibolites and hornblende-plagioclase gneisses which occur at the northwest corner of the area (shaded pattern in Fig. 3.10) and do not constitute a host to ore.

Important minor rock types within the Santunying Formation include quartz-magnetite amphibolites which grade into magnetite quartzites, and hornblendites. The layers of quartz-magnetite amphibolite range in thickness from a few centimeters to about 1 m and are strictly parallel to the surrounding rock structure. They occur in all sections of the Santunying Formation but seem most abundant in the rocks of the middle section in the area of the Sanjia deposit. The hornblendites occur as discontinuous lenses, some showing boudinage structure, or as isolated xenoliths in the amphibolites of all sections of the Santunying Formation. These ultramafic rocks probably represent relics of former dikes in the protolith sequence.

All of the rocks in the Santunying Formation are strongly foliated, with foliation parallel to lithologic layering, and small-scale isoclinal folds are commonly seen in outcrop. Details of the structure are discussed in Chapter 3.2.2.

3.2.1.2 Granite and Dikes

Several intrusive stocks of presumed Yanshanian age intrude the Archean basement in the Sanjia district (Fig. 3.10). Two of these intrusions (Wangtoushan and Sanyihe) are locally mineralized although the gold concentrations are subeconomic. The Wangtoushan Granite is directly associated with the Wangtoushan gold deposit. The Sanyihe Granite is located about 3 km southwest of the Sanjia deposit.

The Wangtoushan Granite is a small pluton of medium-grained leucocratic pinkish granite (outcrop area $0.25\,km^2$) with several NE–SW- and NW–SE-striking apophyses. On the southeastern border of the pluton is a breccia zone consisting of decimeter- to meter-size angular blocks of granite cemented by quartz and graphic granite/pegmatite. The granite consists of approximately 40% albite, 40% K-feldspar, 20% quartz, and 1–2% biotite. The chemical composition reflects the highly leucocratic nature of the granite, with an average 76 wt% SiO_2, 9 wt% total alkalis (K_2O/Na_2O near 1), and the sum of total Fe as FeO, MgO, MnO, CaO, and TiO_2 is less than 1.5 wt%. The concentrations of Ba (average 185 ppm), Sr (average 13 ppm), and Rb (average 247 ppm) are typical for a moderately differentiated granite. The chondrite-normalized REE pattern (not shown) has a large negative Eu anomaly and nearly equal light and heavy REE enrichments. A summary of analytical data is given in Appendix 1.

The Sanyihe Granite forms a small intrusion (about 3 km^2 in outcrop) on the southwestern edge of the Sanjia district. The light gray granite is medium-grained, equigranular, and consists of approximately 35% oligoclase, 40% K-feldspar, 20% quartz, and 5% biotite, with accessory titanite, rutile, apatite, and primary white mica. The chemical composition is very similar to that of the Wangtoushan Granite summarized above, although it is slightly less leucocratic and has correspondingly higher Fe, Mg, and Ti concentrations (see Appendix 1).

Igneous dikes of both mafic and felsic composition are abundant in the Sanjia district. Three groups of dikes are distinguished: porphyritic diorite, granitic (with aplitic or pegmatitic texture), and lamprophyre. All three groups intrude along steeply westward-dipping NE–SW- and N–S-trending faults and fracture zones. The most prominent dikes in terms of size are the granitic dikes, which are typically several meters thick and are exposed over several hundred meters along strike. In the Wangtoushan area it is clear that many of the granitic dikes are apophyses of the Wangtoushan Granite, and it is possible that the other dikes in the district are likewise connected to larger granitic intrusions at depth. Field relations show that all of the dikes cut the granitic stocks at the present erosional level. Cross-cutting relations among the different dikes are not abundant. In some cases, the dioritic dikes are cut by granitic dikes although relations to the contrary can also be found. Both the dioritic and granitic dikes are cut by the ore veins. It is clear that the lamprophyre dikes are the latest intrusions, and they also clearly postdate the mineralization. The largest dikes are shown in Fig. 3.10 but are not differentiated by composition.

3.2.2 Host Rock Structures

The Archean basement rocks in the Sanjia district are isoclinally folded, and the associated axial-planar foliation strikes NE–SW and dips steeply NW. Extensive systems of fracture and fault zones postdate the folding. The granites and dikes intruded after the folding episode and are affected only by brittle deformation.

3.2.2.1 Folds and Foliation

The Sanjia district is located on the eastern limb of the NNE trending Dushan Anticlinorium which, according to Sun et al. (1989), belongs to the early generation of folds, i.e., Archean/Early Proterozoic (see Chap. 2.3.1). The folds of this generation dominate the structure of the Archean basement rocks in the district. They are tight to isoclinal folds overturned to the east with northwest-dipping axial planes. The foliation in the amphibolites and gneisses is axial planar to these folds, strikes generally NE–SW and dips 50°–70° to the NW. The foliation is parallel with lithologic layering and it postdates the migmatization, i.e., the leucosomes are also folded and foliated with the surrounding rock.

3.2.2.2 Faults and Fractures

There are two main orientations of faults and fracture zones in the Sanjia district, namely NE–SW and N–S. Most of the mineralization and most of the igneous dikes are associated with the NE- to NNE-trending structures. A few faults of NW–SE trend also occur, and many of these are later than the previously mentioned structures and also postdate the mineralization.

NE–SW-Trending Faults
A number of NE–SW-trending faults extend through the entire district and these are designated on the geologic map (Fig. 3.10) as F3, F7, and F8 (no age sequence is implied by the numbers). This group of faults strikes 20°–35° and dips 50°–80° to the NW. They are sinistral oblique-slip faults which consist of brecciated and sheared zones several meters to tens of meters wide with gently undulating fault surfaces. Most of the ore veins in the Sanjia and Xinglonggou deposits occur in faults interpreted to be secondary splays of the F3 and F7 faults.

N–S-Trending Faults
Faults and fractures with a N–S strike direction have strike-slip characteristics or are tensional in nature. Many of the tensional N–S fault zones have been intruded by dikes (Fig. 3.10). The main map-scale fault with a N–S orientation is the F4 fault which dips 70°–80° to the west and is characterized by a brecciated zone which is locally silicified and mineralized.

NW–SE-Trending Faults
NW–SE-trending faults and fractures have been divided into two groups according to their relative age. The earlier group of faults are dextral strike-slip faults interpreted as conjugate faults to the sinistral NE–SW-trending faults discussed above. A map-scale example is the F5 fault (Fig. 3.10). The later group of NW-trending faults cuts igneous dikes and ore-bearing veins.

An example is the F6 fault, which is a strike-slip fault striking 300° and dipping 65° to the SW.

3.2.3 Gold Mineralization

The gold mineralization in the Sanjia district occurs in quartz-sulfide veins which cross-cut both amphibolite and also Yanshanian Granite (Wangtoushan and Sanyihe Granites); however, only those veins within amphibolite wall rocks contain economic ore bodies. The style of mineralization and the ore paragenesis in the Sanjia, Wangtoushan, and Xinglonggou deposits are very similar. The following descriptions are generalized from observations of all three deposits except where stated otherwise.

3.2.3.1 *Form of the Ore Bodies*

All of the economic ore bodies in the Sanjia district occur in veins within Archean metamorphic rocks. Where the mineralized quartz veins cut the Wangtoushan and Sanyihe Granites, they splay out into thin veinlets in a zone of pervasively altered (sericite-quartz-pyrite) granite. These zones contain only subeconomic gold values.
In the *Sanjia deposit* the ore-bearing veins strike 60–70° and dip 25–50° to the NW. The host fault surfaces are planar and display indications of dextral movement. These faults are considered to be secondary splays of the main F7 fault (see Fig. 3.10) although the sense of offset on F7 is sinistral.
In the *Xinglonggou deposit* the ore-bearing veins also occupy fault zones showing evidence of shear. Unlike Sanjia, both NE–SW faults with dextral shear and NW–SE faults with sinistral shear occur, and these are interpreted as a conjugate pair of structures related to E–W-directed stress.
In the *Wangtoushan deposit* most of the veins occur in WNW-trending tensional faults which show only minor shearing. The ore-bearing veins have a maximum length of 600 m and a width of 10 to 60 cm. The veins dip 10–45° NE. One NNW-trending gold-bearing quartz vein also contains an economic ore body.

3.2.3.2 *Macroscopic Description of the Ores*

Because only local, subeconomic mineralization occurs in the granites of the Sanjia district, the following discussion is confined to ores in amphibolite wall rocks. The mineralization typically forms in milky white massive vein quartz. The veins pinch and swell and show evidence of multiple re-opening. Rich parts of the veins may be strongly brecciated and cemented with pyrite and base metal sulfides. The wall rocks are generally highly sheared and

Fig. 3.11. *Above*: Photograph of ore veins in underground workings of the Wangtoushan deposit. *Below*: Photomicrograph of ore from the Xinglonggou deposit. Tetrahedrite (*te*), chalcopyrite (*cp*), and galena (*ga*) occur with gangue (*black*) in fractured pyrite (*py*)

altered but rarely are they significantly mineralized except directly at the vein contact. Slivers of wall rock are common in the veins near the walls. The sulfide minerals occur along the vein selvage and in seams and nests within the veins. Locally, an early mineralization by pyrite can be distinguished macroscopically from a later pyrite-galena-sphalerite mineralization based on different generations of vein opening and filling. The typical sulfide concentrations in the mineralized portions of the veins is 5 to 10 vol%. Carbonates typically occur as late-stage gangue minerals filling cross-cutting fractures or disseminated in the altered wall rocks. A typical example of ore veins in amphibolite host rock is shown in Fig. 3.11.

The veins at the Wangtoushan deposit have some special features which are not found in the Sanjia or the Xinglonggou deposits. Reddened K-feldspar commonly occurs in the quartz veins near the wall rock selvages, and in some cases fluorite accompanies the K-feldspar in the veins. More often, fluorite occurs in the altered selvage zones. A third mineralogical peculiarity of the Wangtoushan deposit is the occurrence of accessory molybdenite. These features are thought to reflect the proximity of the Wangtoushan Granite.

3.2.3.3 Ore Petrography and Paragenesis

The ore paragenesis in the three deposits of Sanjia, Xinglonggou, and Wangtoushan is nearly identical. All three deposits contain chalcopyrite, galena, native gold, pyrite, sphalerite, and tetrahedrite. Pyrrhotite and native bismuth were found only at the Sanjia deposit, covellite occurs as a secondary mineral at Xinglonggou, and the mineralization at Wangtoushan contains accessory molybdenite and scheelite.

The following descriptions apply in general to the Sanjia district except where otherwise indicated.

Pyrite

Pyrite is the main sulfide mineral and it occurs in both the quartz veins and altered wall rocks. In the wall rocks pyrite occurs as scattered grains associated with mafic minerals (chlorite, hornblende), and it contains numerous silicate inclusions. In the veins pyrite is the oldest sulfide mineral and it occurs in grains and grain aggregates with individual crystals up to 5 mm in size. Locally, pyrite forms nearly monomineralic seams of some centimeters thickness in vein quartz. The pyrite is strongly fractured and filled by galena, chalcopyrite, tetrahedrite, and quartz (Fig. 3.11). Pyrrhotite (Sanjia deposit only) and chalcopyrite occur rarely as inclusions of a few microns in diameter. A younger pyrite generation occurs together with carbonate in late-stage veinlets which cut the earlier ore and gangue minerals. This late pyrite generation is not associated with other sulfides.

Chalcopyrite, Sphalerite, and Galena

Chalcopyrite is found almost exclusively in the veins with only rare grains dispersed in the wall rock selvages. Chalcopyrite in the veins commonly occurs intergrown with galena, sphalerite and tetrahedrite in fractured pyrite. Chalcopyrite is also common as exsolution blebs and inclusions in sphalerite. Rarely, fracture fillings of massive chalcopyrite with inclusions of galena occur in quartz. Finally, a late stage of chalcopyrite may be found locally in fractures with carbonate. At the Xinglonggou deposit, covellite locally rims chalcopyrite in weathered samples.

Sphalerite is not abundant in the Sanjia district. The mineral most commonly forms as fracture fillings in pyrite together with galena, chalcopyrite, and tetrahedrite. Isolated grains and grain aggregates of sphalerite occur in quartz, and sphalerite exsolution starlets in chalcopyrite also occur.

Galena occurs mainly in fracture fillings in pyrite and quartz. Galena veins sphalerite and is intergrown with tetrahedrite and chalcopyrite. Native gold is frequently associated or intergrown with galena.

Native Gold

Native gold occurs mainly intergrown with galena, chalcopyrite, and tetrahedrite in fractures within pyrite. Minor amounts of gold are also found in fractures within quartz. Gold occurs locally as inclusions in pyrite, tetrahedrite, and even sphalerite. The size of the gold grains is mostly between 0.1 and 0.3 mm with rare coarse aggregates of up to 5 mm in size. SEM-EDS analysis of gold grains showed three compositional groups as follows:

– gold grains associated with sulfides in fractured pyrite have 35–45 wt% Ag,
– isolated gold inclusions in pyrite have concentrations of 20–30 wt% Ag,
– gold in cracks of quartz show the highest Ag concentrations of approximately 55 wt%.

Tetrahedrite

Tetrahedrite typically occurs intergrown with galena, chalcopyrite, and sphalerite in cracks of pyrite and quartz. It overgrows and veins chalcopyrite and galena and is therefore clearly younger than those minerals. The size of the tetrahedrite aggregates can reach several millimeters.

Pyrrhotite

Pyrrhotite is a rare mineral and it was found only in minor amounts as some micron-sized inclusions in pyrite at the Sanjia deposit.

Molybdenite

Molybdenite occurs only in the Wangtoushan deposit, where it forms irregular, felty aggregates of up to 2 mm in diameter in the quartz veins within and near the Wangtoushan Granite, and in the altered wall rocks associated with fluorite, carbonate, and rutile. In rare cases, molybdenite occurs in cracks of pyrite.

Native Bismuth

Native bismuth was found in samples from the Sanjia deposit as micron-sized inclusions in galena.

3.2.3.4 Chemical Composition

The compositions of 17 grab samples of well-mineralized ore taken from the Sanjia district are compiled in Table 3.5. The purpose of the analyses is to

Table 3.5. Chemical composition of ore samples from the Sanjia district, eastern Hebei province

Deposit	Xinglonggou					Wangtoushan								Sanjia			
Sample	6002	6003	6293	6294	6088	6262	6264	6272	6305	6314	6212	6214	6222	6223	6225	6227	6246
Elements in wt %																	
Cu	0.10	0.10	0.52	0.64	0.08	0.01	<0.01	0.01	2.56	0.72	0.59	0.18	0.24	2.35	0.99	0.59	0.08
Fe	27.1	26.7	10.8	9.6	29.5	18.7	25.8	15.8	5.4	30.4	4.6	3.4	8.2	11.8	7.1	2.6	15.1
Mn	<0.01	<0.01	0.01	0.05	<0.01	0.04	0.03	0.08	0.29	0.03	0.49	0.36	0.18	0.21	0.75	0.26	0.05
Pb	0.56	0.42	0.84	1.27	0.37	0.68	0.34	0.29	6.88	0.67	0.47	1.02	0.61	18.3	2.91	6.96	0.35
S (total)	22.0	24.0	11.7	11.5	25.0	19.3	30.1	17.9	12.0	34.7	10.7	3.5	10.1	22.4	10.8	8.3	17.1
Zn	0.01	0.01	0.02	0.02	0.07	0.25	<0.01	<0.01	12.68	0.18	<0.01	<0.01	12.8	2.0	<0.01	2.0	<0.01
Elements in ppm																	
Ag	133	133	158	488	140	298	200	228	98	60	31	51	51	139	126	55	186
As	13	50	55	607	10	25	25	25	311	25	453	25	25	353	353	269	25
Au	19	27	31	81	27	0.7	66	13	25	30	31	23	48	99	54	39	173
Bi	170	160	179	404	320	525	448	484	126	94	24	72	95	178	240	57	760
Co	16	20	22	17	35	14	12	19	30	39	14	18	16	54	42	13	22
Cr	21	23	3	1	6	0.5	0.5	15	11	0.5	40	60	7	13	4	2	4
Mo	<5	<5	18	14	110	704	<5	239	<5	14	2.5	2.5	21	2.5	2.5	2.5	2.5
Ni	10	14	30	50	33	19	24	24	91	52	45	117	36	300	73	32	40
Sb	5.6	16	<5	23	2.6	<5	<5	<5	<5	<5	<5	<5	<5	123	<5	40	<5
W	1.5	1.5	15	34	1.5	31	12	13	100	30	100	14	23	100	100	100	24
Zn	–	–	–	–	–	–	25	36	–	–	16	29	–	–	12	–	33
Elements in ppb																	
Pd	<1	<1	4	5	<1	2	5	6	3	3	3	3	4	6	4	4	8
Pt	5	5	14	25	10	2	23	32	13	16	15	12	15	30	17	15	37

Analyses by Bondar-Clegg laboratories, Ottowa. Fire-assay/DCP (Au, Pd, Pt), all other elements by ICP.

reveal typical element associations in the ore and to give a rough idea of the concentrations; they are not necessarily representative for the bulk deposits. Characteristic element associations of the ores in the Sanjia district are Au-Ag-Cu-Pb-Bi $\pm$Zn $\pm$ Sb $\pm$W. Mo is significant only in the Wangtoushan deposit, where molybdenite occurs in the veins. Gold concentrations in the Sanjia district reach over 100 g/t, but values of 20 to 30 g/t can be considered typical. The Ag/Au weight ratios are invariably greater than one, and with a few exceptions the ratios range from 1 to 2 in the Sanjia deposit, up to 4 to 8 in the other deposits. The base metals Cu and Pb are each present in concentrations of greater than 0.1 wt%. The Zn concentration is usually less than 200 ppm, although it reaches several percent in exceptional samples.

3.2.4 Wall Rock Alteration

Wall rock alteration is well developed around the veins in both the amphibolite and granite wall rocks. The igneous dikes also produce intense wall rock alteration, and the effects of both dike and vein emplacement may be superimposed.

Alteration of Amphibolite
The alteration of amphibolite is characterised macroscopically by a bleaching of the rock due to the replacement of hornblende and/or biotite by chlorite, sericite, epidote, quartz and carbonate. The bleached zones are commonly sheared and permeated by stringers of quartz and carbonate. Pyrite and rarely chalcopyrite form isolated grains in the mafic-rich portions of the wall rcks. In the Wangtoushan deposit the alteration zones also include red K-feldspar and fluorite.
The chemical changes brought about by alteration (Fig. 3.12) include strong and consistent increases in the ore-forming elements Cu, Pb, Zn, W, Bi, Au, and in the volatiles S and CO_2. Elements leached from the rocks include Si, Na, Fe, Mg, and also the rare earths and Y. The graphical "isocon" method of Grant (1986) was used to confirm that the alteration involved negligible changes in total mass of the system, and therefore the relative changes shown are significant.
A special variety of wall rock alteration in the amphibolites affects layers of magnetite-rich amphibolite and magnetite quartzite. In these rocks the magnetite is replaced by pyrite and in strongly pyritized rocks the gold values may reach into the g/t range. The pyritization of magnetite in the wall rocks and its significance for gold mineralization is discussed in detail in Chapter 4.3.

Alteration of Granite
The Wangtoushan and Sanyihe Granites show the same type of alteration where they are cut by mineralized quartz veins. The alteration is charac-

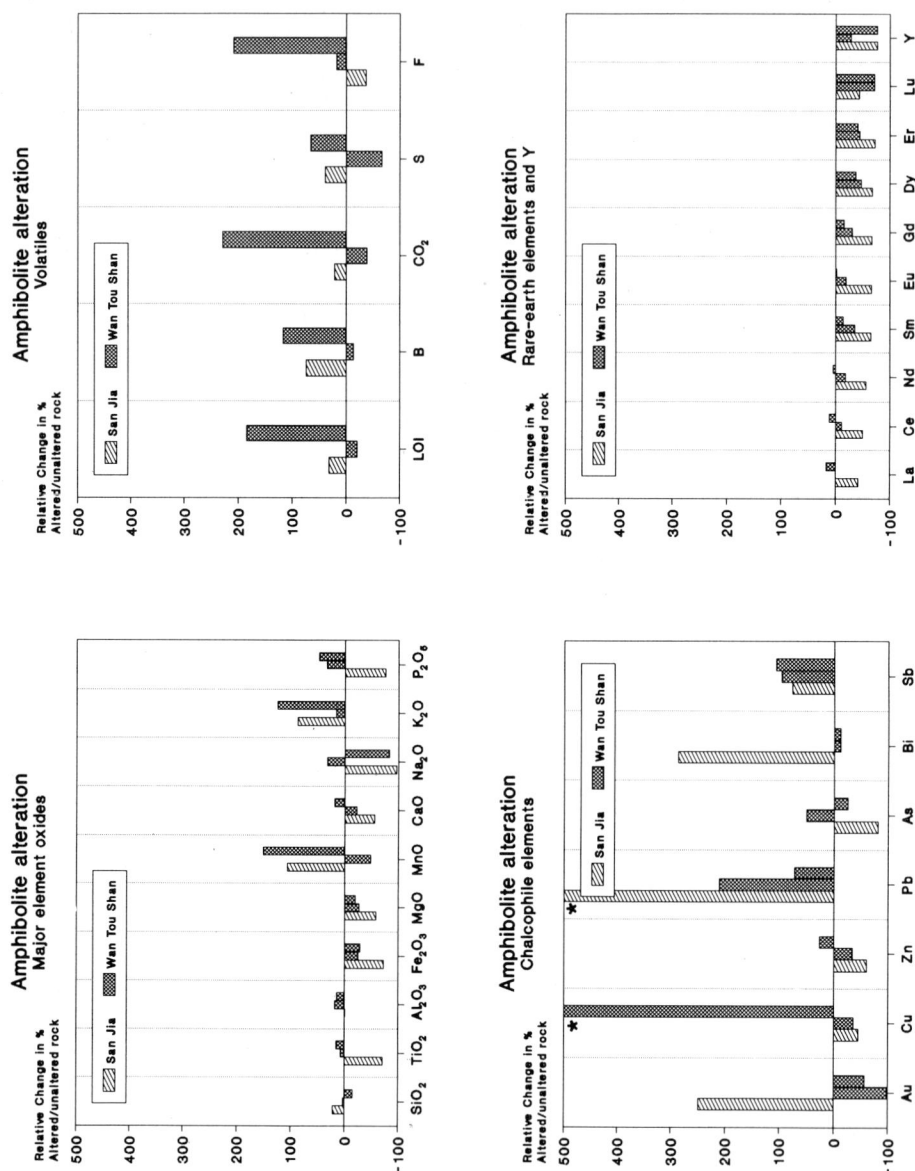

Fig. 3.12. Chemical changes accompanying wall rock alteration of amphibolite around ore veins from the Sanjia and Wangtoushan deposits. *Asterisks* denote element enrichments greater than 500%

terized by silicification and sericitization of both plagioclase and K-feldspar with minor growth of disseminated submillimeter sized euhedra of pyrite. Pyrite rarely reaches more than accessory concentration. Fluorite is rarely developed in the altered granite. The alteration extends outward up to 1 or 2 m from a swarm of quartz veinlets. The maximum gold concentration, according to exploration work done on these zones, is 4 g/t. The chemical effects of alteration (not shown on Fig. 3.12) include a loss of Na, Ca, Ba, and Sr; and the gain of Fe, Mg, S, F, W and the chalcophile ore elements relative to the unaltered granite.

3.2.5 Age of Mineralization

The field evidence in the Sanjia district indicates that the mineralized veins formed after the emplacement of the Wangtoushan and Sanyihe Granites and their associated dikes, and before the intrusion of lamprophyre dikes. The only isotopic age data available from the granites is an unpublished Rb-Sr whole rock isochron of the Sanyihe Granite obtained by the Ministry of Metallurgical Industry (European Community 1990). The isochron age of the Sanyihe Granite is 166 ± 2 Ma and the initial $^{87}Sr/^{86}Sr$ ratio is 0.7047 ± 4 (two sigma uncertainties). This age is interpreted as the intrusion age of the granite.

To the authors' knowledge there have been no previous isotopic studies on the age of mineralization in the Sanjia district. Our investigations involved Rb-Sr dating of hydrothermal vein sericite and K-feldspar from the Wangtoushan deposit, and dating of vein quartz from the Sanjia deposit by the $^{39}Ar/^{40}Ar$ incremental heating method. The Rb-Sr analytical data are given in Table 3.6 and the $^{39}Ar/^{40}Ar$ results are given in Fig. 3.13.

The Rb-Sr age of sericite collected from the Wangtoushan deposit (sample 6313) is 184 Ma. This is considered to be a reliable estimate of the mineralization age since the calculation is not sensitive to the initial $^{87}Sr/^{86}Sr$ ratio. The K-feldspar sample 6273 yields a concordant age of 179 Ma but a

Table 3.6. Rb and Sr isotopic data from hydrothermal minerals from the Wangtoushan deposit

Sample	Mineral	Rb	Sr	$^{87}Rb/^{86}Sr$	$^{87}Sr/^{86}Sr$[a]	Age[b]
6313	Sericite	717	9.70	226	1.3005(1)	184 ± 2
6271	K-feldspar	618	312	5.75	0.71938(5)	115 ± 25
6273	K-feldspar	469	224	6.09	0.72550(4)	179 ± 25

[a] Numbers in parentheses give uncertainty of last digits.
[b] Age in Ma with uncertainty based on 1% relative error in $^{87}Rb/^{86}Sr$ and an initial $^{87}Sr/^{86}Sr$ ratio of 0.710.

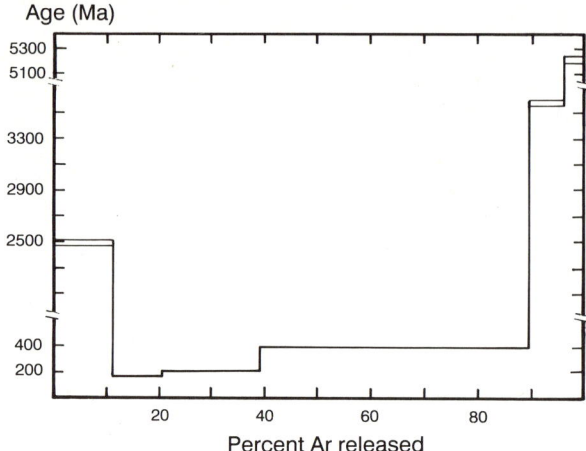

Fig. 3.13. Ar-Ar age-release curves of a sample of vein quartz from the Sanjia deposit. *Double lines* reflect analytical uncertainty. Analyses performed by the Ministry of Metallurgical Industry, Beijing

second sample from the same area (6271) gives a much younger age of 115 Ma. The difference in age between the two samples cannot be real since both came from neighboring veins in the same fracture system. It is concluded that the younger age represents loss of radiogenic ^{87}Sr from the sample.

These mineral ages are slightly older than that of the Sanyihe Granite, in apparent contradiction to the field relationships. This may not be a real discrepancy, since the hydrothermal minerals were taken from the Wangtoushan deposit some kilometers from the Sanyihe Granite, and the Wangtoushan Granite has not been dated. More dating should be done in the Sanjia district, but it suffices for the present purpose to note that gold mineralization and Yanshanian granites are nearly contemporaneous.

$^{39}Ar/^{40}Ar$ Dating

The sample used for dating by the ^{39}Ar/^{40}Ar incremental heating method was vein quartz from the Sanjia deposit. The results shown in Fig. 3.13 indicate a plateau age of 168 ± 3 Ma, which is interpreted as the age of quartz crystallization in the vein. This agrees fairly well with the Rb-Sr ages from the Wangtoushan deposit, and it confirms a Mesozoic age for the mineralization in the district.

3.2.6 Fluid Inclusions

The data on fluid inclusions from the Sanjia district are based on analyses performed in the course of this project. The investigation involved microthermometric analyses of samples of fluorite and quartz from the Wangtoushan deposit, and chemical analyses of bulk fluid released by decrepitation from samples of vein quartz from the Wangtoushan and Sanjia deposits.

Microthermometry

Most vein quartz in the Sanjia district is clouded with minute secondary inclusions and therefore not suited for microthermometry. However, fluorite contains measureable inclusions which, based on their size, regular form, and random arrangement in the host, are thought to be primary. In one sample, quartz inclusions in fluorite were free enough of the secondary fluid inclusion "clouds" that measurements on primary inclusions (based on the criteria above) could be made. Table 3.7 gives a summary of microthermometric data from fluorite and quartz samples from the Wangtoushan deposit.

The inclusions in fluorite are large (10 to 25 microns in diameter) and regular in shape. All inclusions contain mixed CO_2-rich fluids, as evidenced by the formation of clathrates on cooling. Only rarely is liquid CO_2 visible in these inclusions at room temperature or on cooling. The degree of fill is 70 to 80%. The "primary" inclusions in quartz are rare, but the few examples

Table 3.7. Summary of microthermometric data from samples of fluorite and quartz from the Wangtoushan deposit

Host mineral	Sample	T_m CO_2	T_m clathrate	T_h CO_2	T_h final
Fluorite	6580a	−56.9	7.6	28.1	193
	(n = 10)	(x)	(0.3)	(1.9)	(12.8)
	6580b	−56.6	8.0	22.8	193
	(n = 14)	(x)	(0.1)	(2.1)	(20)
	6267a	−58.0	6.8	−5.0	335
	(n = 13)	(x)	(0.2)	(3.5)	(x)
Quartz	6580-2	−58.3	6.2	22.2	>290
	(n = 8)	(0.1)	(0.3)	(5.7)	−

All temperatures represent average values in °C.
T_m, melting temperature; T_h, homogenization temperature; n.d., not determined; (x), number of measurements too small for statistical analysis.
The number of measurements (n) and the standard deviation are given in parentheses.

found have properties similar to the inclusions in fluorite, and are probably of the same generation.

Salinities based on clathrate melting temperatures in both host minerals range from 6–8 wt% NaCl equivalent. The CO_2 melting temperatures indicate nearly pure CO_2 in some samples and minor impurity of the CO_2 phase in others. The final homogenization temperature of inclusions in both host minerals was difficult to determine because of decrepitation. In fluorite, a number of inclusions homogenized to the liquid phase in the range 180–240 °C, a few isolated inclusions homogenized at 330–345 °C and many inclusions decrepitated at about 290 °C. In quartz, most inclusions also decrepitated at about 290 °C. Therefore, a miminum of about 300 °C is taken as a reasonable estimate of the homogenization temperature. From the position of the CO_2-H_2O solvus at the appropriate salinity given by Brown and Lamb (1989), a minimum trapping pressure of about 2.5 kbar can be derived from these data. The true conditions of trapping can potentially be estimated using the fluid isochores combined with oxygen isotopic thermometry of vein quartz and K-feldspar. Unfortunately, the analyzed quartz and feldspar from the Wangtoushan deposit are not in isotopic equilibrium, and therefore no meaningful temperatures can be calculated.

Chemical Analyses of Fluid Contents

The average composition of bulk fluid released from inclusions in vein quartz of the Sanjia and Wangtoushan deposits is shown in Fig. 3.14. It must be emphasized that the fluids analyzed may represent a mixture of several generations, although the samples were decrepitated above 250 °C to minimize the contribution from low-temperature secondary fluids. The fluid composition in both deposits is very similar in terms of the dissolved cations. These are dominated by Na, with much less K and Ca, and very minor Mg. The CO_2 concentration is about 4 mol% from the Wangtoushan samples and only 1.6 mol% from Sanjia. Note that the lower CO_2 concentration in the Sanjia samples may simply reflect a larger component of aqueous secondary inclusions in these samples compared with those from Wangtoushan.

3.2.7 Stable Isotopic Data

This section presents oxygen and carbon isotopic data from quartz, K-feldspar, and carbonate gangue from ore veins in the Wangtoushan, Sanjia and Xinglonggou deposits. The main purpose of the analyses was to provide estimates of the temperature of mineralization, and only this aspect is discussed here. The implications of the data to the source of mineralizing fluids are discussed in Chapter 4.6.2.

Table 3.8 lists the analytical data. The isotopic composition of quartz falls in the range of $\delta^{18}O$ (SMOW) from 10.2 to 11.4‰, which is identical to vein

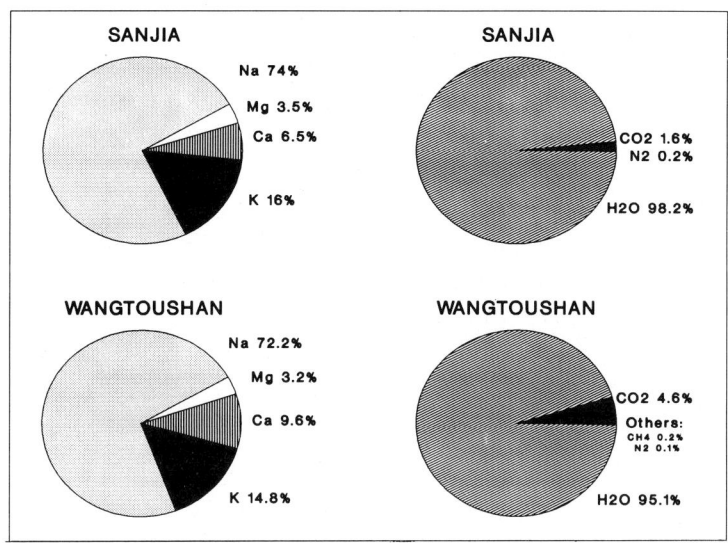

Fig. 3.14. Pie diagrams showing the average composition of bulk fluid inclusion contents from vein quartz in the Wangtoushan and Sanjia deposits. From unpublished analyses of the Ministry of Metallurgical Industry, Beijing

Table 3.8. Carbon and oxygen isotopic composition of carbonate, quartz, and K-feldspar from hydrothermal veins in deposits of the Sanjia district

Sample	Deposit	Mineral	δ^{13}C PDP	δ^{18}O SMOW
6271	Wangtoushan	K-feldspar	–	9.9
6271	Wangtoushan	Quartz	–	11.4
6273	Wangtoushan	K-feldspar	–	11.2
6273	Wangtoushan	Quartz	–	10.2
6309	Wangtoushan	K-feldspar	–	11.3
6309	Wangtoushan	Quartz	–	10.6
6275	Wangtoushan	Dolomite	−6.7	13.5
6309	Wangtoushan	Dolomite	−4.8	13.6
6285	Xinglonggou	Dolomite	−2.7	8.3
6289	Xinglonggou	Dolomite	−6.8	13.2
6210	Sanjia	Dolomite	−5.5	11.4

The precision of analyses is better than ±0.2‰.

quartz from the Niuxinshan deposit (Table 3.4). However, the composition of K-feldspar samples are anomalous in that, in three out of four cases, they are richer in ^{18}O than coexisting quartz. This is contrary to the equilibrium fractionation trend (O'Neil 1986), and therefore the data cannot be used for thermometry and no temperatures are indicated in Table 3.8.

The carbon and oxygen isotopic compositions of carbonate minerals define a narrow range. The interpretation of these compositions is deferred to Chapter 4.6.2, where the data from all deposits are discussed together.

3.3 Yuerya District

The Yuerya gold district is located about 200 km northeast of Beijing, in Kuancheng county, eastern Hebei province. The location is shown in Fig. 3.1. Strictly speaking, only one gold deposit, the Yuerya deposit, occurs in the mining district but smaller deposits of the same geologic type occur within a few tens of kilometers to the northeast of the Yuerya deposit. These include the Baizhangzi, Yangzhangzi, and Maojiadan gold deposits. Only the Yuerya deposit is described in this text. The Yuerya deposit serves as the type deposit for the Yuerya type of gold deposits, i.e., those hosted by Mesozoic granites, discussed by Yu and Jia (1989). Wei (1989) gave a brief description of the Yuerya deposit.

After its discovery in 1887 the Yuerya gold deposit was operated on a small scale until 1965, when systematic prospecting and exploration work by the Ministry of Metallurgical Industry was completed. The present mine plant with an ore dressing and smelting facility was finished in 1968. The mine is operated by the state government.

3.3.1 Host Rock Lithology

The geology of the Yuerya deposit is shown on a simplified geologic map in Fig. 3.15. The host rocks consist of Middle Proterozoic very low-grade metamorphic carbonate rocks intruded by a Yanshanian granite stock and associated mafic and felsic dikes.

3.3.1.1 Proterozoic Rocks

The Proterozoic rocks in the Yuerya area comprise a marine sedimentary sequence of limestones, dolomites, and minor shales which belong to the upper part of the Gaoyuzhuang Formation, the uppermost formation of the Changcheng System. The lithologic sequence at Yuerya comprises, in ascending order, shales, interbedded shales and limestones, manganiferous dolomites, thickly bedded limestones, calcretes, and thinly bedded limestones. The entire sequence strikes NE–SW and dips 50°–70° to the NW. Minor folds and bedding-parallel faults occur, as described more fully in Chapter 3.3.2, but the sequence in general has a monoclinal form. The maximum age for the Gaoyuzhuang Formation is 1678 Ma based on isotopic dating of the underlying formation. The only isotopic constraint on the

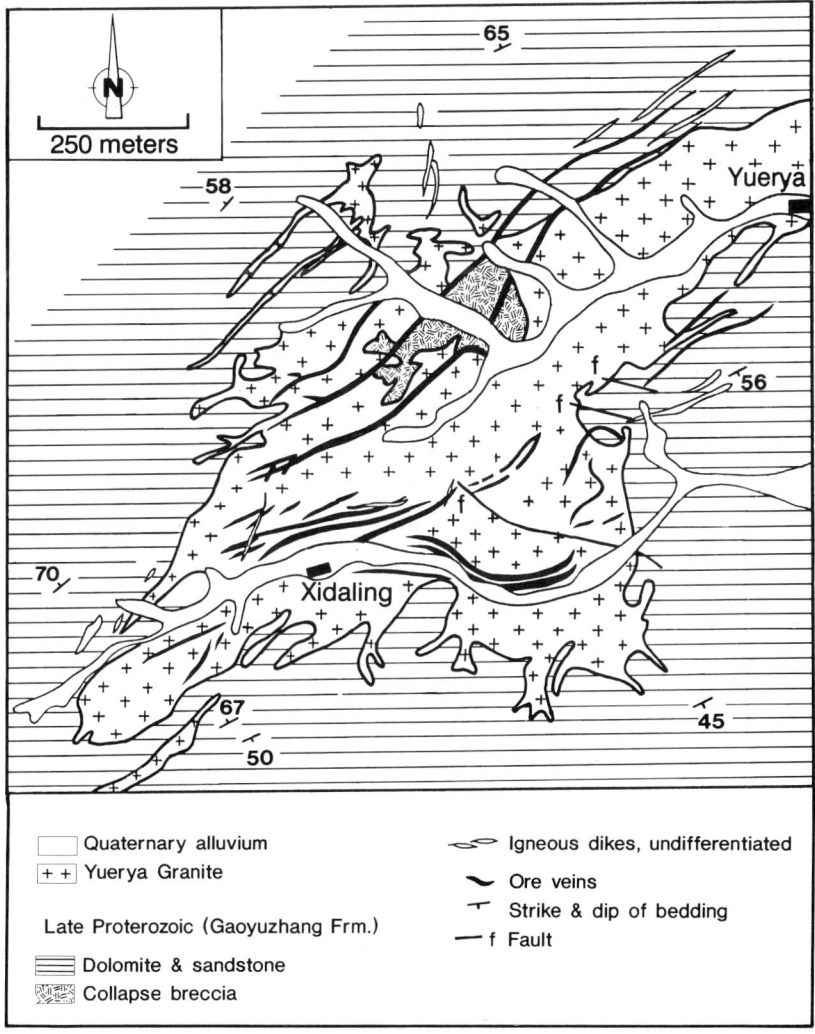

Fig. 3.15. Simplified geologic map of the Yuerya gold deposit

minimum age is a 1200 Ma age from the top of the succeeding Jixian system (see Chap. 2.2.2).

3.3.1.2 Granite and Dikes

The Yuerya Granite is about 2 km long and 700 m wide in outcrop extent, and is elongated NE–SW parallel to the regional strike of the country rocks (Fig. 3.15). The intrusion is highly irregular in form, with numerous apophyses of granite along bedding-parallel fractures in the country rocks. Many country rock inclusions are present in the granite, and in the western part of the intrusion a collapse breccia of roof fragments occurs. Previous radiometric dating has not given an unequivocal age for the granite. Yu and Jia (1989) give K-Ar ages of 149 and 169 Ma. Recent unpublished K-Ar determinations by the Ministry of Metallurgical Industry yielded three ages of 168 ± 3, 166 ± 3, and 163 ± 2 Ma. It seems therefore most likely that the age of the granite is around 165–170 Ma.

The Yuerya Granite consists of two intrusive phases. The earlier phase, and the only one exposed at the surface, is a light-colored medium- to fine-grained biotite granite. A later intrusive phase, which is known from mine workings and drill core, consists of reddish medium- to coarse-grained biotite granite. The mineral compositions of both granite types are similar, with quartz, K-feldspar, oligoclase, biotite, and apatite; however, the red granite contains less biotite than the light granite. The chemical compositions of the two granite phases are also very similar. The red granite is richer in SiO_2 (73–75 wt% vs 70–73 wt%), and slightly poorer in Fe, Mg, Ti, and Ca than the light granite, although in both granite types the sum of total Fe as FeO, MgO, CaO, and TiO_2 is generally less than 3 wt%. Total alkali concentrations are near 8%. The weight ratio of K_2O/Na_2O is near unity in fresh samples but rises rapidly with alteration. The moderate concentrations of Rb (150 ppm) and the relatively high Sr (150 ppm) and Ba (450 ppm) suggest a low degree of differentiation. Analytical data are summarized in Appendix 1.

Three groups of igneous dikes intrude both the granite and the country rocks along fracture zones striking NE–SW and NW–SE. The earliest dikes are granitic dikes of aplitic or rhyolitic texture which may be cogenetic with the Yuerya Granite. The granitic dikes are cut by ore veins. A second group of dikes, which postdates the ore vein formation, consists of porphyritic diorite. Lamprophyre dikes also occur locally and these, too, postdate mineralization. No radiometric age data are available from the dikes.

3.3.2 Host Rock Structures

As described above, the Late Proterozoic sequence has a monoclinal form striking 30°–35° and dipping 50° to 70° NW. Minor folds with NE-striking axes are locally present, one example being a small syncline near the southeast margin of the granite. Apart from minor folds and flexures in the Proterozoic rocks, the deformation in the district is dominated by faults and fractures.

The Yuerya deposit and the other gold deposits of similar type (Baizhangzi, Yangzhangzi, and Maojiadan) are located along the southern portion of the regional Tangdaohe-Lingyuan deep fracture zone which was described in Chapter 2.3.3 and shown in Figs. 2.5 and 2.6. Two major groups of faults and fracture zones are recognized within the mining district. The first group is related to the regional Tangdaohe-Lingyuan fracture zone and comprises reverse and oblique-slip faults which strike NE–SW (55°–65°) and dip 30°–70° to the NW. These faults are present both within the Yuerya Granite and in the Proterozoic sequence. The mineralized veins and alteration zones generally occur along these NE-trending structures. A second group of faults and fracture zones strikes WNW 280°–290° and dip 5°–30° to the NE; these are not significant hosts for mineralization, and usually show evidence of postmineralization movement.

3.3.3 Gold Mineralization

The gold mineralization in the Yuerya deposit is almost exclusively confined to quartz veins and/or disseminated alteration zones within the Yuerya Granite. In 1989, 20 ore-bearing vein zones were known. The veins and associated alteration zones strike NE–SW and dip moderately to the NW. The greatest concentration of veins and the richest mineralization occurs in the southern and eastern parts of the Yuerya intrusion. Most of the ore occurs within the light granite near its (underground) contact with the red granite; a second favorable site for mineralization is at the contact of the granite with the country rocks. Although the fractures which host the veins continue from the granite into the carbonate rocks, mineralization rarely extends more than 50 m out from the granite contact.

3.3.3.1 Form of the Ore Bodies

The ore bodies in the Yuerya deposit may be subdivided into two types based on their form, namely vein-type and disseminated type. The vein-type ore bodies occur both within the granite and at the granite-country rock contact. Within the granite the veins are typically 30–50 cm thick and the ore contains up to 100 g/t gold, on average 50 g/t. Bordering the veins are relatively narrow selvages of altered rock with disseminated mineralization. Thinner quartz veinlets with lower grade often occur in secondary fractures associated with the main veins. At the granite-country rock contact the vein zones are characterized by more intense shearing than within the granite. Ore bodies in this setting are irregular lenses of sheared sulfide-rich quartz veins. The thickness of the ore bodies and the extent of alteration and mineralization are greatest in extensional "flats", where the dip of the host fractures abruptly changes. This ore type contains up to 50 g/t gold. Where the ore veins extend into the country rocks the grade falls rapidly. Individual mineralized zones are typically between 100 and 900 m long (average 200 m) and up to 5–10 m wide (average 0.3–1 m). Present data show mineralization persisting to 300–400 m down dip.

The disseminated type of mineralization is found only within the granite. The disseminated ore bodies are developed around networks of fine secondary fractures associated with the main NE–SW-trending fracture zones. In this type of ore there is a continuous transition between economic ore bodies and the wall rock. In general the economic ore bodies are about 1–2 m thick (up to 10 m), whereas the entire mineralized zone is commonly more than 10 m thick. Gold concentration averages 5–10 g/t and ranges to a maximum of 30–50 g/t.

3.3.3.2 Macroscopic Description of the Ores

The vein-type ores consist of sheared or brecciated quartz with dominantly pyrite and occasionally pyrrhotite as the main sulfide mineral. The richest ores consist of well over 50 vol% sulfides. Galena and sphalerite are commonly developed on the margins of the ore veins. Rare veinlets and massive patches of sulfide minerals with little or no quartz may occur in the altered wall rocks adjacent to the quartz veins. These consist of intergrown pyrite, chalcopyrite, galena, and sphalerite, with accessory tetrahedrite and rare calaverite. The gangue minerals of the vein-type ore in granite are mainly quartz, sericite, calcite, and minor barite. The calcite is generally found in late cross-cutting veinlets. Where the mineralization extends into the country rocks the above-mentioned gangue minerals may be joined by chlorite.

The disseminated ores consist of pervasively silicified and sericitized granite which is permeated by thin quartz and sulfide veinlets (10–30 cm thick, locally up to 10 cm thick). Pyrite occurs as scattered grains in the rock, or as concentrated centimeter-sized nests and patches. Gangue minerals in the disseminated type of ore include quartz, sericite, albite, carbonate, and kaolinite. The carbonatization and kaolinization postdate mineralization.

3.3.3.3 Ore Petrography and Paragenesis

The following ore minerals have been found in the Yuerya deposit: azurite, bismuthinite, bornite, calaverite, chalcocite, chalcopyrite, galena, hessite, malachite, molybdenite, native gold, pyrite, pyrrhotite, scheelite, sphalerite, tennantite, and tetrahedrite. The paragenetic sequence of mineralization at Yuerya is complex. The mineralization can be divided into four main phases from early to late as follows:

a) pyrite-pyrrhotite ± quartz phase,
b) quartz-pyrite phase,
c) quartz-polymetallic sulfide phase,
d) telluride-carbonate-sulfosalt phase,
e) secondary sulfide stage.

Detailed petrographic descriptions are available only for the occurrence of native gold. Most of the gold formed in the second and third phases of mineralization (b and c above) where gold is mainly associated with pyrite. Minor amounts of gold also formed later in the paragenetic sequence in phase d together with telluride minerals. Gold has been observed in the following settings:

a) at the rims or grain boundaries of pyrite,
b) associated with sphalerite, quartz and galena in fracture-fillings in the early stage pyrite,
c) associated with telluride (hessite) aggregates,
d) along grain boundaries or in cracks of fine-grained vein quartz or, rarely, feldspar,
e) with secondary chalcocite filling cracks in late-stage pyrite.

The native gold grains are generally between 0.1 and 0.4 mm in diameter. Grains up to 1 mm in diameter and stringers of gold up to 3 mm long occur as well. Microprobe analyses of gold grains showed 23 wt% Ag (Yu et al. 1989).

3.3.4 Wall Rock Alteration

Alteration of Carbonate Rocks
In the limestone/dolomitic country rocks of Yuerya Granite the effects of alteration due to the mineralized quartz veins are superimposed on an earlier contact metamorphism. The contact metamorphism produced recrystallization of limestone, the development of hornfels in the shaley horizons, and local zones of skarn minerals (diopside, tremolite, ± grossular). The alteration associated with mineralization involved intense silicification, lesser chloritization and sericitization, and minor pyritization.

Alteration of Granite
Wall rock alteration within the granite is associated with both the vein type and the disseminated type of mineralization. The alteration mineralogy in both types is essentially the same, the only difference being that the latter affects a greater volume of rock, and that in the disseminated type of ore, the altered rock is mineralized to ore grade. The alteration involves pyritization, sericitization, silicification, and albitization, with minor chloritization and kaolinization. Of these, the silicification, pyritization, sericitization, and albitization are closely related to the gold mineralization; carbonate and kaolin generally formed later.

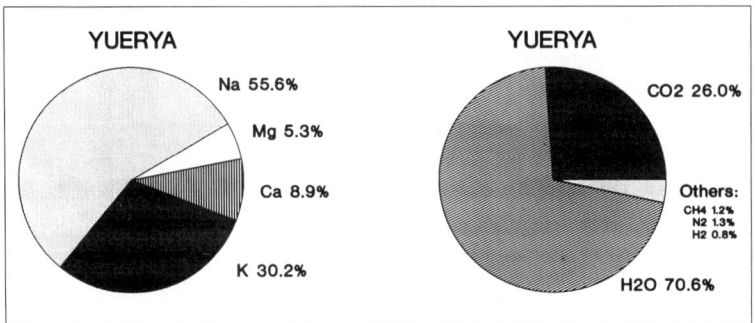

Fig. 3.16. Pie diagrams showing the average composition of bulk fluid inclusion contents from vein quartz in the Yuerya deposit. Source of data: Yu and Jia (1989) and Yu et al. (1989)

3.3.5 Age of Mineralization

The mineralization of the Yuerya deposit clearly cross-cuts the Yuerya Granite and must therefore be younger than that intrusion. The age of the Yuerya Granite is a matter of some controversy as discussed above, but the most likely age is considered to be 165–170 Ma. The only isotopic age data obtained from hydrothermal minerals at Yuerya is a K-Ar age of 200 Ma from "fine scaly sericite" obtained by Yu and Jia (1989). Either this age is too old, for example because of excess Ar, or the granite ages are too young. More work is needed to clear up this discrepancy.

3.3.6 Fluid Inclusions

Data from studies of fluid inclusions in quartz from the Yuerya deposit are reported in Yu and Jia (1989) and Yu et al. (1989). The reports include total homogenization and decrepitation temperatures and chemical analyses of bulk inclusion contents. According to Yu and Jia (1989), the final homogenization temperatures of inclusions in three samples range from 259–390 °C, with homogenization to the liquid phase. The maximum decrepitation temperature peak for the same samples ranges from 250–273 °C. Yu et al. (1989) reported a higher range of decrepitation temperatures (291–345 °C) from ten analyses.

Figure 3.16 shows the average chemical composition of bulk inclusion fluids plotted from the data given by the above-mentioned authors. The results show that Na forms only about half of the dissolved cations, the remainder being mostly K with lesser Ca and very minor Mg. Carbon dioxide makes up 26 mol% of the fluid, and other gases combined constitute about 3 mol%.

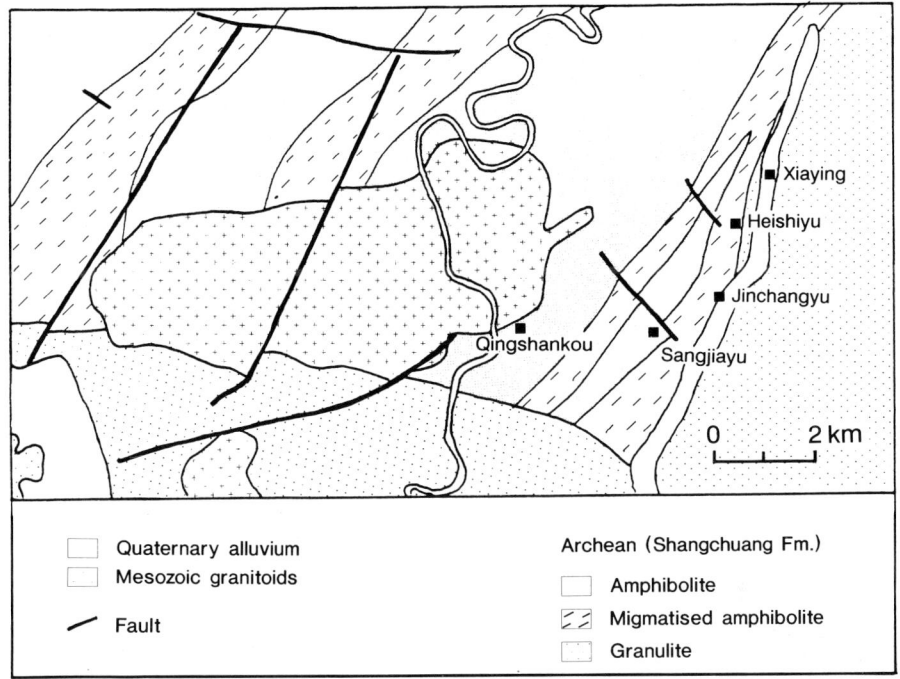

Fig. 3.17. Simplified geologic map of the Jinchangyu district

3.4 Jinchangyu District

The Jinchangyu deposit is located about 150 km northeast of Beijing in Kuancheng county, Hebei province. (see Fig. 3.1). It is the largest gold deposit in eastern Hebei province and one of the most important in China. Gold was mined at Jinchangyu during the Tang Dynasty (600–900 A.D.) and it was one of the three largest gold producers in China during the Qing Dynasty (1644–1911 A.D.). After the founding of the People's Republic, the deposit was systematically reexamined, beginning in 1963, and production renewed in 1968. The Jinchangyu mine is operated by the state government with entirely underground workings. The Jinchangyu deposit covers an area of about 6 km long and up to 900 m wide. It is divided into three geographic sections from north to south: Heishiyu section, Jinchangyu section, and Sanjiayu section (see Fig. 3.17). Some authors refer to each section as a separate deposit; however, in this text all are treated together. Figure 3.18 shows a simplified geologic map of the deposit.

The geology of the Jinchangyu deposit has been reviewed briefly by Gao (1986), Sang and Ho (1987), L.S. Yang (1988), and in more detail by Yu and Jia (1989). It serves as the type deposit for the Jinchangyu type of metamorphic-hosted gold deposits proposed by Zhu (1989).

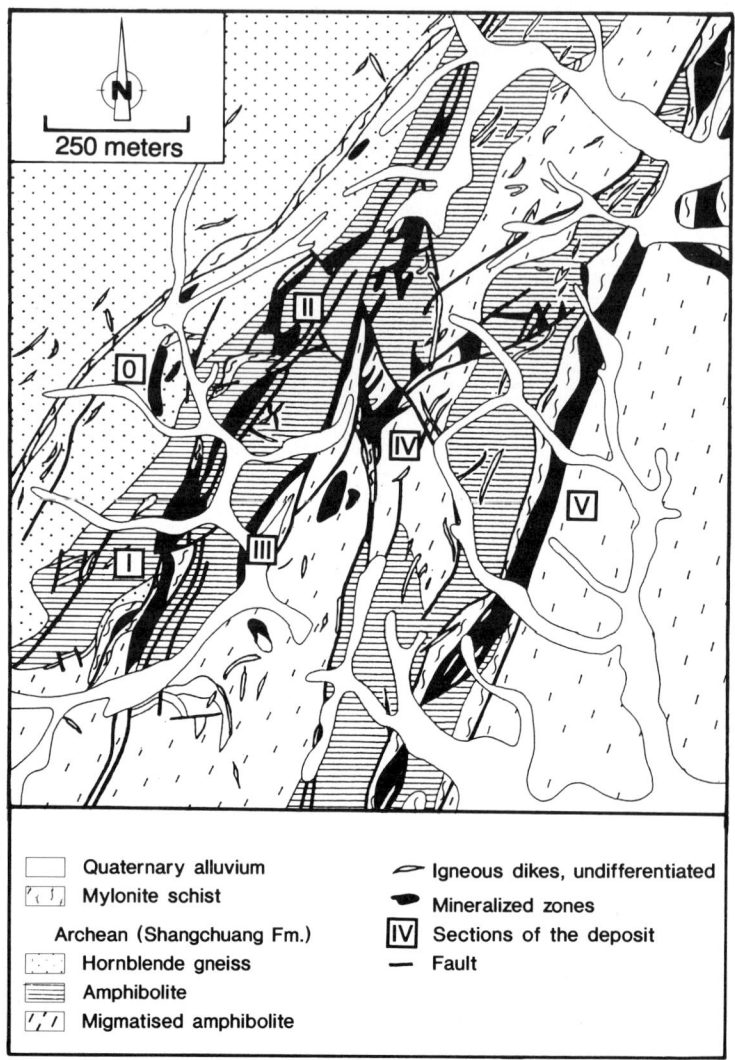

Fig. 3.18. Simplified geologic map of the Jinchangyu deposit

3.4.1 Host Rock Lithology

The dominant country rocks in the Jinchangyu district are Archean amphibolites, gneisses and granulites of the Shangchuang Formation, Qianxi Group. Igneous rocks are represented by a Yanshanian pluton of biotite granite (Qingshankou Granite) and by numerous dikes of various composition whose age is also presumed to be Yanshanian.

3.4.1.1 Archean Rocks

The Archean host rocks in the vicinity of Jinchangyu belong exclusively to the Shangchuang Formation of the Qianxi Group and contain the following main rock types:

- migmatized amphibolites, locally containing biotite or garnet,
- magnetite-quartz amphibolites grading into magnetite quartzites,
- two-pyroxene granulites with layers of amphibolite, the latter probably due to retrograde metamorphism (K.Y. Wang et al. 1985; Jahn et al. 1987),
- hornblende-plagioclase orthogneisses (metatonalites).

The main type of country rock in the vicinity of the Jinchangyu deposit is migmatized amphibolite which contains local magnetite-quartz rich layers. Minor amounts of garnet amphibolite and biotite amphibolite also occur. Migmatization in the Shangchuang Formation is intense in the Jinchangyu area (Fig. 3.17). The migmatization produced K-feldspar blastesis and abundant veins and schlieren of leucosome material. Retrograde metamorphism is commonly shown by replacement of plagioclase by albite and sericite, and the replacement of pyroxene and hornblende by fibrous amphibole, biotite, and chlorite. In the vicinity of some fault zones. the amphibolite and granulite and shered and altered to chlorite-sericite schists.

3.4.1.2 Granite and Dikes

There is no granite intrusion directly within the Jinchangyu mining district. The nearest granite, the Qingshankou Granite, crops out about 3 km to the west (see Fig. 3.17). The Qingshankou Granite is a multiple intrusion of Early Yanshanian age (K-Ar age 196 Ma according to Yu and Jia 1989). The early phase of the intrusion consists of medium to coarse-grained biotite-hornblende quartz diorite. This was followed by the main intrusive phase of coarse-grained biotite granite consisting of K-feldspar (50%), oligoclase (20%), quartz (25%), and biotite (5%), with accessory muscovite and zircon. The latest phase of the pluton is made up of leucocratic alkali-feldspar granite with accessory muscovite. The chemical composition of the Qingshankou Granite (main phase, biotite granite) is characterized by SiO_2 concentrations of 73 wt%, total alkalis near 9 wt%, (K_2O/Na_2O weight ratio near 1), and low concentrations of Fe, Mg, Ti, and Ca (the sum of total Fe as FeO, MgO, TiO_2, and CaO is less than 3 wt%). The moderate concentration of Rb (150 ppm) and the relatively high Sr (120 ppm) and Ba (450–600 ppm) suggest a low degree of differentiation. The chondrite-normalized REE distribution pattern of the granite (not shown) has a smooth decrease in enrichment from the light to the heavy REE and a weak negative Eu anomaly. The composition is summarized in Appendix 1.

Several groups of igneous dikes occur in the district (not differentiated in Fig. 3.18). The most common dikes consist of granitic porphyry. Other dikes include albitic aplite, trachyte, diorite porphyry, and hornblende-phyric lamprophyre. All of the dikes strike NE–SW to NNE–SSW, parallel to the main fault and fracture directions in the mining district. Field relations do not reveal the relative timing of all types of dikes with mineralization; however, the granitic porphyry dikes clearly predate mineralization, and the lamprophyres are clearly later.

3.4.2 Host Rock Structures

The structures of the basement rocks at the Jinchangyu district are characterized by at least two periods of folding and by later ductile and brittle faulting. The Qingshankou Granite and igneous dikes postdate all folding episodes and show only brittle deformation.

3.4.2.1 Folds and Foliation

The main trend of foliation in the Archean rocks strikes NE–SW (40°–60°) and dips to the NW at 40°–70°. This foliation is axial planar to tight folds which L.S. Yang (1988) attributed to the Fuping Orogeny at about 2500 Ma. According to L.S. Yang (1988), these NE–SW-directed folds overprint earlier Archean folds with E–W-trending axes. Evidence of later E–W-trending open folds is lacking at Jinchangyu although such folds are present regionally (see Fig. 2.5).

3.4.2.2 Faults and Fractures

The structural style of the Jinchangyu district is dominated by a complex series of faults and fracture zones which include both Early Proterozoic and Mesozoic elements. The Early Proterozoic faults are oriented NNE to NE, and they consist of chlorite and sericite-rich "mylonite schist" which, according to L.S. Yang (1988), formed during the Fuping Orogeny. The nature of these Precambrian shear zones is obscured by the fact that they have been reactivated by the Yanshanian deformation, and intruded by Mesozoic dikes and quartz veins. The Early Proterozoic fault zones apparently formed under conditions of N–S-directed stress, which produced conjugate NE–SW and NW–SW-trending shear zones, E–W-striking reverse faults, and N–S-striking normal faults. The Yanshan Orogeny produced intense and widepread faulting at Jinchangyu which reactivated and partly overprinted the older structures. The Yanshanian compressive structures (including reverse and strike-slip components) trend NNE–SSW, and associated tension fractures are oriented WNW–ESE. These later faults offset the early mylonite-schist zones and many of the mineralized structures as well (Fig. 3.18).

3.4.3 Gold Mineralization

Gold mineralization in the Jinchangyu ore deposit is found in steeply dipping NE–SW-trending shear zones on the NW limb of the Jinchangyu anticline. The Jinchangyu deposit is divided into six sections of vein zones numbered O-V from west to east (Fig. 3.18). Each section is truncated by cross-faults. Present workings and drill hole data indicate mineralization to a depth of at least 500 m.

3.4.3.1 Form of the Ore Bodies

There are a total of 17 producing ore bodies in the Jinchangyu deposit (as of 1989). The ore bodies are 50–150 m long (maximum 300 m) and 1–6 m thick (maximum over 30 m). In general, the ore bodies are in the form of quartz or quartz-albite veins within sheared fault zones (shown in black in Fig. 3.18) although mineralization is also found disseminated in intensely sheared and altered host rocks. The host shear zones strike NE–SW and dip 70°–80° variably NW or SE. According to L.S. Yang (1988), the shear zones show evidence of mylonitization under greenschist-facies conditions, i.e., they are synmetamorphic, and the gold-bearing quartz or quartz-albite veins were introduced later. The veins themselves show evidence of both pre- and postmetamorphic phases of mineralization. Premetamorphic, barren, or subeconomic veins are concordant with foliation of the host rocks and may show ptygmatic folding, whereas the economic veins are discordant, unfolded, and clearly postmetamorphic.

The host shear zones have been divided into three groups according to their strike direction. These are designated simply as the 0°, 20°, and 60° groups. The 20° group is the most intensely mineralized and an estimated 60% of the ore in the deposit is mined from this group of structures. The areas of intersection of two or more shear zones are particularly favorable for mineralization.

3.4.3.2 Macroscopic Description of the Ores

The ore bodies in the Jinchangyu deposit show evidence of several generations of movement and refilling by quartz and other gangue minerals. Three stages are recognized (unpublished reports, Ministry of Metallurgical Industry). The first two stages, involving quartz and quartz-albite filling, were poorly mineralized, and in some cases these feldspathic veins are clearly metamorphic, being folded and concordant with the host rock foliation. The main stage of mineralization is characterized by gray to white quartz gangue lacking albite, and veins of this generation are typically discordant, although some of the earlier folded veinlets were also enriched by the third-stage mineralization. The latest veining is by carbonate, which postdates mineralization.

There are systematic differences in the mineral assemblage of veins with different orientations. Thus, the 0° group of faults contains simple, weakly mineralized quartz veins with little wall rock alteration, the 20° group contains rich veins showing multiple stages of mineralization and intense wall rock alteration, and the 60° group is characterized by early-stage quartz-albite veins with chloritized wall rocks and only minor mineralization. The occurrence of sulfide minerals in the veins may be disseminated, concentrated in vein-like seams within the quartz (reopening structures), or along the vein walls. In the richest ore the sulfides have a massive structure. Sulfide minerals typically make up about 10 vol% of the ore-bearing veins of the 20° group, and correspondingly less in the other vein groups.

3.4.3.3 Ore Petrography and Paragenesis

The following ore minerals were found in the Jinchangyu deposit: argentite, bornite, calaverite, chalcocite, chalcopyrite, galena, hessite, magnetite, malachite, molybdenite, native gold, pyrite, pyrrhotite, and sphalerite. Despite the importance of this deposit, no systematic studies of ore paragenesis have been published. The only detailed petrographic descriptions are of pyrite and gold, taken from unpublished reports of the Ministry of Metallurgical Industry.

Pyrite
Pyrite is the most abundant ore mineral and it occurs both early and late, and in both wall rocks and quartz veins. The early generation of pyrite is characteristically euhedral in shape with a grain size of 3–5 mm. Later pyrite forms fine-grained anhedral aggregates in stringers filling cracks in quartz, early pyrite, and other gangue minerals. The richest ore is associated with this generation of fine-grained anhedral pyrite. The latest pyrite generation is associated with galena, chalcopyrite, and bornite in cracks of early-stage pyrite.

Gold
Gold occurs most typically associated with fine-grained anhedral pyrite of the second generation mentioned above. The gold occurs as fracture fillings, as replacements on pyrite rims and grain boundaries, and as inclusions in pyrite. Associated minerals are chalcopyrite, calaverite, and argentite.

Pyrite-associated gold makes up about two-thirds of the gold in the ores. The remaining third occurs within quartz. The grain size of gold ranges from about 5 to 20 microns. The silver concentrations in gold range from about 5 to 28 wt%.

3.4.4 Wall Rock Alteraton

Wall rock alteration of the metamorphic host rocks at Jinchangyu is ubiquitous. The width of the alteration zones varies according to the size of the associated vein and, especially, on the degree of shearing of the host rocks. The simple quartz veins of the 0° group, as mentioned above, have developed weak alteration zones with only a few decimeters to meters thickness whereas the richly mineralized and complex veins of the 20° group are associated with intense alteration of the host rocks, with sericitization zones reaching 40 m in thickness. The selvages of altered rock around the quartz veins typically show a systematic zonation of mineral assemblage, with an inner zone of pyritization, silicification, and sericitization followed outward by zones of chloritization with carbonatization, and of weak chloritization alone. Pyritization, sericitization, and silicification are most closely related to the gold mineralization. Carbonatization is generally later than the other alteration phases.

3.4.5 Age of Mineralization

Field evidence for an early, pre-metamorphic stage of mineralization in the Jinchangyu deposit includes folded, concordant quartz-albite veins, and greenschist-facies ductile shear zones which are mineralized to subeconomic grades. On the other hand, there is abundant evidence to show that the main stage of mineralization occurred much later. Most of the economic ore bodies show brittle deformation and occupy discordant structures. Undeformed, discordant granitic dikes are commonly cut by mineralized veins, and these dikes are interpreted to be of Yanshanian age, perhaps related to the nearby Qingshankou Granite, whose isotopic age is 196 Ma. No age dating of the igneous dikes has yet been made.
Published ages of hydrothermal sericite from the Jinchangyu deposit support the view that the mineralization is Mesozoic in age. Yu and Jia (1989) reported two sericite K-Ar ages of 170 and 155 Ma, and Yu et al. (1989) reported a K-Ar age of 192 Ma of sericite from a hydrothermally altered (unmineralized) fault zone. Sang and Ho (1987) cited a further K-Ar age of 197 Ma from unspecified material of wallrock alteration. Further evidence of a Mesozoic age for the Jinchangyu mineralization is a Pb-Pb model age of 133 Ma cited by Yu and Jia (1989) (see Chap. 4.2.3). The agreement among these ages is not close, but they suffice to confirm the field evidence that the main stage of mineralization was Mesozoic in age.

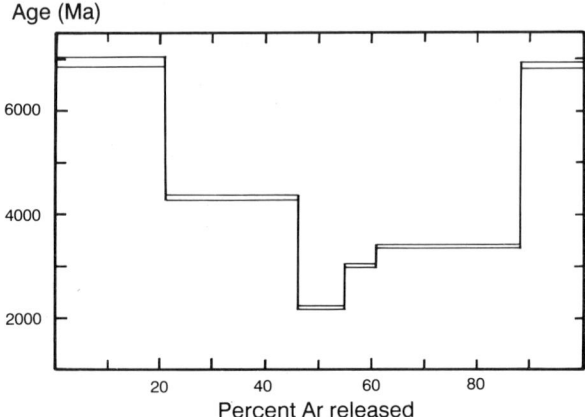

Fig. 3.19. Ar-Ar age-release curves from a sample of vein quartz from the Jinchangyu deposit. *Double lines* reflect analytical uncertainty. Analyses performed by the Ministry of Metallurgical Industry, Beijing

$^{39}Ar/^{40}Ar$ Dating

The results of $^{39}Ar/^{40}Ar$ dating of vein quartz from the Jinchangyu deposit by the incremental heating method are shown in Fig. 3.19. The analyses were performed by the Ministry of Metallurgical Industry, Beijing. The results show a highly disturbed Ar system with no evidence of Mesozoic age (compare the results from the Niuxinshan, Sanjia deposits in Figs. 3.7 and 3.13. This result is geologically unrealistic because the sample was taken from a quartz vein which cross-cuts Yanshanian dikes and must therefore be Mesozoic. The early age probably reflects Ar derived from the wall rocks and trapped in quartz as mineral or fluid inclusions.

3.4.6 Fluid Inclusions

Data from studies of fluid inclusions in quartz from the Jinchangyu deposit are reported in Yu and Jia (1989), Sun et al. (1989), and Yu et al. (1989). These authors give chemical analyses of bulk fluid contents and some microthermometric data.

According to Yu and Jia (1989), the final homogenization temperatures of inclusions in 17 samples range from 256–370 °C, with homogenization to the liquid phase or critical. The decrepitation temperatures for the same samples range from 134–325 °C. Yu et al. (1989) reported decrepitation temperatures ranging from 140–365 °C (mean 319 °C) from 14 samples.

The average chemical composition of inclusion contents from Yu and Jia (1989) and Yu et al. (1989) is replotted in Fig. 3.20. Sodium constitutes only about half of the dissolved cations, the rest being mainly Ca and K, with

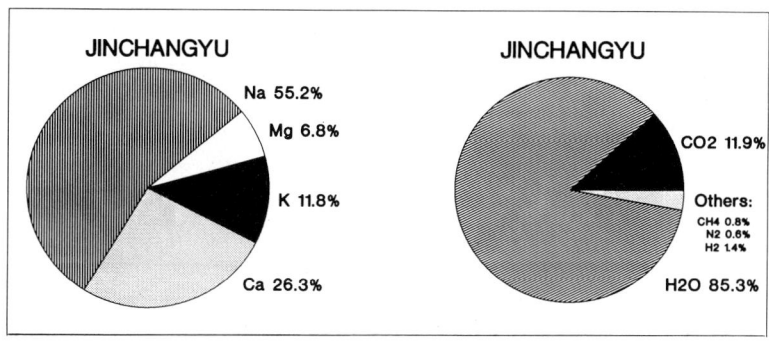

Fig. 3.20. Pie diagrams showing the average composition of bulk fluid inclusion contents from vein quartz in the Jinchangyu deposit. Analytical data from Yu and Jia (1989) and Yu et al. (1989)

minor Mg. Carbon dioxide makes up about 12 mol% of the fluid, the other dissolved gases together constitute about 3 mol%.

3.5 Banbishan District

The Banbishan gold district is located near the Qinglong River in eastern Qinglong county, Hebei province (Fig. 3.1). Mining at Banbishan began in 1982, and in 1985 the operation was taken over by the Qinglong county government. The gold district occurs in a 12-km-long zone, elongate NE–SW, which includes several gold occurrences. Apart from the Banbishan deposit, the following gold deposits and prospects occur in the area: Dayuzhangzi, Miaozhangzi, Zhangzhangzi, Wangzhangzi, Heluobao, Dakuaidi, and Shajinggou. The deposits are small in scale and many are subeconomic. Placer mining is also done on a small scale in the area along the Qinglong River. The following description concerns only the Banbishan deposit. A simplified geologic map of the deposit is shown in Fig. 3.21.

3.5.1 Host Rock Lithology

The host rocks of the Banbishan gold deposit mainly consist of a series of low- to medium-grade metamorphosed volcano-sedimentary rocks belonging to the Early Proterozoic Zhuzhangzi Group. These are cut by mafic and felsic igneous dikes of presumed Yanshanian age (Fig. 3.21).

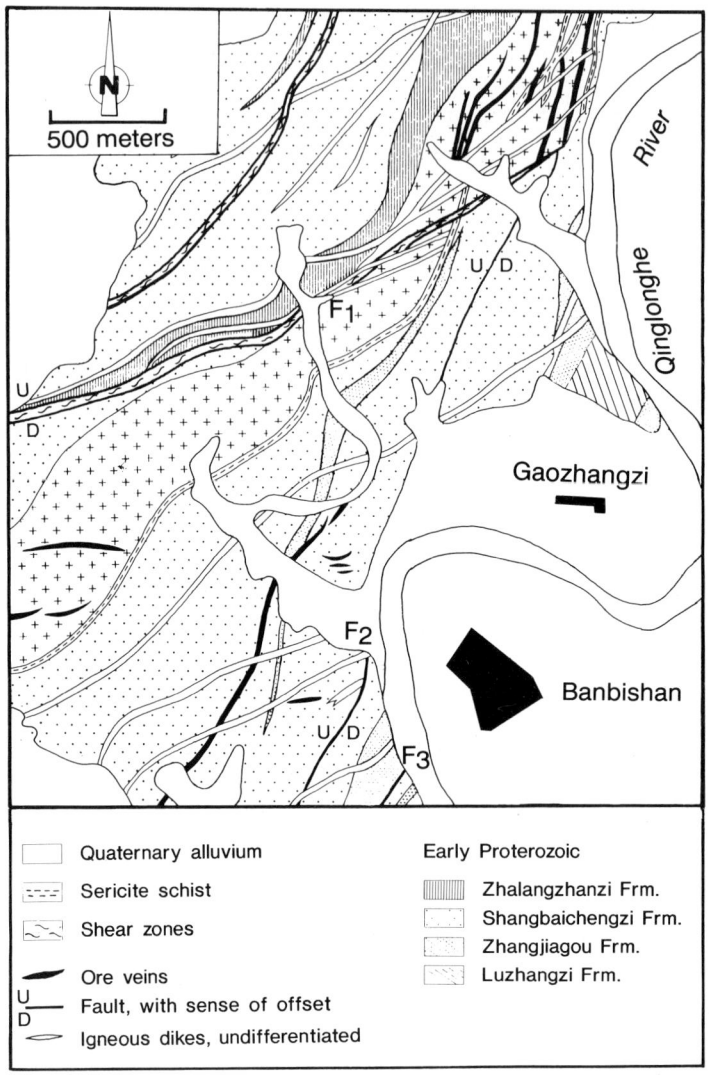

Fig. 3.21. Simplified geologic map of the Banbishan gold deposit

3.5.1.1 *Proterozoic Rocks*

The upper four formations of the Early Proterozoic Zhuzhangzi Group occur in the Banbishan district. According to the existing isotopic age data discussed in Chapter 2.2.2, the Zhuzhangzi Group spans an age of about 2200 to 1800 Ma. The metamorphic mineral assemblages suggest that the rocks were metamorphosed to the greenschist or lower amphibolite facies. From oldest to youngest the Proterozoic sequence includes:

Luzhangzi Formation
The lower part of the formation consists of orthoamphibolites with relict pillow structures, amygdales, vesicles, and doleritic texture. Overlying the amphibolites is a unit of hornblende-biotite schists and leptites whose protoliths were probably andesitic tuffs or lavas.

Zhangjiagou Formation
This formation contains metamorphosed agglomerate lavas intercalated with metaconglomerates and overlain by biotite leptites. The metaconglomerates consist of a biotite leptite matrix with stretched clasts of intermediate-felsic volcanic rocks and minor vein quartz. The conglomerates grade upward into biotite leptites, and they also grade laterally by a change of facies into the agglomerate lavas.

Shangbaichengzi Formation
This formation is the main host to ore in the Banbishan deposit. The rocks consist of weakly banded hornblende-biotite leptites in the lower unit succeeded by biotite-muscovite leptites. The protoliths are thought to be graywacke-type sedimentary rocks. Relict cross-bedding has been observed in parts of the lower unit.

Zhalanzhangzi Formation
This formation contains very fine-grained biotite schists and leptites.

3.5.1.2 Granites and Dikes

The nearest Yanshanian granite intrusion is the Louzishan Granite, located about 8 km SSE of Banbishan (not shown on Fig. 3.21). Within the mining district, igneous rocks are represented by four compositional groups of dikes. None of the dikes has been isotopically dated, but they are assumed, from structural evidence, to be of Yanshanian age. The earliest dikes consist of porphyritic aplite or rhyolite. These dikes strike NE–SW and dip about 50° to the NW. They intruded along bedding parallel fracture and fault zones in the Proterozoic rocks. The most important of the granitic dikes extends across the entire area of Fig. 3.21 and is up to 500 m in outcrop width. The granitic dikes are cut and mineralized by the ore-bearing veins. Rare dikes of porphyritic diorite cut the granitic dikes and are in turn cut by the later dike groups. No cross-cutting relationships with ore veins were observed. Lamprophyre dikes in the district are several tens of meters long, 2–5 m wide, and have variable strikes from nearly E–W to NNE–SSW, with moderate dips 40°–60° to the N and NW. No cross-cutting relationships were found between lamprophyre and mineralized veins. The latest and most common group of dikes in the district consists of equigranular diorite. The dikes intrude NE–SW-striking faults and fracture zones dipping 60°–80°

to the NW. The diorite dikes cut across mineralized quartz veins and shear zones, and therefore postdate mineralization.

3.5.2 Host Rock Structures

The two major structural units in the Banbishan district are the NE–SW-trending Qinglonghe Anticlinorium, which is a late-stage (Proterozoic) fold zone made up of a series of tight anticlines and synclines, and the Qinglonghe Fracture Zone, which is a complex NE–SW-striking, NW-dipping zone of thrust and strike-slip faults (see Fig. 2.5).

3.5.2.1 Folds and Foliation

The folds of the Qinglonghe Anticlinorium are tight and overturned to the east. The axial planes strike NE–SW and dip NW. Both the bedding and the foliation in the metamorphic rocks strike 15°–30° and dip NW at an angle of 40–60°. The Qinglonghe folds belong to the late-stage series of Sun et al. (1989), and no evidence of earlier folding in the Proterozoic rocks has been reported.

3.5.2.2 Faults and Fractures

The Qinglonghe Fracture Zone is an important structural unit affecting the entire Banbishan district. It is a NE–SW-trending (strike 5°–35°) zone of reverse and strike-slip faults. Most faults within the district strike NNE–SSW to NE–SW and dip to the NW. There are two main generations of faults judging from the mineralogy and texture of the fault zones. The older group of faults shows ductile deformation features and consists of biotite-chlorite-sericite schists and mylonites. These may be Proterozoic in age. The later faults are characterized by brittle deformation, with zones of fault breccia, cataclasite, and fault gouge. The late faults cut igneous dikes attributed to the Yanshanian Orogeny and are therefore thought to be Mesozoic in age or younger.

The largest of the early group of faults at Banbishan is a shear zone consisting of sericite-quartz schists which strikes 40°–50° and dips 50°–70° NW. The zone is 5–20 m wide and cuts through the entire mining district (Fig. 3.21). Tourmalinization is extensive in altered portions of the shear zone, and minor arsenopyrite and pyrite also occur. Another example of early faults in the Banbishan area is a chloritized mylonitic shear zone in the metaconglomerate unit of the Zhangjiagou Formation which strikes 10°–25°, dips 40°–60° NW, and is 1200 m long and 4–8 m wide. The zone contains minor gold mineralization associated with chlorite and pyrite alteration.

The most important of the late faults are designated F1, F2, and F3 (Fig. 3.21). All three are reverse faults dipping 20°–80° NW. They are characterized by meter-wide zones of fault breccia. None of the faults is significantly mineralized and, at least in the case of the F1 fault, the last movement clearly postdates mineralization and displaces a postmineralization diorite dike.

3.5.3 Gold Mineralization

3.5.3.1 Form of the Ore Bodies

The gold mineralization in the Banbishan district occurs in groups of quartz veins and alteration selvages in sheared and altered host rocks. The vein groups are associated with NE–SW-striking, NW-dipping faults. The main ore-bearing fault zone strikes 20°–40° and dips 28°–40° NW. The zone is 2–5 m wide and 1120 m long. Gold ore occurs in discontinuous quartz veins within altered and sheared wall rocks of the Shangbaichengzi Formation, and to a lesser extent in granitic dikes. The veins are 100–300 m in length and 1–2 m wide. The gold tenor ranges from 4 to 15 g/t.

3.5.3.2 Macroscopic Description of the Ores

The ores in the Banbishan deposit include both oxidized and primary types. The oxidized zone is 5–10 m thick. The ore is limonitic with a spongy texture. Apart from quartz, primary minerals are completely replaced. This type of oxidized ore has been mined out.
The primary ore can be divided into three parageneses according to the ore mineral assemblage and the nature of wall rock alteration. Most of the gold occurs in the first two types of ore.
The main ore type of the Banbishan deposit is referred to as the chlorite-silica type, and it consists of highly fractured rocks disseminated with abundant, evenly distributed quartz stringers and quartz replacements. The chlorite-silica type ore contains a relatively high-temperature mineral paragenesis with pyrite, pyrrhotite, arsenopyrite, and occasional scheelite and wolframite.
A second type of ore is termed biotite leptite type. This type is gradational between the chlorite-silica type described above and unaltered host rock. It may be very difficult to distinguish from unaltered host rock by macroscopic appearance. The ores are compact and hard due to silicification and/or contact metamorphism from igneous dikes. The ore paragenesis is the same as given above, but the concentrations are lower.
The third type of ore is termed silicified type. This type of ore has a gray-white color, contains open fractures, and is characterized by a lower-

temperature ore paragenesis including pyrite, chalcopyrite, sphalerite, minor arsenopyrite, and local antimonite. Quartz occurs as massive replacements in the host rock, and as veinlets or as individual crystals in fractures. This type of ore mainly occurs in tensional parts of brittle fault zones and it is clearly Mesozoic in age or younger since the host faults cut Yanshanian igneous dikes.

3.5.3.3 Ore Petrography and Paragenesis

The primary ore minerals found in the Banbishan deposit are the following: antimonite, arsenopyrite, chalcopyrite, galena, native gold, pyrite, pyrrhotite, scheelite, sphalerite, and wolframite. No detailed description of ore petrography is available.

Gold occurs mainly in cracks within gangue (quartz, rarely feldspars) and occasionally also in cracks within pyrite and arsenopyrite. Most gold forms in the chlorite-silica and biotite-leptite type ores associated with pyrite and arsenopyrite, but it is also found associated with antimonite in the silicified-type ores. Rarely, grains are visible to the naked eye, but grain size analysis showed that about half of the native gold has a diameter of 0.5–0.04 mm and 30% has a grain size of less than 0.04 mm. The silver concentration in the gold is about 10 wt%.

3.5.3.4 Chemical Composition

The chemical composition of the ores at Banbishan is complicated by the occurrence of different types of primary and oxidized ores. The element association of the primary ores includes As, Ag, Au, Cu, Pb, Zn $\pm$W $\pm$Sb. Table 3.9 lists the range of element concentrations of 20 grab samples representing a mixture of the primary ore types.

3.5.4 Wall Rock Alteration

Three stages of wall rock alteration have been distinguished at the Banbishan deposit. From early to late these are:

a) microcline-quartz-arsenopyrite-pyrite stage,
b) quartz-pyrite-sericite-chlorite stage,
c) carbonate-pyrite stage.

The earliest stage involves the replacement of plagioclase by quartz and microcline, accompanied by early disseminated pyrite and arsenopyrite. Tourmalinization is also locally present, associated with arsenopyrite. The second stage of alteration intensifies and overprints the first. It is confined

Table 3.9. Concentration of selected elements in primary ore of the Banbishan deposit

Element	Concentration (ppm)	Element	Concentration (ppm)
Ag	1–30	Ni	10–30
As	1000–3000	P	1000
Au	10	Pb	15–350
Ba	200–800	Sb	100–300
Bi	3	Sr	100–700
Co	10–20	Ti	40–250
Cr	10–150	V	30–150
Cu	10–250	W	40
Mo	4–50	Zn	30–120
Mn	200–2500		

Source: unpublished analyses by Ministry of Metallurgical Industry, Beijing.

to the extensional zones within the mineralized structures. The alteration involves mainly sericitization, silicification, chloritization, and pyritization. Sericite replaces plagioclase, K-feldspar, and some biotite. The silicification is expressed by quartz replacements of all primary minerals and by the formation of quartz veinlets. Pyrite occurs both as disseminated grains in the rock and in veinlets. Chloritization occurs in the wall rock selvages as replacements of biotite and hornblende. Gold mineralization is best developed in rocks showing the sequential development of both the first and second alteration stages.

The late-stage alteration involves veining by carbonate and local pyritization along open fractures and joint surfaces. This carbonate-pyrite alteration postdates the primary gold mineralization.

3.5.5 Age of Mineralization

No isotopic dates are available to constrain the age of mineralization in the Banbishan district, but the field relations indicate the possibility of two widely separated stages of mineralization (considering only the primary, unoxidized ore). An early, pre- or synmetamorphic stage is suggested by the fact that weak mineralization is present in ductile, greenschist-facies mylonite schist zones. It is possible, however, that the mineralization postdates the formation of the mylonites, and detailed petrographic studies are needed to determine if this is the case. In any case, most of the mineralization, and all of the economic ore at Banbishan, consists of vein stringers and disseminated zones in brittle structures which clearly cut undeformed igneous dikes and are therefore postmetamorphic. The vuggy nature and low-temperature ore assemblages of the silicified type of ore indicate that the late stage of mineralization continued under near-surface conditions.

4 Aspects of Metallogenesis

The similarities in age, geologic setting, and ore association in the various gold districts of eastern Hebei province documented in Chapter 3 suggest the likelihood of a common origin. The purpose of this chapter is to synthesize data and observations from all of the deposits studied in an attempt to constrain their origin. The chapter is organized according to the six metallogenetic questions posed in the introduction, namely:

4.1 The age of mineralization.
4.2 The source of gold.
4.3 The role of iron-rich host rocks.
4.4 The role of granites.
4.5 Structural controls.
4.6 The nature of ore-bearing fluids and conditions of mineralization.

The following discussions are based partly on information from Chapters 2 and 3, and partly on data not previously presented in the text.

4.1 The Age of Mineralization

4.1.1 Field Relations

Field evidence concerning the age of mineralization consists of the nature of the ore-bearing structures (geometry and type of deformation) and cross-cutting relationships between ore veins and igneous intrusions (dikes, plutons) of known or inferred age. The field relations in all of the deposits studied suggest that the main stage of mineralization postdated regional metamorphism. The main-stage ore veins are discordant to the host rock structures and show brittle deformation features. However, it must be noted that there is evidence for a synmetamorphic stage of mineralization in the Jinchangyu and the Banbishan gold deposits.
In the Jinchangyu deposit, the early stage of mineralization is represented by folded and concordant quartz-albite-sulfide veins, and by mylonitic fabrics and greenschist-facies mineral assemblages in some mineralized zones. L.S. Yang (1988) attributes the synmetamorphic mineralization to the Early Proterozoic Fuping Orogeny (ca. 2500 Ma). This early stage of mineralization at Jinchangyu is subeconomic. The main stage of mineralization, which formed most of the ore bodies and/or upgraded the earlier-formed veins, is

represented by quartz veins and altered fault zones which are discordant to the host rock foliation and locally cross-cut undeformed igneous dikes of Yanshanian age (L.S. Yang 1988). In the large shear zone-hosted ore bodies at Jinchangyu, both early and late stages of mineralization may be superimposed.

The gold deposit at Banbishan also shows evidence of two mineralization periods. An early stage is suggested by weakly mineralized, ductile, mylonitic shear zones with greenschist facies mineral assemblages. Detailed petrographic studies of these zones are lacking, however, and it is presently unknown if the mineralization is contemporaneous with the deformation and metamorphism or if it formed later. In any case, the main mineralization at Banbishan, which reaches economic grade, consists of quartz stringers and disseminated zones in semi-brittle faults which crosscut undeformed igneous dikes attributed to the Yanshanian Orogeny. This main stage of mineralization is therefore Mesozoic in age.

In the Yuerya, Niuxinshan, and Sanjia districts there is no evidence for syn-metamorphic mineralization. The mineralized veins cross-cut Yanshanian granite intrusions and/or dikes, some of which have been radiometrically dated at 140–170 Ma. Therefore the maximum age of mineralization in these cases is Jurassic. As discussed later in Chapter 4.5.3, the orientation of mineralized structures in these deposits also suggests that mineralization occurred as a result of the Yanshanian Orogeny.

4.1.2 Isotopic Age Dates

The available isotopic ages of hydrothermal vein minerals from the gold districts of eastern Hebei province are summarized in Fig. 4.1 along with all available ages from Yanshanian granites and dikes in the region. Jurassic ages from hydrothermal minerals have been found in all districts for which data are available. It is remarkable that all of the mineral ages from the Niuxinshan, Wangtoushan, Huajian, and Jinchangyu deposits indicate a mineralization event between 170 and 190 Ma. Based on the few cases where ages from hydrothermal minerals and granites exist from the same district, the hydrothermal minerals are the same age as, or slightly younger than the granites.

The age resolution of the data in Fig. 4.1 is rather poor, but the data suffice to demonstrate that gold mineralization took place during the Yanshanian Orogeny near the time of emplacement of granitic magmas. Further dating studies should attempt to establish a precise chronology of magmatism and gold mineralization. An important step would be to date the igneous dikes which were emplaced after the granites but before the formation of ore veins.

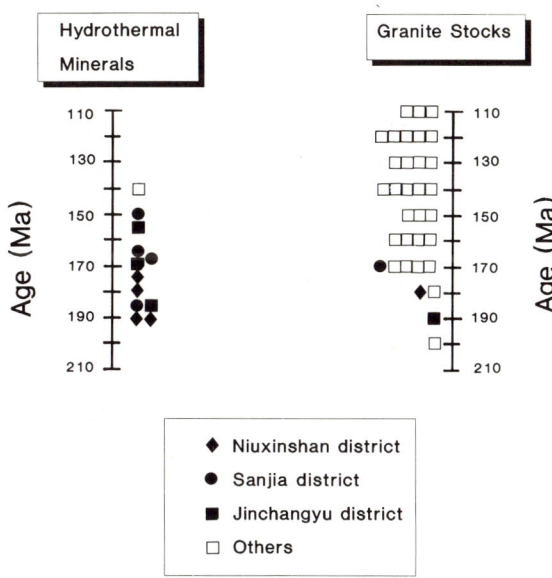

Fig. 4.1. Summary of isotopic age data from hydrothermal minerals and Yanshanian granites in the gold districts of eastern Hebei province described in the text

4.2 The Source of Gold

The source of metals in a given deposit or mining district is one of the most elusive questions in metallogenesis but also one of the most important because of its obvious strategic significance in exploration. The geologic characteristics and age of the gold deposits of eastern Hebei province (Chap. 3) constrain the possible sources of gold practically to three:

1. The gold was leached from the Precambrian metamorphic rocks which surround and/or underlie the deposits.
2. The gold was derived from the Yanshanian granites.
3. The gold was derived from the mantle, and it was transported by juvenile fluids along crustal-scale fault zones.

4.2.1 Gold in the Qianxi Group: The "Source Bed" Concept

One of the most striking features of the gold deposits discussed in this text, and many of the deposits in northeastern China generally, is that they are located in mafic to intermediate high-grade metamorphic rocks of Archean to Early Proterozoic age (Fig. 1.3). Zhu (1989) has estimated that over 50% of all gold deposits in the whole of China are hosted by Early Precambrian metamorphic rocks. The close association of gold with Early Precambrian host rocks in northeastern China suggests that these rocks may be the source of gold. The "source-bed" concept proposes that particular units or beds within the host rocks are gold-rich and, if identified, may guide exploration. There are many proponents of the "source-bed" concept in relation to the metallogenesis of gold in northeastern China. Zhu (1985) pointed out that, in the case of the complex Precambrian basement of northeastern China, "primary" source beds and "derived" source beds should be distinguished, the latter being formed by metamorphic or sedimentary reworking of the former. Guan (1988) surveyed the data on gold concentrations in the Precambrian basement of Liaoning province and concluded that the Archean rocks are depleted in gold relative to similar rocks in greenstone belts of South Africa and Canada, whereas the Early Proterozoic rocks are considerably enriched in gold relative to the crustal average. He suggested that the Early Proterozoic rocks are "secondary source beds" which reworked and concentrated the gold which was presumably present in their Archean predecessors. An interesting further variation on the source-bed concept was discussed by Yang (1989) based on insights provided by the deep drilling project of the Kola Peninsula. Yang pointed out that fluid-saturated zones of high fracture density occur in the Kola well from the 4.9-km level down to about 9 km. The zones are capped by relatively impervious rocks, and they therefore pond crustal fluids. Yang (1989) termed such structurally controlled zones of metal-rich hot brines "deep liquid ore source".

In past efforts to search for a gold-enriched source bed in the Precambrian basement of northeastern China, it proved to be very difficult to reliably determine representative "background" gold concentrations of the various rock units. The reason is that the rocks underwent several metamorphic and tectonic events. Even when interesting gold values are analyzed in apparently unmineralized samples, it is difficult to demonstrate whether these concentrations are the "primary" gold values inherent to the protolith or are due to enrichment or depletion from later metamorphism or metasomatism. This problem can be illustrated from the previously published analyses of "background" gold concentrations in the Qianxi Group rocks from the Jinchangyu district. Zhu (1985) reported an average gold concentration of 71 ppb (21 samples analyzed), which is a tenfold enrichment over the average of 3 to 7 ppb for crustal igneous and metamorphic rocks (Boyle 1979; Crocket 1991). On the other hand, Gao and Lin (1987) reported an average gold concentration of 3.1 ppb (14 samples analyzed) from rocks in the Jinchangyu district. The fundamental question is how to interpret these results. Are the high values representative for the gold concentration in the protolith or have they been influenced by secondary processes?

We consider it very likely that the high Au concentrations reported from the Qianxi Group rocks reflect secondary gold enrichment, which is difficult to avoid if samples are taken in the mining districts. One indication of this is that recent publications consistently report low values for gold concentrations in the Archean rocks collected outside of the mining districts. Yu and

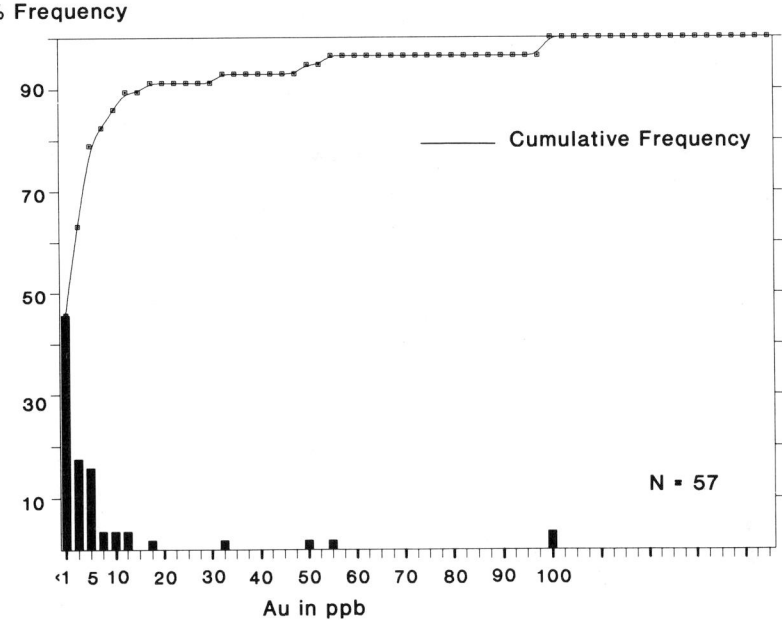

Fig. 4.2. Histogram and cumulative frequency curve of gold concentration in samples of the Archean Qianxi Group collected from outside of the mining districts in eastern Hebei province

Jia (1989) report gold concentrations ranging from 0.5 to 2.3 ppb from 65 samples representing several lithologic units in the Upper Qianxi Group. Yu et al. (1989) reported an average gold concentration of 5 ppb from 55 samples of the Qianxi Group rocks near the Jinchangyu district.
Our own analytical results from 57 samples of the Qianxi Group rocks are presented in Appendix 2. The samples were taken along an east-west profile through the Qianxi Group, located well to the south of the mining districts near Zunhua (see Fig. 1.3). The samples represent a range of rock types from pyroxenites to anorthosites and magnetite quartzites. The gold concentrations are shown in a cumulative frequency diagram in Fig. 4.2. The figure shows that over 80% of the samples have gold values at or under 5 ppb and the rest scatter to higher concentrations, up to a maximum of 100 ppb. A similar distribution of host-rock gold concentrations has been reported, for example, by Saager and Meyer (1984) from the Barberton area of South Africa. These authors suggested that the low "background" gold concentration (geometric mean 1.3 ppb) represents gold contained in the rock-forming minerals, and that the few abnormally high gold values reflect the presence of gold-rich sulfides or native gold on grain boundaries or

microfractures. This would also be a reasonable explanation for the distribution of gold in the Qianxi Group rocks.

Primary Gold Concentrations and the Au-Pd Method

The work of Keays (1984) showed that the gold concentrations measured in metamorphic rocks in greenstone belts are generally not representative of their primary values. Keays and Scott (1976) demonstrated the problem from a study of gold in ocean ridge basalts. They found higher gold concentrations in the glassy margins of basalt pillows than within the spilitized pillow interiors. The gold concentration in the glassy margins was considered to represent that of the quenched lava, whereas the lower concentration in the spilitized pillow interiors was attributed to leaching by the seafloor metamorphism. The implications of this to the problem of determining primary gold concentrations in the high-grade metabasites of the Qianxi Group are disheartening, since these rocks have undergone not only probable seafloor metamorphism, but also at least two periods of high-grade regional metamorphism.

Keays (1984) suggested a potential method to recalculate the primary gold concentrations in altered or metamorphosed rocks based on the geochemical behavior of Au and Pd. He argued that Au and Pd occur in a nearly constant ratio in mafic and ultramafic magmas whereas Au is much more mobile than Pd during metamorphic and metasomatic processes. Keays suggested that the primary Au/Pd ratio of komatiitic magma is 0.37 based on analyses of glassy ultramafic lavas (picrites) of Gorgona Island, Colombia and from Disko Island, Greenland. He then showed that the measured Au/Pd ratios of Archean komatiites from Canada (Munro Township), Zimbabwe (Belingwe), Western Australia (Kambalda and Mt. Clifford), and South Africa (Barberton) are generally lower than the "primary" value, suggesting preferential mobilization of gold. The degree of gold "loss" correlates roughly with the degree of alteration and metamorphic grade of the rocks. Wang (1988) introduced the "gold-palladium method" into the Chinese literature. He used Keays' (1984) results from Archean komatiites in Western Australia and South Africa as evidence that up to 75% of the primary gold in such rocks can be leached after crystallization of the protolith. Wang concluded that the primary gold contents of metamorphic rocks should be recalculated before discussing the source of gold.

Although the qualitative value of the Au-Pd method in distinguishing primary and disturbed noble metal signatures is established, the method may not give a reliable quantitative estimate of primary gold concentrations. One important source of uncertainty is the assumed initial Au/Pd ratio. The primary ratio of 0.37 given by Keays (1984) was based on an average value from analyses of natural picrites which, in fact, showed considerable variation in Au and Pd concentrations. Another source of error is the assumption that Pd is immobile during metamorphism. This seems to be

Table 4.1. Gold and palladium concentrations in ultramafic samples from the Qianxi Group, and their recalculated "primary" gold concentrations

Sample	Rock type	SiO_2	TiO_2	Al_2O_3	Fe_2O_3	MgO	MnO	CaO	Na_2O	K_2O	P_2O_5	Au	Pd	Au/Pd	"Primary Au"
CE102	Websterite	43.88	0.17	5.43	11.44	27.34	0.11	4.63	0.64	0.36	0.18	0.5	32.0	0.02	11.84
CE098	Pyroxene amphibolite	42.98	0.22	5.06	11.58	26.86	0.07	5.88	0.30	0.08	0.05	0.5	28.0	0.02	10.36
CE097	Websterite	42.06	0.23	6.88	15.32	25.52	0.12	5.38	0.34	0.18	0.09	6.0	45.0	0.13	16.65
CE099	Websterite	52.64	0.14	3.62	9.43	24.84	0.12	8.01	0.30	0.08	0.05	10.0	67.0	0.15	24.79
CE101	Websterite	53.18	0.19	3.59	9.90	24.56	0.10	6.76	0.54	0.18	0.01	0.5	14.0	0.04	5.18
YQ8	Pyroxenite	—	0.82	—	16.20	21.56	0.15	7.00	1.05	0.30	0.14	50.0	2.0	25.00	0.74
CE100	Pyroxenite	51.62	0.19	4.82	9.70	18.93	0.10	10.38	1.28	0.28	0.01	0.5	18.0	0.03	6.66
CE201[b]	Hornblendite	49.80	1.46	6.29	15.32	17.96	0.14	6.70	1.32	0.12	0.04	32.0	2.0	16.00	0.74
CE208	Pyroxenite	49.64	0.42	4.05	11.88	17.34	0.18	12.57	0.99	0.25	0.02	0.5	10.0	0.25	3.70
CE209[a]	Hornblendite	47.98	0.50	7.81	12.63	17.10	0.15	11.74	1.27	0.50	0.09	0.5	2.0	0.25	0.74
CE106[a]	Hornblendite	43.78	1.99	6.20	18.05	16.83	0.12	7.59	0.80	0.28	0.23	0.5	5.0	0.10	1.85
CE093[a]	Pyroxene amphibolite	43.06	1.85	5.26	19.80	16.67	0.13	8.75	1.22	0.28	0.46	0.5	3.0	0.17	1.11
CE103	Pyroxene amphibolite	43.96	1.48	6.09	17.36	16.39	0.18	9.25	1.12	0.08	0.16	0.5	4.0	0.13	1.48
CE095[b]	Hornblendite	44.12	1.89	4.68	19.05	15.40	0.12	8.63	1.04	0.18	0.25	98.0	2.0	49.00	0.74
CE096[a]	Hornblendite	44.18	1.77	6.10	17.64	15.40	0.10	9.75	0.88	0.64	0.27	1.0	2.0	0.50	0.74
CE104[a]	Pyroxene amphibolite	41.56	2.17	6.85	19.04	15.29	0.34	10.75	1.04	0.46	0.34	2.0	5.0	0.40	1.85
Q25	Pyroxene hornblendite	48.40	0.65	9.40	9.80	14.65	0.15	12.93	1.22	1.08	0.21	2.0	11.0	0.18	4.07
CE202	Pyroxenite	52.12	0.78	8.44	9.80	13.17	0.12	11.99	2.04	1.40	0.09	2.0	2.0	1.00	0.74
CE105[a]	Hornblendite	43.76	2.02	7.59	17.93	12.97	0.46	12.12	1.46	0.64	0.46	2.0	5.0	0.40	1.85
YQ108	Hornblendite	—	0.73	—	15.70	12.10	0.15	9.79	2.58	0.90	0.48	1.0	2.0	0.50	0.74
YQ124	Amphibolite	—	0.43	—	13.70	11.61	0.13	10.91	1.77	0.42	0.05	1.0	10.0	0.10	3.70
YQ88	Pyroxenite	—	0.62	—	14.70	11.11	0.17	15.39	1.73	1.02	1.81	98.0	3.0	32.67	1.11
YQ123	Pyroxenite	—	0.47	—	12.40	10.94	0.13	7.28	2.78	0.45	0.11	1.0	2.0	0.50	0.74
YQ41	Pyroxenite	—	0.37	—	12.30	10.45	0.13	11.19	2.75	1.01	0.05	2.0	3.0	0.67	1.11
YQ45	Pyroxene amphibolite	—	0.40	—	12.60	10.11	0.12	10.49	2.87	1.06	0.05	3.0	2.0	1.50	0.74

Analyses by XRF and INAA following fire assay (Au) or nickel sulfide (Pd) preconcentration, total Fe as Fe_2O_3.
"Primary Au" = Au × (Au/Pd × 0.37), see text for details.
[a] In contact with BIF lens.
[b] Sample near a fracture zone.

justified for sea-floor metamorphism according to studies of Keays and Scott (1976) and more recent work on precious metals in oceanic basalts by Brugman et al. (1987) and Hamlyn et al. (1985), but the situation may be very different in the high-grade polymetamorphic conditions to which the Archean rocks of northeastern China have been subjected.

We have applied the Au-Pd method to better interpret the Au concentrations of the Qianxi Group rocks. Only samples with MgO contents over 10 wt% were used, because in most other samples, the Pd concentrations are at or below the detection limit of 1 ppb, and because the bulk composition of these rocks justify the application of the "primary" Au/Pd ratio (0.37) derived from picritic basalts and komatiites. Table 4.1 presents the results from 25 samples of the Qianxi Group. Listed in the table are the bulk composition, measured Au and Pd values, Au/Pd ratios, and the calculated "primary" Au concentrations.

The following points can be concluded from Table 4.1:

a) Both the Pd and Au concentrations measured in these samples are highly variable and the Au/Pd ratio is not constant. If the "primary" Au/Pd ratio of 0.37 (or any other fixed ratio) is appropriate for the protoliths of these rocks, then postcrystallization mobility of Au and/or Pd can be inferred.

b) In most samples, the calculated "primary" gold concentrations are higher than the measured concentrations, which suggests leaching of gold (subject to the assumptions given above).

c) The highest measured Pd concentrations are in samples of ultramafic pyroxenites. The gold concentrations in these samples are not correspondingly high, suggesting possible leaching of primary gold from the rocks after crystallization.

d) The highest measured gold concentrations occur in samples taken near fractures. Pd is not correspondingly high in these samples, suggesting possible gold enrichment by postcrystallization processes acting along rock fractures.

e) Most importantly, neither the measured nor the calculated "primary" gold concentrations are significantly higher than the crustal average.

4.2.2 Gold in Yanshanian Granites

The most compelling arguments for the Yanshanian granites (sensu lato) as the source of gold are, first, that the mineralization in most mining districts studied is broadly coeval with the Yanshanian magmatism; and second, the gold deposits are spatially associated with Yanshanian granite plutons and related dikes.

There are much fewer data on gold concentrations from the Yanshanian granites in eastern Hebei province than from the Qianxi Group rocks. Table 4.2 lists the available data from several Yanshanian intrusions based on

Table 4.2. Gold concentration in unaltered samples of granitic plutons associated with mineralization in eastern Hebei province

Name of intrusion	Number of samples	Average Au (ppb)	Reference[a]
Niuxinshan	3	5.3	1
Wangtoushan	1	3	1
Sanyihe	4	3	1
Yuerya (white)	4	4.4	2
Yuerya (red)	4	1.9	2
Maoshan	32	2.5	3

[a] 1, This study, analyses by XRAL laboratories, Ontario, by fire assay, and DCP; 2, Yu et al. (1989), analytical method not given; 3, Yu and Jia (1989), analytical method not given.

our own analyses and on published studies. All of the plutons listed are directly associated with gold deposits, and some are mineralized themselves (Niuxinshan, Yuerya).

The data in Table 4.2 represent only a small number of samples from a few plutons, and more data need to be collected before a definitive statement about the gold potential of the Yanshanian granites can be made. However, at present it appears that the gold concentrations in the Yanshanian granites are less than 5 ppb, i.e., gold does not appear to be enriched in the granites relative to either the crustal average (Boyle 1979; Crocket 1991) or to the Qianxi Group rocks (Fig. 4.2, Appendix 2).

The interpretation of these data can be questioned because the rock samples analyzed do not represent the original magma from which they crystallized, especially because of the loss of volatiles. As discussed by Burnham and Ohmoto (1980), for example, much of the Cl and S in a magma can be removed at a late stage of crystallization by exsolution of volatiles. The importance of Cl and S as ligands for gold complexing suggests that the gold concentration may depend strongly on the behavior of these volatiles in the magma.

4.2.3 Isotopic Constraints

The source of gold may be indirectly constrained by considering isotopic evidence for the source of the ore elements lead and sulfur which accompany gold in the deposits. The following discussion is based on lead and sulfur isotopic analyses of ore and gangue minerals from selected deposits in eastern Hebei province.

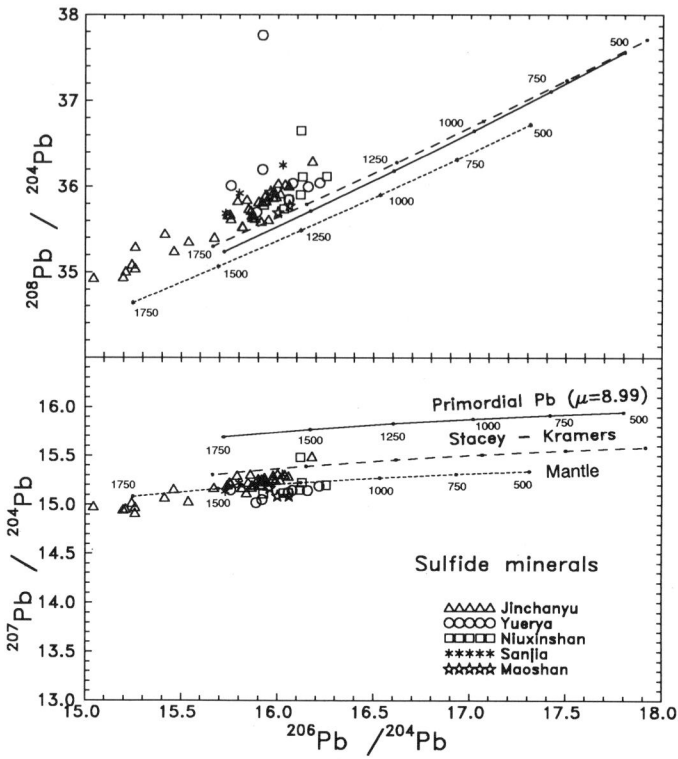

Fig. 4.3. Lead isotopic composition of galena and pyrite from selected gold deposits in eastern Hebei province. *Numbers* indicate age in Ma. Data sources are given in the text

Common Lead Isotopes
The use of common lead isotopes to deduce the source of lead in ore deposits is well established (Doe and Stacey 1974; Doe and Zartman 1979; Kramers and Foster 1984). Previous work on lead isotopes from ore deposits in China is reviewed by Zhu and Chen (1984) and Wang (1989). Wang (1989) concluded that the ore lead in the metamorphic-hosted gold deposits in northeastern China "is mostly derived from old multistage lead of a lower crustal uranium-depleted source." This statement also seems to hold true for the gold deposits from eastern Hebei province discussed below.

Figure 4.3 shows a compilation of lead isotopic data from ore minerals (mostly galena, also pyrite) from the gold deposits of Jinchangyu, Yuerya, Niuxinshan, and Sanjia. Figure 4.4 presents the corresponding lead isotopic compositions of K-feldspars and whole-rock samples from the Yanshanian granites in the respective mining districts. The diagrams combine data from Lin (1985), Yu and Jia (1989) and Yu et al. (1989), together with

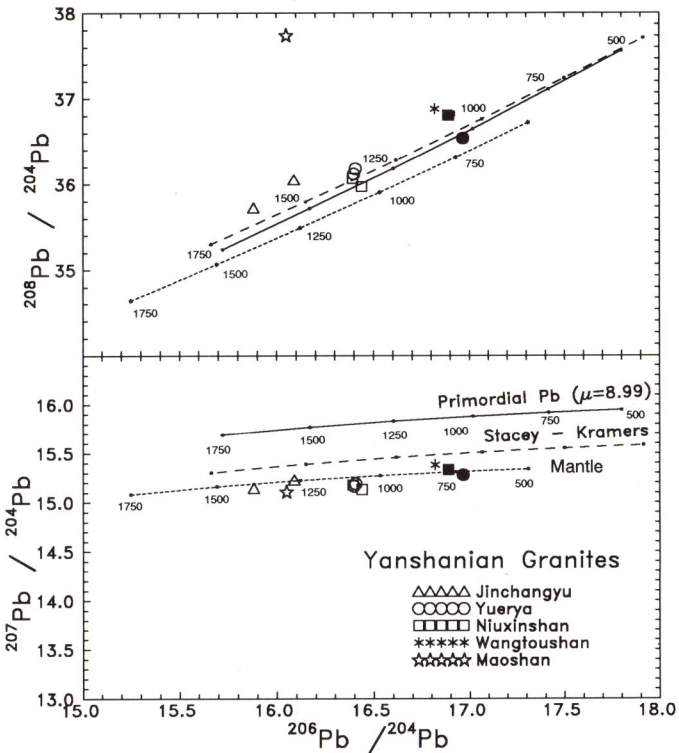

Fig. 4.4. Lead isotopic composition of Yanshanian granite K-feldspar (*open symbols*) and whole rocks (*filled symbols*) from selected gold deposits in eastern Hebei province. *Numbers* indicate age in Ma. Data sources are given in the text

unpublished analyses of the Ministry of Metallurgical Industry. Also shown in each diagram are single-stage lead isotopic growth curves for primeval lead (after Yu and Jia 1989), mantle lead (after Doe and Zartman 1979), and the two-stage terrestrial lead growth curve of Stacey and Kramers (1975).

The ore from all of the deposits shown has quite similar lead isotopic compositions. Except for some samples from the Jinchangyu deposit, the values of $^{206}Pb/^{204}Pb$, $^{207}Pb/^{204}Pb$ and $^{208}Pb/^{204}Pb$ for the ore leads cluster around 16, 15, and 36, respectively. The lead data from the Jinchangyu deposit overlap this range, and extend to lower, less-radiogenic values of $^{206}Pb/^{204}Pb$ and $^{208}Pb/^{204}Pb$. None of the deposits contains conformable, single-stage lead, and all of the deposits contain very nonradiogenic lead for their age; the lead isotopes yield geologically meaningless single-stage model ages (based on Doe and Stacey 1974) between about 1200 and 2000 Ma, whereas the deposits themselves are Mesozoic (see Chap. 4.1). These lead isotopic compositions resemble the examples discussed by Doe and Zartman

(1979) from ore deposits in the "rejuvenated craton" environment. Such lead tends to be low in the uranogenic isotopes ^{207}Pb and ^{206}Pb, and rich in the thorogenic isotope ^{208}Pb compared with crustal, mantle, or average terrestrial lead. Doe and Zartman (1979) suggest that this type of lead could be derived from lower crustal rocks which were depleted in uranium due to granulite-facies metamorphism. This interpretation seems reasonable for the Archean granulite-facies metamorphic terrane of eastern Hebei Province.

Yu and Jia (1989) interpreted the isotopic composition of ore leads in eastern Hebei province based on a two-stage model. The lead isotope data from the Jinchangyu and Yuerya deposits form linear arrays on the diagram of ^{207}Pb/^{204}Pb against ^{206}Pb/^{204}Pb, which the authors interpreted as secondary isochrons. The intersections of the secondary isochron from the Jinchangyu deposit with the primeval lead growth curve indicate model ages of 3480 Ma for the lead source and 133 Ma for the mineralization. The corresponding model ages from the secondary isochron from the Yuerya deposit are 3850 Ma and 230 Ma. This interpretation is in general agreement with the geologic facts (i.e., Early Archean basement, Mesozoic mineralization) but the ages are highly model-dependent and should be considered qualitative at best.

The isotopic composition of lead from the Yanshanian granites associated with the gold deposits also gives important evidence bearing on the source of metals. The comparison of Figs. 4.3 and 4.4 shows that the isotopic compositions of lead from the ores and from the granite K-feldspars are very similar, whereas the lead from granite whole-rock samples is slightly more radiogenic. The more radiogenic whole-rock lead is expected because it can continue to evolve by decay of U and Th after crystallization of the rock, whereas the common lead in K-feldspar is isolated from U and Th. The important point to be made is that the lead from the granites, like that from the ore deposits, is nonconformable, anomalous, and nonradiogenic for its (Mesozoic) age. This suggests that the lead in the granites is also derived, at least in large part, from uranium-depleted metamorphic basement rocks.

In summary, the lead isotopic data from both the granites and from the ores rule out an important contribution of "normal" Mesozoic lead (in the sense of Doe and Stacey 1974) in the deposits studied. The ultimate source of lead must be the uranium-depleted metamorphic basement. Of course, the source of lead in these deposits need not be the same as the source of gold, but there is a strong paragenetic association between gold and galena in the ores.

Sulfur Isotopes

The isotopic composition of sulfur in sulfide minerals can, in favorable cases, constrain the source of sulfur in the ores. Figure 4.5 summarizes the sulfur isotopic compositions of pyrite from five gold deposits in eastern Hebei province taken from Yu and Jia (1989) and Yu et al. (1989). Also shown in the diagram (open circles) are whole-rock δ^{34}S values from

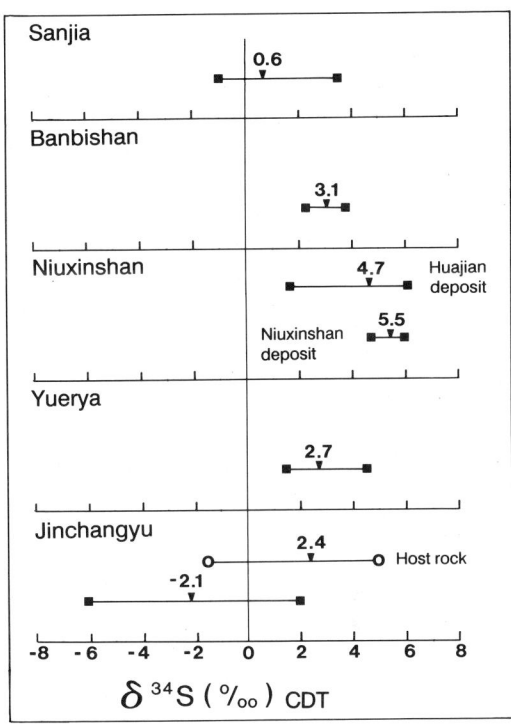

Fig. 4.5. Sulfur isotopic composition of pyrite (*filled squares*) and host rock (*open circles*) from selected gold deposits in eastern Hebei province. *Numbers* indicate mean values. Data replotted from Yu and Jia (1989) and Sun et al. (1989)

amphibolite country rocks from the Jinchangyu district. The pyrites from all of the deposits and the whole-rock amphibolite sample contain sulfur with a narrow range of $\delta^{34}S$ values between −6 and +6‰.

The isotopic compositions shown in Fig. 4.5 are typical for sulfide compositions in mesothermal gold deposits from many parts of the world (Lambert et al. 1984; Kerrich 1987; Peters and Golding 1989; Groves and Foster 1991). Yu and Jia (1989) argued that the similar, low $\delta^{34}S$ values of ore sulfides and amphibolites from the deposits in eastern Hebei province indicate that the sulfur was derived from the Archean basement. This interpretation is geologically reasonable and consistent with the lead isotopic data discussed above, but it must be emphasized that the sulfur data do not rule out other possibilities. According to Ohmoto and Rye (1979) and Ohmoto (1986), such $\delta^{34}S$ values are consistent with a deep-seated source of sulfur either from leaching of metamorphic rocks or from granitoid intrusions. In most rocks, such low values for $\delta^{34}S$ would rule out oxidized oceanic sulfur as a source (modern ocean sulfate has $\delta^{34}S$ values of +20‰). However, as Lambert et al. (1984) pointed out, the situation is different for Archean rocks because the sulfur isotopic composition in the reduced Archean hydrosphere would have had $\delta^{34}S$ values near 0. In addition, the isotopic composition of sulfide minerals depends in large part on the solution chemistry from which they crystallized, in particular the pH and oxygen fugacity, and these parameters are poorly defined for the ores at present. Therefore, the sulfur isotopic data from the ores must be considered ambiguous as to the sulfur source. If one makes the reasonable assumption that the source of sulfur, whatever it was, had $\delta^{34}S$ near zero, then the low positive $\delta^{34}S$ values of pyrite from most of the deposits suggest that the mineralizing fluids were chemically reduced.

Comparing the data from the different eastern Hebei deposits in Fig. 4.5, the Jinchangyu deposit is exceptional in having pyrite with mostly negative values of $\delta^{34}S$ whereas all others show positive values. Assuming that the sulfur source for all of the amphibolite-hosted deposits studied was the same, then the unusually negative $\delta^{34}S$ values of pyrite from the Jinchangyu deposit can be explained simply by a higher oxidation state of the mineralizing fluids in that deposit. Because sulfate concentrates ^{34}S relative to sulfide (Ohmoto 1986), the pyrite precipitating from an oxidized fluid will be isotopically lighter than that from a more reduced fluid, other conditions being equal.

4.2.4 The Mantle Connection

The significance of mantle processes for metallogenesis is a topic of current debate in studies of the Archean gold deposits in Western Australia and the Canadian Shield (Colvine 1989; Fyon et al. 1989; Groves et al. 1989; Perring et al. 1989). Most metallogenetic models which favor the mantle connection do not imply that the gold itself is derived from the mantle. Rather, the role of the mantle is simply to set the metallogenetic process in motion by the introduction of heat and volatiles to the lower crust. This causes granulitization and partial melting of a large volume of lower crustal rocks. The upward transport of metamorphic and/or juvenile fluids and deep-seated magmas has the potential to leach and transport gold. The focusing of fluid flow along regional shear zones provides a mechanism to concentrate gold in upper crustal levels and to ultimately form deposits. Such models offer an explanation for several very common features of mesothermal gold deposits, namely, the occurrence of CO_2-rich, low salinity fluid inclusions, the large-scale carbonatization of wall rocks, the proximity of deposits to regional shear zones with deep-seated intrusive rocks (lamprophyres) and granites, and the mantle signature of stable isotopic data (C-S-O).

The gold deposits in eastern Hebei province have many features in common with those of the Australian and Canadian gold deposits mentioned above, and the ubiquitous presence of lamprophyres in the gold districts described in Chapter 3 indicate the presence of deep-seated magmas closely following the time of mineralization. On the other hand, the lead isotopic evidence discussed above rules out any direct input of lead from the mantle at the time of mineralization. Mantle processes played an important role in the original formation of the Early Archean amphibolites and in their granulite-facies metamorphism around 2.5 to 2.7 Ga (Chap. 2.2.1). However, the main stage of gold mineralization in all deposits studied is Mesozoic in age, and there is no evidence in any of the deposits for Mesozoic lead of either mantle or crustal origin. A further problem is that, if mantle-derived fluids and/or magmas ascendent along major fault zones were important for gold mineralization, then it is odd that the gold in eastern Hebei province occurs almost exclusively in Early Precambrian rocks whereas the major fault zones which might tap mantle fluids are much more common in the areas of Late Proterozoic and Phanerozoic exposures (see Figs. 1.3 and 2.6).

4.2.5 Conclusions

We do not accept the concept of gold-rich source beds within the Qianxi Group. Recent studies of gold concentrations in Early Proterozoic rocks (Zhou 1989) and in the Archean Qianxi Group (this study; Yu and Jia 1989) suggest that these rocks have normal gold concentrations, and that the occasional high values encountered are due to secondary enrichment. Use of the Au-Pd method (Table 4.1) to recalculate the primary, i.e., pre-metamorphic Au concentrations in ultramafic rocks of the Qianxi Group results in values which are still not above the crustal average for such rocks.
The Yanshanian granites are spatially and temporally associated with the gold deposits in eastern Hebei province. They have been less well studied than the Qianxi Group rocks, but available data suggest that the granites, too, contain unexceptional gold concentrations (1–5 ppb) which are in the same range as those of the Archean rocks. In terms of their absolute gold abundances, then, both the granites and the Qianxi Group rocks would be equally favorable as a gold source. However, the lead isotopic data indicate that the lead in the gold deposits is derived from the Archean basement and not from the granites. Furthermore, the Archean rocks constitute a more likely source of gold than the granites simply because they are far more abundant, and they have a higher secondary permeability due to folds, faults, and fractures.
The possibility that gold was derived from the mantle during the Yanshan Orogeny cannot be entirely ruled out, but it is inconsistent with the lead isotopic evidence and it cannot account for the fact that gold deposits are concentrated in the areas of Archean exposures.
We conclude that the gold in the deposits studied was mainly derived from leaching of the Archean metamorphic basement rocks despite the fact that they had average gold concentrations less than 5 ppb. We envision this

leaching as taking place in the brittle regime at the intrusion level of the Yanshanian granitoids where fluid circulation is enhanced by secondary permeability. There is abundant support in the literature for the concept that rocks with low-ppb abundances of gold can be the source of gold for economic deposits (Fyfe and Kerrich 1984; Keays 1984; Phillips et al. 1987; Groves and Foster 1991). Seward (1984), for example, reported analyses of sulfide precipitates from several active geothermal systems in New Zealand which show that ore-grade gold concentrations of 50–80 g/t can precipitate from fluids with low-ppb or even sub-ppb concentrations of gold in solution. The problem of a gold-rich source may, therefore, be less important to the genesis of the deposits than the problem of a large volume of fluid flow and a suitable chemical environment for gold leaching, transportation, and precipitation.

4.3 The Role of Iron-Rich Host Rocks

The Archean and Early Proterozoic metamorphic host rocks in many of the gold districts in northeastern China contain supracrustal sequences including metamorphic banded iron formation (BIF). The nature of these BIF rocks has been recently reviewed by Sills et al. (1987b) and Zhai and Windley (1990). The association of gold with BIF in other Archean cratons in the world has been noted by many authors (Neall 1987; Saager et al. 1987; Groves et al. 1988; Colvine 1989; Foster 1989) but has not been given much attention in northeastern China. For this reason, a discussion of Archean iron formations and their relevance to gold mineralization is appropriate. After a general introduction, the iron formations in the gold districts of eastern Hebei province are described in detail.
Two main classes of iron formations are distinguished based on examples from North America: (1) the Algoma-type, and (2) the Superior-type (Guilbert and Park 1986). The Algoma-type BIFs are directly associated with volcanic rocks, and the iron enrichment is considered to be related to submarine volcanic processes. Algoma-type iron formations are typically of Archean age, although some more modern examples are known. They tend to be smaller and less continuous than the Superior-type. The Superior-type BIFs are typically of early to Middle-Proterozoic age and, although the rock association may include some volcanic input, this is often minimal or absent. The associated rocks indicate a stable shelf depositional environment, and the Superior-type iron formations are often of vast extent. A further important criterion for classifying iron formations is the facies concept. Four facies are distinguished according to the dominant mineralogy of the iron ore, i.e., oxide, silicate, sulfide, and carbonate facies. The type of facies is related to the depositional setting of the iron formations, especially the water depth. The depth of the paleobasin increases in the order oxide-carbonate-sulfide facies (Guilbert and Park 1986).

Gold mineralization in many of the world's Archean cratons, particularly in the greenstone-granite terranes, is closely associated with Archean BIF of Algoma-type. The Superior-type BIF deposits, on the other hand, are rarely mineralized with gold to a significant extent. The metallogenesis of BIF-related gold mineralization is currently disputed (Saager et al. 1987; Foster and Gilligan 1987; Lhotka and Nesbitt 1989; Oberthür et al. 1990). Based on the observations and interpretations given in these studies, it appears that the gold mineralization associated with BIF is obviously stratabound but not always stratiform, being often localized in texturally late quartz stringers, along axial planes of folds or in structural dilatant zones. The formation of ore bodies of economic interest appears to be the product of a polystage process including syn-sedimentary gold enrichment (with barium, arsenic, sulfur), diagenetic reactions, and finally metamorphic and/or postmetamorphic hydrothermal remobilization. Perhaps the most important fact underlying this complexity is that iron-rich units can act from the very beginning of their formation as an effective geochemical trap for gold in both the sedimentary and hydrothermal environment.

4.3.1 Banded Iron Formations in Northeastern China

The distribution, metamorphic grade and geotectonic setting of the Archean and Early Proterozoic BIFs in China have been discussed in some detail by Sills et al. (1987b) and by Zhai and Windley (1990), and the reader is referred to those references for general information. Zhai and Windley (1990) emphasized the fact that many of the BIFs in northeastern China are found in the Archean high-grade granulite terrane and that this rock association is rare in other cratons, a notable exception being Isua in western Greenland. In the Archean rocks of northeastern China, the BIF layers are generally associated with amphibolites and mafic granulites interpreted to be metabasalts. For this reason, Zhang (1987) and Sills et al. (1987b) equate the Archean BIF-metabasalt association of China with the Algoma-type. The early Proterozoic BIFs in northeastern China are comparable to the Superior-type because they lack a major volcanic association, but in northeastern China these Superior-type BIFs are much less extensive than in North America, and most of the iron ore comes from the Archean Algoma-type BIF.

The iron formations in northeastern China are almost exclusively of the oxide facies (dominated by magnetite), with subordinate iron silicates. One reason for the lack of carbonate-facies iron formation and for the relatively low oxidation state of the Chinese BIF may be the high-grade metamorphism which the rocks have undergone. Lower crustal oxygen fugacities are typically below the magnetite-hematite buffer, and carbonate minerals in association with silica would be destroyed by decarbonation reactions during prograde metamorphism such as the following:

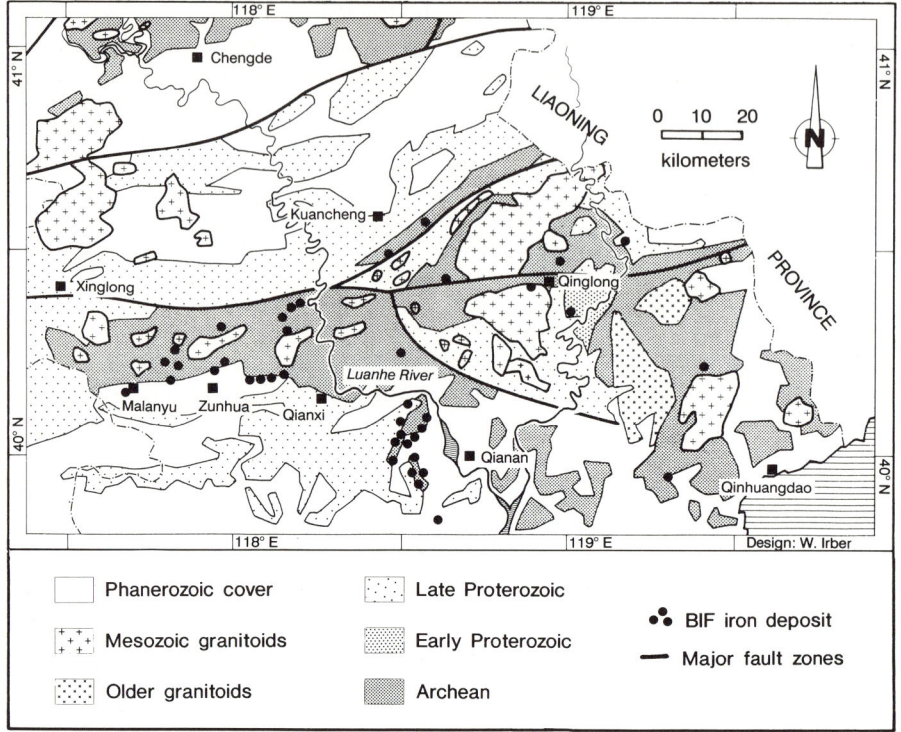

Fig. 4.6. Simplified geologic map of part of eastern Hebei province showing the distribution of BIF-type iron deposits

$$Ca(Fe, Mg)(CO_3)_2 + 2SiO_2 = Ca(Fe, Mg)Si_2O_6 + 2CO_2.$$

$$(Fe, Mg)CO_3 + SiO_2 = (Fe, Mg)SiO_3 + CO_2.$$

Turning our attention to eastern Hebei province, BIF occurs as discontinuous, stratiform lenses in the Archean Qianxi and Dantazi Groups, and to a lesser extent in the Early Proterozoic Zhuzhangzi Group. Figure 4.6 shows the distribution of the largest iron deposits in this area. The comparison of this map with the distribution of gold deposits in the same area shown on Fig. 1.3 indicates a poor correspondence of iron and gold deposits, a fact also noted by Shen et al. (1989). The largest iron deposits in eastern Hebei province are found in the Archean Santunying Formation in the Qianan area south of the Luanhe River. In this area, BIF layers are continuous along strike for up to several kilometers and reach a thickness of up to 100 m. These BIFs have been described by Zhai and Windley (1990). The BIF layers north of the Luanhe River, where almost all of the gold districts are located, occur in amphibolites and gneisses as discontinuous, stratiform, mostly lens-shaped bodies of minor economic importance. The observed thickness of the iron-rich lenses in this area is mostly some decimeters to several meters, and their lateral extent is some tens to hundreds of meters, depending on local structure. Banding of quartz-rich and magnetite-rich portions in the iron-rich rocks is locally present, but it is by no means ubiquitous, and the term banded iron formation is often not justified. In the Chinese literature the iron-rich rocks are commonly called magnetite quartzites and this term will also be used here.

4.3.2 Petrography and Composition of Magnetite Quartzites

The magnetite quartzites of the Qianxi Group exposed in the gold districts north of the Luanhe River grade continuously over a distance of a few decimeters into normal amphibolites. In the most iron-rich layers magnetite and quartz occur in approximately equal proportions, and hornblende and plagioclase are reduced to accessories. Such rocks possess a foliation and banding which is continuous with that of the surrounding amphibolites.

Like their amphibolite country rocks, the magnetite-rich rocks have been metamorphosed to granulite or upper amphibolite facies conditions and show abundant evidence of later retrograde metamorphism in the form of fibrous blue-green actinolite pseudomorphs after pyroxene and hornblende, chlorite after garnet, and sericitization of amphibole and plagioclase. The rocks have a hypidiomorphic granular texture with weak foliation, and are locally banded, with quartz-rich and magnetite-rich layers. Magnetite in the rocks is intergrown with quartz and/or retrograde fibrous amphibole. The magnetite has a grain size of about 0.2 to 1 mm.

Chemical analyses of selected samples of magnetite quartzites collected from areas north of the Luanhe River are shown in Table 4.3. Some samples were taken from outside the gold mining districts and others from outcrops in the mineralized areas of the Niuxinshan and Sanjia districts. The table is divided into two sections. In section (a) those samples are listed which show little or no secondary alteration (based on petrography and total S content). Table 4.3b lists analyses of samples affected by secondary sulfidization. The latter are discussed separately in the following section. The total iron concentrations of unaltered samples (as Fe_2O_3) range from 28 to 47 wt%. The concentrations of MgO and CaO range from about 1 to 2 wt%. The range of Al_2O_3 is from less than 1 to about 3 wt%. The trace element concentrations are all quite low with the exception of chalcophile elements in some samples affected by sulfidization as discussed below. These chemical compositions compare favorably with those given in Zhai and Windley (1990) for BIF ores from various parts of northeastern China except that the total iron contents reported here are lower, and the Al_2O_3 concentrations are higher than the range reported by Zhai and Windley (1990). This discrepancy is probably due to the fact that the samples reported here were

Table 4.3. Partial chemical analyses of magnetite quartzite samples from the Qianxi Group

Locality[a]	a (Unaltered)						b (Sulfidized)						
Sample No.	NXS 6126	SJ 6203	STY 6101	NXS 6166	NXS 6122	NXS 6128	WJ 6321	STY 6093	STY 6095	NXS 6170	NXS 6185	NXS 6523	STY 6102
TiO_2	0.09	0.22	0.04	0.41	0.63	1.55	0.01	0.16	0.06	0.37	0.01	0.05	0.32
Al_2O_3	1.24	6.10	1.37	1.17	0.96	12.29	0.23	2.58	1.98	4.20	0.55	3.77	1.14
Fe_2O_3	49.01	26.03	33.20	45.42	47.06	14.43	45.42	25.61	37.31	28.32	42.30	32.66	32.70
Mn	449	534	527	774	790	1626	372	457	534	984	4848	7977	1967
MgO	1.18	1.90	2.18	1.34	0.85	5.41	0.55	1.86	1.38	3.23	1.94	1.22	0.77
CaO	1.35	3.20	2.90	1.69	0.81	6.21	1.87	2.51	3.01	3.64	1.75	1.52	2.59
Na_2O	0.13	0.89	0.05	0.06	0.03	3.57	0.01	0.22	0.04	0.74	0.01	0.02	0.02
K_2O	0.13	1.90	0.00	0.04	0.35	1.22	0.00	1.48	0.25	0.25	0.19	0.56	0.05
P_2O_5	0.25	0.25	0.21	0.23	0.23	0.13	0.28	0.58	0.22	0.19	0.22	0.13	0.20
Rb	25	99	25	25	60	144	25	104	56	25	57	141	25
Sr	59	300	34	11	13	337	49	99	55	73	48	28	25
Ba	48	1190	19	12	59	522	25	355	59	31	39	58	21
V	1	24	1	5	55	314	1	21	3	44	1	9	26
Cr	3	18	1	1	1	42	2	31	3	40	1	5	1
Co	15	9	1	15	8	38	1	3	1	37	1	14	21
Ni	6	18	6	20	8	35	1	24	5	96	1	28	28
Y	9	12	8	8	6	30	8	20	8	11	6	7	8
Zr	1	14	12	1	1	7	1	2	15	4	1	9	1
Total S (wt%)	0.01	0.01	0.01	0.04	0.05	0.10	0.51	0.71	0.95	2.64	2.72	7.45	14.27
Cu	11	5	6	10	29	58	29	114	100	644	209	1195	844
Zn	57	66	36	113	115	158	21	29	120	81	277	384	214
Pb	32	5	5	5	5	34	5	15	5	5	49	221	14
Ag	0.8	0.6	0.6	0.6	0.9	0.6	0.3	1.2	1.1	1.0	1.5	5.0	3.0
W	27	5	16	15	36	5	17	25	5	15	33	306	36
Au (ppb)	1	33	1	35	17	287	2	33	299	28	87	461	4590

Oxides in wt% elements in ppm unless otherwise stated, total Fe as Fe_2O_3.
[a] Localities: NXS, Niuxinshan; SJ, Sanjia; WJ, Wangjiangzi; STY, Santunying.

not taken from iron ore but represent the typical subeconomic magnetite quartzite horizons in the Qianxi Group.

4.3.3 Sulfidization and Gold Mineralization

The gold concentrations in the non-sulfidized samples of magnetite quartzite in Table 4.3a are at or below the Clarke average, and they are comparable to those of the Qianxi Group amphibolites in general (Fig. 4.2, Appendix 2). This suggests that the iron formations themselves are not primarily enriched in gold. Any gold enrichment noted in the samples from the mining districts can be attributed to secondary sulfidization.

Petrography of Sulfidization
Sulfidization is manifested by the replacement of magnetite by sulfide minerals including mostly pyrite and lesser pyrrhotite and chalcopyrite. Typical of the newly formed pyrite grains are numerous minute inclusions of silicate minerals which were present as inclusions and interstices within magnetite aggregates. The sulfidization front can be seen in some samples as a clearly delineated zone which forms around a central quartz vein. An example is shown in the photomicrographs in Fig. 4.7. The ore minerals found in samples of sulfidized magnetite quartzite include: magnetite, pyrite, pyrrhotite, chalcopyrite, native gold. They show the following paragenetic features:

Magnetite
Magnetite is usually found in aggregates of up to a few millimeters in size within or in the interstices of the silicate minerals. The magnetite enrichment occurs in bands which parallel the foliation of the rock. The magnetite grains are euhedral to subhedral, and commonly fractured and partially replaced by Fe-hydroxides, chlorite, carbonates, and sulfides.

Pyrite and Chalcopyrite
Pyrite occurs in the magnetite quartzite within the selvage zone of quartz-sulfide veins as cubes of some millimeters in size and as irregularly shaped aggregates pseudomorphous after magnetite. Pyrite replaces magnetite along fractures and grain boundaries. The pyrite pseudomorphs after magnetite contain numerous inclusions of silicates, chalcopyrite, pyrrhotite, and relict magnetite grains. An example is shown in Fig. 4.7.
Chalcopyrite forms irregular aggregates of sub-millimeter size at the replacement front between magnetite and pyrite. It can also be observed to fill cracks in cataclastic pyrite and it occurs in minor amounts disseminated as small anhedral grains associated with mafic silicates.

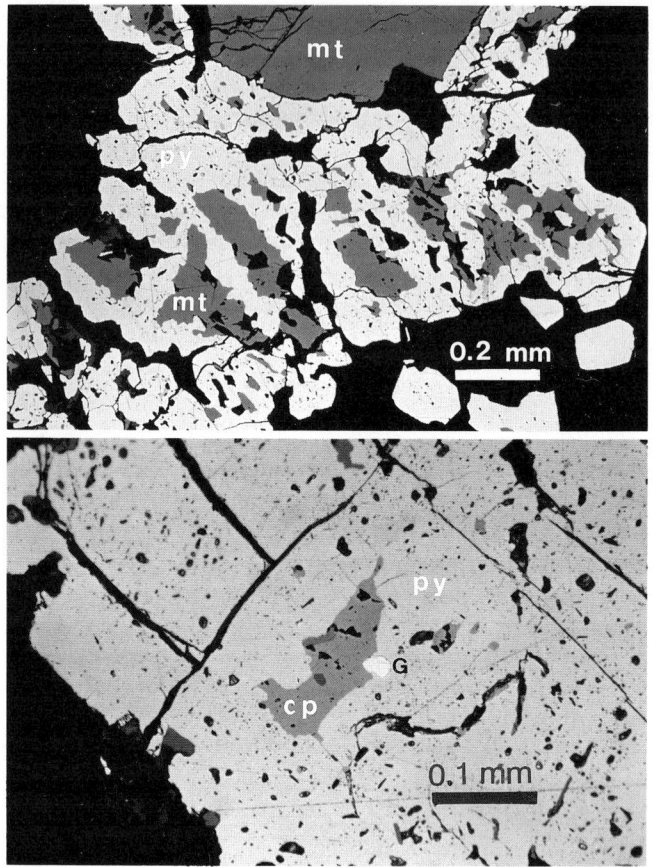

Fig. 4.7. *Above*: Photomicrograph of nearly complete replacement of magnetite (*mt*) by pyrite (*py*) in sulfidized magnetite quartzite from the Sanjia deposit. *Below*: Gold (*G*) and chalcopyrite (*cp*) in pyrite (*py*) in sulfidized magnetite quartzite from the Sanjia deposit

Native Gold

Gold is quite rare in the sulfidized magnetite quartzites. Single, free gold grains up to about 0.01 mm in size occur within pyrite grains along the sulfidization front. An example is shown in Fig. 4.7 (below). The gold grains may be intergrown with chalcopyrite. The EDS microanalysis of gold (one sample) showed 25 wt% Ag, which is not appreciably different from the composition of gold from ore in the normal amphibolite host rocks.

Geochemistry of Sulfidization

The degree of alteration of the samples is reflected in their chemical compositions by variations in the K_2O and total S concentrations (cf. Table 4.3a

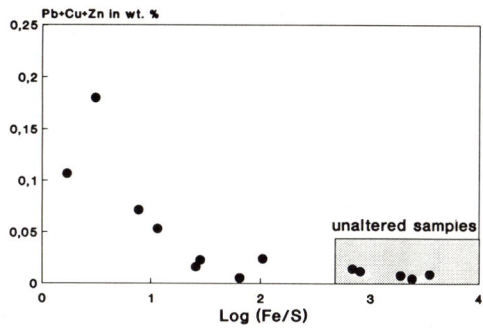

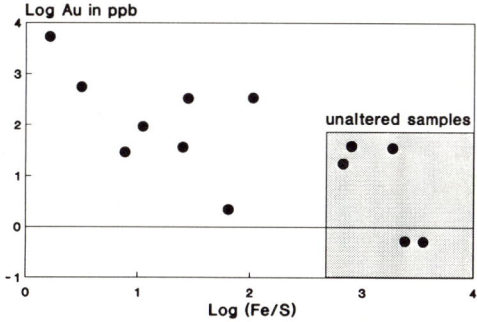

Fig. 4.8. Diagrams showing the variation of base metals concentrations (*upper*) and gold (*lower*) with the degree of sulfidization in magnetite quartzites from the Qianxi Group

and b). Along with the increase in sulfur, the chalcophile elements Cu, Pb, Zn, and Au are also enriched relative to the unaltered magnetite quartzites. The effect of sulfidization on gold and base metal concentration is examined in Fig. 4.8, which shows the element concentrations plotted against the weight ratio of Fe/S as a measure of the sulfidization degree. The increase in total base metal concentration of the rocks with sulfidation is clearly demonstrated. An increase in gold concentration with degree of sulfidization is apparent but the trend is much less regular.

Precipitation Mechanisms

According to the present knowledge of gold geochemistry (Seward 1991), gold will be present as both chloride- and sulfur complexes at the physical conditions of ore formation discussed in Chapter 4.6 (ca. 300–350°C and 2–4 kbar). The bisulfide complex of gold [Au(HS)$_2^-$] can be de-stabilized by sulfidization of magnetite during wall rock alteration because these reactions

141

remove reduced sulfur from the hydrothermal fluid (Neall 1987). An overall model reaction for this process is:

$$6Au(HS)_2^- + 2Fe_3O_4 + 0.5O_2 = 6Au° + 6FeS_2 + 3H_2O + 6OH^-.$$

Note that the formation of pyrite from iron-rich silicate minerals would have the same effect of consuming sulfide from the fluid. Phillips and Groves (1984) proposed the following model reaction for the replacement of iron-rich chlorite by pyrite and magnesian chlorite:

$$3Fe_4Mg_2Si_2O_{10}(OH)_8 + 12H_2S + 3O_2 =$$
$$6FeS_2 + 2Fe_3Mg_3Si_4O_{10}(OH)_8 + 4SiO_2 + 16H_2O.$$

4.3.4 Conclusions

There is no evidence that the iron-rich rocks (magnetite quartzites) in the gold districts of eastern Hebei province have a primary, syngenetic gold enrichment. Instead, the high gold concentrations measured in some samples of these rocks are a result of secondary sulfidization of the rocks caused by hydrothermal alteration. The reactions forming pyrite from magnetite or from iron-rich silicate minerals should favor precipitation of gold carried in solution as a sulfur complex. The observed positive correlation of gold concentration with degree of sulfidization is good evidence that sulfur complexes were in fact involved in the transport of at least some of the gold present in these rocks.

At present there is no direct confirmation from mine records that magnetite quartzites and/or iron-rich horizons in the host rocks are particularly well mineralized with gold. On the contrary, it was noted above that the large iron deposits in eastern Hebei province are not notably mineralized with gold (see also Shen et al. 1989). However, the iron deposits do not occur in exactly the same geologic setting as the gold deposits, and in the gold mining districts themselves this aspect of host-rock control of mineralization has not previously been considered. A reexamination of drill core logs in this light might give valuable information for further gold exploration. If a connection is found, tracing the magnetite quartzite layers in the field by inexpensive magnetometry would be an effective exploration tool.

4.4 The Role of Yanshanian Granites

The field relations in the individual mining districts of eastern Hebei province discussed in Chapter 3 and the evidence from isotopic dating summarized in Chapter 4.1 clearly demonstrate that gold mineralization is closely related in time and space with certain Yanshanian granite plutons and associated dikes. In most districts studied, the ore veins cut the associated granites and are penecontemporaneous with post-granite mafic and felsic dikes. Some field relations are ambiguous, but in general it can be stated that the mineralization occurred in a late stage of Yanshanian magmatism. Other workers have also proposed that the Precambrian-hosted gold deposits in northeastern China are genetically related to Yanshanian granites (M.Z. Yang 1988; Liu 1989; Zhou 1989), and the same conclusion was reached by Shelton et al. (1988) in a study of similar Archean-hosted gold deposits in South Korea.

Of course, it is well known that the Yanshanian magmatism (in the broad sense, Mesozoic–Tertiary, see Chap. 2.4) was important to the formation of Sn, W, Cu, and Mo ore deposits in eastern Asia generally. Well-documented areas include southeastern Asia (Hutchinson and Taylor 1978), southeastern China (Guo 1982; Ishihara and Sato 1982; Wu 1985), southern Korea (Lee 1981; Iyama and Fonteilles 1981; Kim and Lee 1983), and Japan (Ishihara 1981; Ishihara et al. 1981). The information from northeastern China and Siberia is less complete, but in these areas, too, a strong correlation of ore deposits with Yanshanian magmatism has been noted (Zonenshain et al. 1974; Guo 1982; Ishihara 1984).

Despite this supporting evidence, the connection between granitic intrusions and gold mineralization is not unambiguous, and the role of granites in the genesis of gold deposits is not so well understood as in the case of Sn, W, Cu, and Mo deposits. It is important to note, too, that granite-related gold metallogenesis in northeastern China is not entirely restricted to the Yanshanian Orogeny. In some gold mining districts in Jilin and Heilongjiang province discussed in Chapter 1.2, the granites associated with gold deposits are Variscan in age.

4.4.1 Granite Compositions

The spatial distribution of Yanshanian granites and gold deposits in eastern Hebei province (Fig. 1.3) raises the question of why certain granites are associated with gold and others are not. This is of obvious strategic importance to further exploration, and one important aspect of the problem is the composition of the various plutons. Unfortunately, there have been relatively few studies done on the Yanshanian granites in northeastern China, and there are no comprehensive data with which to compare the granites associated with gold deposits and those with no gold association. The authors began such a study in eastern Hebei province with a geochemical reconnaisance of 16 Yanshanian plutons as presented in Chapter 2.4.3. The results of this study which are relevant to the granite–gold relationship are discussed below.

According to the work of Ishihara (1984) and Wu (1985) on granite-related metallogeny in eastern Asia as a whole, it might be expected that granites associated with gold deposits would be intermediate in composition and belong to the magnetite series, in contrast to the ilmenite-series leucogranites associated with Sn and W deposits. This idea is supported by Tu (1989), who stated that the granitoids associated with gold deposits in China tend to have "dioritic" compositions. M.Z. Yang (1988) proposed three genetic categories of granites associated with gold deposits in northern China based on their geologic setting, initial $^{87}Sr/^{86}Sr$ and oxygen isotope ratios. The categories are: anatectic crustal source granites, deep-source granites, and a transitional type termed strata-bound deep source granites. Gold deposits occur with granites of all three categories according to M.Z. Yang (1988), and he gives no indication that any one granite type is more important than the others for gold metallogenesis. It may also be relevant to this discussion that the magmatogenic Late Tertiary gold deposits in western Pacific island arcs are associated with both rhyolitic-rhyodacitic rocks and andesitic-dacitic rocks, although the latter predominate (Sillitoe 1989).

The compositions of 16 Yanshanian granites from eastern Hebei province are summarized in Appendix 1 and were discussed in Chapter 2.4.3. Two compositional groups were recognized, the dominant one characterized by relatively felsic, moderately differentiated granites; and a second group containing only a few plutons which are more mafic and weakly differentiated. Table 4.4 and Figs. 4.9 and 4.10 show selected geochemical features of the plutons grouped according to the presence or absence of gold deposits

Table 4.4. Selected chemical features of gold-related and not-gold-related Yanshanian granites in eastern Hebei province

Pluton	SiO_2	Fe index	Rb/Sr	K/Rb	Na_2O/K_2O
Gold-related granites					
Laochengling	76.66	0.63	–	–	1.13
Sanyihe	73.93	0.49	1.5	245.7	1.07
Madi	74.15	0.24	367.6	18.9	1.50
Yuerya	73.97	0.32	0.9	260.0	0.81
Maoshan	74.46	0.33	1.4	96.4	1.03
Niuxinshan	74.25	0.57	10.0	144.6	0.65
Qingshankou	73.57	0.37	1.4	235.1	0.99
Wangtoushan	75.69	0.51	0.9	237.7	0.62
Gaojiadian	56.30	0.40	0.1	492.2	1.56
Not-gold-related granites					
Xiaoyingzi	68.79	0.47	0.1	590.1	1.03
Wangpingshi	73.36	0.44	1.7	159.3	0.94
Doushan	70.07	0.34	0.1	512.0	0.99
Luowenyu	75.35	0.28	5.4	124.1	1.02
Qianfenshuiling	69.76	0.52	–	–	1.29
Jiajiashan	73.93	0.38	2.1	223.9	1.16
Shitaizi	73.52	0.59	–	–	0.81

Fe index: atomic ratio $Fe_2O_3/(Fe_2O_3 + FeO)$.
A value of 0.35 divides the ilmenite and magnetite series of Ishihara (1984).

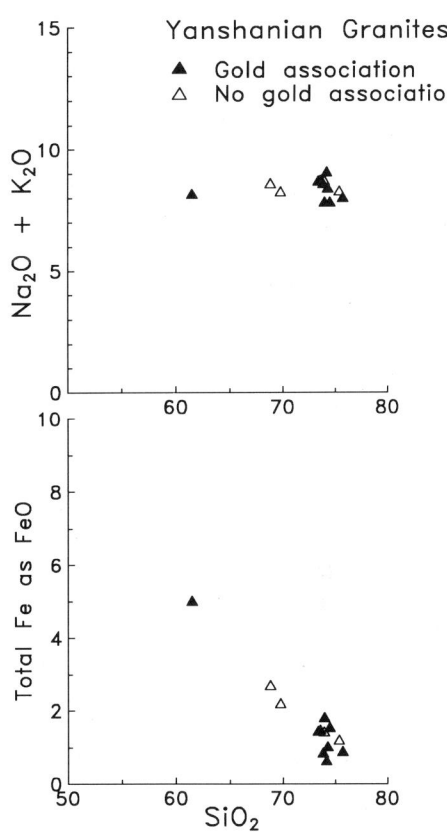

Fig. 4.9. Harker diagrams showing the average composition of Yanshanian plutons in eastern Hebei province with spatially associated gold deposits and plutons with no gold association

spatially associated with them (gold-related and not gold-related plutons). The average compositions of the plutons were used to avoid overcrowding the diagrams and to give equal weight to plutons from which many samples were analyzed and those represented by only one or two analyses. The data show that the gold-related and the not-gold-related plutons both cover a wide range of compositions, and that these ranges overlap. The two compositional groups of Yanshanian plutons identified in Chapter 2.4.3 do not correlate with the presence or absence of gold mineralization. The gold-related plutons in Table 4.4 belong mostly to Ishihara's (1984) magnetite series according to their whole-rock oxidation index (atomic $Fe_2O_3/Fe_2O_3 + FeO > 0.35$), but this does not distinguish them from the plutons not related to gold deposits.

All available data on gold concentrations in Yanshanian granites from eastern Hebei province were presented in Table 4.2. It suffices to reiterate

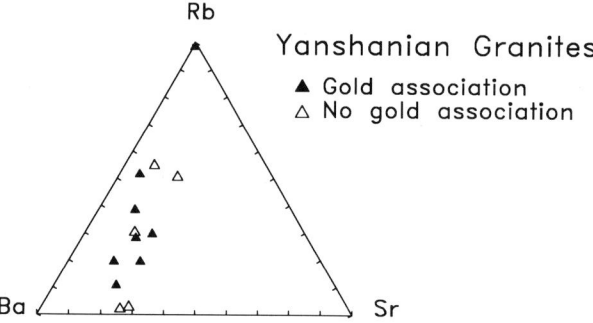

Fig. 4.10. Rb-Ba-Sr diagram showing the average composition of Yanshanian plutons in eastern Hebei province with spatially associated gold deposits and plutons with no gold association

here that the granites associated with gold deposits have "normal" background gold concentrations at or below 5 ppb. There are not enough data at present to compare the gold concentrations in gold-related and in not-gold-related plutons, and this aspect should be pursued in future studies.

4.4.2 Heat Production

Recently, the concept of high heat production granites was proposed as an important factor in granite-related metallogenesis. A high heat production granite is one with a high concentration of radioactive elements (mainly K, Th, and U), which constitute a significant heat source long after the magmatic heat has dissipated. The consequence is that hydrothermal circulation around such granites can last much longer than otherwise, and this factor alone may increase the mineralization potential of such granites. It is thought that, for example, the hydrothermal ores associated with the Cornubian batholith of southwestern England were produced or enhanced by this process, and even today the area exhibits anomalously high surface heat flow and a high geothermal gradient (Stone and Exley 1985).

The heat production of a granite can be calculated from a chemical analysis, and the results for selected plutons in the mining districts in eastern Hebei province are shown in Table 4.5. Unfortunately, the requisite U and Th data are presently available for only three granites, and all three are associated with gold deposits. The heat production value of the Niuxinshan granite is comparable with that of the Cornubian batholith, which may be considered the "type" high-heat production granite, but the other two Chinese granites have lower heat production values than even the average granite. Therefore, it seems that there are both "normal" granites and granites of the high-heat production type in eastern Hebei province. However, more data are

Table 4.5. Radiogenic heat production of selected granites from eastern Hebei province

Pluton	U (ppm)	Th (ppm)	K_2O (%)	Heat production ($10^{-6} W/m^3$)
Niuxinshan	7.6	32	4.79	4.66
Sanyihe	2.7	11.3	4.50	1.88
Wangtoushan	3.1	7.0	5.15	1.72
Average granite[a]	3	17	5.06	2.49
Cornubian batholith[b]	11.3	19.1	4.3	4.7

Heat production calculated from average composition of the granites using the equation of Rybach (1976) assuming a density of 2.7 for all granites.
[a] Compositional data from Rösler and Lange (1972).
[b] Data from Brown et al. (1979).

needed, including analyses from plutons not related to gold deposits, before the significance of this distinction can be discussed.

4.4.3 Conclusions

The field relationships and radiometric age data demonstrate that gold mineralization in eastern Hebei province is related in space and in time to certain of the Yanshanian granites and/or their related igneous dikes. However, the relation is not a direct one; that is, the granites themselves are seldom mineralized and in most cases they were in place and solid before mineralization commenced.

The chemical composition of 16 Yanshanian granites from eastern Hebei province, including both gold-related and not-gold-related plutons, and the lead isotopic composition of ore minerals from the deposits (Chap. 4.2.3) suggest the following conclusions:

1. Apart from local high values due to alteration, the gold concentrations (<1 to 5 ppb) of the gold-related granites (i.e., Niuxinshan, Wangtoushan, Sanyihe, Maoshan, Yuerya) are not above average, and the concentration of gold in these granites is lower than or equal to that in the Archean country rocks.
2. The lead isotopic compositions of galena and iron sulfides from the ore veins suggest that the lead in the gold deposits was derived from the Early Precambrian metamorphic basement and not from the Yanshanian granites.
3. The compositions of individual granites in eastern Hebei province do not correlate with the presence or absence of associated gold mineralization. Gold deposits are associated with granites having a wide range of composition.

4. Based on whole-rock Fe_2O_3 and FeO concentrations, both the granites associated with gold deposits and those with no gold association belong predominantly to the magnetite series of Ishihara (1984).
5. Both low- and high-heat production granites occur in the gold mining districts of eastern Hebei province. More studies are needed to assess the importance of radiogenic heat production to mineralization potential in this area.

In summary, the available evidence suggests that the chemical composition of the Yanshanian granites has no bearing on the presence or absence of gold mineralization, and that the granites were not the source of ore-forming elements found in the deposits. However, the close spatial and temporal relationships of Yanshanian granites and associated dikes with gold mineralization in all districts studied cannot be coincidental. If the granites made no material contribution to the deposits, the only reasonable explanation for the relationship is that the heat and/or deformation attending the intrusion of granites created conditions favorable for hydrothermal circulation. The nature of faults and fractures in the gold districts would play a vital role in focusing or dispersing hydrothermal circulation, and it may be that the difference between gold-related and not-gold-related granites lies in the local structural environments, and has nothing to do with the composition of the granites themselves.

4.5 Structural Controls

Rock structures, in particular fault zones and fractures, are the most direct factors controlling the form, distribution and intensity of gold mineralization in eastern Hebei province on both a regional and a local scale. This section summarizes the most important features of structure relevant to gold mineralization based on the information given in Chapter 2.3 (regional structure) and Chapter 3 (local structures in the mining districts). We then attempt to interpret these features in relation to regional tectonic movements in northeastern China, especially those of the Yanshanian Orogeny.

4.5.1 Regional Structures

On a regional scale, the distribution of gold mining districts in eastern Hebei province and surrounding areas is closely bound to uplifts of Early Precambrian basement rocks. Within these, the mining districts are associated with major fault zones. The structural fabric of the metamorphic basement rocks (i.e., folds and foliation) has little direct influence on the distribution of gold deposits, although it may locally exert an indirect influence inasmuch as the locus of faulting and igneous intrusion in some districts (e.g., Niuxinshan) coincides with the hinge lines of major folds.

The regional-scale fault zones in eastern Hebei province and surrounding areas form two main groups, striking roughly E–W and NE–SW respectively, and a third, less well-developed group with NW–SE strike direction (Fig. 2.6). Most of the faults formed in a compressive tectonic regime and show reverse or oblique-slip senses of offset. In general, the E–W-trending faults are earlier than, and are offset by, the NE–SW faults. The NW–SE-trending faults cross-cut both of the other fault groups and are therefore later. Both the E–W and NE–SW groups of faults show evidence of movement beginning in the Early Proterozoic, with episodes of later reactivation. However, the most active period of faulting in northeastern China was during the Mesozoic Yanshanian Orogeny (Ren et al. 1987). Much of the Yanshanian faulting involved a reactivation of earlier structures, especially those oriented NE–SW. In addition, faults with NE–SW and NW–SE trends were newly formed.

The gold districts in eastern Hebei province and surroundings are located within a few kilometers of the major fault zones, and they are especially common near the intersections of E–W- and NE–SW-trending fault zones. Individual ore deposits occur along subsidiary faults, and the major faults themselves are barren. In this sense, the deposits in eastern Hebei province are similar to many Archean mesothermal gold deposits in Western Australia (Eisenlohr et al. 1989) and Canada (Colvine 1989). A general discussion of possible factors relating gold mineralization to deformation processes in shear zones is given by Eisenlohr et al. (1989).

4.5.2 Local Structures

The gold mineralization on the scale of mining districts or single deposits is strictly controlled by faults and fracture zones. Most of the ore-controlling faults form brittle or brittle-ductile shear zones a few decimeters to meters wide which show reverse or oblique-slip sense of offset. The ore veins have a pinch-and-swell structure and the vein-filling took place partly during shear, as is shown by schlieren of phyllosilicates and strained, recrystallized quartz subgrains oriented parallel to the vein borders. Local dilation of the veins is evidenced by laminar structure produced by multiple episodes of opening and quartz filling (crack-seal mechanism).

The dilation responsible for vein-filling can be explained by a number of possible factors (Harris 1987): (1) secondary dilational structures within major shear zones, (2) irregularities along faults due to different rock competency (pull-apart zones), (3) intersections with zones of preexisting weakness. Factors which could cause district-wide dilation of pre-existing faults include: (1) changes in the regional stress orientation, and (2) uplift caused by granite intrusion.

Structural studies of ore-bearing veins in the Niuxinshan and Sanjia districts by the Ministry of Metallurgical Industry suggest that rotation of the regional stress field and local uplift due to granite intrusion were the main causes of vein-filling. No detailed studies of ore field structures have been made in the other districts. Zhai (1984) emphasized the importance of changes in the regional stress orientation with time as a metallogenetic factor in many vein-type ore deposits in northeastern China.

4.5.3 Regional Tectonic Interpretation

It is well known from regional studies that the main orogenic compressional direction in northeastern China has changed with time (Ren et al. 1987), and this rotation of the regional stress field with time forms the basis of a tectonic interpretation linking local structures in the mining districts with regional orogenic events.

From the Early Proterozoic until the Mesozoic, the main direction of orogenic compression in northeastern China was N–S, related to convergence along the northern and southern margins of the Sino-Korea platform. This compression produced E–W-trending fold axes which refolded Early Archean structures and gave rise to the present NE- and SE-trending structural grain of the basement. Related Proterozoic strike-slip or reverse faults trend E–W or ENE–WSW.

At the end of the Triassic period, convergence of the Izanagi plate with the Sino-Korean Platform began on the Pacific margin and caused a rotation of compression to ESE–WNW. However, the N–S direction of compressional stress still dominated. In the course of the first and second stages of the Yanshanian Orogeny (late Jurassic and Early Cretaceous) the main compression direction rotated from N–S to ESE–WNW. NNE-striking faults resulted, and open folds formed in Jurassic strata with NNE-striking axial planes. During the Cretaceous and Early Tertiary (third Yanshanian stage) the direction of main compression shifted to NNE–SSW (Wan and Zhu 1989).

A comparison of the time-dependent regional stress orientation summarized above and the orientation of local principal stress directions inferred from structural analysis in the mining districts is shown in Fig. 4.11. For each mining district in which structural studies were done, the figure indicates the orientation of maximum bulk compressive stress (σ_1) for the periods of time before, during, and after mineralization. The orientations of the principle stress axes are based on field measurements of inferred conjugate shear planes showing the sense of movement and a clear age relationship to ore veins. Note that all measured structures, including those predating the mineralization, are post metamorphic, brittle structures. There are slight differences in the plunge of the maximum principle stress direction from one mining district to another but all show a very similar SE–NW orientation. This orientation fits with the regional stress field at the time of the first stage of the Yanshanian Orogeny. It is inconsistent with the tectonic regimes of

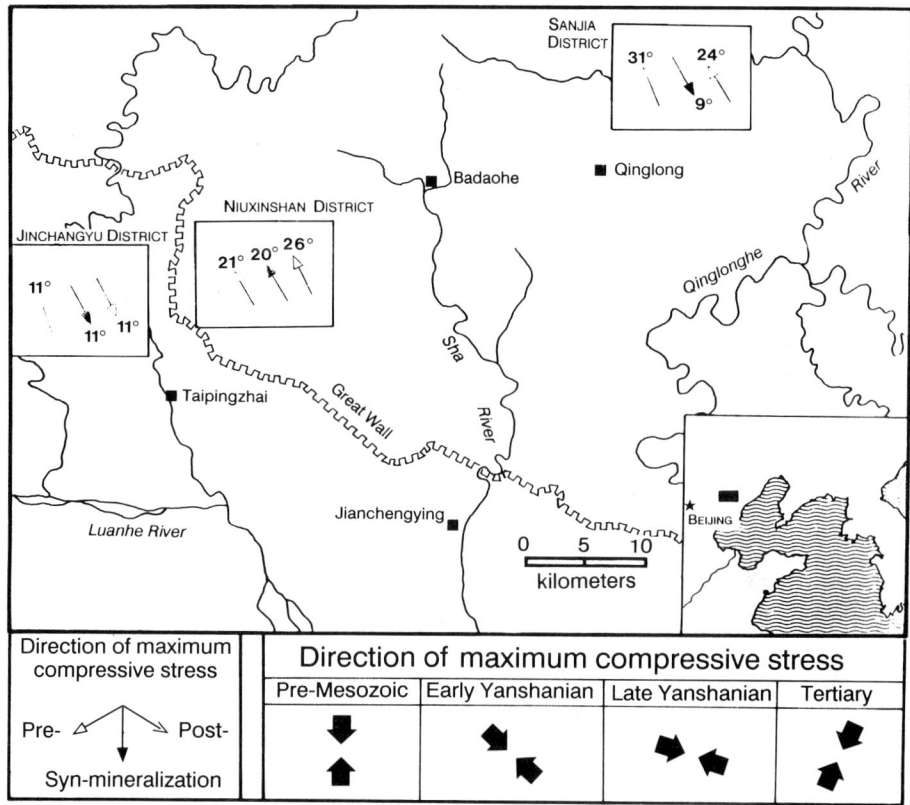

Fig. 4.11. Inferred directions of maximum compressional stress derived from pre-, syn-, and postmineralization structures in selected gold mining districts in eastern Hebei province. See text for explanation. The *inset* shows the directions of maximum compression during the main orogenies affecting northeastern China

both the pre-Mesozoic orogenies and the Cretaceous/Early Tertiary third stage of the Yanshanian Orogeny. In fact, even the post-mineralization structures show no evidence of the NNE–SSW Cretaceous compressional direction.

In summary, the orientation and sense of movement of the ore-controlling structures in the gold districts of eastern Hebei province suggest that the main period of mineralization was during the first stage of the Yanshanian Orogeny. This age constraint agrees with the radiometric dates obtained from the vein minerals and with the relations of mineralization with granites and dike intrusions of Early Yanshanian age.

4.6 Fluid Composition and P-T Conditions of Mineralization

4.6.1 Evidence from Fluid Inclusions

Table 4.6 gives a summary of the fluid inclusion characteristics from gold deposits in eastern Hebei province for which data is available. The data from the Jinchangyu and Yuerya deposits were taken from Yu and Jia (1989) and Yu et al. (1989); the data on the other deposits are from investigations carried out in the course of this project. More detailed descriptions of the inclusions are given for each deposit separately in the respective sections of Chapter 3. The microthermometric data in Table 4.6 refer to the primary inclusions only. The compositional data are based on chemical analyses of bulk inclusion contents which unavoidably represent mixtures of primary and secondary inclusions. The contribution of the latter was minimized by analyzing only the fluid released after most secondary inclusions had decrepitated. Nevertheless, the compositional data should be interpreted with caution.

Table 4.6. Summary of fluid inclusion characteristics and composition from selected gold deposits of eastern Hebei Province

Deposit name	Inclusion characteristics
Niuxinshan	*Microthermometric data* H_2O-CO_2, 3-phase inclusions at room temperature Salinity: 6–9 wt% NaCl equivalent, 9–12 mol% CO_2 Final homogenization T: 270–315 °C Bulk fluid density: 0.9–0.96 *Fluid composition from bulk analysis, average mole fraction* X_{Na}: 0.72 X_K: 0.10 X_{Ca}: 0.12 X_{Mg}: 0.05 X_{CO_2}: 0.051
Wangtoushan	*Microthermometric data* H_2O-CO_2, 3-phase inclusions at room temperature Salinity: 6–8 wt% NaCl equivalent, 10–14 mol% CO_2 Final homogenization T: 190–340 °C Bulk fluid density: 0.91–1.01 *Fluid composition from bulk analysis, average mole fraction* X_{Na}: 0.72 X_K: 0.15 X_{Ca}: 0.10 X_{Mg}: 0.03 X_{CO_2}: 0.046
Yuerya	*Microthermometric data* H_2O-CO_2, 2- and 3-phase inclusions at room temperature Final homogenization T: 260–390 °C *Fluid composition from bulk analysis, average mole fraction* X_{Na}: 0.66 X_K: 0.33 X_{Ca}: 0.01 X_{Mg}: 0.01 X_{CO_2}: 0.260
Jinchangyu	*Microthermometric data* H_2O-CO_2, 2- and 3-phase inclusions at room temperature Final homogenization T: 256–370 °C *Fluid composition from bulk analysis, average mole fraction* X_{Na}: 0.58 X_K: 0.16 X_{Ca}: 0.21 X_{Mg}: 0.06 X_{CO_2}: 0.030

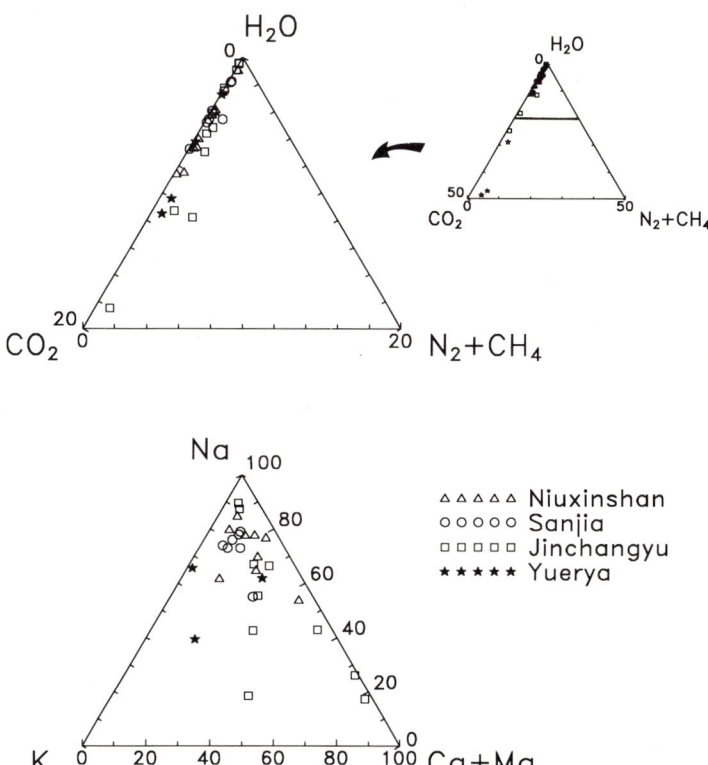

Fig. 4.12. Summary of bulk fluid composition from selected gold deposits in eastern Hebei province

Figure 4.12 summarizes the compositional data from the inclusion studies. Subject to the caveat given above, the similarity of fluid characteristics in these deposits is remarkable. In all of the investigated deposits, the inclusion fluids are dominated by H_2O with typically about 10 mol% of CO_2 (based on microthermometry and visual volume estimates), and they contain minor but detectable quantities of CH_4 and N_2 (based on chemical analysis of inclusion contents). Microthermometric data indicate low salinities, from 6 to 8 wt% NaCl equivalent, and bulk densities of 0.9 to 0.95 g/cm^3. Chemical analyses of bulk inclusion contents indicate that the dissolved cations are dominated by Na, but K, Ca, and Mg are also important constituents.

It may be significant that the fluid inclusion compositions from amphibolite-hosted deposits closest to Yanshanian granites, in which the alteration zones contain K-feldspar and fluorite (Niuxinshan and Wangtoushan), are no different from those where the nearest granite is a few kilometers distant (Jinchangyu and Sanjia), suggesting that a granitic fluid input in these deposits was minimal. The inclusions from the Yuerya deposit are rich in

CO_2 and K compared with those from the other deposits. This difference may be due to the host rocks. The Yuerya deposit is hosted in a potassic granite near the contacts with carbonate rocks, whereas all of the other deposits are hosted in amphibolites, which have much higher whole-rock Na/K and Na/Ca + Mg ratios than the host rocks at Yuerya.

The final homogenization temperatures of the primary inclusions measured range from 190–390 °C, but the inclusions in most deposits show a clustering of homogenization temperatures in the narrow range of 250–350 °C (Table 4.6). These temperatures are not pressure-corrected and therefore represent the minimum estimates of mineralization temperature. The minimum pressure, based on the CO_2-H_2O solvus with 6 wt% NaCl according to Brown and Lamb (1989), is about 2–4 kbar for the range 250–350 °C. There is no evidence of heterogeneous trapping in the inclusions studied, and it is therefore likely that the trapping temperatures were higher than the homogenization temperatures recorded. An independent estimate of the mineralization temperature is given by oxygen isotope thermometry of hydrothermal quartz and K-feldspar pairs. The temperatures from the Niuxinshan deposit are 430–490 °C (see Chap. 3.1.7), and the intersection of this temperature range with the fluid inclusion isochores indicates model pressures for mineralization of 3.5 to 5 kbar. These estimates seem high considering the brittle nature of the mineralized veins. Furthermore, one of the four samples analyzed for oxygen isotope thermometry from the Niuxinshan deposit gave an impossibly high temperature of cover 1000 °C, and the oxygen isotopic data from the Wangtoushan deposit showed isotopic disequilibrium. Therefore the results of isotopic thermometry are of questionable validity, and the microthermometric data are considered to provide the most reliable estimates for the P–T conditions of mineralization. The type of fluid inclusions found in these deposits and the range of homogenization temperatures recorded are similar to those reported for mesothermal gold deposits from Archean terranes elsewhere (Ho et al. 1990; Groves and Foster 1991), but also for metamorphic-hosted lode gold deposits of Phanerozoic age (Nesbitt 1991). As discussed by these authors, such low-salinity, CO_2-rich fluids are not diagnostic of any one fluid regime. Possibilities include metamorphic devolatilization, but in the case of eastern Hebei province, this hypothesis (metamorphic fluids) can be disregarded since the gold mineralization took place long after the last phase of regional metamorphism. Fluid inclusions typical for granitic-related deposits such as tin, porphyry, copper, or molybdenum deposits tend to have high salinities, common daughter minerals, and low CO_2 contents (Roedder 1984). This would seem to disfavor a magmatic origin for the fluid in the gold deposits reported here.

4.6.2 Stable Isotopic Data

This section summarizes the available carbon, oxygen, and hydrogen isotopic data from the deposits in eastern Hebei province and discusses their implications for the nature and source of the ore-forming fluids. The sulfur isotopic data from these deposits were discussed in Chapter 4.2.3, and will not be repeated here. The use of stable isotopes for mineral-pair geothermometry was attempted only for the Niuxinshan deposit and the Wangtoushan deposit (Sanjia district), and the results are discussed in Chapters 3.1.7 and 3.2.7.

Carbon Isotopes

A number of studies have attempted to use the carbon isotopic composition of carbonates from mesothermal gold deposits in order to constrain the source of ore-bearing fluids (Kerrich 1987, 1989; Golding et al. 1989; Peters and Golding 1989). Analyses of the carbon and oxygen isotopic composition of vein carbonates from the Niuxinshan and Sanjia districts are shown in Fig. 4.13 together with the fields of possible carbon reservoirs (mantle, metamorphic rocks, and marine limestones) taken from the literature. Also shown for comparison are carbonate compositions from the Archean gold deposits of Canada (Kerrich 1989) and Australia (Golding et al. 1989).

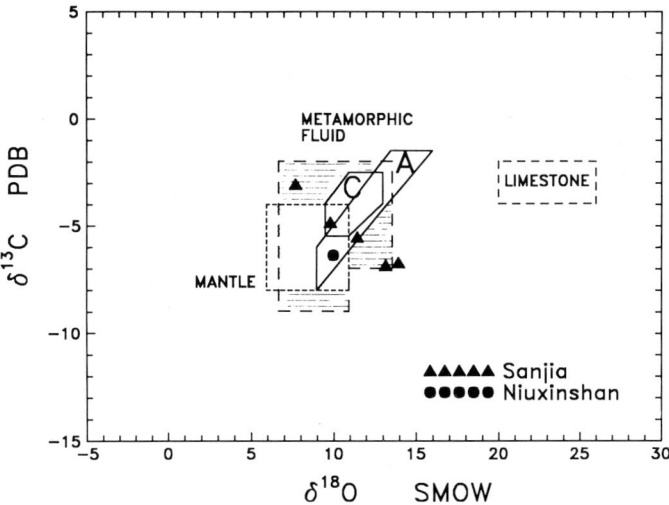

Fig. 4.13. Carbon and oxygen isotopic composition of vein carbonates from the Niuxinshan and Sanjia gold deposits. Also shown for comparison are fields of carbonate composition from Archean gold deposits in Australia (*A*) and Canada (*C*). (Kerrich 1989). Isotopic composition of possible C-O reservoirs are taken from Faure (1986), Valley (1986), and Kerrich (1989)

The number of samples analysed from the Chinese deposits is small (data are given in Tables 3.4 and 3.8), yet all show a restricted range of $\delta^{13}C$ values between -3 and $-6.8‰$, and a wider range of $\delta^{18}O$ values of $+7.7$ to $+13.9‰$. These isotopic compositions of carbonate from the Chinese gold deposits are in the same range as those reported from gold deposits of the Canadian shield and Western Australia. There are two problems with interpreting these data to constrain the source of the ore-bearing fluids. The first is that carbonate minerals in the Chinese gold deposits formed later than the sulfide ore minerals (and gold), and therefore it is not certain that the carbon isotopic data are pertinent to the ore-forming stage of hydrothermal activity. Secondly, as discussed in some detail by Kerrich (1989), values of around $-5‰$ for $\delta^{13}C$ in carbonates are not diagnostic of any single carbon reservoir. The data are consistent with derivation from mantle CO_2 (Golding et al. 1989), magmatic CO_2 from a granitic magma (Burrows and Spooner 1987), or from thoroughly mixed average "crustal carbon" (Ohmoto and Rye 1979). Moreover, the carbon isotopic composition of carbonates is a function of the pH and oxygen fugacity of the fluid from which they formed, because of the strong isotopic fractionation between reduced and oxidized carbon compounds (Ohmoto and Rye 1979). Therefore, it must be concluded that the carbon isotopic data are of little use to constrain the source of ore-bearing fluids.

Oxygen and Hydrogen Isotopes

A compilation of all available oxygen and hydrogen isotopic data from vein minerals in the gold deposits of eastern Hebei province is given in Table 4.7. The hydrogen data represent analyses of fluid released from fluid inclusions in quartz. The table also shows the calculated oxygen isotopic composition of the hydrothermal fluid from each deposit based on a model temperature for mineralization (from fluid inclusion data) and quartz-water fractionation factors of Matsuhisa et al. (1979).

The isotopic composition of quartz is similar for all the deposits, ranging between $+10$ and $+14‰$ relative to SMOW. These values, and the estimated $\delta^{18}O$ values of about $+4$ to $+8‰$ for the hydrothermal fluids, are typical for Archean gold deposits worldwide, as summarized by Groves and Foster (1991), and they are somewhat lower and less variable than those of vein quartz from Phanerozoic mesothermal lode gold deposits as reviewed by Nesbitt (1991). The oxygen isotopic composition of vein quartz in the Chinese deposits overlaps with the reported isotopic composition of quartz from the Archean metamorphic country rocks (i.e., $+13$ to $+15‰$ for quartz from metamorphic iron formations of the Qianxi Group, Qian et al. 1985; and $+11.6‰$ for amphibolite from the Jinchangyu district, Sun et al. 1989). This suggests that the hydrothermal fluids were in isotopic equilibrium with the metamorphic country rocks. It is important in this light to note that there is no difference in the oxygen isotopic composition

Table 4.7. Oxygen and hydrogen isotopic data from quartz veins in gold deposits of eastern Hebei province

Deposit	Sample	Mineral	$\delta^{18}O$ (SMOW) Quartz	δD (SMOW) Fluid inclusion	$\delta^{18}O$ (SMOW) Fluid	Reference[a]
Niuxinshan	6111	Quartz	10.6		3.7	1 TUM
	6020	Quartz	10.9		4.0	1 TUM
	6555	Quartz	11.7		4.8	1 TUM
	6181	Quartz	11.6		4.7	1 TUM
	6111	K-feldspar	8.7			1 TUM
	6020	K-feldspar	9.2			1 TUM
	6555	K-feldspar	11.2			1 TUM
	6181	K-feldspar	10.0			1 TUM
	21	Quartz	13.0	−85.5	6.1	1 MMI
	50	Quartz	12.1	−133.4	5.2	1 MMI
Huajian	CE89059	Quartz	13.3	−64	6.4	1 MMI
Sanjia	64	Quartz	14.4	−85.5	7.5	1 MMI
	CE89020	Quartz	12.5	−81	5.6	1 MMI
	91-1	Quartz	12.8	−48.9	5.9	1 MMI
Wangtoushan	6309	Quartz	10.6		3.7	1 TUM
	6271	Quartz	11.4		4.5	1 TUM
	6273	Quartz	10.2		3.3	1 TUM
	6309	K-feldspar	11.3			1 TUM
	6271	K-feldspar	9.9			1 TUM
	6273	K-feldspar	11.2			1 TUM
Jinchangyu	54-2	Quartz	11.4	−50	4.5	2
	65-3	Quartz	11.2	−73.9	4.3	2
	69-1	Quartz	13.5	−67.7	6.6	2
	70-5	Quartz	11.3	−86.5	4.4	2
	CE89150	Quartz	10.9	−75	4.0	1 MMI
	–	Quartz	10.9			3
	–	Quartz	10.8			3
Yuerya	74-1	Quartz	10.3	−69.4	3.4	2
	Q3	Quartz	13.7	−88.6	6.8	1 MMI
	Q4	Quartz	12.6	−88.6	5.7	1 MMI

[a] References: 1 TUM, this study, analyses by Technical University of Munich; 1 MMI, this study, analyses by Ministry of Metallurgical Industry; 2, Yu and Jia (1989); 3, Yu et al. (1989).

of quartz from the amphibolite-hosted deposits (Niuxinshan, Sanjia, Jinchangyu) and of quartz from the Yuerya deposit, which is hosted by Proterozoic carbonate rocks and granite. This suggests a uniformity of fluid composition which disregards local lithology, i.e., a deep and extensive circulation of fluids on a subregional scale.

The genetic interpretation of this range of $\delta^{18}O$ values is difficult because fluids of both a magmatic and metamorphic source would be consistent with these isotopic values (Taylor 1979). Meteoric water is generally much

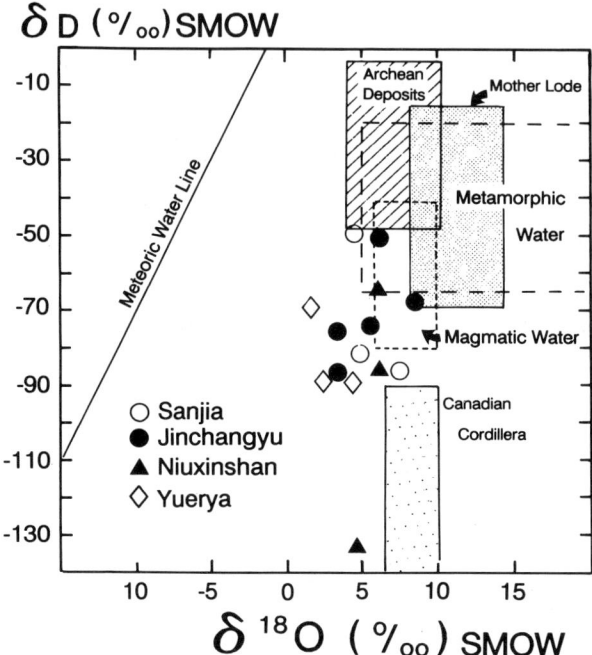

Fig. 4.14. Hydrogen and oxygen isotopic composition of ore fluid from selected gold deposits of eastern Hebei province. Data sources are given in Table 4.7. Also shown for comparison are fields of ore fluid composition from other mesothermal gold deposits (Archean, Mother Lode, Canadian Cordillera) after Nesbitt and Muehlenbachs (1989). Isotopic composition of magmatic and metamorphic fluids are taken from Taylor (1979)

lower in ^{18}O, unless it had thoroughly exchanged oxygen with crustal rocks. Further constraints on fluid source can be made by combined oxygen and hydrogen isotopic analyses. Figure 4.14 shows the limited data available relating to ore fluid from the Chinese gold deposits. The hydrogen values represent measured δD of fluid released from inclusions in vein quartz, and oxygen isotopic compositions of ore fluid were calculated from the $\delta^{18}O$ values of quartz as given in Table 4.7. The position of the meteoric water line and fields of magmatic and metamorphic fluids are from Taylor (1979). Also shown for comparison with the Chinese deposits are the inferred compositions of ore fluids reported from other mesothermal gold deposits by Nesbitt and Muehlenbachs (1989).

The hydrogen and oxygen isotopic compositions of ore fluids from all of the Chinese deposits are quite similar, and they plot far to the right of the meteoric water line near the fields of magmatic and metamorphic fluids. A metamorphic fluid can be ruled out because the quartz veins postdate any known regional metamorphism in the area by more than one billion years, and furthermore, the petrographic evidence in the rocks indicates that the youngest metamorphic event was retrograde, which would consume and not release fluid. Yu and Jia (1989) interpreted their oxygen and hydrogen isotopic data from the Jinchangyu deposit as indicating a mixed magmatic-meteoric fluid. The hypothesis of magmatic water may be questioned because the ore veins clearly postdate the emplacement of granites in the mining districts, and because there is no granite in the immediate vicinity of some deposits (notably Jinchangyu). On the other hand, late magmatic dikes are coeval with quartz veins in most districts, and therefore a magmatic origin for the fluids cannot be dismissed. The hypothesis of thoroughly equilibrated "crustal water" of meteoric origin is consistent with the uniformity of fluid inclusion and stable isotopic compositions (S, C, H, O) from vein minerals among several districts, and it would also fit the lead isotopic evidence that the ore lead was leached from a high-grade metamorphic basement. The oxygen isotopic evidence given above for equilibration of the ore-fluids with the metamorphic country rocks also supports the possibility that the fluids were "disguised" meteoric waters.

We conclude that the stable isotopic evidence is permissive of more than one explanation for the source of ore fluids. We consider that the best explanation of the isotopic, fluid inclusion, and geologic evidence is given by the hypothesis that the ore fluids were meteoric waters whose isotopic composition was thoroughly equilibrated with the metamorphic basement rocks.

4.6.3 Gold Transport and Precipitation

The evidence discussed above suggests that the ore-bearing fluids in the gold deposits of eastern Hebei province were at a temperature of at least 300 °C (fluid inclusion homogenisation), and consisted of water with about 10 mol% CO_2 and a total salinity of about 1 M NaCl equivalent (4–8 wt%). The coexistence of K-feldspar and sericite in the wall-rock selvages of most veins suggests near-neutral pH. The sulfur isotopic evidence, lack of sulfate minerals, and the detection of coexisting CH_4 and CO_2 in inclusion fluids suggest that the fluids were reduced. With these fluid characteristics as constraints, the possible mechanisms of gold transport and deposition can be discussed.

Seward (1984, 1989, 1991) has summarized the hydrothermal geochemistry of gold, and an important conclusion is that there is still much uncertainty about the speciation of gold in solution, thermodynamic data being absent for many potential gold complexes, particularly at high temperature. It is commonly assumed that the solubility of gold in natural hydrothermal fluids depends on the stability of one or both of the two gold complexes shown by the following equations:

$$Au^\circ + H_2S + HS^- = Au(HS)_2^- + 0.5H_2, \qquad (1)$$

$$Au^\circ + H^+ + 2Cl^- = AuCl_2^- + 0.5H_2. \qquad (2)$$

The bisulfide complex (1) is dominant under reducing conditions at near-neutral pH, and at relatively low temperature; and there is little doubt that this species is important for gold transport and deposition in epithermal deposits and active geothermal systems (Berger and Henley 1989; Seward 1989). At the higher temperatures of ore formation in mesothermal gold deposits, however, both the bisulfide and the dichloride complexes may be important. Many studies of Archean greenstone-belt gold deposits have emphasized the role of the bisulfide complex (Groves and Foster 1991) because of the following lines of evidence:

1. the low salinity, neutral pH, and reducing conditions of the ore fluids,
2. the association of gold with sulfidization of high Fe/Fe + Mg rocks, and
3. the very low enrichments of Cu, Pb, and Zn, which are typically carried in solution as metal-chloride complexes.

The fluid composition inferred for the Chinese gold deposits is similar to the composition of ore fluids in the Archean examples cited by Groves and Foster (1991). Furthermore, as discussed in Chapter 4.3.3, a correlation of gold with sulfidization of iron-rich rocks can be locally observed in the Chinese deposits. This suggests that a significant amount of gold in the Chinese examples was also transported in the ore fluid as sulfide complexes. On the other hand, the Chinese ore fluids are slightly more saline than many of the Archean examples cited by Groves and Foster (1991), and many of the Chinese ores contain large amounts of base metal sulfides. Therefore, the role of chloride complexes for the transport of gold in these deposits may also be important. Sang and Ho (1987) stated that gold was transported as chloride complexes in the Mesozoic gold districts of northeastern China which they investigated.

We conclude that both sulfide and chloride complexes were probably important for the transport of gold in the deposits of eastern Hebei province. Possible causes of gold precipitation can be inferred from the stability of these complexes, but critical data about the ore fluids are lacking (i.e., pH, oxygen fugacity, concentration of total sulfur, etc.) to evaluate their real importance. Both complexes would be destabilized by mixing of ore fluid with cooler, more dilute fluids. Seward (1991) pointed out that boiling (or effervescence) of ore fluids would also cause the deposition of gold from both sulfide and chloride complexes. However, the limited fluid inclusion data available from the Chinese deposits suggest that the ore fluids were not boiling at the time of trapping.

The ubiquity of intense wall-rock alteration around the ore veins in the Chinese deposits suggests that fluid-rock interaction may be important in gold precipitation. Breakdown of the bisulfide complex due to pyritization of wall rocks (removal of reduced sulfur from the fluid) was discussed in Chapter 4.3.3 as one probable mechanism of gold precipitation. The sericitization of feldspars is a very common type of wallrock alteration in the Chinese deposits. This reaction consumes hydrogen ions and therefore raises the fluid pH, which would have the effect of destabilizing the gold-chloride complex (Seward 1984). Redox reactions will also affect the solubility of gold, with opposite affects on chloride complexes (stable under oxidizing conditions) and on sulfide complexes (stable under reducing conditions), but the redox state in the veins and alteration zones around the Chinese deposits has not been studied and the importance of this factor cannot be evaluated at present.

5 Towards a Metallogenetic Model

Table 5.1 summarizes the main characteristics of the gold deposits in eastern Hebei province documented in this study. The most important geologic and geochemical constraints on a successful metallogenetic model are listed here together with chapter references to where the evidence was introduced in the text:

1. There is some evidence for a relict, subeconomic, syn-metamorphic mineralization in the Jinchangyu and Banbishan deposits (Chap. 3.4.5, 3.5.5), but the main-stage ore veins in all districts studied are discordant and post-metamorphic. On a regional scale, the deposits are related to major NE–SW-striking crustal-scale faults and lineaments. The ore-bearing veins occur in subsidiary compressional (reverse and oblique-slip) faults formed or reactivated in the Early Yanshanian Orogeny (Jurassic). Dilation and vein filling may have been caused by a rotation of the regional stress field (Chap. 4.5.2).
2. The ore paragenesis in all districts studied is simple and uniform. The paragenetic sequence begins with barren vein quartz and pyrite. Most of the gold occurs later, together with galena, sphalerite and chalcopyrite in fractures of early formed pyrite. Accessory ore minerals include tetrahedrite, tetradymite, native bismuth, molybdenite, tellurides, and scheelite. The fineness of the gold is fairly uniform at 600 to 800. The bulk Au/Ag ratio in the ores is generally less than one (Chap. 3).
3. Most gold deposits and occurrences are found within exposures of high-grade metabasic rocks of the Archean Qianxi Group (Chap. 1.3). Of secondary importance are Early Proterozoic metasedimentary host rocks. Granites are rarely host to ore, with the important exception of the Yuerya deposit.
4. The gold concentrations determined in unmineralized host rocks of the Qianxi Group fall in the range of average crustal values (1–5 ppb) in most samples (Chap. 4.2.1). These values may not represent the primary gold concentrations, but the available evidence suggests that the protoliths were not enriched in gold. Nevertheless, the Qianxi Group rocks are considered to be the ultimate source of gold in the deposits (Chap. 4.2.5).
5. The gold deposits and occurrences are closely related both spatially and temporally to Late Mesozoic Yanshanian granites and associated igneous dikes. The gold-bearing quartz veins generally cut the Yanshanian

Table 5.1. Summary of the main characteristics of the investigated gold deposits in eastern Hebei province

Deposit	Type of ore body	Ore minerals	Alteration minerals	Host rocks	Age of mineralization	Stable isotopes (vein minerals)	P-T and fluid conditions
Niuxinshan	Quartz veins in amphibolite, Disseminations in granites	Pyrite, chalcopyrite, sphalerite, galena, gold, covellite tetradymite, bismuth scheelite	Sericite, quartz, carbonate, pyrite, chlorite, minor K-feldspar, fluorite	Archean amphibolites, migmatite gneisses, magnetite amphibolites; Yanshan granites and dikes	190 ± 2 Ma (Rb-Sr, sericite) 174 ± 25 Ma (Rb-Sr, K-feldspar) 176 ± 3 Ma (Ar-Ar, quartz) 188 Ma (K-Ar, sericite)	Carbonate: $\delta^{13}C = -6.3$, $\delta^{18}O = +9.7$ Pyrite: $\delta^{34}S = +4.9$ to $+6.0$ Quartz: $\delta^{18}O = +10.6$ to $+11.7$ Fluid inclusions: $\delta D = -85.5$	CO_2-H_2O fluid, 10 mol% CO_2, 6-9 wt.% NaCl equiv. Minimum temperature = 270–315 °C Minimum pressure = 1.5–2 kbar
Sanjia	Quartz veins in amphibolite	Pyrite, chalcopyrite, galena, sphalerite, gold, tetrahedrite, bismuth, pyrrhotite	Sericite, quartz, carbonate, pyrite, chlorite	Archean amphibolites, magnetite amphibolites; Yanshan dikes	168 ± 3 Ma (Ar-Ar, quartz)	Carbonate: $\delta^{13}C = -5.5$, $\delta^{18}O = +11.4$ Pyrite: $\delta^{34}S = -1.0$ to $+3.6$ Quartz: $\delta^{18}O = +12.5$ to $+14.4$ Fluid inclusions: $\delta D = -81$ to -85	CO_2-H_2O fluid, No microthermometric data available
Xinlonggou	Quartz veins in amphibolite	Pyrite, chalcopyrite, galena, sphalerite, gold, covellite, tetrahedrite	Sericite, quartz, carbonate, pyrite, chlorite	Archean amphibolites, magnetite amphibolites; Yanshan dikes	No data available	Carbonate: $\delta^{13}C = -6.8$ Carbonate: $\delta^{18}O = 13.2$	CO_2-H_2O fluid, No microthermometric data available

Deposit	Style	Ore minerals	Alteration	Host rocks	Age	Isotopes	Fluid
Wangtoushan	Quartz veins in amphibolite, Disseminations in granite	Pyrite, chalcopyrite, galena, sphalerite, gold, tetrahedrite, molybdenite, scheelite	Sericite, quartz, carbonate, pyrite, chlorite, minor fluorite, K-feldspar	Archean amphibolites, migmatite gneisses, magnetite amphibolites; Yanshan granites and dikes	184 ± 2 Ma (Rb-Sr, sericite) 179 ± 25 Ma (Rb-Sr, K-feldspar)	Carbonate: $\delta^{13}C = -5.8$ Carbonate: $\delta^{18}O = +11.9$ Quartz: $\delta^{18}O = +10.2$ to $+11.4$	CO_2-H_2O fluid, 10 mol% CO_2 6–8 wt.% NaCl equiv. Minimum temperature = 190–340 °C Minimum pressure = 2.5 kbar
Yuerya	Quartz veins, disseminations in granite	Pyrite, chalcopyrite, galena, sphalerite, gold, pyrrhotite, molybdenite, tetrahedrite, chalcocite, calaverite	Albite, sericite, chlorite, quartz, pyrite	Yanshan granite and dikes; Proterozoic limestone	<165 ± 5 Ma (K-Ar, granite) 200 Ma (K-Ar, sericite)	Pyrite: $\delta^{34}S = +1.5$ to $+4.5$ Quartz: $\delta^{18}O = +10.3$ to $+13.7$ Fluid inclusions: $\delta D = -69$ to -88	CO_2-H_2O fluid, no salinity data Minimum temperature = 260–390 °C No pressure estimate
Jinchangyu	Quartz veins in amphibolite	Pyrite, chalcopyrite, galena, sphalerite, gold, calaverite, argentite, molybdenite, pyrrhotite, chalcocite, hessite	Sericite, carbonate, quartz, pyrite, chlorite	Archean amphibolites, migmatic gneisses, magnetite amphibolites; Yanshan dikes	192 Ma (K-Ar, sericite) 169 Ma (K-Ar, sericite) 155 Ma (K-Ar, sericite) 133 Ma (Pb-Pb, galena)	Pyrite: $\delta^{34}S = -6$ to $+2.5$ Quartz: $\delta^{18}O = +10.8$ to $+13.5$ Fluid inclusions: $\delta D = -68$ to -85	CO_2-H_2O fluid, no salinity data Minimum temperature = 256–370 °C No pressure estimate

Table 5.1 (*continued*)

Deposit	Type of ore body	Ore minerals	Alteration minerals	Host rocks	Age of mineralization	Stable isotopes (vein minerals)	P-T and fluid conditions
Banbishan	Quartz veins in leptite, Disseminations in shear zones	Pyrite, chalcopyrite, galena, sphalerite, gold, arsenopyrite, pyrrhotite, wolframite, scheelite, antimonite	Sericite, K-feldspar, quartz, carbonate, chlorite, pyrite	Proterozoic leptite, metadiorite; Yanshan dikes	No data available	No data available	No data available

intrusions and are coeval with some of the dikes. This suggests that mineralization took place at a late stage of the Yanshanian magmatism (Chap. 3).
6. The radiometric dating of mineralization confirms the Late Mesozoic age inferred from field relations. In the gold deposits of eastern Hebei province for which data are available (Niuxinshan, Huajian, Wangtoushan, Jinchangyu, Yuerya) the ages of hydrothermal minerals range from 150 to 190 Ma (Chap. 4.1.2).
7. The role of the Yanshanian granites in mineralization is not entirely clear. Gold is associated with both magnetite-series hornblende-biotite granodiorites and with ilmenite-series leucocratic biotite granites. The granites apparently did not constitute the source of gold or other ore-forming elements in the deposits studied (Chap. 4.4).
8. The physical conditions of mineralization were similar in all districts studied. Fluid inclusion studies suggest that the mineralization occurred at a minimum of about 300–350 °C and 2–4 kbar pressure. The ore fluid had low to moderate salinity and about 10 mol% CO_2 (Chap. 4.6.1).
9. Wall rock alteration is strongly developed to a distance of a few centimeters to some meters from the veins. The alteration involved the breakdown of feldspars, amphiboles, pyroxene, and biotite, and the formation of chlorite, pyrite, sericite, and hydrothermal quartz. Carbonate is also common in the alteration zones, but was generally later than the main phase of alteration and mineralization (Chap. 3).
10. The sulfidization of magnetite to pyrite in magnetite-rich host rocks is an important type of wall rock alteration which locally caused gold precipitation. However, magnetite-rich lenses are thin and discontinuous in the gold districts of Niuxinshan, Sanjia, and Jinchangyu, and do not constitute a major host to ore (Chap. 4.3).
11. The common lead isotopic composition of galena from ore veins suggests that the lead was derived from Early Precambrian U-depleted rocks (Chap. 4.2.3). Carbon and sulfur isotopic data permit the interpretation that the the Precambrian basement rocks were also the source of sulfur and carbon in the fluids; however, the data do not rule out a magmatic origin for these elements (Chap. 4.2.3, 4.6.2).
12. The oxygen and hydrogen isotopic compositions of ore fluid, calculated from analyses of vein quartz and of water from fluid inclusions, are similar in all deposits studied despite local differences in wallrock composition (Chap. 4.6.2). The isotopic data suggest that the hydrothermal fluid was either of magmatic origin, or was meteoric water thoroughly equilibrated with the Precambrian metamorphic rocks. The latter interpretation better fits the geologic evidence (Chap. 4.6.2).

5.1 Previous Models

The gold deposits of eastern Hebei province have been studied by Chinese geologists for many years and several hypotheses of their origin have been proposed. Following Zhu (1989), the models can be divided essentially into two rival types as follows:

1. Metamorphic-Hydrothermal Models
The metamorphic hydrothermal models consider that the ultimate source of gold is in the mafic and ultramafic Archean rocks of the lower crust. The agent for leaching and transporting the gold and other ore-forming elements is considered to be low salinity CO_2-H_2O fluid developed by devolatilization reactions during prograde metamorphism of the lower crust. The fluids are channeled by crustal-scale fault zones, along which the gold deposits eventually form. Recent proponents of the metamorphic model include Metamorphic models are also favored by some authors for the Archean greenstone-belt gold deposits in Australia (Groves et al. 1987, 1988) and Canada (Card et al. 1989; Colvine 1989). In these cases, there is a general concordancy of the age of mineralization and the age of regional metamorphism. However, the main problem with a metamorphic model for the eastern Hebei deposits is that the age of mineralization is Mesozoic, whereas the last regional metamorphic event in the area is Late Proterozoic. There is, in fact, some evidence for a minor syn-metamorphic gold mineralization in the Jinchangyu and Banbishan deposits (Chap. 3.4.5, 3.5.5) but this early mineralization is of no economic significance.
A second problem with the metamorphic model is that it fails to explain the strong spatial association of gold deposits and Mesozoic granites. Some proponents of the metamorphic-hydrothermal model recognize this problem and suggest that the granites remobilized an earlier, synmetamorphic mineralization (Zhu 1989; Wang and Sun 1989).

2. Magmatic Hydrothermal Models
The magmatic hydrothermal models are presently most favored for the gold deposits in northeastern China (Sang and Ho 1987; Wang and Cheng 1988; M.Z. Yang 1988; Feng and Yang 1989; Liu 1989; Zhou 1989). These models propose that the Yanshanian granites were the agent of gold transport and concentration from the source area to the site of intrusion. The primary source of gold and other ore-forming elements is not tightly constrained by the models. Many authors consider that the granites are derived by anatexis of lower crustal rocks, and that the gold originates in that source (Sang and Ho 1987; M.Z. Yang 1988; Zhu 1989). The source of hydrothermal fluids in the various models may be either magmatic volatiles or meteoric water which is brought into circulation by the heat of the intrusions.

The magmatic models have the important advantage that they are consistent with the mineralization ages in the gold deposits of eastern Hebei province, and they explain the spatial relationships between gold deposits and Yanshanian granites. However, the models are not without problems. First, the question must be raised of why only some of the Yanshanian granites are associated with gold deposits whereas most are not. Second, the style of the supposed granite-related gold mineralization is quite different from that of unequivocal granite-related deposits of Cu, Mo, Sn, and W. In the latter cases, mineralization is clearly centered on granite intrusions or their contacts with the country rocks, and the granites themselves are important hosts of ore. In the gold deposits of eastern Hebei province, the granites are rarely mineralized and the locus of gold-bearing veins is by no means centered around the intrusions.

5.2 The Preferred Model for Eastern Hebei Province

The authors believe that the geologic and geochemical constraints listed above are best explained by a "magmatic-hydrothermal" model, to use the terminology of Zhu (1989). The deposits were directly caused by processes related to the Yanshanian Orogeny, but we also stress the role of the Archean basement rocks as a source of gold and other ore elements. The preferred model is based on three indisputable facts:

First, the mineralization is epigenetic; second, the gold deposits occur almost exclusively within Early Precambrian metamorphic terranes; and third, the main stage of mineralization in all the gold districts studied is Mesozoic in age.

The source of gold in the deposits is considered to be the Early Precambrian metamorphic basement, which consists mostly of an Archean high-grade gneiss terrane (not a greenstone belt) containing mantle-derived metabasalts, iron formations, and TTG-type orthogneisses metamorphosed to upper amphibolite and granulite facies conditions. The present gold concentration in the Archean rocks is generally in the range of 1–5 ppb. Whether this range reflects the original gold contents of the protoliths is unknown. The granulite-facies metamorphism at about 2500 Ma (Fuping Orogeny) and a subsequent medium-grade metamorphic event at about 1800 Ma (Zhongtiao Orogeny) may well have mobilized gold from the protoliths, but evidence of syn-metamorphic mineralization is very rare, the only known examples being at Jinchangyu and, possibly Banbishan (see Chap. 4.1.1). The mobilization of gold by metamorphic fluids and its concentration in higher-level shear zones, which is thought to be important for the formation of greenstone-belt gold deposits worldwide (Groves et al. 1987; Colvine 1989), was either unimportant in the Chinese examples or evidence for it has been removed by erosion. It must be kept in mind that the crustal level exposed in the Chinese Archean terrane spans the granulite-amphibolite facies transition, whereas in the Western Australian and Canadian greenstone terranes, the greenschist facies is exposed.

The most significant event for the formation of the gold deposits in northeastern China, indeed, for metallogeny in eastern Asia as a whole, was the Mesozoic Yanshanian Orogeny. In eastern Hebei province, the Yanshanian Orogeny mainly caused widespread compressional faulting, often along preexisting structures, and the intrusion of numerous relatively small granitic plutons and multifarious dikes. The ultimate cause of the Yanshanian magmatism is considered to be the subduction of oceanic lithosphere beneath the Sino-Korean Platform (Takahashi 1983; Ishihara 1984; Wu 1985). Shallow subduction of relatively hot lithosphere can be inferred from the plate reconstructions, and this explains the wide belt of Yanshanian magmatism extending far inland from the continental margin (Takahashi 1983). Kerrich and Wyman (1990) have suggested that mesothermal gold deposits of Archean and Phanerozoic age are preferentially located in convergent margin settings, and are ultimately caused by subduction-related crustal underplating and attendant processes. This tectonic setting is valid for the deposits in northeastern China as well.

According to the few isotopic data available (low initial $^{87}Sr/^{86}Sr$ ratios, nonradiogenic common Pb), the Yanshanian granites in eastern Hebei province apparently formed by partial melting of the lower crust in response to this broad thermal disturbance (M.Z. Yang 1988). Their intrusion was facilitated by pre-existing major fault zones, so that they now occur along regional lineaments and at their mutual intersections. The intrusion of many individual granites in a narrow time interval represents a very significant convective transfer of heat into the upper crust. This heat is considered to be far more important for the formation of the gold deposits than the magmas themselves, since the gold deposits are associated with granites of quite different bulk compositions, and there is no compelling evidence that any of the ore constituents were derived from the granites.

Equally important for the metallogenetic model as the granitic magmatism was the creation and/or reactivation of major compressional fault zones during the Yanshanian Orogeny. These brittle and brittle-ductile faults and fracture zones acted as zones of weakness which facilitated granite intrusion and subsequent dike formation. Additionally, the fault zones provided a focus for fluid circulation which was driven by temperature gradients around the cooling plutons, perhaps aided in the brittle regime by a seismic-pumping mechanism (Eisenlohr et al. 1989). Gold mineralization formed in secondary splays of the major faults, in dilatent zones which formed either as a result of local fault geometry (intersections, jogs, competency contrasts) or due to changing regional stress patterns. The association of ore veins with granites may be partly due to the structural effect of competency contrast.

The source of ore fluid can be only poorly constrained. Hydrogen and oxygen isotopic data from vein quartz are permissive of magmatic, metamorphic, or surface water thoroughly exchanged with crustal rocks. Metamorphic fluids can be ruled out because prograde metamorphism had long ceased before mineralization. Unadulterated meteoric water can also be ruled out, but a choice between magmatic and "equilibrated" surface water, or an admixture of the two, is difficult. The low salinity of the ore fluids argues against a magmatic fluid since fluid inclusions from magmatogenic porphyry deposits are characteristically very saline (Roedder 1984; but see Burrows and Spooner 1987). Furthermore, the mineralization postdates crystallization of the main granites, being coeval only with volumetrically minor dikes. We therefore favor the interpretation that the ore fluids were derived from surface waters whose isotopic composition was thoroughly equilibrated with the basement rocks. Extensive interaction of ore fluids with the metamorphic basement rocks on a regional scale is attested to by the following lines of evidence:

1. The uniform composition of ore fluids from widely-separated gold deposits, inferred from the similarity of wallrock alteration and fluid inclusion data, and from isotopic measurements of ore and gangue minerals (C, S, Pb, O, H), could best be achieved by large-scale equilibration of fluid with the basement rocks.
2. The isotopic composition of lead in vein sulfides from all of the deposits studied (including those hosted in granite) suggest that the lead was derived from leaching of the basement rocks. The carbon and sulfur isotopic data are not diagnostic of a single source, but the data are consistent with a derivation of these elements from the basement rocks as well.

The gold in solution was most likely transported at the conditions of mineralization (300–350 °C, 2–4 kbar) as both chloride and sulfide complexes. Sulfide complexes are suggested by the clear correlation of gold with sulfidization of wallrocks (see below), and the presence of chloride complexes is inferred from the relatively high temperatures, moderate salinities (equivalent to about 1 M NaCl) of the fluids, and the association of abundant base metals in the ores (see also Sang and Ho 1987).

Precipitation of gold from either sulfide or chloride complexes would be effected by cooling of the hydrothermal fluid or by phase separation (boiling or CO_2 effervescence) caused by local pressure release. The association of gold with other ore minerals near wallrock selvages and rarely within the vein quartz suggests that chemical effects of wallrock interaction must have played the most important role in precipitation. However, the lack of quantitative estimates of the pH, oxidation potential, activity of sulfide and chloride ligands in the fluid, etc., and the fact that some of these parameters have opposite effects on the stability of chloride and sulfide complexes of gold, preclude a complete description of how gold was precipitated in these ores. The almost exclusive occurrence of gold with sulfide minerals in the ores suggests that the precipitation of gold relates to the sulfides. The explanation for this may be that sulfide formation lowered the activity of reduced sulfur in solution and thereby caused the instability of the bisulfide gold complex. This is certainly the case for gold enrichment in pyritized lenses of magnetite quartzite, and it is a common mechanism suggested for gold precipitation in other mesothermal deposits (Neall 1987; Groves and Foster 1991). A possible precipitation mechanism involving the chloride gold complex could be the sericitization of feldspars, which is a very common type of wall rock alteration. The stability of the gold-chloride complex is highest at low pH. Sericitization would have the effect of neutralizing acidic fluids, and this could cause the breakdown of the complex.

The significance of the metallogenetic model to exploration for gold deposits in this setting is that deposits are most likely to be found in areas where the three elements: major fault zones, Archean crust, and Yanshanian granites, occur together. The country rocks around granites in zones of high fault density, especially those which occur at or near intersections of regional fault zones, are favourable targets for exploration. On a local scale, gold mineralization is most likely to be found in sulfide-rich veins in mafic host rocks with well-developed alteration zones.

5.3 Open Questions

Several questions about the genesis of gold deposits in eastern Hebei province remain only partially answered, partly due to lack of data and partly due to the geologic and geochemical complexity of the problem. Some of the more important points which need further study are suggested here.

The reader will have noticed that the amount of information presented is not uniform from all deposits. In particular, studies on fluid inclusions, age dating, and stable isotopic work are lacking or have been done only in a reconnaisance fashion in several deposits. The most severe lack of information at the time of writing concerns the deposits located in the Early Proterozoic metamorphic rocks (Banbishan and related districts), and these should perhaps be a priority for further research.

It is still uncertain to what extent pre-Yanshanian mineralization is important to the distribution or grade of the gold deposits. The evidence is overwhelming that the main stage – and in many deposits the only detectable stage – of mineralization is Mesozoic, but there is also clear evidence for pre-Mesozoic mineralization in the Jinchangyu and Banbishan deposits. It may be significant that the largest deposit in eastern Hebei province, Jinchangyu, is the one which shows the clearest evidence for an earlier stage of mineralization.

An important point which needs further work is the significance of iron-rich host rocks in localizing ore formation. Field observations indicate that lenses of metamorphosed iron formation which occur in the gold mining districts are strongly sulfidized where crossed by ore veins, and the available analyses show a significant correlation between sulfidization and gold concentration. The importance of iron-rich host rocks has been abundantly demonstrated in Western Australian gold deposits (Neall 1987; Groves and Foster 1991). On the other hand, the major iron mines operating in Archean BIF in eastern Hebei province do not encounter gold mineralization to any significant extent (Shen et al. 1989).

The true relationship between Yanshanian granites and gold metallogeny is still poorly defined. In particular, it is impossible at present to understand why certain granites are associated with gold and others are not. A major hindrance to this understanding is the lack of data on the precise age, composition, petrographic nature, and intrusive style of the dozens of Yanshanian granites in eastern Hebei province and surroundings. As a single example, the lack of U and Th data makes it impossible to discuss the importance of internal heat production as a factor in promoting hydrothermal circulation around certain granites.

The igneous dikes associated with granites have been only cursorily studied. Many districts display a common intrusive sequence beginning with granitic dikes followed by dioritic dikes and ending with lamprophyre dikes, with mineralization generally coeval with the diorite dikes. The significance of this sequence has not been explored. Note, too, that the possible role of lamprophyres in gold metallogeny of Western Australia and Canada has recently been stressed by Rock et al. (1989) and Wyman and Kerrich (1989).

More detailed mineralogical-geochemical studies aimed at determining the critical parameters of ore fluid composition are needed to constrain models of gold transport and deposition, and to better interpret the sulfur and carbon isotope data. More fluid inclusion studies, including Raman spectroscopic data instead of bulk fluid analyses, and detailed studies of alteration geochemistry would be particularly helpful.

6 Comparison with Other Archean-Hosted Gold Provinces

The amount of research and published information on mesothermal vein-type gold deposits in general, and in Archean terranes especially, has increased dramatically in recent years. The intention of this chapter is not to review the nature of mesothermal gold deposits in general, but simply to point out some important similarities and differences between the Archean-hosted gold deposits in eastern Hebei province and the well-known Archean-hosted gold deposits of the Canadian shield, Western Australia, and Southern Africa. For information on the latter areas we depend heavily on previous reviews by Hutchinson and Vokes (1987), Groves et al. (1988), Card et al. (1989), Foster (1989), Vearncombe et al. (1989), and Groves and Foster (1991). Before discussing individual features of the Chinese deposits, it is worth stating that there are far more similarities than differences between these deposits and other Archean-hosted mesothermal gold deposits. In fact, Nesbitt (1991) and Kerrich and Wyman (1990) have stressed that mesothermal gold deposits of all ages share a great many features and should perhaps be treated as a single class of ore deposit.

Host Rocks

The gold deposits in eastern Hebei province are hosted almost exclusively in Early Precambrian metamorphosed supracrustal rocks, and by far the most important examples are hosted in multiply deformed, high-grade Archean metabasic rocks (migmatitic amphibolites and mafic granulites). Orthogneisses are common in the Archean exposures but they rarely host important gold mineralization. It must be stressed that the Archean terrane in northeastern China represents a high-grade gneiss terrane in the sense of Windley (1984) and it is not just an intensely metamorphosed greenstone belt. In this sense the Chinese example is unusual, since most of the Archean-hosted gold deposits in other cratons are located in greenstone belts and the adjacent gneiss terranes are unimportant (Groves et al. 1987; Card et al. 1989). A further important point is that, although BIF horizons are common in the Archean terrane in northeastern China, they do not host gold deposits. In contrast, BIF is a very important host to ore in Western Australia and Zimbabwe (Groves et al. 1988; Foster 1989).

The close spatial association of gold deposits with granite intrusions is an important feature of eastern Hebei province. Similar associations have been noted for the Canadian shield by Card et al. (1989), and for the Norseman-

Wiluna belt in Western Australia by Groves et al. (1988). The significance of the granite association is controversial in both cases, and as noted in Chapter 5.3, the role of granites in gold metallogeny of eastern Hebei province is also not completely clear.

Structural Control

The gold deposits in eastern Hebei province are strictly confined to faults and/or fracture zones of brittle and brittle-ductile nature. On a district scale the deposits are located near major, regional faults of a compressional nature. These features are common to a great many other gold provinces in Archean terranes around the world (Vearncombe et al. 1989; Groves and Foster 1991), and point to the importance of regional-scale faults in focusing hydrothermal circulation.

Ore Fluids

Like the structural setting, the fluid inclusion characteristics form one of the unifying aspects of mesothermal gold deposits worldwide. The data from deposits in eastern Hebei province indicate that ore fluids were of low to moderate salinity (4–8 wt% NaCl equivalent), contained about 10 mol% CO_2, and were trapped in vein minerals at temperatures of at least 300–350°C. With the exception that many Archean deposits have somewhat lower ranges of salinity (often less than 4 wt% NaCl equiv.), these fluid characteristics are identical with those from many Archean examples (Ho et al. 1990; Groves and Foster 1991) and Phanerozoic examples (Nesbitt 1991). The source of ore fluids is also fully as ambiguous in the Chinese examples as in many others (Groves et al. 1988)!

Metal Association

The element association in gold ores from eastern Hebei province (Au, Ag, Cu, Pb, Zn, Bi, W, ±Mo) is somewhat different from that in many Archean-hosted gold deposits. The latter have been called gold-only deposits because of the lack of base metal enrichment and the high Au/Ag ratios of about 10 in bulk ores (Groves and Foster 1991; Fyfe and Kerrich 1984). In the Chinese examples reported here, in contrast, base metals are commonly present at the percent level in the ores, and the bulk Au/Ag ratios are invariably less than unity. Both of these features could be explained by a higher salinity of the ore fluids in the Chinese case, since the transport of base metals is primarily as chloride complexes, and silver is incorporated in galena.

Tectonic Setting

Recent integrated studies of the tectonic setting of Archean gold deposits in the Norseman-Wiluna Belt suggests an assocation of the deposits with accretionary continental margins (Barley et al. 1989). Similar ideas have been expressed for the Superior Province in Canada by Card et al. (1989). Kerrich and Wyman (1990) suggested that mesothermal lode gold deposits of all ages share a common geodynamic setting of continental margin accretion. According to these authors, the unifying features of mesothermal gold deposits including late- to postmetamorphic timing, association with crustal-scale faults, low salinity C-O-H fluids, and dominantly volcanic host rocks can be explained by processes following accretion by subduction of oceanic crust.

The gold deposits in eastern Hebei province, and probably elsewhere in northeastern China as well, formed in an unambiguous convergent margin setting. The deposits formed during the Mesozoic Yanshanian Orogeny, which involved eastward subduction of oceanic crust beneath the Sino-Korean platform margin. The gold deposits therefore were the result of the magmatic and tectonic activity associated with this Mesozoic reactivation of the Archean craton.

Appendix 1. Average composition of selected Yanshanian granitic plutons from eastern Hebei province

Pluton	Sanyihe	Dushan	Niuxinshan	Wangtoushan	Xiaoyingzi	Gaojiadian	Jiajiashan	Laochengling
SiO_2	73.93	70.07	74.25	75.69	68.79	61.48	73.93	76.66
TiO_2	0.12	0.24	0.07	0.08	0.38	1.18	0.10	0.07
Al_2O_3	13.42	14.68	13.12	12.91	14.26	15.91	13.82	12.62
Fe_2O_3	1.06	1.99	1.15	1.00	3.01	5.58	1.59	1.15
MgO	0.18	0.57	0.13	0.12	1.01	1.61	0.21	0.20
MnO	0.22	0.03	0.17	0.01	0.08	0.08	0.05	0.05
CaO	0.54	1.54	0.58	0.96	1.83	3.53	0.49	0.37
Na_2O	4.54	4.32	3.32	3.06	4.37	4.66	4.68	4.27
K_2O	4.25	4.37	5.09	4.96	4.23	3.52	4.05	3.77
P_2O_5	0.02	0.14	0.05	0.01	0.16	0.84	0.11	0.02
LOI	0.36	0.40	1.17	0.73	0.65			
Total	98.51	98.05	98.59	99.11	98.23	98.39	99.00	99.18
Rb	144	71	292	173	60	157	150	
Sr	93	721	29	195	554	508	70	
Ba	272	2113	230	651	1394	1823	127	
Cr	22	46	4	6	17	9	8	
Zr	99	43	85	96	228	18	88	
Zn	44	48	90	37	40	60	32	
Y	14	6	29	9	16	26	4	
Nb	26	13	64	20	12	27	43	
La	16.7	30.0	8.7	7.5		53.3	11.7	
Ce	35.8	51.9	19.3	17.5		131.0	32.4	
Nd	14.7	16.0	9.9	8.0		40.7	7.7	
Sm	2.9	2.2	2.9	1.4		7.1	1.4	
Eu	0.4	0.5	0.2	0.2		1.8	0.3	
Gd	2.3	1.6	2.4	0.9		5.4	1.0	
Tb	0.7	0.3				0.8	0.3	
Dy	1.9	0.9	2.5	0.8		4.1	1.0	
Yb	2.7	0.4	0.3	0.2		2.3	0.8	
Lu	0.2	0.1				0.4	0.2	
n	7	9	12	7	13	6	2	1

n, number of samples.
Total Fe as Fe_2O_3.

Appendix 1 (*continued*)

Pluton	Louwenyu	Madi	Maoshan	Qianfengshuiling	Qingshankou	Shitaizi	Wangpingshi	Yuerya
SiO_2	75.35	74.15	74.46	69.76	73.57	73.52	73.36	73.97
TiO_2	0.10	0.03	0.13	0.24	0.20	0.18	0.18	0.12
Al_2O_3	13.18	14.61	13.29	15.45	13.67	12.82	14.07	13.09
Fe_2O_3	1.34	0.73	1.72	2.44	1.64	2.57	1.61	2.02
MgO	0.28	0.11	0.28	0.82	0.38	0.43	0.31	0.25
MnO	0.18	0.12	0.12	0.09	0.07	0.03	0.09	0.06
CaO	0.56	0.29	1.32	1.62	0.59	1.03	0.67	0.80
Na_2O	4.18	5.44	3.97	4.66	4.34	3.70	4.22	3.51
K_2O	4.11	3.63	3.86	3.62	4.39	4.57	4.48	4.33
P_2O_5	0.08	0.07	0.14	0.18	0.57	0.18	0.12	0.06
LOI								
Total	99.37	99.17	99.28	98.87	99.40	99.02	99.11	98.21
Rb	275	1590	333		155		233	138
Sr	51	4	239		113		138	158
Ba	196	10	551		524		495	403
Cr	7	8	7		8		6	8
Zr	73	73	97		44		73	166
Zn	46	59	52		53		35	256
Y	29	10	28		11		12	22
Nb	46	166	58		29		35	24
La		8.8	20.3		46.0		21.3	
Ce		32.4	48.2		109.4		46.0	
Nd		14.0	19.0		47.1		12.0	
Sm		5.9	4.8		9.0		2.2	
Eu		0.1	0.6		2.2		0.3	
Gd		4.8	4.6		7.3		1.8	
Tb		0.8	0.8		1.1		0.4	
Dy		2.7	4.7		5.7		1.6	
Yb		0.5	3.6		2.6		2.2	
Lu		0.1	0.7		0.4		0.5	
n	2	4	4	3	2	2	3	12

n, number of samples.
Total Fe as Fe_2O_3.

Appendix 2. Partial analyses including gold of rocks from the Qianxi Group in eastern Hebei province

Sample Rock type	CE97 Websterite	CE98 Hornblendite	CE99 Websterite	CE100 Websterite	CE101 Websterite	CE102 Websterite	CE103 Amphibolite	Q25 Amphibolite	CE208 Granulite
SiO_2	42.06	42.98	52.64	51.62	53.18	43.88	43.96	48.40	49.64
TiO_2	0.23	0.22	0.14	0.19	0.19	0.17	1.48	0.65	0.42
Al_2O_3	6.88	5.06	3.62	4.82	3.59	5.43	6.09	9.40	4.05
Fe_2O_3	15.32	11.58	9.43	9.70	9.90	11.44	17.36	9.80	11.88
MgO	25.52	26.86	24.84	18.93	24.56	27.34	16.39	14.65	17.34
MnO	0.12	0.07	0.12	0.10	0.10	0.11	0.18	0.15	0.18
CaO	5.38	5.88	8.01	10.38	6.76	4.63	9.25	12.93	12.57
Na_2O	0.34	0.30	0.30	1.28	0.54	0.64	1.12	1.22	0.99
K_2O	0.18	0.08	0.08	0.28	0.18	0.36	0.08	1.08	0.25
P_2O_5	0.09	0.05	0.05	0.01	0.01	0.18	0.16	0.21	0.02
S(tot)	–	–	–	–	–	–	–	–	–
Au (ppb)	6	<1	10	1	1	1	1	2	1
Pd (ppb)	45	28	67	18	14	32	4	11	10
Ag	–	–	–	–	–	–	–	–	–
Cu	–	–	–	–	–	–	–	–	–
Zn	–	–	–	–	–	–	–	–	–
Pb	–	–	–	–	–	–	–	–	–
W	–	–	–	–	–	–	–	–	–
Cr	–	–	–	–	–	–	–	–	–
Co	–	–	–	–	–	–	–	–	–
Ni	–	–	–	–	–	–	–	–	–

Appendix 2 (*continued*)

Sample	CE209	CE106	CE93	CE96	CE104	CE105	CE95	CE201
Rock type	Hornblendite[a]	Hornblendite[a]	Amphibolite[a]	Hornblendite[a]	Amphibolite[a]	Hornblendite[a]	Hornblendite[b]	Hornblendite[b]
SiO_2	47.98	43.78	43.06	44.18	41.56	43.76	44.12	49.80
TiO_2	0.50	1.99	1.85	1.77	2.17	2.02	1.89	1.46
Al_2O_3	7.81	6.20	5.26	6.10	6.85	7.59	4.68	6.29
Fe_2O_3	12.63	18.05	19.80	17.64	19.04	17.93	19.05	15.32
MgO	17.10	16.83	16.67	15.40	15.29	12.97	15.40	17.96
MnO	0.15	0.12	0.13	0.10	0.34	0.46	0.12	0.14
CaO	11.74	7.59	8.75	9.75	10.75	12.12	8.63	6.70
Na_2O	1.27	0.80	1.22	0.88	1.04	1.46	1.04	1.32
K_2O	0.50	0.28	0.28	0.64	0.46	0.64	0.18	0.12
P_2O_5	0.09	0.23	0.46	0.27	0.34	0.46	0.25	0.04
S(tot)	–	–	–	–	–	–	–	–
Au (ppb)	1	1	1	1	2	2	98	32
Pd (ppb)	2	5	3	2	5	5	2	2
Ag	–	–	–	–	–	–	–	–
Cu	–	–	–	–	–	–	–	–
Zn	–	–	–	–	–	–	–	–
Pb	–	–	–	–	–	–	–	–
W	–	–	–	–	–	–	–	–
Cr	–	–	–	–	–	–	–	–
Co	–	–	–	–	–	–	–	–
Ni	–	–	–	–	–	–	–	–

Appendix 2 (*continued*)

Sample Rock type	CE202 Pyroxenite	CE203 Hornblendite[b]	CE205 Hornblendite[a]	CE204 Amphibolite	YQ26 Granulite	YQ28 Leptite	YQ31 Leptite	YQ56 Amphibolite
SiO_2	52.12	40.90	42.10	50.52	50.96	48.84	54.84	48.84
TiO_2	0.78	0.74	1.66	0.66	0.72	0.92	0.54	1.25
Al_2O_3	8.44	11.59	10.52	12.17	14.82	14.20	16.39	12.84
Fe_2O_3	9.80	28.09	24.10	11.20	11.73	13.81	8.34	14.24
MgO	13.17	7.90	9.32	9.28	8.10	6.65	5.45	6.95
MnO	0.12	0.36	0.08	0.09	0.19	0.25	0.13	0.19
CaO	11.99	8.26	10.03	9.86	10.60	12.40	8.80	11.95
Na_2O	2.04	1.48	1.56	2.90	3.38	3.04	4.22	4.80
K_2O	1.40	0.94	0.58	1.24	1.32	1.00	1.68	0.64
P_2O_5	0.09	0.04	0.10	0.18	0.23	0.13	0.22	0.14
S(tot)	–	–	–	–	–	–	–	–
Au (ppb)	2	16	2	1	1	2	1	4
Pd (ppb)	2	3	2	5	12	7	8	22
Ag	–	–	–	–	–	–	–	–
Cu	–	–	–	–	–	–	–	–
Zn	–	–	–	–	–	–	–	–
Pb	–	–	–	–	–	–	–	–
W	–	–	–	–	–	–	–	–
Cr	–	–	–	–	–	–	–	–
Co	–	–	–	–	–	–	–	–
Ni	–	–	–	–	–	–	–	–

Appendix 2 (continued)

Sample Rock type	YQ90 Amphibolite[a]	YG124 Amphibolite	YQ8 Pyroxenite	YQ14 Plagiogneiss	YQ19 Plagiogneiss	YQ22 Plagiogneiss	YQ25 Amphibolite	YQ26 Amphibolite
SiO_2	48.22	49.00	–	–	–	–	–	–
TiO_2	1.36	0.94	0.82	0.65	0.58	0.50	0.47	0.55
Al_2O_3	13.20	13.39	–	–	–	–	–	–
Fe_2O_3	16.26	12.42	16.20	6.41	9.39	13.40	12.80	11.60
MgO	6.50	8.70	21.56	5.31	7.63	7.30	6.96	8.12
MnO	0.29	0.17	0.15	0.08	0.09	0.18	0.14	0.13
CaO	11.15	12.74	7.00	6.02	5.88	11.89	9.93	8.54
Na_2O	3.00	2.72	1.05	4.03	3.41	3.28	3.49	3.45
K_2O	0.88	0.48	0.30	2.77	1.57	0.67	0.72	0.81
P_2O_5	0.09	0.09	0.14	0.27	0.32	0.07	0.14	0.23
S(tot)	–	–	–	–	–	–	–	–
Au (ppb)	1	1	50	53	3	4	2	1
Pd (ppb)	4	10	2	2	3	2	3	12
Ag	–	–	<0.5	<0.5	<0.5	<0.5	<0.5	<0.5
Cu	–	–	200	140	150	200	150	83
Zn	–	–	120	91	110	96	94	120
Pb	–	–	10	18	18	10	16	14
W	–	–	–	–	–	–	–	–
Cr	–	–	1200	140	490	320	250	360
Co	–	–	90	23	36	54	40	39
Ni	–	–	800	59	160	120	88	76

Appendix 2 (*continued*)

Sample Rock type	YQ28 Leptite	YQ30 Felsic gneiss	YQ31 Leptite	YQ38 Pyroxenite	YQ41 Gneiss	YQ45 Amphibolite	YQ48 Orthogneiss	YQ56 Amphibolite
SiO_2	–	–	–	–	–	–	–	–
TiO_2	0.73	0.75	0.45	0.72	0.37	0.40	0.22	0.87
Al_2O_3	–	–	–	–	–	–	–	–
Fe_2O_3	14.70	14.10	9.33	14.20	12.30	12.60	35.40	16.80
MgO	6.30	7.30	5.64	4.81	10.45	10.11	2.49	6.63
MnO	0.17	0.17	0.10	0.14	0.13	0.12	0.07	0.17
CaO	10.91	10.77	7.00	12.03	11.19	10.49	4.20	9.23
Na_2O	3.38	3.44	4.52	3.29	2.75	2.87	1.61	3.14
K_2O	0.63	0.58	1.05	0.43	1.01	1.06	0.22	0.53
P_2O_5	0.14	0.11	0.21	0.09	0.05	0.05	0.16	0.16
S(tot)	–	–	–	–	–	–	–	–
Au (ppb)	2	1	1	6	2	3	5	4
Pd (ppb)	7	7	8	3	3	2	3	22
Ag	<0.5	<0.5	<0.5	<0.5	<0.5	<0.5	<0.5	<0.5
Cu	140	320	85	140	90	130	270	63
Zn	110	100	90	89	83	76	73	130
Pb	10	14	24	12	18	14	8	14
W	–	–	–	–	–	–	–	–
Cr	250	150	220	140	270	480	30	170
Co	46	60	30	35	51	50	11	55
Ni	72	81	52	40	130	140	16	83

Appendix 2 (*continued*)

Sample Rock type	YQ72 Orthogneiss	YQ73 Gneiss	YQ78 Websterite	YQ82 Amphibolite	YQ87 Plagiogneiss	YQ88 Pyroxenite	YQ95 Gneiss	YQ98 Amphibolite
SiO_2	–	–	–	–	–	–	–	–
TiO_2	0.68	0.48	0.70	0.60	0.53	0.62	2.00	0.57
Al_2O_3	–	–	–	–	–	–	–	–
Fe_2O_3	16.90	12.60	27.20	14.70	12.90	14.70	17.70	14.80
MgO	6.47	5.47	4.15	7.13	8.29	11.11	4.48	8.29
MnO	0.19	0.12	0.18	0.17	0.14	0.17	0.22	0.14
CaO	10.21	7.84	6.72	9.37	8.40	15.39	9.09	8.12
Na_2O	2.34	3.91	2.34	2.70	2.96	1.73	2.98	3.16
K_2O	0.33	0.65	0.36	0.84	0.95	1.02	0.75	0.67
P_2O_5	0.09	0.11	0.21	0.09	0.07	1.81	0.23	0.07
S(tot)	–	–	–	–	–	–	–	–
Au (ppb)	3	10	1	4	11	98	4	1
Pd (ppb)	2	9	2	2	2	3	2	2
Ag	<0.5	<0.5	<0.5	<0.5	<0.5	<0.5	<0.5	<0.5
Cu	190	88	84	65	80	120	240	260
Zn	120	75	140	110	88	170	130	110
Pb	10	10	12	16	12	14	12	18
W	–	–	–	–	–	–	–	–
Cr	430	300	310	280	390	330	160	260
Co	60	33	32	55	48	45	60	56
Ni	120	86	28	95	94	130	39	120

Appendix 2 (*continued*)

Sample Rock type	YQ101 Pyroxenite	YQ108 Hornblendite	YQ111 Pyroxenite	YQ123 Plagiogneiss	YQ124 Amphibolite	YQ130 Amphibolite	YQ133 Amphibolite
SiO_2	–	–	–	–	–	–	–
TiO_2	1.27	0.73	0.52	0.47	0.43	3.34	0.04
Al_2O_3	–	–	–	–	–	–	–
Fe_2O_3	17.50	15.70	12.40	12.40	13.70	17.00	53.20
MgO	5.64	12.10	7.30	10.94	11.61	6.13	3.65
MnO	0.21	0.15	0.12	0.13	0.13	0.15	0.15
CaO	8.54	9.79	8.54	7.28	10.91	6.16	5.04
Na_2O	3.18	2.58	4.00	2.78	1.77	3.76	0.08
K_2O	0.76	0.90	0.46	0.45	0.42	0.84	0.04
P_2O_5	0.14	0.48	0.16	0.11	0.05	0.25	0.18
S(tot)	–	–	–	–	–	–	–
Au (ppb)	2	1	1	1	1	1	12
Pd (ppb)	2	2	2	2	10	2	2
Ag	<0.5	<0.5	<0.5	<0.5	<0.5	<0.5	<0.5
Cu	240	130	290	180	130	200	190
Zn	110	160	120	88	83	130	39
Pb	16	10	16	12	12	12	8
W	–	–	–	–	–	–	–
Cr	160	420	190	310	220	10	20
Co	65	57	42	52	56	53	5
Ni	95	110	71	120	130	59	1

Major element oxides in wt%, trace elements in ppm or ppb as indicated, total Fe as Fe_2O_3. Au and Pd analyses by INAA following fire assay (Au) or nickel sulfide (Pd) concentration.
[a] Sample taken from BIF zone.
[b] Sample taken from fracture zone.

References

Barley ME, Eisenlohr B, Groves DI, Perring CS, Vearncombe JR (1989) Late Archean convergent margin tectonics and gold mineralization: a new look at the Norseman-Wiluna Belt, Western Australia. Geology 17: 826–829

Berger BR, Henley RW (1989) Advances in the understanding of epithermal gold-silver deposits, with special reference to the western United States. Econ Geol Monogr 6: 405–423

Boyle RW (1979) The geochemistry of gold and its deposits. Geol Surv Can Bull 280

Brown GC, Plant J, Lee MK (1979) Geochemical and geophysical evidence on the geothermal potential of Caledonian granites in Britain. Nature 280: 129–131

Brown PE (1989) FLINCOR: A microcomputer program for the reduction and investigation of fluid-inclusion data. Am Mineral 74: 1390–1393

Brown PE, Lamb WM (1989) P-V-T properties of fluids in the system $H_2O \pm CO_2 \pm NaCl$: New graphical presentations and implications for fluid inclusion studies. Geochim Cosmochim Acta 53: 1209–1221

Brugman GE, Arndt T, Hofmann AW and Tobschall HJ (1987) Noble metal abundances in komatiite suites from Alexo, Ontario, and Gorgona Island, Colombia. Geochim Cosmochim Acta 51: 2159–2169

Burnham CW, Ohmoto H (1980) Late-stage processes of felsic magmatism. Mining Geol Spec Issue 8: 1–11

Burrows DR, Spooner ETC (1987) Generation of a magmatic H_2O-CO_2 fluid enriched in Au and W within an Archean sodic granodiorite stock, Mink Lake, northwestern Ontario. Econ Geol 82: 971–986

Card KD, Poulsen KH, Robert F (1989) The Archean Superior Province of the Canadian shield and its lode gold deposits. Econ Geol Monogr 6: 19–36

Chen GD (1989) Tectonics of China. International Academic Publishers, Pergamon Press, Oxford

Chinese Academy of Geological Sciences (1979) Tectonic Map of the People's Republic of China, scale 1:4000000. Cartographic Publ House, Beijing

Clayton N, Goldsmith JR, Mayeda TK (1989) Oxygen isotope fractionation in quartz, albite, anorthite, and calcite. Geochim Cosmochim Acta 53: 725–733

Colvine AC (1989) An empirical model for the formation of Archean gold deposits: products of final cratonization of the Superior Province, Canada. Econ Geol Monogr 6: 37–53

Crocket JH (1991) Distribution of gold in the Earth's crust. In: Foster RP (ed) Gold metallogeny and exploration. Blackie, London, pp 1–36

Dickinson WR (1979) Plate tectonic evolution of the north Pacific rim. In: Uyeda S, Murphy RQ, Kobayashi K (eds) Geodynamics of the Western Pacific. Advances in Earth Planet Sci 6. Center for Academic Publ, Tokyo, pp 1–20

Doe BR, Stacey JS (1974) The application of lead isotopes to the problems of ore genesis and ore prospect evaluation: A review. Econ Geol 69: 757–776

Doe BR, Zartman RE (1979) Plumbotectonics, the Phanerozoic. In: Barnes HL (ed) Geochemistry of hydrothermal ore deposits. Wiley, New York, pp 22–70

Eisenlohr BN, Groves D, Partington GA (1989) Crustal-scale shear zones and their significance to Archaean gold mineralization in Western Australia. Mineral Depos 24: 1–8

Ernst WG, Cao R, Jiang J (1988) Reconnaisance study of Preambrian metamorphic rocks, northeastern Sino-Korean shield, People's Republic of China. Geol Soc Am Bull 100: 692–701

European Community (1990) Gold deposits prospection and exploration technology (China). Final Rep Proj No CI1*-0127-D(BA). Commission of the European Communities, Directorate-General for Science, Research and Technology DGXII, Brussels (unpubl Tech Rep)

Faure G (1986) Principles of isotope geology, 2nd edn. Wiley, New York

Feng SZ, Yang TD (1989) On magmatic hydrothermal metallogenesis of gold in Archean greenstone belts in the North China Platform. In: Guan GY, Zhu FS (eds) Proc Int Symp on Gold geology and exploration, 26–30 June 1989, Shenyang. Northeast University of Technology Publ House, Shenyang, pp 63–69

Foster RP (ed) (1984) Gold '82: The geology, geochemistry and genesis of gold deposits. AA Balkema, Amsterdam

Foster RP (1989) Archean gold mineralization in Zimbabwe: implications for metallogenesis and exploration. Econ Geol Monogr 6: 54–70

Foster RP (ed) (1991) Gold metallogeny and exploration. Blackie, London

Foster RP, Gilligan JM (1987) Archean iron-formation and gold mineralization in Zimbabwe. In: Appel UPW, Laberge GL (eds) Precambrian iron-formations. Theophrastus, Athens, pp 635–674

Fyfe WS, Kerrich R (1984) Gold: Natural concentration processes. In: Foster RP (ed) Gold '82: the geology, geochemistry and genesis of gold deposits. AA Balkema, Amsterdam, pp 99–128

Fyon JA, Troop DG, Marmont S, Macdonald AJ (1989) Introduction of gold into Archean crust, Superior Province, Ontario—coupling between mantle-initiated magmatism and lower crustal thermal maturation. Econ Geol Monogr 6: 479–490

Gao DY (1986) Geological features and metallogenic mechanism of Jinchangyu gold deposit in Hebei province. Changchun Insititute of Gold Research, Ministry of Metallurgical Industry, Gold and Silver Anthology 5: 140–148 (in Chinese)

Gao ZL, Lin EW (1987) The study of the whole-rock gold abundance of the Jinchangyu gold mine. J Changchun Coll Geol 17: 65–72 (in Chinese)

Grant JA (1986) The isocon diagram, a simple solution to Gresens' equation for metasomatic alteration. Econ Geol 81: 1976–1982

Golding SD, McNaughton NJ, Barley ME, Groves DI, Ho SE, Rock NMS, Turner JV (1989) Archean carbon and oxygen reservoirs: their significance for fluid sources and circulation paths for Archean mesothermal gold deposits of the Norseman-Wiluna Belt, Western Australia. Econ Geol Monogr 6: 376–388

Groves DI, Foster RP (1991) Archean lode gold deposits. In: Foster RP (ed) Gold metallogeny and exploration. Blackie, London, pp 63–103

Groves DI, Phillips N, Ho SE, Houstoun SM, Standing CA (1987) Craton-scale distribution of Archean greenstone gold deposits: predictive capacity of the metamorphic model. Econ Geol 82: 2045–2058

Groves DI, Ho SE, McNaughton NL, Mueller AG, Perring CS, Rock NMS, Skwarnecki MS (1988) Genetic models for Archean lode gold deposits in Western Australia. In: Ho SE, Groves DI (eds) Advances in understanding Precambrian gold deposits, vol II. The Geology Department and University Extension Publ 12, University of Western Australia, Nedlands, pp 1–22

Groves DI, Barley ME, Ho SE (1989) Nature, genesis, and tectonic setting of mesothermal gold mineralization in the Yilgarn Block, Western Australia. Econ Geol Monogr 6: 71–85

Guan GY (1988) Secondary source beds and Precambrian lode gold deposits in the northern China platform. In: Goode ADT, Smyth EL, Birch WD, Bosma LI (eds) Abstracts and proceedings, gold '88. May 1988, Melbourne. Geol Soc Aust Abstr Ser 23, pp 593–595

Guan GY, Zhu FS (eds) (1989) Proc Int Symp on Gold Geology and Exploration, 26-30 June 1989, Shenyang. Northeast University of Technology Publ House, Shenyang

Guan GY, Jin CZ, Wu XH (1989) Monosource-polygenetic model of gold deposits in Liaoning Province and its adjacent areas. In: Guan GY, Zhu FS (eds) Proc Int Symp on Gold geology and exploration, 26-30 June 1989, Shenyang. Northeast University of Technology Publ House, Shenyang, pp 72-76

Guilbert JM, Park CF Jr (1986) The geology of ore deposits. WH Freeman, New York

Guo WK (1982) On granitoids relevant to metallogeny. Reg Geol China 2: 15-30 (in Chinese)

Guo WK (1987) Metallogenic map of endogenic ore deposits of China with guide, scale 1:4000000. Cartographic Publ House, Beijing (in Chinese and English)

Hamlyn PR, Keays RR, Cameron W, Crawford AJ, Waldron HM (1985) Precious metals in magnesian low-Ti lavas: implications for metallogenesis and sulfur saturation in primary magmas. Geochim Cosmochim Acta 49: 1797-1811

Hao ZP (1989) Geochemical feature of the Dongfengshan gold deposit. In: Guan GY, Zhu FS (eds) Proc Int Symp on Gold geology and exploration. 26-30 June 1989, Shenyang. Northeast University of Technology Publ House, Shenyang, pp 330-333

Harris LB (1987) A tectonic framework for the Western Australian Shield and its significance to gold mineralization: a personal view. In: Ho SE, Groves DI (eds) Recent advances in understanding Precambrian gold deposits. Geology Department and University Extension Publ 11. The University of Western Australia, Nedlands, pp 307-320

Ho SE, Groves DI, Phillips GN (1990) Fluid inclusions in quartz veins associated with Archean gold mineralization: clues to ore fluids and ore depositional conditions and significance to exploration. In: Herbert HK, Ho SE (eds) Stable isotopes and fluid processes in mineralization. Geology Department and University Extension Publ 23. The University of Western Australia, Nedlands, pp 35-50

Hu AG (1989) Geological setting and the genesis of Jiapigou gold deposit. In: Guan GY, Zhu FS (eds) Proc Int Symp on Gold geology and exploration. 26-30 June 1989, Shenyang. Northeast University of Technology Publ House, Shenyang, pp 346-352

Huang DY (1986) Fundamental metallization pattern of gold-silver deposits in the northwestern part of Shandong Peninsula. Geol Prospect 12: 10-15 (in Chinese)

Huang JQ (1945) On major tectonic forms of China. Natl Geol Surv China Geol Mem Ser A 20 (in Chinese)

Huang X, Bi Z, DePaulo DJ (1986) Sm-Nd isotope study of Early Archean rocks, Qianan, Hebei province, China. Geochim Cosmochim Acta 50: 625-635

Hutchinson CS, Taylor D (1978) Metallogenesis in SE Asia. J Geol Soc Lond 135: 407-428

Hutchinson RW, Vokes FM (1987) Introduction: special issue on Precambrian gold deposits. Econ Geol 82: 1991-1992

Ikonnikov AB (1975) Mineral resources of China. Geol Soc Am Microform Publ 2, Boulder, CO

Ishihara S (1981) Granitoid series and mineralization. Econ Geol 75th Anniversary Vol, pp 418-484

Ishihara S (1984) Granitoid series and Mo/W-Sn mineralization in east Asia. Geol Surv Jpn Rep 263: 173-208

Ishihara S, Sato T (1982) Mineral resources of China. Part 3. Granitoids of southern China. Chishitsu News 340: 34-45

Ishihara S, Lee DS, Kim SY (1981) Comparative study of Mesozoic granitoids and related W-Mo mineralization in southern Korea and southwestern Japan. Mining Geol 31: 311–320

Iyama JT, Fonteilles M (1981) Mesozoic granitic rocks of southern Korea reviewed from major constituents and petrography. Mining Geol 31: 281–296

Jahn BM (1990) Origin of granulites: geochemical constriants from Archean granulite facies rocks of the Sino-Korean craton, China. In: Vielzeuf D, Vidal P (eds) Granulites and crustal differentiation, NATO ASI Series. Kluwer, Dordrecht, pp 471–492

Jahn BM (1991) Early Precambrian rocks of China. In: Hall RP, Hughes DJ (eds) Early Precambrian basic magmatism. Blackie, Glasgow, pp 294–315

Jahn BM, Ernst WG (1990) Late Archean Sm-Nd isochron age for mafic-ultramafic supracrustal amphibolites from the northeastern Sino-Korean craton, China. Precambrian Res 46: 295–306

Jahn BM, Zhang ZQ (1984) Archean granulite gneisses from eastern Hebei province, China: rare earth geochemistry and tectonic implications. Contrib Mineral Petrol 85: 224–243

Jahn BM, Auvray B, Cornichet J, Bai YL, Shen QH, Liu DY (1987) 3.5 Ga old amphibolites from eastern Hebei province, China: field occurrence, petrography, Sm-Nd isochron age and REE geochemistry. Precambrian Res 34: 311–346

Keays RR (1984) Archean gold deposits and their source rocks: the upper mantle connection. In: Foster RP (ed) Gold '82: The geology, geochemistry and genesis of gold deposits. AA Balkema, Amsterdam, pp 17–51

Keays RR, Scott RB (1976) Precious metals in ocean-ridge basalts: implications for basalts as source rocks for gold mineralization. Econ Geol 71: 705–719

Keays RR, Ramsay WRH, Groves DI (eds) (1989) The geology of gold deposits: the perspective in 1988. Econ Geol Monogr 6

Kerrich R (1987) The stable isotope geochemistry of Au-Ag vein deposits in metamorphic rocks. Mineral Assoc Canada Short Course Handbook 13, Toronto, pp 287–336

Kerrich R (1989) Archean gold: relation to granulite formation or felsic intrusions? Geology 17: 1011–1015

Kerrich R, Wyman D (1990) Geodynamic setting of mesothermal gold deposits: an association with accretionary tectonic regimes. Geology 18: 882–885

Kim OJ, Lee DS (1983) Summary of igneous activity in South Korea. Geol Soc Am Mem 159: 87–104

Klimetz MP (1983) Speculations on the Mesozoic plate tectonic evolution of eastern China. Tectonics 2: 139–166

Kramers JD, Foster RP (1984) A reappraisal of lead isotope investigations of gold deposits in Zimbabwe. In: Foster RP (ed) Gold '82: the geology, geochemistry and genesis of gold deposits. AA Balkema, Rotterdam, pp 569–582

Lambert IB, Phillips GN, Groves DI (1984) Sulphur isotope compositions and genesis of Archean gold mineralization, Australia and Zimbabwe. In: Foster RP (ed) Gold '82: the geology, geochemistry and genesis of gold deposits. AA Balkema, Rotterdam, pp 373–388

Large RR, Huston DL, McGoldrick PJ, Ruxton PA, McArthur G (1988) Gold distribution and genesis in Australian volcanogenic massive sulfide deposits and their significance for gold transport models. Econ Geol Monogr 6: 520–533

Lee M (1981) Geology and metallic mineralization associated with Mesozoic granitic magmatism in South Korea. Mining Geol 31:235–244

Lhotka PG, Nesbitt BE (1989) Geology of mineralized and gold-bearing iron formation, Contwoyto Lake-Point Lake region, Northwest Territories, Canada. Can J Earth Sci 26: 46–64

Li CF, Liu XS (1986) Geological feature of porphyritic gold deposit in Tuanjiegou. Changchun Institute for Gold Research, Ministry of Metallurgical Industry. Gold Silver Anthol 4: 69–73 (in Chinese)

Li CY, Wang Q, Zhang ZM, Liu XY (1980) A preliminary study of plate tectonics of China. Chin Acad Geol Sci Bull Ser I 2: 11–22

Li CY, Wang Q, Liu XY, Tang YQ (1982) Tectonic Map of Asia, scale 1:8 000 000 with Explanatory Notes. Research Institute of Geology, Chinese Academy of Geological Sciences. Cartographic Publ House, Beijing

Li J (1988) Geological feature and genesis of gold deposits in east Hebei province. Geol Prospect 1: 5–8 (in Chinese)

Lin EW (1985) Research on Pb isotopes in gold deposits in the central part of E. Hebei province. J Changchun Coll Geol 4: 1–9 (in Chinese)

Liu DY, Shen QH, Zhang ZQ, Jahn BM, Auvray B (1990) Archean crustal evolution in China: U-Pb geochronology of the Qianxi complex. Precambrian Res 48: 223–244

Liu LD (1989) A new understanding of magmatic hydrothermal gold deposits. In: Guan GY, Zhu FS (eds) Proc Int Symp on Gold geology and exploration. 26–30 June 1989, Shenyang. Northeast University of Technology Publ House, Shenyang, pp 120–122

Liu JL (1987) Gold deposits in Precambrian BIF. Geol J 1: 58–71 (in Chinese)

Lu GY, Huang JH (1987) New results of Rb-Sr isotopic age for eastern Hebei low grade metamorphic rocks and their geological significance. China Reg Geol 3: 219–224 (in Chinese)

Lu ZX, Fan YX, Sun FY (1989) Structural and magmatic controls over gold mineralization in the Zhaoye gold ore zone, Shandong Province. In: Guan GY, Zhu FS (eds) Proc Int Symp on Gold geology and exploration. 26–30 June 1989, Shenyang. Northeast University of Technology Publ House, Shenyang, pp 135–140

Ma XY, Wu ZW (1981) Early tectonic evolution of China. Precambrian Res 14: 185–202

Maruyama S, Liou JG, Seno T (1989) Mesozoic and Cenozoic evolution of Asia. In: Ben-Avraham Z (ed) The evolution of the Pacific ocean margins. Oxford Monograph on Geology and Geophysics 8, pp 75–99

Matsuhisa Y, Goldsmith JR, Clayton RN (1979) Oxygen isotope fractionation in the system quartz-albite-anorthite-water. Geochim Cosmochim Acta 43: 1131–1140

McElhinny BJ, Embleton BJJ, Ma XH, Zhang ZK (1981) Fragmentation of Asia in the Permian. Nature 293: 212–216

Molnar P, Tapponnier P (1975) Cainozoic tectonics of Asia: the effects of a continental collision. Science 189: 419–426

Neall FB (1987) Sulfidation of iron-rick rocks as a precipitation mechanism for large Archean gold deposits in Western Australia: thermodynamic confirmation. In: Ho SE, Groves DI (eds) Recent advances in understanding Precambrian gold deposits. Department of Geology and University Extension Publ 11. The University of Western Australia, Nedlands, pp 265–270

Nesbitt BE (1991) Phanerozoic gold deposits in tectonically active continental margins. In: Foster RP (ed) Gold metallogeny and exploration. Blackie, London, pp 104–132

Nesbitt BE, Muehlenbachs K (1989) Geology, geochemistry, and genesis of mesothermal lode gold deposits of the Canadian cordillera: evidence for ore formation from evolved meteoric water. Econ Geol Monogr 6: 553–563

Oberthür T, Saager R, Tomschi HP (1990) Geological, mineralogical and geochemical aspects of Archean banded iron formation-hosted gold deposits: some examples from Southern Africa. Mineral Depos 25: 125–135

Ohmoto H (1986) Stable isotope geochemistry of ore deposits. In: Valley JW, Taylor HP Jr, O'Neil JR (eds) Stable isotopes in high temperature geological processes. Reviews in mineralogy 16. Mineralogical Society of America, Washington, pp 491–560

Ohmoto H, Rye RO (1979) Isotopes of sulfur and carbon. In: Barnes HL (ed) Geochemistry of hydrothermal ore deposits. Wiley, New York, pp 509–567

O'Neil JR (1986) Theoretical and experimental aspects of isotopic fractionation. In: Valley JW, Taylor HP Jr, O'Neil JR (eds) Stable isotopes in high temperature geological processes. Reviews in mineralogy 16. Mineralogical Society of America, Washington, pp 1–40

Pearce JA, Harris NBW, Tindle AG (1984) Trace element discrimination diagrams for the tectonic interpretation of granitic rocks. J Petrol 25: 956–983

Perring CS, Barley ME, Cassidy KF, Groves DI, McNaughton NF, Rock NMS, Bettenay LF, Golding SE, Hallberg JA (1989) The association of linear orogenic belts, mantle-crustal magmatism, and Archean gold mineralization in the eastern Yilgarn Block of western Australia. Econ Geol Monogr 6: 571–584

Peters SG, Golding SD (1989) Geologic, fluid inclusion, and stable isotope studies of granitoid-hosted gold-bearing quartz veins, Charters Towers, northeastern Australia. Econ Geol Monogr 6: 260–273

Phillips GN, Groves DI (1984) Fluid access and fluid-wall rock interaction in the genesis of the Archean gold-quartz vein deposit at Hunt mine, Kambalda, Western Australia. In: Foster RP (ed) Gold '82: the geology, geochemistry and genesis of gold deposits. AA Balkema, Rotterdam, pp 389–416

Phillips GN, Groves DI, Brown IJ (1987) Source requirements for the Golden Mile, Kalgoorlie: significance to the metamorphic replacement model for Archean gold deposits. Can J Earth Sci 24: 1643–1651

Pidgeon RT (1980) 2480-Ma-old zircons from granulite facies rocks from east Hebei province, north China. Geol Rev 26: 198–207

Ren JS, Jiang CF, Zhang ZK, Qin DY (1987) Geotectonic evolution of China. Science Press, Beijing

Rock NMS, Groves DI, Perring CS, Golding SD (1989) Gold, lamprophyres and porphyries: what does their association mean? Econ Geol Monogr 6: 609–624

Roedder E (1984) Fluid inclusions. Reviews in mineralogy 12. Mineralogical Society of America, Washington

Rösler HJ, Lange H (1972) Geochemical tables. Elsevier, Amsterdam

Rybach L (1976) Radioactive heat production; a physical property determined by the chemistry of rocks. In: Strens RG (ed) The physics and chemistry of rocks. Wiley, New York, pp 309–318

Saager R, Meyer M (1984) Gold distribution in Archean granitoids and supracrustal rocks from southern Africa: a comparison. In: Foster RP (ed) Gold '82: The geology, geochemistry and genesis of gold deposits. AA Balkema, Amsterdam, pp 53–70

Saager R, Oberthür T, Tomschi HD (1987) Geochemistry and mineralogy of banded iron formation-hosted gold mineralization in the Gwanda greenstone belt, Zimbabwe. Econ Geol 84: 197–198

Sang JH, Ho SE (1987) A review of gold deposits in China. In: Ho SE, Groves DI (eds) Recent advances in understanding Precambrian gold deposits. The Geology Department and University Extension Publ 11. The University of Western Australia, Nedlands, pp 307–320

Seward TM (1984) The transport and deposition of gold in hydrothermal systems. In: Foster RP (ed) Gold '82: the geology, geochemistry and genesis of gold deposits. AA Balkema, Amsterdam, pp 165–182

Seward TM (1989) The hydrothermal chemistry of gold and its implications for ore formation: boiling and conductive cooling as examples. Econ Geol Monogr 6: 398–404

Seward TM (1991) The hydrothermal geochemistry of gold. In: Foster RP (ed) Gold metallogeny and exploration. Blackie, London, pp 37–62

Sha RZ (1986) Ore prospecting types of gold deposits in Shanxi Province. Shanxi Metallurgical and geological information, Ministry of Metallurgical Industry (in-house journal) 2: 21–23 (in Chinese)

Shelton KL, So CS, Chang JS (1988) Gold-rich mesothermal vein deposits of the Republic of Korea: geochemical studies of the Jungwon gold area. Econ Geol 83: 1221–1237

Shen BF, Luo H, Li JJ, Peng XL (1989) The types and evolution of Archean granitoid-greenstone terranes in the North China Platform. In: Guan GY, Zhu FS (eds) Proc Int Symp on Gold geology and exploration. 26–30 June 1989, Shenyang. Northeast University of Technology Publ House, Shenyang, pp 198–203

Shenyang Institute of Geology and Mineral Resources (1988a) Contributions to the project of regional metallogenetic condition of main gold deposit types in China 1: Heilongjiang province. Geological Publishing House, Beijing (in Chinese with English summaries)

Shenyang Institute of Geology and Mineral Resources (1988b) Contributions to the project of regional metallogenetic condition of main gold deposit types in China 4: southern Liaoning province. Geological Publ House, Beijing (in Chinese with English summaries)

Shenyang Institute of Geology and Mineral Resources (1989a) Contributions to the project of regional metallogenetic condition of main gold deposit types in China 2: eastern Hebei province. Geological Publ House, Beijing (in Chinese with English summaries)

Shenyang Institute of Geology and Mineral Resources (1989b) Contributions to the project of regional metallogenetic condition of main gold deposit types in China 3: Xiaoqinling area in Henan and Shaanxi provinces. Geological Publ House, Beijing (in Chinese with English summaries)

Shenyang Institute of Geology and Mineral Resources (1989c) Contributions to the project of regional metallogenetic condition of main gold deposit types in China 5: Jiaodong area in Shandong province. Geological Publ House, Beijing (in Chinese with English summaries)

Shenyang Institute of Geology and Mineral Resources (1989d) Contributions to the project of regional metallogenetic condition of main gold deposit types in China 6: southwestern Guizhou province. Geological Publ House, Beijing (in Chinese with English summaries)

Sillitoe RH (1989) Gold deposits in Western Pacific island arcs: the magmatic connection. Econ Geol Monogr 6: 274–291

Sills JD, Wang KY, Yan YH, Windley BF (1987a) The Archean high grade gneiss terrane in eastern Hebei province, NE China: geological framework and conditions of metamorphism. In: Park RG, Tarney J (eds) The evolution of the Lewisian and comparable Precambrian high-grade terranes. Geological Society of London Spec Publ 27, pp 297–305

Sills JD, Wang KY, Yan YH, Windley BF, Zhai MG (1987b) Banded iron formations in the Early Precambrian of NE China. In: Appel PWU, LaBerge GL (eds) Precambrian iron-formations. Theophrastus, Athens, pp 487–511

Stacey JS, Kramers JD (1975) Approximation of terrestrial lead isotope evolution by a two-stage model. Earth Planet Sci Lett 26: 207–221

Stone M, Exley CS (1985) High heat production granites of SW England and their associated mineralization: a review. In: Halls C (ed) High heat production (HHP) granites, hydrothermal circulation, and ore genesis. Institution of Mining and Metallurgy, London, pp 571–593

Sun DZ (ed) (1984) The Early Precambrian geology of eastern Hebei province. Tianjin Science and Technology Press, Tianjin (in Chinese with English summary)

Sun DZ, Lu SN (1985) A subdivision of the Precambrian of China. Precambrian Res 28: 137–162

Sun DZ, Wang WY (1984) Discussion about geochronology. In: Sun DZ (ed) The Early Precambrian geology of the eastern Hebei province. Tianjin Science and Technology Press, Tianjin, pp 24–34 (in Chinese)

Sun DZ, Wu CH (1981) The principal geological and geochemical characteristics of the Archean greenstone-gneiss sequences in North China. Geol Soc Aust Spec Publ 7, pp 121–132

Sun DZ, Wang KY, Wang JL, Yang CL, Zhao FM (1989) Studies on auriferous rock series of Archean in eastern Hebei province. In: Contributions to the project of regional metallogenetic conditions of main gold deposit types in China 2: eastern Hebei province. Geological Publ House, Beijing, pp 49–98 (in Chinese with English summary)

Takahashi M (1983) Space-time distribution of late Mesozoic to Early Cenozoic magmatism in east Asia and its tectonic implications. In: Hashimoto H, Uyeda S (eds) Accretion tectonics in the circum-pacific regions. Terra Scientific, Tokyo, pp 69–88

Tang SL (1986) Discussion of geological feature and ore prospecting direction of gold deposits in Jilin Province. Treatise Collection of Gold Deposit Geology. Guilin Geological Prospecting Company, Ministry of Metallurgical Industry (internal report), pp 17–23 (in Chinese)

Taylor HP Jr (1979) Oxygen and hydrogen isotope relationships in hydrothermal mineral deposits. In: Barnes HL (ed) Geochemistry of hydrothermal ore deposits. Wiley, New York, pp 236–277

Taylor RP, Fryer BJ (1984) Rare earth element lithogeochemistry of granitoid mineral deposits. Can Mining Metallurgy Bull 76: 74–84

Terman M (1984) The last 200 million years in eastern Asia: Yanshanian subduction and post-Yanshanian extension. Geol Surv Jpn Rep 263: 27

Trumbull RB, Satir M, Sun Q, Quo D (1990) Geochemistry, Rb-Sr and oxygen isotopic composition of Yanshanian granitoids in the Anjiaygzi gold district, Inner Mongolia, P.R. China: constraints on the age of mineralization. In: International Mineralogical Association 15th General Meeting Abstracts, Beijing, June 28–July 3, 1990. Chinese Institute of Geology and Mineral Resources Printing House, p 278

Tu GZ (1989) Gold Deposits in China. In: Guan GY, Zhu FS (eds) Proc Int Symp on Gold geology and exploration. 26–30 June 1989, Shenyang. Northeast University of Technology Publ House, Shenyang, pp 2–5

Tu GZ, Wang XZ, Chen XP, Li CY, Zhang GX, Zhao ZH (1984) Geochemistry of strata-controlled ore deposits in China, vol 1. Science Publ House, Beijing (in Chinese)

US Bureau of Mines (1990) Mineral commodity summaries, 1990. US Government Printing Office No 1990-254-368/01089

Uyeda S, Miyashiro A (1974) Plate tectonics and the Japanese Islands: a synthesis. Geol Soc Am Bull 85: 1159–1170

Valley JW (1986) Stable isotope geochemistry of metamorphic rocks. In: Valley JW, Taylor HP Jr, O'Neil JR (eds) Stable isotopes in high temperature geological processes. Reviews in mineralogy 16. Mineralogical Society of America, Washington, pp 445–489

Vearncombe JR, Barley ME, Eisenlohr BN, Groves DI, Houstoun SM, Skwarnecki MS, Grigson MW, Partington GA (1989) Structural controls on mesothermal gold mineralization: examples from the Archean terranes of Southern Africa and Western Australia. Econ Geol Monogr 6: 124–134

Wan TF, Zhu H (1989) The tectonic stress field of the Cretaceous-Early Eocene in China. Acta Geol Sin 63: 14–25 (in Chinese)

Wang AJ (1988) The study and discrimination of the source rocks in gold deposits. Contrib Geol Mineral Resour Res 1: 29–38 (in Chinese)

Wang HZ (ed) (1985) Atlas of the paleogeography of China. Institute of Geology, Chinese Academy of Geological Sciences and Wuhan College of Geology, Cartographic Publ House, Beijing (in Chinese with English summaries)

Wang HZ (1987) Geological feature of the Xiaoqinling gold field and genesis of the deposit. Ore Depos Geol 1: 57–67 (in Chinese)

Wang KY, Sun DZ (1989) Gold mineralization in the eastern part of Hebei province, China. In: Guan GY, Zhu FS (eds) Proc Int Symp on Gold geology and exploration. 26–30 June 1989, Shenyang. Northeast University of Technology Publ House, Shenyang, pp 493–494

Wang KY, Yan YH, Yang RY, Chen YF (1985) REE geochemistry of Early Precambrian charnockites and tonalitic-granodioritic gneisses of the Qianan region, eastern Hebei, north China. Precambrian Res 27: 63–85

Wang KY, Zhang RH, Chen YF (1987) Rb-Sr age of the Shanhaiguan polyphase granitic gneisses. Sci Geol Sin 2: 148–151 (in Chinese)

Wang KY, Windley BF, Sills JD, Yan YH (1990) The Archean gneiss complex in eastern Hebei province, north China: geochemistry and evolution. Precambrian Res 48: 245–265

Wang LK, Zhu WF, Zhang SL, Yang WJ (1983) The evolution of two petrogeno-mineralization series and Sr isotopic data from granites in South China. Mining Geol 33: 295–303

Wang RM, He S, Chen Z, Li P, Dai F (1985) Geochemical evolution and metamorphic development of the Early Precambrian in eastern Hebei, China. Precambrian Res 27: 111–129

Wang XZ, Cheng JP (1988) Major geological characteristics and origin of gold deposits in China. In: Goode ADT, Smyth EL, Birch WD, Bosna LI (eds) Abstracts and proceedings, bicentennial gold '88 May 1988 Melbourne. Geol Soc Aust Abstr Ser 23, pp 408–413

Wang YW (1989) Studies of stable isotopic geochemistry of gold deposits in China. In: Guan GY, Zhu FS (eds) Proc Int Symp on Gold geology and exploration. 26–30 June 1989, Shenyang. Northeast University of Technology Publ House, Shenyang, pp 782–789

Wei J (1989) Discussion of the geological character and genesis of the Yuerya gold deposit, Hebei province, PRC. In: Guan GY, Zhu FS (eds) Proc Int Symp on Gold geology and exploration. 26–30 June 1989, Shenyang. Northeast University of Technology Publ House, Shenyang, p 498

Wiley TJ, Howell DG, Wong FL (1990) Terrane analysis of China and the Pacific rim. Circum-Pacific Council for Energy and Mineral Resources. Earth Science Series 13. The Circum-Pacific Council for Energy and Mineral Resources, Houston

Wilson M (1989) Igneous petrogenesis. Unwin Hyman, London

Windley BF (1984) The evolving continents, 2nd edn. Wiley, Chicester New York

Wu LR (1985) Mesozoic granitoids in East China. In: The crust—the significance of granites-gneisses in the lithosphere. Theophrastus, Athens, pp 201–215

Wu SQ (1985) Research on mineralogy and genesis of pyrite in Jiapigou gold mining district, Jilin Geol 2: 28–35 (in Chinese)

Wyman D, Kerrich R (1989) Archean shoshonitic lamprophyres associated with Superior Province gold deposits: distribution, tectonic setting, noble metal abundances and significance for gold mineralization. Econ Geol Monogr 6: 651–667

Xia ZP (1986) Cambrian geology of Xuanhuacongli of Hebei province and study of gold ore metallogenic regularities. Zhangjiakou Geol 8: 1–48 (in Chinese)

Xu KQ, Sun N, Wang DZ, Liu CS, Chen KR (1982) Two genetic series of granitic rocks in southeastern China. Acta Petrol Mineral Anal 1: 1–19 (in Chinese)

Yang K (1981) Gold leaching experiments of amphibolite rock in the Qinglong district of eastern Hebei province. Gold 6: 28–30 (in Chinese)

Yang LS (1989) The metallogenetic model of Jinchangyu gold deposit in the Archean greenstone belt, Hebei province, China. In: Goode ADT, Smyth EL, Birch WD, Bosma LI (eds) Abstracts and proceedings bicentennial gold '88 May 1988 Melbourne. Geol Soc Aust Abst Ser 23, pp 137–139

Yang LS (1989) Endogenic gold metallogenesis in connection with deep-seated source and prospecting prediction. In: Guan GY, Zhu FS (eds) Proc Int Symp on Gold geology and exploration. 26–30 June 1989 Shenyang. Northeast University of Technology Publ House, Shenyang, pp 664–668

Yang MZ (1988) Tectonics—granites—hydrothermal gold ore belts and the evolutionary geochemical characteristics in northern China. In: Goode ADT, Smyth EL, Birch WD, Bosma LI (eds) Abstracts and proceedings bicentennial Gold '88 May 1988 Melbourne. Geol Soc Aust Abstr Ser 23, pp 658–659

Yang ZY, Cheng YQ, Wang HZ (1986) The geology of China. Oxford Monographs on Geology and Geophysics No 3. Oxford University Press, Oxford

Yu CT, Jia B (1989) Study on the genesis of major types of gold deposits and its mechanism of formation in eastern Hebei. In: Contributions to the project of regional metallogenetic conditions of main gold deposit types in China 2: eastern Hebei province. Geological Publ House, Beijing, pp 1–48 (in Chinese with English summary)

Yu RL, Li WL, Gu SZ, Li JL, Wang FZ, Zhao WH, Liu S, Zhang HX (1989) Metallogenetic conditions of major gold ore types and ore-searching orientation in Eastern Hebei. In: Contributions to the project of regional metallogenetic conditions of main gold deposit types in China 2: eastern Hebei province. Geological Publ House, Beijing, pp 99–146 (in Chinese with English summary)

Zhai MG, Windley BF (1990) The Archean and Early Proterozoic banded iron formations of North China: their characteristics, geotectonic relations, chemistry and implications for crustal growth. Precambrian Res 48: 267–286

Zhai MG, Yang RY, Lu WJ, Zhou J (1985) Geochemistry and evolution of the Qingyuan Archean granite-greenstone terrain, NE China. Precambrian Res 27: 37–62

Zhai MG, Windley BF, Sills JD (1990) Archean gneisses, amphibolites and banded iron formations from the Anshan area of Liaoning Province, NE China: their geochemistry, metamorphism and petrogenesis. Precambrian Res 46: 195–216

Zhai YS (1984) Outline of ore field tectonics. Ministry of Metallurgical Industry Publ House, Beijing (in Chinese)

Zhang J (1979) Features of the main types of gold deposits in northeast China and their ore potential, part 1. Research Institute, Jilin Geological Prospecting Company, Ministry of Metallurgical Industry, pp 23–30 (in Chinese)

Zhang QS (1987) Banded iron formations in China. In: Appel PWU, LaBerge GL (eds) Precambrian Iron-formations. Theophrastus, Athens, pp 423–448

Zhang QS, Liu LD, Zhu YZ, Yang LS (1984) Geology and metallogeny of the Early Precambrian in China. IGCP Proj 91. Report of the National Working Group of China. People's Publishing House of Jilin, Changchun

Zhang RY, Cong BL (1982) Mineralogy and T-P conditions of crystallization of Early Archean granulites from Qianxi county, NE China. Sci Sin Ser B 25: 96–112

Zhang WG (1986) Geological feature and genesis of the Gengzhuang gold-silver deposit, Shanxi Province. Shanxi Metallurgical Geol 2: 1–31 (in Chinese)

Zhang ZM, Liou JG, Coleman RP (1984) An outline of plate tectonics of China. Geol Soc Am Bull 95: 295–312

Zhao YZ (1989) Mathematical and mechanical model and prediction of metallogenic structure system and gold concentration in the Niuxinshan region, Kuancheng County of Hebei province. Technical University of Northeast China Publ House, Qinhuangdao (in Chinese)

Zhong FD (1975) K-Ar isochron age of Precambrian rocks in northeast China. Geochemistry 2: 114–122 (in Chinese)

Zhou QH, Fan YX (1989) On ore-forming geochemistry of Jiaojia gold deposit, Shandong province, China. In: Guan GY, Zhu FS (eds) Proc Int Symp on Gold geology and exploration. 26–30 June 1989 Shenyang. Northeast University of Technology Publ House, Shenyang, pp 829–836

Zhou ST (1989) Genesis of gold deposits in Archean metamorphic series of North China Platform. In: Guan GY, Zhu FS (eds) Proc Int Symp on Gold geology and exploration. 26–30 June 1989 Shenyang. Northeast University of Technology Publ House, Shenyang, pp 277–283

Zhu BC (1979) Metallogenic law and ore prospecting direction of Heilongjiang gold deposits. Main types and ore prospecting direction of gold deposits in NE China. Jilin Geology Institute, Ministry of Metallurgical Industry (internal report), pp 1–24 (in Chinese)

Zhu BQ, Chen YW (1984) Features of Pb isotopic composition of ores and evolution of continental crust of China. Sci Sin Ser B 27: 635–646

Zhu FS (1985) The gold ore deposits geology and metallogeny of Precambrian metamorphic complex in China. Gold 6: 1–7 (in Chinese)

Zhu FS (1989) Study on genetic types of gold deposits in China and their basic geologic features. In: Guan GY, Zhu FS (eds) Proc Int Symp on Gold geology and exploration. 26–30 June 1989 Shenyang. Northeast University of Technology Publ House, Shenyang, pp 18–31

Zonenshain LP, Kuzmin MI, Kovalenko VI, Saltykovsky AJ (1974) Mesozoic structural-magmatic pattern and metallogeny of the western part of the Pacific belt. Earth Planet Sci Lett 22: 96–109

Subject Index

Aikinite 67
Albitization 101
Algoma-type iron formation 134
Altay mountains 21
Amphibolite facies 36, 39
Antimonite 116
Anziling migmatitic granite 30
Archean rocks
    Age dates 34
    Chemical composition 31–34
    Metamorphism 35
    Stratigraphy 27–31
Argentite 108
Arsenopyrite 116
Au/Ag ratio 68, 89, 163, 176
Au/Pd ratio 124–126
Azurite 100

Badaohe Group 28
Baimiaozi Formation 31
Baizhangzi gold district 15, 96
Banbishan gold deposit 111–118
Banded iron formation 26, 29, 135
    Relation to gold metallogeny
    134–142
Barite 100
Bismuth, native 68, 87
Bismuthinite 100
Bornite 100, 108
Bulgugsa Group 50

Calaverite 100, 108
Caledonian Orogeny 21
Canadian Shield 155, 175
Carbon isotopes 155
    Niuxinshan deposit 78
    Sanjia deposit 95
Carbonatization, see Wallrock alteration
Chalcocite 100, 108
Chalcopyrite 67, 86, 101, 108, 116
Changcheng System 38, 96
Changlingou Formation 38
Changzhougou Formation 38
Charnockite 30, 32

Chengjiang Event 20
Chloride-gold complexes, see Gold, transport and deposition
Chloritization, see Wallrock alteration
Circum-Pacific magmatic province 46
Covellite 67, 86

Daebo Group 50
Dahongyu Formation 38
Dakuaidi gold prospect 111
Dantazi Group 31, 34–35
Daoliushui gold district 16
Dashuiqing gold deposit 10
Daxing–Anling fold belt 6
Dayuzhangzi gold prospect 111
Deep fault zones 41–45
    Relation to gold metallogeny 148
Dongfengshan gold deposit 7
Dushan Anticlinorium 83
Dushan Granite 45, 55

E'erguna fold belt 6
E'erguna gold province 6
Eastern Hebei gold province, see Yanshan gold province
Element association 68, 89, 116, 163, 176
Epithermal gold deposits 6, 8, 10
Erdaodianzi gold subprovince 8

Fenghuangzui Formation 31
Fengning–Longhua fault zone 44
Fengning–Ningcheng fault zone 44
Fluid inclusions 152–154
    Jinchangyu deposit 110
    Niuxinshan deposit 74–77
    Sanjia deposit 93–94
    Yuerya deposit 102
Fluorite 62, 65, 74, 86, 91, 93
Fujian volcanic belt 49
Fuping Orogeny 19

Galena 67, 86, 100, 108, 116
Gaojiadian 16

Gaoyuzhuang Formation 38, 96
Gengzhuang gold deposit 11
Gneiss domes 19, 30
Gold
　Concentration in Archean rocks
　　121–126
　Concentration in granites 126
　Metallogenetic provinces 5–13
　Native gold 68, 87, 101, 108, 116
　Relation to BIF 134–142
　Relation to deep faults 148
　Relation to granites 142–148
　Transport and precipitation 141,
　　159–161
Granites
　Heat production 146
　Ilmenite and magnetite series 51,
　　143–45
　North China and Korea 50
　South China 49
Granite-hosted gold deposits 13, 58
Granulite facies 25, 35
Granulite – gneiss belt 26
Great Wall of China 57, 59
Greenschist facies 39
Greenstone belts 26–27, 175
Greisenization, see Wallrock alteration
Gubeikou – Pingquan fault zone 43

Hadaling gold province 8
Heilongjiang fold belt 2, 6
Heishiyu 103
Heluobao gold prospect 111
Henan Uplift 12
Hessite 100, 108
Himalayan Orogeny 22
Honghuagou gold deposit 10
Hongshweizhuang Formation 39
Huajian gold deposit 58
Huanan – Laoyeling gold province 7
Huanan River placer gold deposit 7
Huashi gold district 16
Hydrogen isotopes 156–159

Indosinian Orogeny 21
Inner Mongolian Axis 4
Inner Mongolian eugeosyncline, see
　Inner Mongolian Axis
Inner Mongolian – Great Hinggan fold
　system 3
Izanagi plate 47
Isua 27

Jialingkou quartz diorite 30
Jiamosi Uplift 7
Jianchang – Chaoyang fault zone 45
Jianchangying – Shangying fault zone
　45
Jianping gold district 45
Jiaojia gold deposit 12
Jiaoliao Uplift 11
Jiapigou gold deposit 9
Jiapigou gold province, see Longgang –
　Mudanling gold province
Jiayin – Luobei gold province 7
Jilin – Heilongjian fold system 2
Jinchanggouliang gold deposit 10
Jinchangyu gold deposit 103–111
Jineryu Formation 39
Jinning Event 20
Jinpen gold deposit 10
Jinshan 16
Jixian 38
Jixian System 38
Juifa River 8

Kangbao – Chifeng fault zone 44
Kaolinization, see Wallrock alteration

Lamprophyres 62, 82, 98, 106, 113, 132
LANDSAT lineaments 41
Lead, common Pb isotopes 128–130
Lengkou fault zone 45, 64
Leptite 30
Linglong gold deposit 12
Lingyuan 15
　Gold district 43
Little Qin Hill gold province, see
　Xiaoqinling gold province
Longgang – Mudanling gold province 9
Longhua gold district 44
Louzishan Granite 113
Luanhe River 34–35
Ludong gold province 11
Luliang Orogeny 20
Luzhangzi Formation 37, 113

Madi gold district 15
Magnetite quartzite 29, 61, 81, 105,
　137–141
Majiayu gold district 16
Malachite 100, 108
Malanyu Formation 30
Malanyu gold district 16
Malanyu – Taipingzhai Anticlinorium
　40

Mantle, role in gold metallogenesis   132
Maodougou syncline   63
Maojiadan gold deposit   96
Maoshan gold district   16
Maoshan Granite   16
Maweigou   58
Metamorphic-hosted gold deposits   13, 58
Miaozhangzi gold prospect   111
Microthermometry, *see* fluid inclusions
Migmatite   29, 81, 105
Migmatitic granite   26, 30, 61
Miyun – Longhua – Mijiayingzi fault zone   44
Miyun – Qinglong fault zone   43
Molybdenite   87, 100, 108
Mylonite schist   106, 117

Nandianzi Formation   31
Niuxinshan – Laocheng anticline   63
Niuxinshan gold deposit   58–78
Niuxinshan Granite   61–62
North China Continent   21
North China Platform, *see* Sino – Korean Platform

Ore bodies
    Banbishan deposit   115
    Jinchangyu deposit   107
    Niuxinshan deposit   65
    Sanjia deposit   84
    Yuerya deposit   99
Orogenic events   17–23
Orthogneiss   26, 30
Oxidized zone   115
Oxygen isotopes
    Geothermometry   78
    Jinchangyu deposit   157
    Niuxinshan deposit   77, 157
    Sanjia deposit   94, 157
    Yuerya deposit   157

P-T conditions of metamorphism   35
Paired plutonic belts   51
Paleoplacer gold deposits   6, 10
Paomaochang   15
Paraplatform   4
Pingquan   43
Pingquan – Balihan – Hongshan fault zone   45
Placer gold deposits   6, 7, 9, 11, 12
Plate tectonics   46–47
Platformal fold belts   4

Porphyry copper-type gold deposits   6, 7, 12
Proterozoic stratigraphy   36–39
Pyrite   67, 86, 100, 108, 116
Pyritization, *see* Wallrock alteration
Pyrrhotite   87, 100, 108, 116

Qianan Complex   30
Qianan Gneiss Dome   30
Qianxi Complex   29
Qianxi Group   29–31, 34, 121
Qianxi Orogeny   19
Qianxi – Longhua fault zone   45
Qianzhangzi – Longwangmiao Anticlinorium   40
Qing Dynasty   58, 80, 103
Qingbaikou System   39
Qingling suture   47, 49
Qinglonghe Anticlinorium   114
Qinglonghe Fracture Zone   114
Qingquan terrane   27
Qingshangkou Granite   105

Radiometric ages
    Granites   52, 62, 91, 98, 105, 120
    Hydrothermal minerals   73, 91, 102, 109, 120
    Metamorphic rocks   34
REE, *see* Wallrock alteration
Regional stress field   150
Retrograde metamorphism   29, 36

Saddle-reef veins   8
Sanhedian Formation   37
Sanjia gold deposit   78–96
Sanjiayu   103
Santunying Formation   29, 60, 80
Sanyihe Granite   82, 91
Scheelite   67, 86, 100
Sericitization, *see* Wallrock alteration
Shajinggou gold prospect   111
Shangbaichengzi Formation   37, 113
Shangchuang Formation   29, 60, 105
Shanhaiguan Granite   30
Shanxi Uplift   11
Shihu gold deposit   11
Shuangshanzi   15
Sibazi   16
Sichuan Orogeny   22
Silicification, *see* Wallrock alteration
Sinian System   36
Sino-Korean Platform   2–5
Skarn-type gold deposits   6, 9, 10

Source bed concept, *see* Source of gold
Source of gold   121–134
Southern Liaoning gold province, *see* Yingkou-Kuandian gold province
Sphalerite   67, 86, 100, 108, 116
Subduction   46
Sulfide-gold complexes see Gold, transport and precipitation
Sulfosalts   68, 100
Sulfur isotopes   130–132
Superior-type iron formation   134
Supracrustal rocks   25, 29

Taipingguo Anticline   7
Taipingling gold province   8
Tancheng-Luliang fault   12
Tang Dynasty   103
Tangdaohe – Kalaqin fault zone   45
Tangdaohe – Lingquan fault zone   45
Tectonic division of China   2
Tectonic stages   17
Tennantite   100
Tetradymite   67
Tetrahedrite   87, 100
Tianshan mountains   21
Tieling Formation   39
Tourmalinization   116
Tuangshanzi Formation   38
Tuanjiegou gold deposit   7

Variscan Orogeny   21

Wall rock alteration
   Banbishan deposit   116
   Jinchangyu deposit   109
   Niuxinshan deposit   69–72
   Sanjia deposit   89–91
   Yuerya deposit   101
Wangcheng Formation   35
Wangtoushan gold deposit   80–96
Wangtoushan Granite   81
Wangzhangzi gold prospect   111
Western Australia   155, 175

Wokenhe Basin   7
Wolframite   116
Wulaga Basin   7
Wumishan Formation   39
Wutai – Taihang gold province   11
Wutai Orogeny   20

Xiamaling Formation   39
Xiaoqinling gold province   12
Xiaoxing-Anling gold province   6
Xiaoyingpan gold deposit   10
Xiaying   15
Xingkai Event   21
Xinglonggou gold deposit   80–96

Yanbian fold belt   8
Yangtze Orogeny   20
Yangzhangzi gold deposit   96
Yangzhuang Formation   38
Yanshan
   Fold Belt   4
   Gold province   10
   Granites   46–55, 142–148
   Orogeny   22
Yingkou – Kuandian gold province   9
Yinshan – Nuiu'erhushan gold province   9
Yixinzhai gold deposit   11
Yongji – Panshi gold subprovince   8
Yuerya gold deposit   96–102
Yuerya Granite   97
Yuerya-type gold deposits   96
Yümoling   58

Zhalangzhangzi Formation   37, 113
Zhangjiagou Formation, 37, 113
Zhangzhangzi gold deposit   15, 111
Zhaoye gold province, *see* Ludong gold province
Zhongtiao Orogeny   20
Zhongtiaoshan gold province   12
Zhuzhangzi Group   37, 111
Zunhua Belt   30